Routledge Revivals

Ways to Paradise

First published in 1979, in *Ways to Paradise* Michael Loewe, an internationally recognised authority on Han China, assesses a wealth of an archaeological evidence in an attempt to uncover the attitudes of the pre-Buddhist Chinese to matters relating to death and hereafter. Dr Loewe examines in particular three major subjects of Han art and iconography: a recently found silk painting from Central China dating from around 168 BC; the numerous bronze mirrors of the so-called TLV pattern that came into fashion at the beginning of the Christian era, and which are especially rich in cosmological symbolism; and the representations of the Queen Mother of the West which appear as a leading motif of Chinese art from perhaps a century later. These Dr Loewe sets within a framework of contemporary literature and historical incident to create a wonderfully vivid picture of religious life and thought in this early and fascinating period of Chinese history which was to contribute so much to later developments in Far Eastern Philosophy, religion and art.

Ways to Paradise
The Chinese Quest for Immortality

Michael Loewe

First published in 1979
by George Allen and Unwin Ltd.

This edition first published in 2022 by Routledge
4 Park Square, Milton Park, Abingdon, Oxon, OX14 4RN

and by Routledge
605 Third Avenue, New York, NY 10017

Routledge is an imprint of the Taylor & Francis Group, an informa business

© Michael Loewe 1979

All rights reserved. No part of this book may be reprinted or reproduced or utilised in any form or by any electronic, mechanical, or other means, now known or hereafter invented, including photocopying and recording, or in any information storage or retrieval system, without permission in writing from the publishers.

Publisher's Note
The publisher has gone to great lengths to ensure the quality of this reprint but points out that some imperfections in the original copies may be apparent.

Disclaimer
The publisher has made every effort to trace copyright holders and welcomes correspondence from those they have been unable to contact.

A Library of Congress record exists under ISBN: 0041810252

ISBN: 978-1-032-26832-3 (hbk)
ISBN: 978-1-003-29013-1 (ebk)
ISBN: 978-1-032-26834-7 (pbk)

Book DOI 10.4324/9781003290131

Ways to Paradise

The Chinese Quest for Immortality

MICHAEL LOEWE

London
GEORGE ALLEN & UNWIN
Boston   Sydney

First published in 1979

This book is copyright under the Berne Convention. All rights are reserved. Apart from any fair dealing for the purpose of private study, research, criticism or review, as permitted under the Copyright Act, 1956, no part of this publication may be reproduced, stored in a retrieval system, or transmitted, in any form or by any means, electronic, electrical, chemical, mechanical, optical, photocopying, recording or otherwise, without the prior permission of the copyright owner. Enquiries should be sent to the publishers at the undermentioned address:

GEORGE ALLEN & UNWIN LTD
40 Museum Street, London WC1A 1LU

© Michael Loewe, 1979

British Library Cataloguing in Publication Data

Loewe, Michael
  Ways to Paradise.
  1. Art, Chinese – Ch'in-Han dynasties, 221 B.C.
  –220 A.D. 2. Immortality in art
  I. Title
  704.94′9′12960931   N7343.23   78–41229

ISBN 0–04–181025–2

Typeset in 11 on 12 point Times by Bedford Typesetters Ltd
and printed in Great Britain
by Fakenham Press Limited, Fakenham, Norfolk

Preface

This book is concerned with three subjects of Chinese art and iconography of the Han period: a recently-found silk painting from central China, which may be dated very close to 168 BC; bronze mirrors of the well-known TLV pattern, which came into fashion at about the beginning of the Christian era; and the representations of the Queen Mother of the West which appear as a leading motif of Chinese art from perhaps a century later. The subjects are alike in so far as they all derive from burial furnishings; all were designed with the same purpose, that of conferring a benediction on the deceased person; and for this reason they may each be studied with a view to understanding the underlying beliefs of the Han Chinese regarding death and the hereafter.

The three subjects are examined in conjunction with the evidence of literature and historical incident; they reveal the development of Chinese ideas of the cosmos and immortality during the three centuries in question, towards the end of which Buddhism was beginning to take root in Chinese town and country-side. The subjects and their treatment reflect a change whereby the hopes of an after-life were directed first towards a paradise of the east and thereafter towards one of the west. While the magical Isles of P'eng-lai and the Eastern Seas attracted prayer and devotion during the second century BC, by the eastern Han period (AD 25–220) hopes were centred on the Queen Mother of the West, to whom were ascribed certain powers of controlling the universe.

Such a change is fully consistent with contemporary developments in the religious, intellectual and political outlook of Han China. Fortunately the evidence permits general chronological distinctions. The beliefs that are expressed in the painting of Ma-wang-tui, which need not be regarded as untypical, hark back to the visions and beliefs of the pre-imperial age, as may be seen in some of the poems of the *Ch'u tz'u*. The appearance of TLV mirrors with their definite intellectual functions reflects the growing acceptance of the cosmic scheme that is associated with Han Confucianism. That scheme was formulated by about 100 BC; it was promoted by leading statesmen some fifty years later; and it was fully adopted under the regimes of Wang Mang and the eastern Han emperors. The iconography of the Queen Mother of the West enters into Chinese art during the eastern Han period; and the theme is subsequently developed in the literature of the *San-kuo*, Chin and *Nan-pei-ch'ao* periods (220–589).

Ways to Paradise

Some of the ideas that are incorporated below can only remain matters of speculation. As each of the chapters has been designed so that it may be read independently there is a certain amount of repetition between each one, and it is hoped that this will not irk a reader of the whole volume unduly. Since the main part of the research was completed, several discoveries have been made which concern the subjects of the book, but full details of such finds have yet to be published. In particular, at the time of going to press, only the preliminary reports were available for the important paintings found in the tomb of Pu Ch'ien-ch'iu, near Lo-yang.

My thanks are due to a number of friends and colleagues who have helped me by discussion of these themes and examination of the evidence. I single out the names of a few to whom I am especially grateful and whose ideas have been most fruitful; Carmen Blacker, of Cambridge; Nathan Sivin, of the University of Pennsylvania; and the curator of the museum erected at Ch'ang-sha to house the relics found at Ma-wang-tui. I am glad to thank Mr Richard Wang, of the Chinese Language Project, Cambridge, for writing the Chinese text for the book; Mr Bernard Thomason, of the Department of Aerial Photography, Cambridge, for the preparation of Figures 2, 17, 23 and 25; and Mr Kominami Ichiro, of the Research Institute for Humanistic Studies, Kyoto, for permission to reproduce Figures 15, 17, 18 and 22. I am grateful to the following for permission to reproduce illustrations: the Trustees of the British Museum (Plates II, IV, V, XXIV and XXV); the Trustees of the Victoria and Albert Museum (Plates III, XII–XIV and XXII); Mr Inoue Masashi of the Kyoto National Museum (for plates of mirrors in the Moriya collection); and the present owner of a mirror which was formerly in the Cull collection (Plate X).

Cambridge M.L.
March 1978

Contents

Preface		*page* vii
List of illustrations		xi

Chapter One	The Han frame of mind	1
Chapter Two	The painting from tomb no. 1, Ma-wang-tui	17
Chapter Three	TLV mirrors and their significance	60
Chapter Four	The Queen Mother of the West	86
Chapter Five	The bird in the sun and the hare in the moon	127

NOTES

Chapter One	134
Chapter Two	136
Chapter Three	144
Chapter Four	148
Chapter Five	156

APPENDIX

One	Classification and list of TLV mirrors	158
Two	Select inscriptions of TLV mirrors	192
Three	The diviner's board	204
Four	Types of mirrors and their distribution	209
Five	Mirrors dated to a specified year	223
Six	Decorative features and calligraphic styles in mirrors	227

List of books cited and abbreviations used	230
Glossary of Chinese and Japanese proper names and terms	247
Index	264

List of Illustrations

PLATES
- I Queen Mother of the West; from a brick from Ssu-ch'uan (*Ssu-ch'uan Han tai tiao-su i-shu*, Peking 1959 no. 61).
- II *Ts'ao-yeh* mirror, from the collection in the British Museum.
- III *Ts'ao-yeh* mirror with TLV marks, A 0005; from the collection in the Victoria and Albert Museum.
- IV *Shou-chou* mirror; from the collection in the British Museum.
- V *Shou-chou* mirror with TLV marks, B 0006; from the collection in the British Museum.
- * VI TLV mirror (C 1101).
- * VII TLV mirror (C 1201).
- * VIII TLV mirror (C 1902).
- * IX TLV mirror (C 1903).
- X TLV mirror (C 2104); purchased from Spink and Son by a private collector, and formerly in the Cull collection.
- * XI TLV mirror (C 2404).
- XII TLV mirror (C 3101); detail. From the collection in the Victoria and Albert Museum.
- XIII TLV mirror (C 3101). From the collection in the Victoria and Albert Museum.
- XIV TLV mirror (C 3101); detail. From the collection in the Victoria and Albert Museum.
- * XV TLV mirror (C 4126).
- * XVI TLV mirror (C 5002).
- * XVII TLV mirror (D 1007).
- * XVIII TLV mirror (D 2009).
- * XIX TLV mirror (X 1004).
- * XX TLV mirror (X 9003).
- XXI Pillow-shaped object from tomb no. 2, Wang-tu, Ho-pei, possibly showing the Queen Mother of the West. (Wang-tu (1959) p. 29 fig. 37).
- XXII Mirror in high relief, with Queen Mother of the West. From the collection in the Victoria and Albert Museum.
- XXIII Screen, of jade, showing the Queen Mother of the West and her partner. From tomb no. 43, Ting-hsien, Ho-pei (WW 1973.11 Plate 1).
- XXIV Mirror in high relief, with inscription arranged in blocks. From the collection in the British Museum.

* For the sources of these illustrations see the entries in Appendix One.

Ways to Paradise

XXV Late mirror, with decorative devices, of the Sui period. From the collection in the British Museum.
XXVI Devices on a coffin from Sha-tzu-t'ang, Ch'ang-sha (WW 1963.2, colour plate).
XXVII Decorated ends of third coffin, tomb no. 1, Ma-wang-tui (MWT (Report) Plates 35–6).
XXVIII The suppliant's path to paradise; from a fresco at Ying-ch'eng-tzu, Liao-ning. (Ying-ch'eng-tzu, Plate XXXVIa.)

FIGURE ILLUSTRATIONS

		page
1	Religious building, Ch'ang-an (KK 1963.9 fig. 21).	14
2	The Han empire, 168 BC.	19
3	Tomb no. 1, Ma-wang-tui: cross-section (MWT (Report) vol. 1 fig. 3).	22
4	Tomb no. 1, Ma-wang-tui: coffin-structure (MWT (Report) vol. 1 fig. 6).	23
5	Second coffin, tomb no. 1, Ma-wang-tui: detail of decor (MWT (Report), vol. 1 fig. 19).	24
6	Painting from tomb no. 9, Chin-ch'üeh-shan, Lin-i, Shantung (WW 1977.11, inside cover).	32
7	Painting from tomb no. 1, Ma-wang-tui (MWT (Report) vol. 1 fig. 38).	36
8	Interlaced dragons, from a tomb in Kiangsu (KK 1966.2 p. 70 fig. 4.2).	41
9	Fu Hsi and Nü Kua, with interlaced tails (WW 1975.8 p. 63 fig. 1).	41
*10	TLV mirror (C 4111).	65
11	Diviner's board (WW 1972.12 p. 15 fig. 8).	76
12	Diviner's board, as reconstructed (Lo-lang (Harada) Pl. CXII).	80
*13	TLV mirror (C 4312).	81
14	*Liu-po* board (WW 1973.9 p. 34 fig. 39).	85
15	Queen Mother of the West; from a stone relief in Shantung (Kominami p. 62 fig. 17).	91
16	Roof paintings from the tomb of Pu Ch'ien-ch'iu (Lo-yang) (WW 1977.6 pp. 10–11 figs. 33–4).	102
17	The *sheng*, or Queen Mother's crown (Kominami p. 42 figs. 3 and 5; Umehara and Fujita Pl. 65).	104
18	Queen Mother of the West; from a stone relief in Shantung (Kominami p. 63 fig. 20).	107
19	Queen Mother of the West; from a stone relief in Shantung (Finsterbusch no. 271).	109

List of illustrations

20	The constellations of the Weaver and the Oxherd (Kominami p. 34 fig. 1).	113
21	Queen Mother of the West and King Father of the East; from I-nan, Shantung (I-nan Plates 25, 26).	123
22	Queen Mother of the West; from a stone relief in Shantung (Kominami p. 60 fig. 15).	130
*23	TLV mirror (D 2004).	164
*24	TLV mirror (X 1007).	171
*25	TLV mirror (X 2010).	172
*26	TLV mirror (X 1005).	211

* For the sources of these illustrations see the entries in Appendix One.

WAYS TO PARADISE

Chapter One

The Han frame of mind

Under the western Han dynasty (202 BC–AD 9), China achieved a new measure of imperial unity, dynastic stability and administrative intensity. Despite a number of occasions of violence and bitter disputes regarding the succession, the house of Liu survived as the acknowledged masters of the empire. But in the meantime the principles of government that had been inherited from the Ch'in dynasty had undergone reform, and simultaneously the period had witnessed major changes in religious practice and intellectual attitudes. The deities who had been worshipped by the kings and emperors of Ch'in and the first nine of the Han rulers had yielded place to heaven as the prime object of the imperial cult. A new view of the universe and of mankind, which had been formulated by an unsuccessful official (Tung Chung-shu), was incorporated into the orthodox philosophy of state. The idea of imperial rule, conducted by a central government, became accepted as the normal and ideal way of governing mankind, despite the criticism that had been levelled against Ch'in's practices. New ways had been set for training and recruiting officials, which were to leave their stamp upon social hierarchies for some two thousand years of China's future. All these developments formed part of a single process, manifested in the expression of commonly held beliefs.

Just as the transitional nature of the times stands revealed in a number of historical incidents and developments, so too may it be marked in a number of significant intellectual, scientific and cultural changes.[1] The adoption of the new calendar from 104 BC followed the evolution of a new type of water-clock, which could measure time continuously instead of simply for short, defined periods. Poets such as Ssu-ma Hsiang-ju (died *c.* 177 BC) were experimenting with the new literary form, of the *fu*. Writers such as Tung Chung-shu (*c.* 179–104 BC) and the unnamed authors of the *Huai-nan-tzu* were penning philosophical treatises that attained a new depth, and which were laid out more systematically than their predecessors. At just this time Ssu-ma Ch'ien's history was nearing

1

completion. Perhaps some thirty years or so after the reform of the calendar in 104 BC and the affirmation of modernist principles of that year, Han mathematicians produced a systematic textbook of algebra.[2] In 52 BC the construction of new instruments, termed the *Ch'ih-tao-i*, may have enabled astronomers to measure the movements of the heavenly bodies in relation to the equator with greater precision than hitherto. It was probably with the use of that equipment, which had not been available to the astronomers of Ssu-ma Ch'ien's generation, that Liu Hsin (died AD 23) made the calculations necessary for the calendar which was introduced in the first decade of the Christian era.[3]

These developments were followed by notable intellectual advances during the eastern Han period (AD 25–220). Manuscripts found recently at Wu-wei, in north-west China, reveal the extent of the medical skills achieved in the first decades of that period.[4] A calendar that was yet further refined was introduced in AD 85; at much the same time Fu An, who was probably the first Chinese astronomer to measure the obliquity of the ecliptic, evolved a more accurate set of astronomical instruments; this was the *Huang-tao-i*, constructed in AD 103. Wang Ch'ung, whose radical scepticism had cast a new light on China's scientific outlook, had died a few years previously. The beginning of the second century AD saw the introduction of a more accurate system of measuring time; the manufacture of a paper-like substance that was intended for writing; and the compilation of the *Shuo-wen* dictionary. In this last work Hsü Shen provided a tool that has been the first call of scholars and textual critics ever since. These advances led in turn to the dramatic achievements of Chang Heng, whose armillary sphere of AD 124 was shortly followed by his famous seismograph.

Engaged as they were in achieving these results and applying their skills to the solution of everyday problems of agriculture, engineering and transport, the philosophers and scientists of the Han age were also addressing their intellects to other, major problems. Three particular issues recur in the writings of contemporary philosophers; the problem of evil, the authority of government and the question of a life after death. Two of these are frequently reflected in Han art; it may be noted that in two of the subjects which are considered below (i.e., TLV mirrors and the Queen Mother of the West) Han artists have associated the last of these questions with the first.

The problem of evil was concerned with calamities which apparently took place without cause, and which wrought violence and havoc on all men alike, be they just or unjust, good or wicked, nobleman or slave. The question arose of what steps could be taken, if any, to avert such calamities and to prevent the disruption of the normal conditions of peaceful and prosperous living. As such steps would devolve on those

The Han frame of mind

who claimed the right to act on behalf of the whole population and to order their activities, the second question was immediately involved. It became necessary to determine the capacity, religious or civil, in which an emperor and his government were entitled to act, and to determine the nature of the authority whereby an emperor and his officials could claim obedience and loyalty. These issues soon involved consideration of a cosmic scheme which would encompass the activities of man on earth. Han artists, if not Han philosophers, were also sometimes tempted to associate the third major problem in the same context. This concerned the fate that awaited man after death, were it to be happy or distasteful. This in turn provoked other enquiries; what elements of man, if any, could be expected to survive the death of the body; and what steps could be taken to provide for the welfare or happiness of those elements.

To the Han Chinese the problem of evil was a matter of cosmic order rather than theology, ethics or psychology. Indeed, long before the Han period Chinese thinkers had addressed themselves to the need to find a scheme of ordered regulation of the universe. The initial enquiries were probably started as a result of observations that must surely be made, even if they are not recorded, by all pioneer scientists, be they from Babylonia, Greece or China, be they of Jewish, Christian or Buddhist persuasion. This is the realisation that all that may be observed, of mind or matter, is subject to change. The regular and irregular movements of the heavenly bodies illustrate this truth in the skies; the growth and decay of the trees and plants that bedeck the earth display the beautiful workings of the principle below; and the rise of man to the heights of fortune one day, his fall to the depths of despair the next, showed the Chinese that he too, despite all his wisdom and cleverness, is likewise subject to the same recurring process.

It is within this *perpetuum mobile* that there occur those apparently causeless acts of violence to which human frailty is often exposed. Like others, the Chinese were anxious to seek the reasons for such occurrences, in the hope that they could be averted, or at least understood, or even predicted. The search for reason, for cosmic pattern or regularity, led to three possible solutions, all of which commanded a following in western Han times. The first of these theories or attitudes was centred on nature; it may be loosely described as naturalist, or Taoist, so long as it is distinguished both from the mysticism associated with Chuang tzu, and from the religious observances and disciplines evolved by the Taoist church at the end of the Han period. The second explanation looked to the force of destiny and its arbitrary whim; it afforded scope for divination in an attempt to avert the worst consequences of change. The third solution was the one that was to become accepted as official and orthodox dogma; this looked to the part played by man in determining the cosmic order and it recognized a positive controlling influence that was exercised by heaven. This scheme may be described loosely as Confucian, provided that it is distinguished clearly both from the personal and ethical teachings ascribed to Confucius, and from the social and political hierarchies of state which were later laid at his door.

The naturalist scheme is expounded in the *Huai-nan-tzu*, a fascinating and difficult text which still awaits the full attention of scholars and textual critics.[5] Probably the book includes opinions which were held in some of the highest and noblest circles of the empire during the reigns of Wen ti (180–157 BC) and Ching ti (157–141 BC), when it is known that the Dowager Empress favoured a Taoist approach.[6]

The scheme saw the universe as a single organic whole which was partly comparable with the human body and its organs. The heavens were divided into twelve sections, being held together by two 'ropes', and marked by four specially important nodal points at the corners.[7] Corresponding to the brain and heart, which exercise a paramount influence over the decisions and movements of the body, the *Tao* constituted the inbuilt natural rhythm of the universe, regulating the orbits of the celestial bodies, the succession of the seasons on earth, the growth and death of living creatures, and other regular systematic changes. The question is therefore raised why calamities and acts of violence occur, in a universe that is informed by this all-pervasive rhythm and pattern. The answer is to be found, regrettably, in man who, while but a single one of the myriad objects of creation, is nonetheless capable of exerting undue pressures on the other objects of his environment. For, thanks to his superior capacity, he can interfere in the workings of the cosmos to a violent and wholly disproportionate extent.

Provided that man will be ready to obey his natural instincts without indulging in greed, his pressures will not be excessive. The results of his activities will be satisfactory so long as he will conform with the natural order of creation rather than challenge its regimen. Human activities will then correspond with the movements in the heavens and on earth; and they will not run counter to the variations in climate and season. There will follow an abundant prosperity of the natural creative work of the earth and an absence of untoward manifestations in the skies. However, totally different results follow if man abuses his superior powers so as to denude nature of her riches. They ensue if he never ceases to tear jade and precious metals from the earth's body so as to adorn his person; if he destroys forest and vegetation, or sacrifices animal life, solely in the pursuit of artificial pleasures or ephemeral values. There will then follow a general upset of the natural order, or *Tao*, together with its consequential calamities. Mankind will suffer the effects of uncontrolled competition and greed; plants and trees will fail to sprout or blossom, in an earth that lies wounded; and thunder and storm will reverberate in the heavens. In this way violent and strange phenomena take place when mankind ignores or infringes the natural order of the cosmos, in order to indulge his material pleasures.[8]

According to the second scheme the cosmos should be viewed as a series of situations which develop from one to the next by means of very simple and gradual changes. Strange phenomena, including those incidents which appear to be of extreme violence, are no more than examples of these different situations, which all possess equal validity and significance in the cosmos. The nature of change, if correctly understood, is thus gradual rather than precipitate; it comes about as part of the world order rather than as a result of episodic or purposeful action. This scheme is ascribed to the *Book of Changes* (*I-ching*) and is expounded in its many accretions. The eight trigrams symbolize the two basic estates of heaven and earth and the six elements of creation, i.e. thunder, wind, water, fire, mountain and lake. The sixty-four hexagrams symbolize the situations that have been evolved by combinations of the two estates and the six elements; they represent the complex situations of which one is in existence at any single moment of time.

Violent forces then are not to be regarded as abnormal; change comes about from one situation to another as easily as the single line of a pattern is transformed into a broken line. If one could but ascertain which one of the sixty-four situations prevails, it would be possible to adjust one's behaviour accordingly so as to attain conformity. Various techniques of divination were therefore applied to the *I-ching* with a view to ascertaining the future. It became an approved source of counsel to which officials and governments could respectfully resort; and its importance was well recognized during the Ch'in and western Han periods.[9]

From the Han period onwards the Taoist approach and the attention paid to the *I-ching* developed in manifold ways and exerted major influences on Chinese thought. But neither scheme could provide a satisfactory answer to the problem of evil which could bring immediate comfort or conviction. According to the naturalist scheme, while man is capable, at his best moments, of living in accord with nature, and, in his worst moments, of upsetting the natural order, he cannot take positive steps to control violence or to avert disruptive change. The injunction of the *I-ching* to look at the place of particular events within this major cosmic context could hardly divert an observer from the immediate havoc wrought by storm or the fears engendered by an eclipse. The new attitude to the cosmos which became formulated shortly before 100 BC derived partly from the other two and filled some of their deficiencies. It conceded that man possessed some means of preventing the worst occurrences from taking place; it did not seek to explain the freaks of nature merely as incidents of gradual change from one normal situation to another.

The Confucian scheme conceived the cosmos as consisting of the three estates of heaven, earth and man, whose activities were ordered by the two basic powers of Yin and Yang working through five phases. As it imposed considerable responsibilities on man, it may be described as a man-centred scheme; and its adoption from about 70 BC or so is sometimes described rather loosely as the victory of Han Confucianism.

In fact the scheme drew on concepts that had been formulated from the fourth century BC or earlier; it was elaborated by Tung Chung-shu, shortly before 100 BC, so as to incorporate the imperial government of man as part of the cosmic order. Its adoption as the orthodox creed of state has exercised a paramount influence on China's subsequent intellectual and political development; and its theme appears in the work of Han artists from perhaps 50 BC.

The complementary forces of Yin and Yang permeate all aspects of the spiritual, natural and animal worlds, accounting for growth and decay, and being discernible in material and abstract forms alike. The alternation of the two forces may perpetually be traced in five phases;[10] in the first two, Yang rises to its zenith and then declines to its point of origin. The third phase is one of equilibrium; Yang's force is spent, and he has come to rest, while Yin has yet to rise. In the fourth and fifth phases Yin in her turn rises to her zenith and then declines to her original level. This rhythm underlies the natural and regular changes of the universe, be they concerned with the birth and death of organic beings, the rise and fall of temporal powers, the waxing and waning of the moon, or the daily movements of the sun. Long before the Han dynasty the Chinese had become accustomed to denote these five phases by means of symbols, chosen from the materials and phenomena of the visible world, i.e.:

Wood: for Yang rising to his peak
Fire: for Yang at his full brilliance
Earth: for the central point of balance
Metal: for Yin growing to her sharpest point
Water: for Yin at her most receptive and coldest point

Owing to this close association of these elements with the rhythmic phases of nature, the theory has frequently been described as that of the Five Elements, *Wu hsing*. In elaborating the theory, Han philosophers sought to answer the second, as well as the first, of the major problems of the day. By stressing the interdependence of the three estates of heaven, earth and man, and the integral part played by the government of man within the cosmic system, they drew attention to the proper authority and responsibilities of government, within a scheme that encompassed an explanation for the occurrence of violent incidents.

The cosmic system of the Confucian order, then, comprised the three estates mentioned; it included the realms of human, animal and vegetable life, and the activities, thoughts and emotions of both a temporal and a spiritual nature. It was a system which regulated both the processes of natural growth and decay on earth, and the institutions whereby mankind is governed in an orderly manner. As each one of the three estates is but a single component part of a unity, activities within any one of the three give rise to corresponding movements in the other two. Human actions thus provoke reactions of a comparable nature in heaven and earth. Heaven, which remains a somewhat ill-defined controlling power, regulates the movements of the constellations; it deputes to its son the power and authority to guide the activities of man on earth; and the effective exercise of that rule takes its proper place as one of the ordered rhythms of the universe.

These rhythms bring about a state of perfect balance and harmony, which stands revealed in the regular movements of the heavenly bodies within clearly defined orbits. It is seen in the recurrence of the seasons in their due order, thereby inaugurating the appropriate phases of birth and decay on earth. It is also seen in the amity and concord of man, living at peace with his neighbour and in a contented acceptance of the temporal government of the emperor's officials.

In this ideal state the problem of evil raises its ugly head when the skies are darkened out of turn, and no man can tell the reason; when strange phenomena are witnessed on earth, such as the snows which fall upon a summer's day, or the trees which blossom in mid-winter; and when strife breaks out amongst mankind, unwilling to accept the heaven-blest order of the cosmos.

The Han Confucianists saw the reason for this apparent disruption of the cosmic order in the beneficent and fatherly intentions of heaven, who continually keeps man, his activities and his government under observation. Heaven deliberately brings about calamities if it observes mankind being oppressed by its duly appointed servant, or if it sees that an emperor is failing to live up to the qualities demanded of his high office. Such failings, which involve the mismanagement of human affairs, are followed by the disruption of the natural order, in the form of eclipse or earthquake, the birth of a freak or other phenomena.[11]

Ways to Paradise

These constitute heaven's warning to his son. Just as he by his actions has disrupted the political or social order on earth, so too has heaven brought about a catastrophe of the same type in one of the other estates; and just as heaven can repair the damage by restoring the regular orbits of the constellations, so too can the emperor, once made aware of the faults committed in his name, repair the damage wrought by misgovernment or oppression. The just government of man, as conducted by the emperor, forms one of the essential principles of the cosmos; provided that it is conducted satisfactorily the emperor's claim to govern must be regarded as legitimate.

The scheme thus explained the occurrence of evil and afforded a legitimate basis for imperial government. In so doing it could answer some of the questions that the Taoist attitude and the dependence on the *I-ching*'s theories left open. A new stress was being placed on the powers of heaven, with all-important results. Han would now be able to claim a legitimate place as the successor of the kings of Chou and their heaven-blest order. For the first century of its existence Han had been content to lay claim to its authority by virtue of conquest of Ch'in; in its second century the Han emperors looked to the kings of Chou, who had worshipped heaven, as their spiritual ancestors; and until the twentieth century Chinese governments were proud enough to seek inspiration in a similar way from Chou, its culture and its Confucian tradition. Before the Confucian scheme had been adopted as orthodox, the Han emperor had worshipped those spirits or powers (*Ti*) whose cult had been perpetuated by Ch'in. From 31 BC a new era started in imperial religious practice, when an emperor sacrificed to heaven for the first time;[12] such sacrifices continued at irregular intervals until 1915.

One further result of the state's adoption of this philosophy needs to be mentioned, i.e. its appearance in Han art. From about 50 BC or perhaps a little earlier the motif of Yin Yang and the Five Elements or Phases is seen with increasing frequency.[13] The animals which symbolized four of the Five Phases appear on the designs of mirrors and as guardian talismans in tombs. Man must conduct himself in life so as to conform with the ordered configuration of the Five; so too in his death he must be surrounded by appropriate symbols which serve to keep him in the right context, lying in his proper place and set in his proper direction within the cosmos.

For all the philosophers' attempts to explain the universe, man's place therein and the government of man, there remained two major problems which faced the mind of the Han Chinese. First there was no means of access between one of the estates and the others. It was thought that

The Han frame of mind

such a connection had been severed at some very early point of time.[14] With no means of physical access there was a manifest need of divination as a means of ascertaining facts about the future;[15] and there was a similar need for a way to present oneself before the gods and report on the current state of the world.

The second problem, which was by no means new to China in the Han period, was that of death and its consequences. For centuries, men and women had been anxious to serve the spirits of their deceased ancestors in the same way as they had wished to respect them in their lifetime. It was this desire, to continue the service and to avert the evil consequences of failing to do so, that had given rise to some of the earliest evidences of civilized life in the valleys of the Yellow River, the Huai and the Yangtse. In Han times it was still believed that the spirits of the departed were capable of malevolent actions which could be directed in anger against the living. However convincing the explanation of nature according to the Yin Yang and *Wu hsing* theories might be, it could do little to allay these deep-rooted fears. Many features of the natural burial practices of the Han people may be traced to this cause, which also accounts for some of the motifs that are conspicuous in Han works of art.

There is no direct statement or systematic explanation of the attitude to life and death that was adopted by the various leaders of Han thought. It would in any event be inappropriate to seek precision or uniformity in a subject which the Chinese, like others, have often preferred to leave in the realms of mystery, as matters of faith and conviction, rather than to define as objects of quantifiable proof. The ideas and beliefs described below were not necessarily acceptable to all schools of thought during the period under discussion.

Chinese of the Han age distinguished between three constituent elements in human nature, one bodily and two spiritual. This is clear from a passage in the *Lun-heng*, which quotes and criticises a citation from the *Tso chuan*. That passage refers to events of the year 534 BC, and was presumably compiled *c.* 350 BC. The tone of Wang Ch'ung's criticism is such that he appears to be writing in protest against a belief that was currently and generally held in his own time (AD 27–*c.* 100).[16]

The physical form of man, or *hsing*, may be regarded as the wick and substance of the candle. Of the two spiritual elements, the *p'o* was regarded as being like the force that keeps the candle alight; it keeps the body alive, controlling its five organs. The other spiritual element, the *hun*, was thought to be like the light that emanates from the candle, endowing a human being with intelligence and spiritual qualities. Later, the *p'o* was characterized as *yin*, female and receptive, having been

Ways to Paradise

evolved at the moment of conception; and the *hun* was regarded as *yang*, male and active, coming into being at the moment of birth.

In normal circumstances the *p'o* and the *hun* were believed to separate at the moment of death; but the point of the passage from the *Tso chuan* lies in the assumption that in cases of death by violence this norm is frustrated. In exceptional circumstances of that type, the *p'o* and the *hun* remain bound together; although they are separated from the body, they retain the power of assuming another bodily form. This capacity permits them to avenge the violence practised on the body which they formerly inhabited; such vengeance is exacted by various forms of malevolence. While the *p'o* and the *hun* of ordinary mortals may possess this power, it is much stronger for members of the higher orders of humanity; for, by virtue of the higher type of existence that they have practised, they have acquired a richer and more powerful store of essential quality or spirituality (*ching*).

Normally however the *p'o* and the *hun* separate at death. In fortunate cases, such as those of kings, the *hun* proceeds to paradise, the abode of *Shang ti*, God on high, where a strictly hierarchical manner of existence is practised, no less in heaven than on earth. However there are formidable difficulties that a *hun* will encounter on its road to paradise, such that it may well be driven back from attaining its goal. It is not clear where a *hun* would go if it failed to reach its proper destination.

Provided that certain conditions are satisfied, the *p'o* continues to exist with the corpse, i.e. the *hsing*. Probably the beliefs regarding such conditions varied somewhat. According to one idea, the *p'o* remained with the body so long as adequate nourishment had been provided by descendants of the deceased, at the time of death. If however they had failed in this duty, the *p'o* would express its dissatisfaction in a manner that was highly dangerous to mankind; for it would return to the land of the living as a demon (*kuei*) or revenant (*kuei*), to demand satisfaction or to exact vengeance. According to other views the *p'o* remained with the *hsing* during the statutory period of three years' mourning. Thereafter its malevolence could be prevented by the provision of regular offerings at the ancestral shrine; but once these were interrupted, the *p'o* was liable to act as an evil-minded demon. Yet a further possibility may also have been envisaged: that the *p'o* was willing to remain with the body after the three years had passed so long as it was preserved from decomposition.

In addition, from the eighth century BC the Chinese had envisaged the existence of the sub-terranean world known as the *Huang ch'üan*, or Yellow Springs.[17] This world was populated by *p'o*; it existed in parallel with the paradise to which the *hun* tried to proceed, and was likewise characterized by an hierarchical form of existence. But unlike the life

The Han frame of mind

that was enjoyed under the aegis of *Shang ti*, existence in the Yellow Springs was miserable. Souls were held there as wretched prisoners in bondage within the gaol of *Hou t'u*, Lord or Queen of the Earth.

Burial practices and some of the symbols of Han art were designed to alleviate the fears of these consequences. They were intended to provide some form of guidance for the *hun*, so that it could be safely escorted on its journey to paradise, through the many dangers that were known to beset the path. Symbolical measures were taken to bring this about. At the same time, steps were taken to ensure that the *p'o* would remain satisfied, appeased and benevolent for as long as possible, so as to prevent its appearance as an evil-minded *kuei*. For this purpose large supplies of material goods were buried for its gratification and use, or attempts were made to preserve the body for eternity. While there was no contradiction in providing for both of these contingencies for one and the same person, it was also only right and proper to provide for the further possibility that the soul should find itself in the grim and dour life of the Yellow Springs. For this reason steps were taken to ensure that the soul possessed the requisite equipment for such a life, and a retinue of servants that corresponded with the rank to which it could aspire.

The effect of these ideas on the burial practices and art motifs of Han China is seen in much of the archaeological evidence that has come to light in recent years; the beliefs may also be traced in literature. We hear of the practice of summoning the soul (*hun*) of a newly-deceased person to return to its original home in the body, rather than risk the hazards of the journey to paradise. As part of the ceremony of the summons, a man would ascend to the roof of the deceased's house, carrying his official robes; and facing north he would call upon the soul to return, no less than three times.[18] Invocations of this type also appear in two poems of the *Ch'u tz'u*; these are the *Chao-hun* and the *Ta-chao*, which may be tentatively dated at *c.* 241 and 208 BC.[19] It is of deep significance that the splendid imagery of these poems, which is imbued with the southern culture of Ch'u, also appears in the features of the two paintings found in the tombs of Ma-wang-tui, lying in the old kingdom of Ch'u. The following citation (from the *Chao-hun*) exemplifies the fears that were felt on behalf of the deceased's *hun*, and the heartfelt attempt to induce it to return to the body:[20]

> O soul, come back! In the south you cannot stay.
> There the people have tattooed faces and blackened teeth;
> They sacrifice flesh of men, and pound their bones to paste.
> There are coiling snakes there, and the great fox that can run
>   a hundred leagues,

Ways to Paradise

> And the great Nine-headed Serpent who darts swiftly this way and that,
> And swallows men as a sweet relish.
> O soul, come back! In the south you may not linger.

It is suggested below that the paintings found in the two tombs of Ma-wang-tui were likewise concerned with the *hun*; but whereas the *Chao-hun* and *Ta-chao* poems are prayers intended to prevent the soul's suffering, and restrain it from proceeding to a far-off land, the paintings were designed as symbols intended to escort the soul to its proper destination. Some scholars, however, take the view that the paintings, like the poems and certain ceremonies, were intended as an invocation to bring the soul down from heaven.[21] It is further suggested below that some of the features of TLV mirrors, as well as their inscriptions, were designed for the same purpose, of conveying the soul to the land of the immortals; and the same result would, it was hoped, follow service duly paid to the Queen Mother of the West.

The form of the two paintings itself supports the suggestion that is adopted below. It is clear that they were shaped as banners, and it is very likely that these were intended to be carried in the funeral processions of the deceased. These took place when all hope that the *hun* would return to the body had been abandoned. The intimate association of the banner with the deceased individual is seen in the later use of such banners in funerals, with the name of the dead persons lovingly and meticulously inscribed upon them.

Other funerary practices derived from the attentions due to the *p'o* rather than the *hun*. In the hope that the *p'o* would remain with the body as long as possible, a number of precautionary measures, ranging from the simplest to the most elaborate, were possible. Some of the orifices of the body could be sealed with tablets, to discourage the soul from escaping. It was probably for this purpose that a jade stopper was placed in the mouth of the Countess of Tai who was buried at Ma-wang-tui.[22] There were also more effective precautions, whose use was limited to the highest of the land by virtue of the rules of rank and convention, and to the wealthiest members of society by virtue of the expenses that were entailed. These included the encasement of the body in a tailor-made suit of jade. The prescriptions for the manufacture of these suits were laid down in the manuals on ritual, so as to ensure that the correct hierarchies of rank were maintained; from the dynastic histories we hear of cases of special privilege when such rules were laid aside in order to gratify a favourite of the court.[23] The recent discovery of fragments of jade-suits and their remarkable reconstruction as whole shrouds testifies to this practice. However, in all the examples that

The Han frame of mind

have come to light, the body of the deceased person has been reduced to dust; and the belief that the properties of jade included the power of preservation from corruption remains without corroboration.

The same objective, of preserving the body intact, was responsible for the elaborate and highly effective burials of south China that are seen at sites such as Ma-wang-tui and Sha-tzu-t'ang. Chemical processes were used in an attempt to embalm the corpse; this was then buried within a series of multiple coffins whose mighty timbers and expert joinery prevented the intrusion of the noxious and corrupting vapours of the upper atmosphere. The success of these methods has been illustrated dramatically at tomb no. 1, Ma-wang-tui.[24]

In addition the *p'o* was provided with the essential commodities that he might need in his continued existence with the body and with valuables that would make such an existence attractive. These were the *ming-ch'i* 'sacred equipment', such as model granaries, wells or farmyards which provided for the demands of daily life. Necessities of food, clothing or cash were packed in highly valuable containers, which were the products of the potter, the lacquer-painter or the bronze-smith. To identify these goods with the deceased, beyond any shadow of doubt, an inscription was often appended to the article.[25] At the same time the rank, position or degree of wealth of the deceased was made clear by the burial of treasures whose possession had been limited to persons of the deceased's social status. Such precious articles included bronze mirrors or jades, and occasionally the text of an imperial decree or a work of literature with which the deceased had been intimately associated.

For the same reason, and possibly to provide the dead person with a suitable retinue should he be relegated to an existence in the Yellow Springs, the dead were provided with groups of attendants. There is a suggestion in the *Lun-heng*[26] that for this purpose individuals, both human and animal, were immolated in order to keep the *p'o* company; but there is no material evidence to show that this practice, which had been current some centuries before Han, was still maintained during that period. Instead the *p'o* was provided with simulacra of servants, entertainers or colleagues, so that it could be seen to be playing a role that accorded with his appropriate place in the social hierarchy. These took the form of figurines, frescoes or low-relief sculptures.

The style of these practices varied from region to region, as may be seen by comparing the archaeological evidences from, e.g. Ssu-ch'uan and Shantung. Similarly the structure of the tombs evolved in different ways, leading eventually to the multi-chambered and richly carved mausolea of Wang-tu or I-nan. The pattern of such tombs may be traced in subsequent edifices, such as the tombs of the imperial T'ang and Ming families which may be seen today near Si-an and Peking.

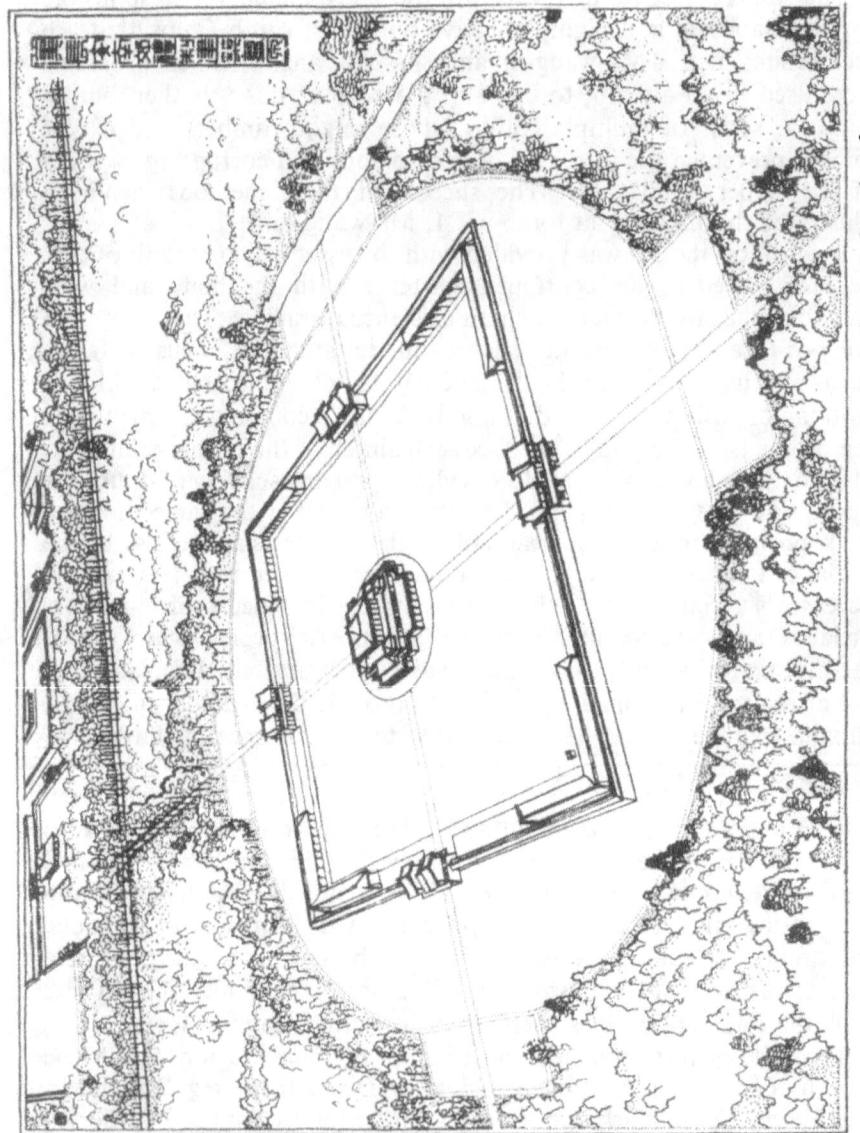

Fig. 1. Religious building, Ch'ang-an, as reconstructed; estimated length of surrounding walls, including gateway, 235 metres

The Han frame of mind

The symbols that appear and re-appear in Han art and objects reflect the strength of the foregoing beliefs. The circular heaven and square earth, that formed one of the basic principles of Han cosmology, recur in the shape of bronze mirrors and in the plan of at least one religious building.[27] The eight trigrams remind the owners of certain objects of the gentle processes of change as these are conceived in the *Book of Changes* and its interpretations, many of which were formulated in the Ch'in and Han periods. The four animals – symbols of four of the Five Phases – signify the eternal cycle of birth, decay and rebirth that is accomplished by the forces of Yin and Yang. As a pointer to the development of Han thought, it may be observed that the earliest examples of these symbols are probably to be found in tombs now situated within Lo-yang and dated *c*. 50 BC. In addition the winged creatures of some of the TLV mirrors and of the frescoes of Liao-ning represent that world of the immortals to which the souls of the dead were ideally directed.

The Han concept of immortality was anything but unitary, comprising beliefs in a paradise of the east and of the west.[28] Unfortunately direct statements are lacking in respect of these ideas. Nor are we informed of the role played by the intermediaries (*fang-shih*), or of the way in which the Power of Yellow (*Huang ti*, or the 'Yellow Emperor') could achieve or transmit the blessed state of deathlessness to others. Probably both concepts of an eastern and a western paradise were of early origin. That of the east was associated with the Isles that lay in the sea to the east of China. It may perhaps have been regarded as the abode of Ti or Shang ti as worshipped in the tradition of the Shang people. The paradise of the west came to be associated with the K'un-lun mountains of central Asia or western China, and with the realm over which the Queen Mother of the West presided. It may also be suggested that it was linked with the worship of T'ien that was incorporated within the cultural tradition of Chou.

During the Ch'in period and for at least the first century of Han, attention seems to have been fastened on the paradise of the east, as may be seen in the steps taken in the palace and by officials of state. There is scant evidence to show that much attention was paid to the paradise of the west and the concepts associated with it much before the time of Wang Mang (reigned AD 9–23)[29]. Possibly the ideas of the eastern and western paradises may be linked respectively with the two major attitudes of the modernists and the reformists that affected the development of religious practice, intellectual outlook and political principles during this period.[30]

The persistence and development of some of these ideas may be traced in various ways. During the first century AD some of the Han

Ways to Paradise

Chinese entertained certain well-seated concepts of death and the power of the dead. Evidently these were of sufficient strength to draw Wang Ch'ung's rationalist criticism. In one of his most famous chapters on the subject,[31] he sets out to disabuse his contemporaries of three misapprehensions to which they were prone: that on death a man becomes a spirit capable of taking on bodily form; that the spirits of the dead possess powers of cognition and speech; and that the spirits of the dead are capable of harming living creatures.

But Wang Ch'ung's fulminations may have lacked persuasive power, and we find a reflection of some of the beliefs considered above persisted in a somewhat unexpected source. Chang Heng (AD 78–139) possessed one of the most sophisticated and advanced minds of the eastern Han period. He was a master of mathematics and astronomy; his scientific outlook was put to practical use in the instruments which he had constructed for the aid of the court. These were designed to measure the distances and directions of the heavenly bodies, or to reveal the incidence of earthquake in the remotest parts of the empire. Chang Heng's rationalist attitude is exemplified in the cogent arguments which he raised against the faith placed in the texts of prognostication.

However, the *Hou Han-shu* preserves the text of a further piece of writing that derived from Chang Heng's hand, the *Ssu-hsüan fu*.[32] As part of the visionary experience described in this long poem, he sees himself seeking the mysteries of the cosmos from both the eastern and the western paths.[33] He climbs P'eng-lai and is admitted there. . . . He dallies for a time on Ying-chou, to pluck the Magical Plant, in the hope of achieving long life. He then alights upon a cloud that will take him home where he belongs . . . he sojourns by night on the Fu-sang tree . . . he dreams of the grain growing on the heights of K'un-lun; in the morning he proceeds by the Valley of the Sun. . . . Later in the poem he visits the Queen Mother on her silvery terrace.[34]

One very great difference is to be stressed between the Han beliefs in the hereafter and those that were shortly to gain a following in China, thanks to the arrival of Buddhism. In pre-Buddhist China, immortality was achieved, if at all, by an appeal to cosmic forces or by the symbolical use of certain cosmic patterns. Once Buddhism had taken root in China, it brought with it a totally different concept; that of personal transformation by means of spiritual disciplines and devotions, of types so far unknown in China.

PLATE I
Queen Mother of the West, from a brick from Ssu-ch'uan, 46 by 41 cm. Attributes of the Queen include the dragon and tiger throne, the hare, the toad, the three-legged bird, the armed guardian, the suppliant and the nine-tailed fox.

PLATE II
Ts'ao-yeh mirror (diameter 13.8 cm); Crown copyright, British Museum.

PLATE III
Ts'ao-yeh mirror with TLV marks (A 0005; diameter 13.5 cm); Crown copyright, Victoria and Albert Museum.

Chapter Two

The painting from tomb no. 1, Ma-wang-tui

The painting found recently in tomb no. 1, Ma-wang-tui, may be dated at 168 BC or slightly later. Reverently placed on top of the innermost coffin of the tomb, the painting was clearly one of the most important pieces of funerary equipment to be included. Its function was evidently that of a talisman designed to conduct the occupant, who may be identified as the countess of Tai, to her destination after burial. Much of the imagery and symbolism of the painting may be compared with that of the poems of the *Ch'u tz'u*, or interpreted with the help of passages in the *Shan-hai-ching*; and the painting can be explained as depicting the journey of the deceased person through the Island of P'eng-lai to her final destination in the realm of Ti, or God on high.

This chapter is divided into the following sections:

   i. The evidence from Ma-wang-tui and its value, p. 17
  ii. The kingdom of Ch'ang-sha and its position in the Han empire, p. 20
 iii. Tomb no. 1, Ma-wang-tui: structure (21); funerary furnishings (25); dating and identification of the occupant (27), p. 21
 iv. The function of the painting and the theme of immortality, p. 30
  v. Description of the painting: the vertical part, p. 34
 vi. Description of the painting: the upper part, p. 47

i. The evidence from Ma-wang-tui and its value

The excavation of Han tomb no. 1, Ma-wang-tui, Hu-nan province, was started in the early part of 1972. The preliminary reports of the work, which were published with commendable speed, soon informed the learned world of the discovery of one of the most important archaeological sites in China. The tomb may be dated within a few decades of the establishment of the Han empire in 202 BC, and it constitutes one of the earliest sites known from western Han. The objects found in the tomb bear characteristics that are of supreme significance in tracing the development of Han thought at that early stage in the dynasty; for there are few contemporary works of literature which elucidate the Chinese view of mankind and the world which was prevailing at that time. The evidence of Ma-wang-tui, and particularly that of the painting which was found there, thus fills a gap between the writings of the *Chan-kuo* period and the mythologies and cosmologies of the *Huai-nan-tzu* and the *Shih-chi*, which may be dated at approximately 120 and 90 BC respectively.

Quite apart from the funerary painting, which forms the main subject of this chapter, the site contained striking evidence regarding early Chinese methods of mummification and the construction of tombs. These subjects will be a matter of major concern to students of Chinese archaeology, medicine and chemistry for many years. Comparative evidence may be adduced from archaeology and from both earlier and later literature, with a view to interpreting the painting and its symbols and its connection with Chinese ideas of immortality.

Being situated in the Yangtse valley area, the tomb of Ma-wang-tui includes lacquers whose rich decoration is one of the hallmarks of that southern type of Chinese culture, from Ch'u, that was held in favour at the court of Kao-tsu.[1] It is not surprising to find affinities not only between the particular tomb under study and others of that region, but also between the imagery of the painting and allusions in the literature of the Yangste valley of a slightly different time. In this connection it is the poems of the *Ch'u tz'u* which invite immediate comparison;[2] for although, as will be seen, the underlying motives of the artist who painted the picture and of the author of poems such as *Chao-hun* were fundamentally different, they refer to the same commonly accepted cultural heritage and assume familiarity with the same basic beliefs and mythology.

The *Shih-chi* and the *Han-shu* tell us of the attention paid by the Han court and the imperial house to the various beliefs of the time; these sources may be supplemented from the poems of Ssu-ma Hsiang-ju (died 117 BC) and the chapters of the *Huai-nan-tzu* (completed *c.* 122 BC). Some of the obscurities of the *Ch'u tz'u* gain clarity by comparison with passages from the *Shan-hai-ching*, difficult as it is to date particular parts of that work precisely, and inappropriate as it would be to seek therein a systematic account of early Chinese mythology.

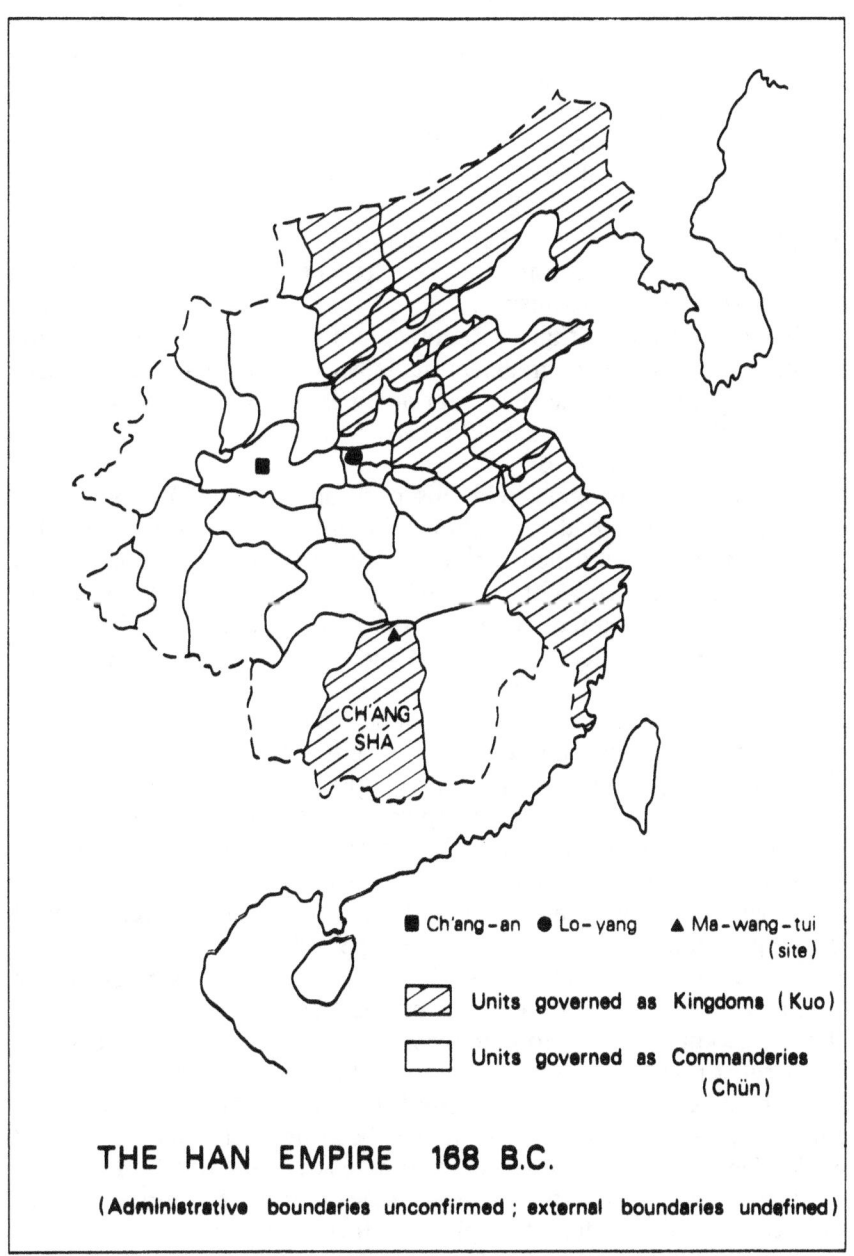

Fig. 2. The Han empire 168 BC

ii. The kingdom of Ch'ang-sha and its position in the Han empire

The painting which forms the subject of this chapter was found in a tomb near Ch'ang-sha, and for reasons that will follow it may be dated shortly after 168 BC. In many ways Ch'ang-sha must be regarded as being remote from the centre of the Han empire and culture. It lay at the southern tip of the Chinese imperium, until the military and territorial advances of 111 BC; its local culture was traditional to the Yangtse River valley rather than to that of the Yellow River; and from the start of the Han empire the area had been subject to somewhat exceptional political treatment.

The very large area that was known as Ch'ang-sha formed the sole lasting exception to the agreement made between the first Han emperor and his supporters, to the effect that only persons of imperial blood, i.e. members of the Liu family, should be invested as kings.[3] However, from the very beginning (202 BC) Wu Jui had been invested as king of the area, and his descendants held this position until 157 BC, when the last king of the line died without successor.[4] Two years later the kingdom was re-established, and the government took the opportunity to bring it into line with regular practice. The new kingdom of Ch'ang-sha was invested in one of the emperor's sons, and this line continued until the death of the last incumbent, without a successor, in 47 BC.[5] In the meantime the extent of Ch'ang-sha kingdom had been considerably reduced, as part of the policy of cutting down the strength of the kings and increasing that of the central government.[6] However, throughout the period with which this chapter is concerned Ma-wang-tui lay within the kingdom of Ch'ang-sha. As far as is known, no exceptional circumstances of an administrative nature prevailed within the kingdom. The government was conducted by officials whose titles and organization were a replica of those of the central government of the empire, and who were under the supervision of the chancellor of the kingdom.[7] As the years passed, several statesmen who served the central government gave warning of the dangers that would follow should the kings become too independent or should they wish to set up a separatist regime which could threaten the imperial house.[8]

At the time when the tomb of Ma-wang-tui was built the concept of empire was still relatively new. It had been derived from Ch'in; and while Han regarded itself as the legitimate successor to Ch'in by right of conquest, the new regime was endeavouring to impart a new characteristic to the idea of empire and to render it more popular and at the same time more efficient. Such measures included the compromise whereby the empire was administered partly as commanderies (*chün*), that were under the direct control of the central government, and partly

The painting from tomb no. 1, Ma-wang-tui

as kingdoms, whose rule had been invested in the kings and was held by them on an hereditary basis.[9]

However, the concept and practice of empire was still largely experimental. Despite its hopes and its pretensions to survive unto eternity, the Ch'in empire had been very short-lived; it could not be foretold whether the Han empire would be any more successful, or whether it would be destined to outlast 40 or 400 years. Indeed, there were several reasons why sceptics could continue to nourish grave doubts. Recently there had occurred a very serious dispute over the imperial succession and a contest between the Liu and Lü families for the supreme position of state; this had only been resolved, at the price of considerable bloodshed, in 180 BC. The institutions of state were relatively new and untried, and the changes introduced in the coinage or in taxation possibly argued some measure of instability. In addition Chinese territory was still open to penetration or invasion, in areas where the Han empire was subject to the will of other parties from central Asia. As late as 166 BC enemy patrols lay in sight of Kan-ch'üan, a summer retreat for the Han emperors; and it was not until the Han victories of 121 BC and 119 BC that the threat of invasion was effectively checked.[10]

In addition intellectual developments were still relatively unsophisticated when compared with later achievements. As yet Tung Chung-shu (*c.* 179–*c.* 104 BC) had not formulated his doctrine of the cosmos which provided for the triad of heaven, earth and man, which firmly incorporated temporal government within the universal order, and which saw imperial authority as the means of maintaining the requisite balance and harmonies of the world. The cults of state of Han were still being directed to the manifold gods and spirits worshipped by Ch'in, and the adoption of heaven as the supreme deity to be revered by the emperor was still a century and more away. It need hardly be mentioned that Buddhism had yet to affect the outlook and practice of the Chinese, and there were no organized institutions of a Taoist church. In addition, as far as may be known, there was no commanding figure corresponding with Socrates or Plato who could analyse man's beliefs of life and death or describe eternal truths in visionary terms.

iii. Tomb no. 1, Ma-wang-tui

Structure
Ma-wang-tui lies four kilometres to the east of the centre of the modern city of Ch'ang-sha.[11] Traditionally the area was believed to be the site of the burial of the Han Kings of Ch'ang-sha and their relations,

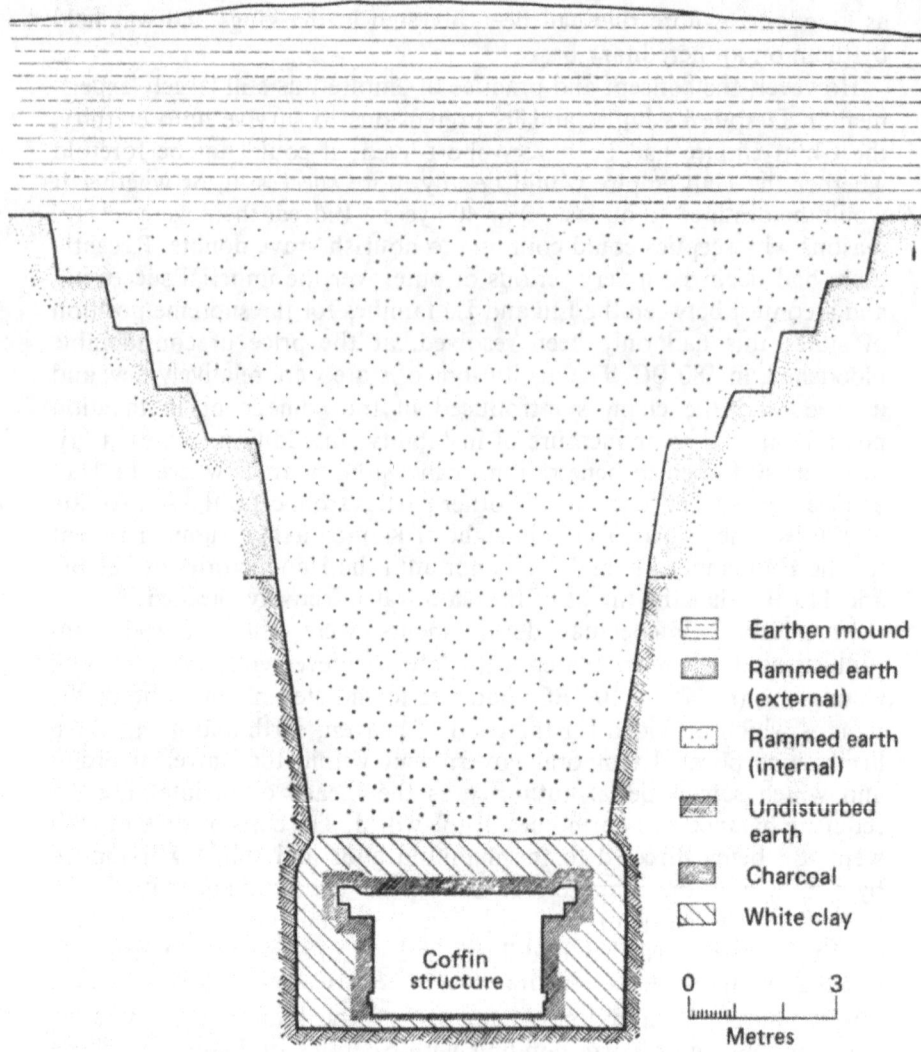

Fig. 3. Tomb no. 1, Ma-wang-tui: cross-section

and this belief was destined to be corroborated in a striking way as a result of the recent excavations of three tombs.[12] Although the importance of the site had been recognized since 1952, it was not until January 1972 that the work of excavation could be put in hand. By the end of April the main results were forthcoming from tomb no. 1; the Chinese archaeologists are to be congratulated both on the speed with which

The painting from tomb no. 1, Ma-wang-tui

Fig. 4. Tomb no. 1, Ma-wang-tui: cross-section (lengthwise) of coffin structure

the work was accomplished and a full-scale report, copiously illustrated in two volumes, was made available to the public by 1973.

The structure of the tomb, its main features and its type of contents, are comparable with those of other tombs found in the same region, such as Han tomb no. 1 at Sha-tzu-t'ang.[13] The rectangular pit, which is stepped at the top, is aligned to meet the four points of the compass.[14] From the lowest of the four steps, inward sloping walls lead downwards to the chamber which was used for interment, and the total depth from the summit of the funerary mound to the lowest point of the tomb is 20 metres. Within the final chamber the body was buried within four coffins, whose joinery had been devised with special care to insulate the contents against air. As a further precaution against damp, layers of white clay and charcoal had been incorporated in the structure of the tomb. Outsize timbers, of catalpa wood, were used for the coffins, which were embellished to a very high standard. No metal pins were used in the coffins, whose construction depended on expert mortise and tenon joints.[15]

The outermost of the four coffins was painted black;[16] the next one was decorated with a wealth of cloud pattern, and mythological creatures, executed in gold and scarlet, on a black background.[17] The third coffin was painted with a scarlet background, embellished with a rich variety of animals such as dragon, tiger or deer in white and gold, and the scarlet bird. As yet these animals have not been grouped in a set fashion so as to correspond with the four directions of which they later came to be the attributes. Usually they are shown in pairs, and sometimes on either side of a triangular device or a circle.[18] There is some resemblance between some of these figures and designs and those that appear on the painting. The innermost of the four coffins was decorated with satin stitch embroidery and an applied fabric.

23

Fig. 5. Second coffin of tomb no. 1, Ma-wang-tui: detail of coffin end, which measures 1.18 by 1.14 metres; original colours scarlet and gold, on a black background

The painting from tomb no. 1, Ma-wang-tui

Funerary furnishings
The very rich supply of artefacts found in the tomb comprises over 1000 objects. Many of these are of types that are regularly expected in burials, but the standard of artistry and beauty that was attained is often exceptionally high as compared with that of other finds. Possibly the high standards of workmanship and quality are a clue to the importance of the tomb. The excellent state in which these objects have been preserved, which is rarely seen elsewhere, is due partly to the care with which the builders had excluded destructive influences; partly to the happy chance that for over two thousand years the tomb has evaded the attentions of robbers. As a result some of the artefacts, such as the lacquer-ware or the textiles, form unique finds for the early part of the western Han dynasty.

The objects had been packed with extreme care, in a manner that is rare.[19] Many had been wrapped within 48 neatly corded and sealed caskets of bamboo which had been set reverently beside the coffins. The method used to fasten the boxes, i.e. by fixing the cords fast in small wooden cases, and attaching labels for identification, confirms many of the inferences that had been drawn from the more fragmentary evidence found at other sites. In addition to the intact cases, found in the state in which they had been left at the time of burial, the tomb included a number of funerary furnishings that had been packed loose at the side of the coffins.[20]

The tomb included a large supply of silken and hempen textiles of various qualities and patterns; some were of polychrome weaves, some of dyed or stamped material. In addition to the articles of clothing and the curtains that were hung within the tomb, there were a number of cases of fabric, made for the care of musical instruments, lacquer-ware vessels, or needles. There was also an embroidered case for the single bronze mirror that was found in the tomb.[21]

Many of the 184 pieces of lacquer were decorated in the characteristic black and scarlet to a very high standard of finish. Some of the lacquer containers for food and drink still retained their contents. There were also platters and cups, spoons and trays; and ladies' toilet sets. Many of these were inscribed, sometimes with the name of the family concerned, sometimes with a note of the capacity of the vessel.[22]

While in other tombs the occupant was provided with attendants in the form of stone reliefs, figurines or frescoes, in no. 1 tomb, Ma-wang-tui, these take the form of small wooden manikins, to the number of 162. There are hatted male figures; clothed female servants; clothed dancers and singers; painted figures standing erect; and musicians, kneeling and playing their instruments. Of particular interest are the 36 talismans, whose function was, it is believed, to avert evil.[23] Some of these were shaped individually and covered in hempen garments; one set of 22 figures, bearing somewhat crudely painted faces, was strung together in the manner in which manuscript strips were tied together to form a book. These are somewhat reminiscent of similar figures found at the sites of Chü-yen, which are however twice the size of those found here.[24]

The furnishings of the tomb included a 25-string zither and its fabric case; an organ of 22 pipes; and a set of twelve pitch pipes, together with the bag in which they were stored.[25] There were also sundry pieces of equipment such as fans and pieces of matting[26] and a total of 51 pottery vessels, mostly intact and embellished with a high standard of artistry.[27] Many of these vessels still contained remnants of the food which they had held on burial, e.g. grain, fruit or ginger; animal or fish. There are also a number of tags which were attached to the pots for purposes of identification.[28]

There was one further type of objects buried in the tomb which has a profound significance in determining its date. These are the clay replicas of two types of coin, comprising 300 specimens of the gold piece (*ying-ch'eng*), and at least 100,000 replicas of the small bronze *pan-liang* coin; these latter were found in 40 basket containers.[29]

Metal hardly features in the equipment of the tomb. Apart from one mirror of an early western Han type,[30] and 16 bell-like objects,[31] metal appears only as parts of other pieces of equipment.

Finally there was a total of 312 bamboo strips used as stationery for recording an inventory of the furnishings. These had been tied up in five bundles, but the cords had mostly rotted before discovery.[32] As none of the strips had been broken they form a refreshing contrast with the major finds of this type of document from Tun-huang and Chü-yen, with which they have many features in common. The strips are inscribed on one side only, and they had been bound together with two cords in the usual way. Some of the inscriptions carry punctuation marks, but there are no numbers written at the foot, as is the case with some of the strips found at Wu-wei.[33] There are no signs of the grooves which were sometimes cut at the side of the strips in order to hold the cords in their correct positions. The length of these strips is 27.6 cm or 1.2 Han feet, i.e. slightly more than that of the standard one-foot strip used for administrative documents at Tun-huang and Chü-yen.

None of these strips were inscribed to the full length of the column, and it is not possible to say for certain whether the record was written before or after the cords had been tied and the strips secured in the form of a scroll.[34] Most of the strips describe the individual articles which comprised the funerary furnishings. A few, which are distinguished by a broad horizontal stroke at the head of the column, act as captions to the entries of the preceding strips.[35]

The painting from tomb no. 1, Ma-wang-tiu

These strips are by no means the only example of an inventory. A longer one, running to over 400 strips was found at tomb no. 3 Ma-wang-tui, and there are other examples both of western Han date and earlier.³⁶

Dating and identification of the occupant
From the foregoing evidence it may be generally inferred that tomb no. 1 may be dated in the early part of western Han. The type of tomb and style of construction is seen in the late pre-imperial tomb of Ch'u at Sha-tzu-t'ang. Tombs of the late *Chan-kuo* period and early Han contain artefacts of the style, shape and decor that are represented at Ma-wang-tui. The choice of funerary furnishings is very similar to that seen at western Han tombs; and while one piece (the bronze mirror) may definitely be assigned to early western Han, there is an absence of articles which may be specifically associated with the time of Wu ti or later. In order to date the tomb more precisely, attention should be paid to four significant factors: the replica coins; the inscriptions on the strips; the evidence of radio-carbon dating; and the inscriptions on some of the vessels.

1. The replica coins. The *Ying-ch'eng* gold coins, represented by the clay models, were current in the pre-imperial kingdom of Ch'u, and their circulation doubtless continued in central China after the foundation of the Han empire. During the first decades of that dynasty a number of experiments were made to control the coinage; and in 175 BC a bronze coin weighing four *shu* was first issued, bearing as its inscription the proud, but untrue, designation *pan-liang*.³⁷ It is clear that the clay replicas of the *pan-liang* coins were made in imitation of this lightweight coin and not of the heavier coins which carried the identical inscription and which had been minted earlier. The tomb included no replicas of the later coins minted in the period of Wu ti (141–87 BC) which were inscribed *wu shu*.³⁸

2. The inscriptions on the strips are written in some of the early forms of *li-shu*, while preserving some of the features of the seal script that was used during the latter part of the *Chan-kuo* period. While this criterion is notoriously imprecise and subjective, it would seem reasonable to suggest that the style of calligraphy is somewhat later than that of the strips of Hsin-yang, of the *Chan-kuo* period, and somewhat earlier than that of the material found at Tun-huang and Chü-yen, which dates from about 100 BC onwards.

3. Radio-carbon dating tests which have been applied to the remnants of fruit and other material give results which vary from 245±95 BC to 145±80 BC. These results suggest that the tomb was sealed at a time between the foundation of the empire (202 BC) and the accession of Wu ti (141 BC).[39]

4. The inscriptions on some of the vessels and the impressions of some of the seals with which the containers were closed bear the imprint of the Noble of Tai, and it is clear that the tomb was associated with that family. For the following reasons it is likely that the fifty-year-old woman buried with such care and attention in the tomb was the first countess of that nobility.

The nobility was created in 193 BC for Li Ts'ang, who was chancellor of the kingdom of Ch'ang-sha; it was held by him and his three descendants as follows:[40]

1 Li Ts'ang   from 193 to 186 BC
2 Li Hsi   from 185 to 165 BC
3 Li P'eng-tsu   from 164 to 141 BC
4 Li Ch'ih (or Fu)   from 140 to 110 BC

It is unlikely that the tomb was associated with the fourth holder of the title. Quite apart from the foregoing considerations which indicate that the tomb should not be dated as late as the time of Wu ti, Li Ch'ih's end was such that it is unlikely that one of his female relatives would have been buried in the style and luxury of tomb no. 1 Ma-wang-tui; for he was appointed to be governor of Tung-hai commandery but came to a dishonourable end, facing a charge which merited execution. He was able to ransom himself from such punishment by forfeiting his nobility, which thereupon came to an end.[41] It is unlikely that his relatives would have been buried down at Ma-wang-tui if they had died after his progress to Tung-hai; and had they died after his disgrace they would hardly have been buried in such style. There remains the somewhat improbable possibility that the fifty-year-old woman buried at Ma-wang-tui was one of his relatives who died prior to these events.

For contrary reasons it is likely that members of the family of the second noble may be discounted. With due allowance for textual corruption,[42] it seems clear that he was appointed to be Superintendent of ceremonial[43] in the central government in 145 BC; presumably he moved to Ch'ang-an to take up his appointment, and he appears to have died while holding the office, in 141 BC. It could therefore be expected that his female relatives had moved to Ch'ang-an with him and that

The painting from tomb no. 1, Ma-wang-tui

they would not have been buried in Ch'ang-sha kingdom, unless they had died earlier.

Some attention should also be paid to the imperial edicts of 179 BC and 176 BC which ordered the nobles to repair to their estates, away from the vicinity of Ch'ang-an.[44] To what extent these orders applied also to the major cities of provinces and to what extent they were operative must remain questionable; but if they had applied to the noble of Tai, he would have been forced to remove from Ch'ang-sha kingdom to the site of his estate, which was situated in Chiang-hsia commandery.[45]

The report on the excavation suggests[46] that the tomb is to be dated after 175 BC, when the new lightweight coinage was introduced, and before 145 BC, i.e. in the time of the second or third nobles of the line. However, evidence has been found subsequently which suggests that the tomb can be identified as the resting place of the first countess. In the course of the excavation of the adjoining tombs, nos. 2 and 3, which was carried out from the end of 1973 onwards[47] it was found that tomb no. 2 contained a seal which was inscribed Li Ts'ang. It could therefore be inferred that the occupant of that tomb was no less a person than the first noble, chancellor of Ch'ang-sha kingdom, who died in 186 BC. In addition there was clear evidence that tombs nos. 1 and 3 had been built after no. 2, and the relative situation of no. 1 suggests that it had been built for the consort of the occupant of tomb no. 2. For these reasons it is believed that the fifty-year-old lady buried with such care and luxury in tomb no. 1 may be identified as the first countess. From the seal which was found inside one of the toilet cases buried in the tomb, she may be identified by name as Lady Hsin Chui.[48]

Tomb no. 3, which is situated to the south of tomb no. 1, included a large number of wooden strips, of which one bore the date in a year corresponding to 168 BC; it has been suggested that the tomb was built in that year for one of the younger sons of the first noble. As tomb no. 3 was also constructed before no. 1, it may be further assumed that the first countess survived until at least that year.

The preservation intact of the body of the first countess of Tai is one of the most remarkable features of the tomb, and as yet only one other example of the successful preservation of a body is known in China.[49] However, a reference may be cited to a similar discovery, made at a much earlier period, in much the same part of the land. In his notes to the *San-kuo chih*, P'ei Sung-chih quotes a statement of Kuo Sung, of the Chin dynasty, to the effect that the tomb of Wu Jui had been discovered towards the end of the Huang-ch'u period (220–226). Wu Jui had been the first of the kings appointed to rule Ch'ang-sha during the Han dynasty, holding the title for six months only, in 202 BC.

The discovery of his body 'just as if it was alive' with clothing intact caused quite a stir at the time.[50] It is open to speculation how far the art of preservation was practised at the court of Ch'ang-sha and to what extent it had been mastered by the officials charged with the burial of more exalted personages in the imperial mausolea near Ch'ang-an.

iv. The function of the painting and the theme of immortality

The painting was found on top of the innermost coffin, face downwards, with its head corresponding to the position of the head of the corpse. At its side lay 33 talismans in the form of manikins made of peachwood.[51] A bamboo rod at the head of the painting had been used to hold it rigid during suspension. A circular disc, such as a jade *pi*, was attached centrally at the head, and the painting was dressed with four tassels at the extremities. The overall length of the T-shaped painting is 2.05 metres, with a width of 92 cm at the upper part, and 47.7 cm at the lower part. The painting was made of three pieces of silk, and the lines of stitching whereby the two wings were joined to the central part may be traced in the photographs. The pigments of scarlet and gold, blue green and white are described variously as vegetable or mineral.[52]

The final position of the painting may have been chosen in order to bring its symbols into as close contact as possible with the body of the deceased countess. The fittings that accompanied the painting show that it could have been suspended on a wall or carried aloft during a funeral procession. Evidence to support this suggestion may be found in passages of the *Shih-chi* and *Han-shu*, which state that the celebrations of the victory achieved by Han arms over Nan-yüeh included a display of a banner which had been decorated with the sun, moon and dipper. From the *Hsü Han-shu* we learn of the part played by banners in the funeral cortège of an emperor. It may be noted that the custom of carrying a banner in funeral processions, on which the name of the deceased had been inscribed, and which was finally buried on top of the coffin, continued right up to 1949.[53]

The suggestion that the painting was used in a processional display is supported by its identification with an item listed in the inventory of funeral furnishings. The entry reads 'One flying mantle, length 12 feet'. It has been calculated that the total length of the painting, with its appurtenances, measures 2.85 metres, a figure which corresponds very closely to 2.82 metres or 12 Han feet.[54]

The painting which is under review may now be compared with a second painting which was discovered in a comparable position in

The painting from tomb no. 1, Ma-wang-tui

tomb no. 3 Ma-wang-tui which is dated in 168 BC. As yet full details have not been made available and no full-scale facsimile has been published. However, it is clear that the painting of tomb no. 3 is very similar to that of no. 1, being of the same shape and much the same size, and being dressed with tassels at the corners. Above all, the greatest point of similarity lies in the design, which appears to include many of the features and details that are seen in the painting of tomb no. 1. It is not yet known in what terms the second painting was described in the inventory of funerary goods of that tomb.[55]

Early Chinese paintings on silk are rare;[56] by virtue of its design and state of preservation, its wealth of detail and its skill of execution, the painting of tomb no. 1 Ma-wang-tui must rank in the forefront of the most significant discoveries made in China recently. Before examining its imagery, we may consider the more obvious dangers to which interpreters of the twentieth century may be prone, i.e. those of excessive rationalization, or attempts to explain all the symbols of the painting in terms of consistency. Eclecticism and a capacity to tolerate many persuasions is one of the characteristics of Chinese thought, if a bold generalization may be allowed; the painting may well have been conceived so as to incorporate a variety of beliefs, without being confined rigidly to a single tradition.

While the evidence at our disposal is tenuous, scanty or fragmentary, it is nonetheless unlikely that a single consistent traditional mythology had gained predominance over others at the time when the painting was composed. Both the painting and the comparable literature probably drew on several existing philosophies or mythologies, and it would be improper to expect identity or to demand consistency. It is perhaps a failure of traditional Chinese scholarship to attempt to seek consistency in this type of material; there are signs of a similar tendency in some modern Chinese publications, where the attempt to relate the features of the painting to literature are sometimes far-fetched or ultra-rational.

Similarly there is a danger of anachronism. No scholar would attempt – and so far as is known no scholar has attempted – to discern Buddhist iconography in a work of art that pre-dates the entry of Buddhism to China by some two centuries; and none would seek the characteristics that marked the Taoist institutions that were formed thereafter. It is however of equally great importance to bear in mind that in 168 BC orthodox Han cosmology with its triad of heaven, earth and man had hardly been formulated; a faith in the almighty powers of Yin and Yang and the Five Elements or Phases had not yet informed the Chinese mind in the marked way that may be discerned from about 50 BC; and heaven had not yet replaced other dignitaries as the objective of the cults of state. Similarly there is nothing to show that the Queen

Fig. 6. Painting from tomb no. 9, Chin-ch'üeh-shan, Lin-i, Shantung, measuring 200 by 42 cm. Subjects include the symbols of the sun and moon, scenes from everyday life and a pair of dragons

PLATE IV
Shou-chou mirror
(diameter 19.4 cm);
Crown copyright,
British Museum.

PLATE V
Shou-chou mirror with TLV marks
(B 0006; diameter 11.5 cm);
Crown copyright, British
Museum.

PLATE VI
TLV mirror (C1101; diameter 18.7 cm).

PLATE VII
TLV mirror (C1201; diameter 22.1 cm).

Mother of the West had yet gathered unto herself a following of the faithful.

Reference has been made above[57] to those poems of the *Ch'u tz'u* which illustrate the attempts made by the Chinese to save an individual from the consequences of death. These attempts included a summons which was issued to the soul (*hun*) of the individual, in order to persuade it to return from its great adventure in the beyond and to rehouse itself in its accustomed home and habitat of the body. As a means of entreaty, poems such as the *Ta-chao* and the *Chao-hun* described in horrifying detail the terrors that would await the soul in the great unknown, and contrasted these perils with the comforts of life in the realm of earth. Two other poems, whose theme is somewhat different, bring out the strength of the same belief; these are the *Ta-ssu-ming* and the *Shao-ssu-ming*, which are concerned with bringing the Lord of the Lives, or Director of Destiny, from heaven to earth, so that he may determine the length of a man's life.[58]

The continuity of this belief is attested in a number of ways. Chu Hsi[59] is cited as an authority who testifies to the practices of the southern Sung period. At that time it was the habit to summon the souls of those who had died recently by mounting to the roof of their house. The clothes of the deceased were carried there; the chief mourner or officiant faced north and cried aloud the name of the deceased thrice; and on his descent the body was wrapped in the clothes. This custom, which was observed in south China, is regarded as being associated with the *Chao-hun* poem and the way of life of Ch'u; and it has been suggested that the use of a painted banner such as the one found at Ma-wang-tui derived from the same motive and ritual. It has also been suggested that some of the funerary furnishings were buried as part of the ritual of summoning the soul.

The descriptions of the next world are carefully and vividly worded in the *Chao-hun* and *Ta-chao* poems; and there is a very clear identity with some of the subjects that are delineated on the painting. However, the purposes that lay behind the poems and the painting were, in the present writer's belief, fundamentally different. While in the poems the object is to deter, in the painting it is to provide guidance, so that the soul of the deceased countess may be escorted to her final goal of paradise.[60] Other examples of Han art, perhaps of a later date, were directed to the same purpose; for example the frescoes found in the tomb of Ying-ch'eng-tzu, which show the progress of a soul from this world to the next. Here the deceased person is shown in three successive postures on earth; and in an upper tableau he is portrayed on his arrival in the next world, accompanied by an acolyte to escort him, among the benign creatures who abound there.[61] It is also possible that

Ways to Paradise

the same theme forms the subject of a famous moulded brick from Ssu-ch'uan, which reveals the Queen Mother of the West in all her glory, and a mortal creature on his journey to the realm over which she presides.[62] Probably this brick dates from *c.* AD 100 to AD 250. It is suggested below that the pilgrim's progress which is depicted in the painting of Ma-wang-tui lay along a different road; for the soul of the countess is journeying to paradise by way of the east rather than the west, by way of P'eng-lai rather than K'un-lun.

v. Description of the painting: the vertical part

Several scholars interpret the painting by dividing it into three parts: (i) the horizontal part which forms the wide cross-bar of the T; (ii) the upper part of the upright section, extending from the canopy (alongside the tassels) to the lower of the two white platforms; and (iii) the lowest portion, lying below the lower platform and forming the smallest of the three parts of the painting. These parts are interpreted variously. They are sometimes taken as representing (i) the world of heaven; (ii) the deceased during her daily life; and (iii) the underworld.[63] Another writer explains the uppermost part as heaven and its gate; the middle part as depicting the journey and ascent from the world of man to heaven; and the lowest part, taken from halfway up the vertical section of the painting, as displaying the feasting which the deceased had enjoyed.[64] At least one scholar[65] interprets some of the characteristics of the painting in terms of the Five Phases, and conceives that their symbols may be traced in the order of 'Mutual Conquest'.[66] This notion depends on the somewhat questionable identification of some of the features of the painting and an association with the Five Phases that is not entirely convincing. In addition, while the 'Mutual Conquest' order of the Five Phases was probably accepted in official circles at this time, by the time that the *Wu hsing* theory had become a compelling belief the order adopted for the Five was that of 'Mutual Production' and not of 'Mutual Conquest'.

In the following account of the various features and the imagery of the painting, the underlying assumption differs somewhat. The painting is considered as comprising two parts, first the vertical part and secondly the broad horizontal part. The vertical part is regarded as depicting the road taken by the soul to its destined abode; and this road passes through the magic and mystery of the Island of P'eng-lai, the Vase. The second part of the painting is conceived as the destination to which the soul was successfully escorted, the world of paradise. The composition of the painting, which was executed with consummate skill, is symmetrical throughout, except for two features; these infuse a degree

The painting from tomb no. 1, Ma-wang-tui

of movement into a painting which might otherwise appear to be static. This movement is suggested by the extension of the lower horizontal platform (feature No. 8) further to the left than to the right; and when the beholder's eye has thus been carried from left to right, it will soon reach the second device, which will carry it higher up the painting, from the right to the left, i.e. the terracotta coloured causeway (No. 6) which leads to the upper horizontal platform.

The review of the painting must start with the vertical part, which includes the following features (an asterisk indicates those features which may be discerned in the available facsimiles of the painting found in tomb no. 3 Ma-wang-tui):

* 1 A lid-like cover, or canopy, on which a pair of double-tailed birds stand perched, and which is surmounted by a fleur-de-lis shaped flange
* 2 A bat or possibly bird, in flight below the lid
* 3 Two dragons, facing outwards; their bodies stretch from the lid to the base of the painting, being entwined and linked by (4)
* 4 A jade ring or *pi*, which divides the lower part of the painting into the two tableaux (5) and (8)
  5 Upper tableau: an elderly woman stands, resting on a stick, with three attendants standing behind her on the right of the painting, and two crouching in front of her at the left of the painting. The tableau rests on a white platform which bears the characteristic markings of jade ornaments. Access to the platform is by way of (6)
  6 Causeway, of a terracotta coloured substance, slanted towards the left and flanked by two leopards
* 7 Polychrome sash tied to the ring (4), and suspending a jade ornament (9), by means of a pole and two rings; two human-headed birds (10) roost on the sash
  8 Lower tableau: six figures face each other across a table, which bears vessels and other equipment upon it; they are attended by a white-robed figure standing behind one of five major vessels, of bronze, which are set in two groups of two and three respectively. Below the table, and set in the background of the tableau, a polychrome rectangular object, with a rounded top, rests on four short legs, with two carrying poles fitted longitudinally. The scene is surmounted by (9), and rests on a white platform
* 9 Jade ornament or *huang*
  10 Two human-headed birds roosting on the sash (7)
  11 Two turtles, standing erect on each side of the platform (in 8), outside the lower coils of the two dragons (3). They hold cloud-

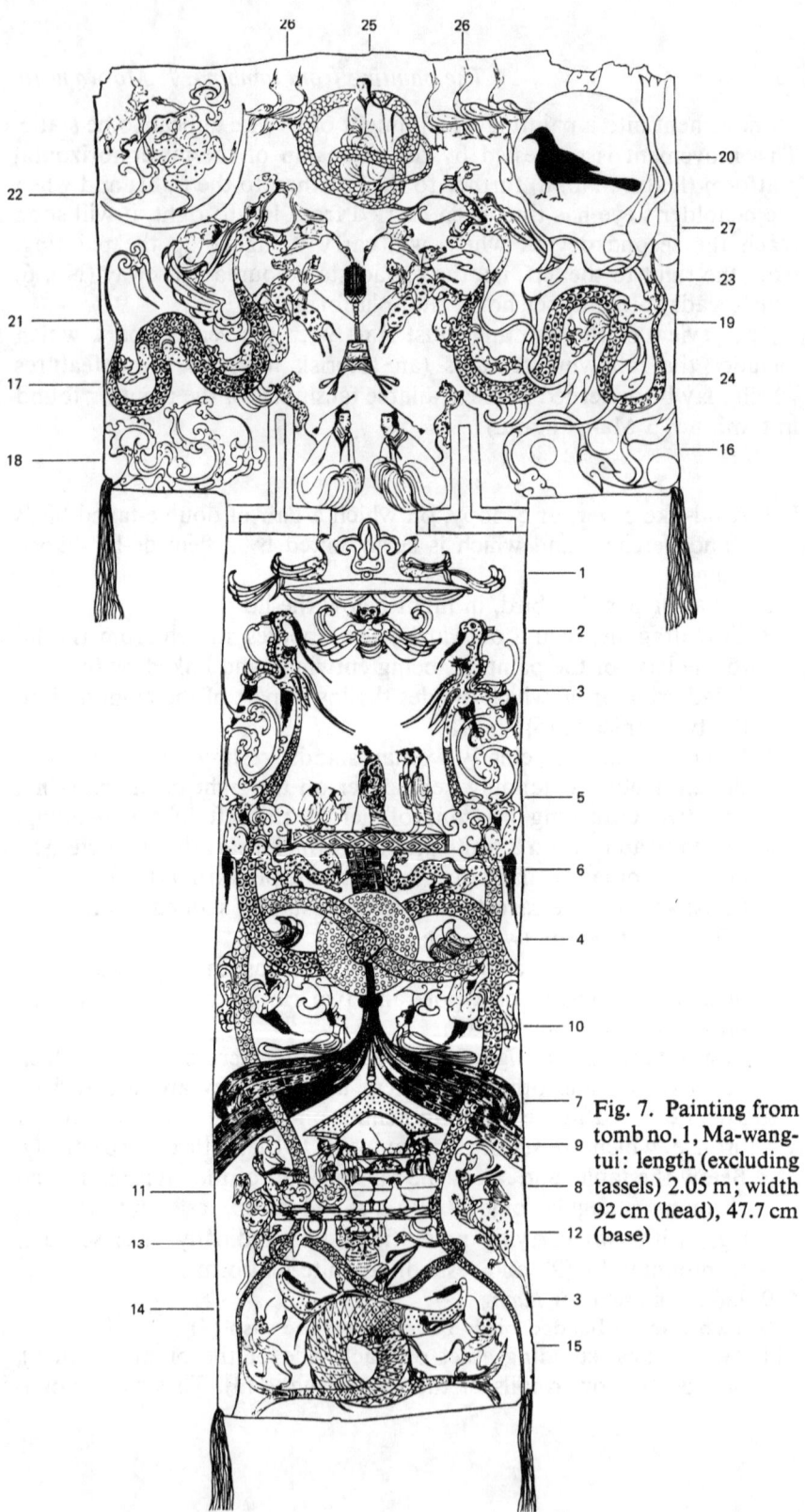

Fig. 7. Painting from tomb no. 1, Ma-wang-tui: length (excluding tassels) 2.05 m; width 92 cm (head), 47.7 cm (base)

The painting from tomb no. 1, Ma-wang-tui

scroll devices in their mouths, and bear owls upon their backs. The turtles are each depicted with four feet and a tail

*12 A giant whose arms uphold the platform of the lower tableau (8). His legs are crossed by (13)
13 A scarlet serpent, whose coils link the two dragons, and whose neck is tied to the left leg of the giant (12)
14 A pair of interlaced leviathan-like creatures
15 A pair of animals with horns, or antennae, whose paws are outstretched, with heads turned inwards

The vertical part of the painting is to be interpreted as a representation of P'eng-lai, the Island of the Vase through which lay the road to eternity and which features in other products of Han artists.[67] According to Chinese mythology, P'eng-lai was one of a group of islands that lay in the eastern seas; it formed the home of various creatures who had been blessed with immortality, and it was a source of the elixirs that could confer that blessing. Quite apart from the attempts of a number of kings of the pre-imperial era to procure these drugs, it was said that the first Ch'in emperor had endeavoured to find the islands and to wrest their secrets from them. Similar stories are told of Han Wu ti during the early years of his reign (141–87 BC),[68] and although the painting predates that period, the principles which those accounts exemplify are probably applicable.

Han Wu ti was subject to the persuasions of various persons who claimed to possess spiritual gifts or magical powers. One particular incident in which such an intermediary was involved illustrates the strength of the belief that the Island of P'eng-lai possessed the secret of the much-wanted gift of immortality.[69] In about 130 BC an intermediary named Li Shao-chün told Wu ti of the complex process of achieving this blessing, which required a belief in certain processes of alchemy.[70] It was first necessary to sacrifice to the spirit or god of the stove in order to acquire the necessary material objects; and with these it would be possible to transmute cinnabar powder into gold. Once gold had been manufactured it could be fashioned into vessels used for eating and drinking; and by these means a man's span of life could be prolonged. With such results, it would be right and proper to visit the immortals of the isles of P'eng-lai; and once such a visit had been paid and ceremonies such as the *Feng* and *Shan* sacrifices performed, one could achieve a state of deathlessness.

Li Shao-chün added that it was precisely this process that had been completed by Huang ti, the 'Yellow Emperor'. Li continued: 'Once when I was travelling by sea, I was received by Mr An Ch'i. The latter person feeds on outsize jujubes which are as large as gourds.[71] He is one of the immortals who is in direct contact with P'eng-lai; and if a man conforms with his ways, Mr An Ch'i will allow himself to be seen; otherwise he remains hidden.'

Wu ti carefully carried out all the prescribed measures, but without immediate results; and some twenty years later another intermediary, named Lüan Ta, claimed that he too had beheld An Ch'i.[72] There is in addition one further incident in which Wu ti was concerned which has a direct bearing on the contemporary belief in P'eng-lai and its properties.

In 115 BC Wu ti had built a terrace which was surmounted by a copper column designed to catch the sweet dews of heaven.[73] The magical qualities of honey dew were recognized elsewhere in Chinese history, as may be seen in the adoption of the term *Kan lu* as a regnal title; and at least one Han engraving shows a worshipper who is hoping to collect the precious liquid.[74] However, to Wu ti's consternation his terrace was burnt down in 104 BC. The precautions which he took to avert further calamity included sacrifice in honour of the inhabitants of P'eng-lai, and he was advised by yet another intermediary, Yung Chih, to take even more measures. According to Yung Chih it was the custom of the men of Yüeh, who lived in the deep south beyond the Yangste river, to replace a burnt building immediately. The new structure which they raised had perforce to be more magnificent than its predecessor, and in this way all evil consequences would be averted. For these reasons, we are told, Wu ti embarked on building the Chien-chang palace. He laid out the palace with the utmost respect to contemporary belief and its symbols, of which one aspect is of direct bearing on the present enquiry.

In the northern part of the site Wu ti had a large lake constructed, which was named T'ai-i, or Grand Unity. In the middle there was a lofty eminence, rising to a height of 200 feet; and the lake encompassed the four islands of P'eng-lai, Fang-chang, Ying-chou and Hu-liang. These symbolized the holy mountains, the turtles and the fish that are to be found within the ocean.

In other passages, that are probably somewhat later, the number of islands varies from three to five; but the association with a vase is explicit. The five mountains which according to the *Lieh-tzu* (3rd to 4th century AD?)[75] rise up in the sea, included one which was named Fang-hu, or 'Square Vase'. Kan Pao, who wrote in the early part of the fourth century, was even more specific:[76] 'The three vases are the three mountains within the sea, namely Fang-hu (Square Vase), P'eng-hu (the vase of P'eng-[lai]) and Ying-hu (the Vase of Ying-[chou]). They were named the vases, as the shapes of the mountains are like vases.'

The features of the vertical or lower part of the painting may be con-

The painting from tomb no. 1, Ma-wang-tui

sidered under three groups. First, those that form integral parts of the vase, i.e. the lid (1), the walls (3), and the ring (4); secondly, the features which indicate the situation of the vase and the means whereby it was fastened, i.e. the human-headed birds (10), turtles (11), giant (12), serpent (13), leviathans (14), and horned animals (15); and thirdly those items which depict the contents of the vase, i.e. the lower tableau (8), polychrome sash (7), jade ornament (9), and stairway (6) which leads to the upper tableau (5) and its winged harbinger (2). In considering these details the progress of the countess may be traced by a number of stages. Her first appearance may possibly be within the object that stands in the background of the lower tableau (8), and which, it is suggested below, may be a coffin. Next she is partaking of the elixir, possibly under the direction of An Ch'i or one of his colleagues. In the upper tableau (5) she has reached a further stage in her journey, properly dressed and accompanied, as before, by her acolytes, and with the bird of heaven acting as a harbinger to waft her on her way to her final destination. This stands revealed in all its glory in the horizontal or upper part of the painting.

Notes on the individual features of the painting follow.

(1) The lid of the vase
This is shaped very much like the lids that were fitted to the bronze or lacquer vases of early western Han. Very often these carried two or three upright flanges, shaped somewhat like a fleur-de-lis, and one of these is clearly visible on the painting.[77] The function of the pair of double-tailed birds who surmount the lid cannot be determined for certain. They are variously identified as phoenixes or other types,[78] and comparison has been drawn with the phoenix that are sometimes portrayed on the roofs of Han buildings. However, the reliefs which are marked by this characteristic date from eastern Han, and the function of the birds there has not been satisfactorily explained. In addition those birds are not double-tailed.

It may be appropriate at this stage to draw attention to the nearly regular alternation whereby the pairs of creatures who figure on the painting are shown facing outwards or inwards, as follows:

No. 15 horned animals		inwards
No. 14 leviathan-like creatures	outwards	
No. 11 turtles		inwards
No. 10 human-headed birds		inwards
No. 6 leopards	outwards	

39

Ways to Paradise

| No. 3 dragons | outwards |
| No. 1 double-tailed birds | inwards |

The same type of alternation may be observed in the composition of the upper part of the painting, where the leopards on the pillars (17) and the wardens (18) face inwards, the horses (23) outwards and the dragons (19 and 21) inwards. In addition there is a further feature of the composition to be noted. The three figures shown with full face (front view) are spaced fairly evenly along the length of the painting, thereby imparting a unity, i.e. the giant (12); the bird or bat in flight (2); and the female figure who stands at the central apex at the head of the painting (25).

(3) *The two dragons*
Coloured blue and red, the sinuous curves of these dragons extend from the base of the painting to the top of the vertical part, thus forming the walls of the vase, from the lower platform (in no. 8) or base, to the lid (1). The two are entwined together in the ring (4); and it is not impossible that, in addition to forming the walls of the vase the two dragons and their union are intended to evoke the concept of Yin and Yang.[79]

(4) *The jade ring*
In view of the characteristic markings of ritual discs, this may be identified as a *pi*.[80] These discs were used symbolically to represent heaven; there would not appear to be direct evidence to show that they were used in everyday life as buckles, and their sacred nature and value would perhaps preclude such a function. The use of the *pi* as the basis of a design is seen elsewhere at Ma-wang-tui, again suspending a sash.[81] In the present context it may perhaps represent the ring that was often attached to the side of Han vases for use in carriage.

(10), (11) *The human-headed birds and the turtles*
These two pairs should be considered together, in view of a passage in the *Lieh-tzu* which may well reflect an earlier tradition. In the *T'ang-wen* chapter there is a beautiful description of the five islands that lay in the eastern seas, including the island of P'eng-lai.[82] The islands are stated to have lacked roots whereby they could be held fast, with the result that they were wont to float to and fro, at the mercy of tide and wind. When the holy immortal beings of the islands complained of these dangers, the supreme power (*Ti*) realized that they were liable to drift beyond the western confines of the world, and that the immortals might be deprived of their home. He therefore commanded Yü Ch'iang to despatch fifteen giant turtles to raise their heads so as to hold the islands

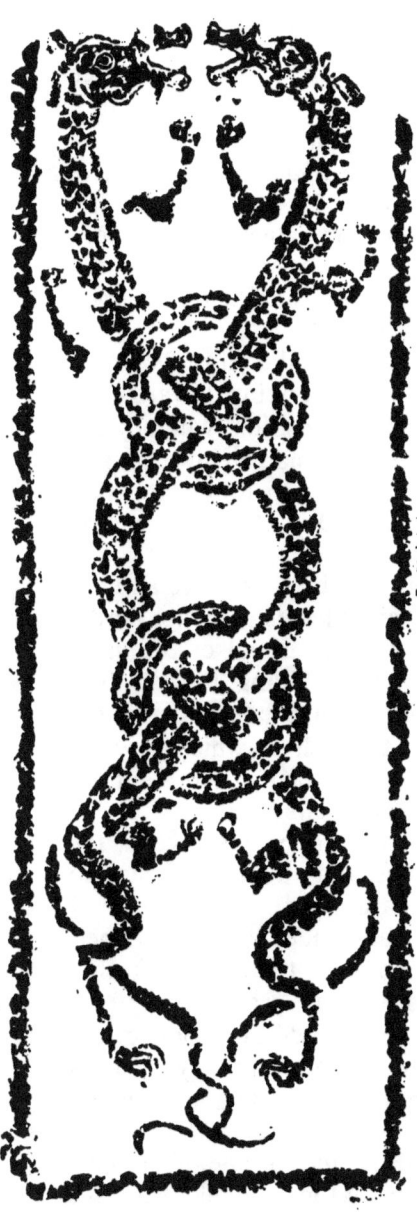

Fig. 8. Interlaced dragons, with two securing rings (105 by 35 cm) from a tomb at Shih-li-p'u, Hsü-chou, Kiangsu

Fig. 9. Fu Hsi and Nü Kua, with interlaced tails; from a stone relief from P'i hsien, Ssu-ch'uan

fast. The turtles obeyed the order by forming themselves into three teams, who took the task upon them turn in and turn about, with a change of rota taking place once every 60,000 years.

The passage may be supplemented from the *Shan-hai-ching*, where the characteristics of Yü Ch'iang are described. He was a spirit, who is described under the entry of Tan-erh, later the name of the modern island of Hainan. 'There is a spirit with a human face and a bird's body; a pair of green serpents hangs down from his ears, and he treads upon a pair of red serpents; he is named Yü Ch'iang.'[83]

The painting provides us with a pair of turtles and a pair of human-headed birds; and as they are both depicted looking inwards, an exception occurs in the arrangement of the composition, whereby the pairs of animals tend to be shown looking alternately inwards and outwards. Possibly this exception provides a clue which indicates that these two pairs of creatures should be considered in close conjunction with each other.

There are several points of variance between these passages and the painting. Although the turtles stand with raised heads, they are hardly using them as a means of anchoring the fugitive island of the vase; possibly their stance suggests that their feet are fulfilling this role. The human-headed birds are dressed with ribbons rather than snakes dangling from their ears, but it is possible that the sash on which they are perched, which is shot with scarlet, may be intended to represent the red serpents who are mentioned in the *Shan-hai-ching*.

No satisfactory explanation can be offered for the presence of the owls who stand upon the backs of the turtles, and no direct allusion to this feature has been found in Chinese literature.[84]

However, the identification of the human-headed birds and their association with the turtles must be considered in the light of further evidence. In the first place, human-headed birds are seen in other Han works of art in an entirely different context;[85] in addition some of the recent writers explain them as Chü-mang (or Kou Mang)[86] who is described in the *Shan-hai-ching* as 'having a bird's body and a human face, and riding on a pair of dragons.' Kuo P'u's note to the passage describes Kou Mang as the spirit of Wood (symbol of one of the Five Phases), and cites a passage from the *Mo-tzu* that may be relevant. This is to the effect that, in order to reward Mu Duke of Ch'in for his spiritual qualities, the supreme power ordered Kou Mang to confer upon him the gift of longevity for 19 (*sic*) years.[87] That this spirit possessed such powers may possibly have been the reason why he was an object for worship; for according to the *Han-shu* he was included among the deities who were worshipped in the time of Wang Mang.[88] The deity also appears in the *Yüan-yu* poem of the *Ch'u tz'u*; here the wandering soul decides to visit Kou Mang in his search for ultimate reality.[89]

Finally the characteristics that are ascribed to Yü Ch'iang and Kou Mang appear in at least one other context in the *Shan-hai-ching*, where they are attributed to Yen Tzu.[90] It is however unlikely that this passage is relevant to the painting, as Yen Tzu derived from the western sea and there is no other suggestion that the painting alludes to that area; there does not appear to be any reason to connect Yen Tzu with longevity or immortality.

The explanations of the human-headed birds as Yü Ch'iang or as Kou Mang are perhaps equally plausible; while Yü Ch'iang was specifically associated with P'eng-lai, he came from the north; Kou Mang was a tutelary god of the east and was capable of conferring immortality. On balance the explanation as Yü Ch'iang has been adopted here, in view of the association with the turtles.

(12), (13), (14), and (15) *The giant, serpent, pair of leviathans and pair of horned animals*

While a number of comparisons have been drawn between these features of the painting and literary passages, no fully convincing explanation has yet been forthcoming, and most writers on the subject agree that interpretation should be held in abeyance pending further research. It is possible that some of the problems may be solved by the discovery of new evidence, such as that of the painting found in no. 3 tomb, whose features are not dissimilar.

If the general interpretation of the painting that is given above is correct, and if it can be accepted that the artist has shown the island of P'eng-lai anchored in the ocean, the presence of two large fish is understandable enough; but the linkage of their tails, as if to form another jade ring (*pi*), has yet to be explained. Shang Chih-t'an[91] considers and rejects the view that the giant is to be identified with Yü Ch'iang, and the two large fish with the turtles ordered to carry out the commands of the supreme power. Other reports[92] seek to associate the scene with a passage in the *T'ien-wen* poem of the *Ch'u tz'u*;[93] this refers to the 'bird-turtles' who were linked together, and to Kun, father of Yü, who had failed to complete the task that his son later accomplished. But whereas the description of 'bird turtles' could apply to feature 11, it could hardly apply to no. 14; and while the bird turtles of no. 11 are carefully separated, it is the leviathan creatures of no. 14 who are linked so inextricably together.

An Chi-min[94] explains the flat disc that rests upon the giant's head, and which is taken here to be the base of the vase of P'eng-lai, as an object which represents the earth. However, there seems to be no literary support for the Atlas-like posture of the central figure. An Chih-min explains the latter as a spirit who upheld the earth, but agrees that there is no source for such a myth and no name for such a spirit. He draws an interesting parallel with a mural from Chi-an, which was dated some time after the painting of Ma-wang-tui. He also draws attention to passages in the *Shan-hai-ching* and *Huai-nan-tzu* which refer specifically to the possibility of rebirth after death, and it is possible that the artist has included an allusion here to the main theme of his painting.[95] However, An Chih-min is surely incorrect in suggesting that the two horned or antenna-bearing animals (15) have been inserted by the artist in order to fill up a blank space in the painting, whose imagery and composition is such that every detail can be expected to bear an ideological or mythological significance.

(7) and (9)   *The sash, pole, ring and jade ornament or canopy*
Some of these features, i.e. the sash, pole and jade ornament, together with the jade ring (4), the leopards (6) and the human-headed birds (10) are also seen in the decorations of west Han tomb no. 1, Sha-tzu-t'ang.[96] However, the combination of the features there is somewhat different (e.g. at Sha-tzu-t'ang the human-headed birds and the leopards are juxtaposed, at Ma-wang-tui they are separated; at Sha-tzu-t'ang the jade ornament or canopy appears directly above a bell; at Ma-wang-tui the bell has been removed aloft and is suspended in the upper part of the painting; see feature no. 24, a bell, below).

An Chih-min[97] interprets the jade ornament as a musical instrument, i.e. a *ch'ing*; and he further regards the other features that are under consideration here as representing the type of frame in which such instruments were suspended. This interpretation depends partly on a passage from the *K'ao-kung-chi* chapter of the *Chou-li*, whenever that may have been compiled;[98] and the various features of the painting are taken as symbolizing the characteristics of the traditional type of decoration of such frames. The explanation of the jade ornament as a *ch'ing* is possibly supported by its close association with a bell, as at Sha-tzu-t'ang; however, this theory is doubted by several scholars, including Mrs Rawson, and Professor Hayashi. The explanation of the other parts as a means of suspending the frame is not altogether convincing.[99] It is more probable, as has been suggested by Mrs Rawson and Professor Hayashi and others,[100] that the canopy is formed of a jade ornament known as a *huang*; while the *ch'ing* was always formed of two limbs of uneven length, the *huang* was characteristically symmetrical, and was marked with the type of decoration that is seen in this feature of the painting. Like the *pi*, the *huang* was used as a pendant.

The painting from tomb no. 1, Ma-wang-tui

(8) *The lower tableau*

This is mounted on a platform whose pattern is again characteristically that of jade ornaments; and the scene of the tableau has been variously interpreted as a banquet or as a preparatory rite observed prior to setting out the banquet.[101] The prominent sets of two and three vessels in the foreground recall the arrangement of the two and three attendants in the upper tableau (no. 5). These are also matched by the two sets of two and three birds at the central apex in the top half of the painting; and in all three cases the set of two appears at the left and the set of three at the right. It is open to question whether these vessels may be identified as equipment used in alchemical processes.[102]

The scene shows a white-robed attendant waiting on six participants, who may be identified as the deceased herself and the five servants who accompany her in the upper tableau (5). Alternatively one writer suggests[103] that the figures are all male, in view of the style of their headdress. The white robes of the attendant perhaps recall a statement in the *Lieh-tzu*[104] that all the animals and birds of P'eng-lai were clad in pure white.

Set more deeply in the background there lies a rectangular object. This is rounded at the top; it rests on four feet, and carrying poles are attached. This object stands below an inner table or platform, which bears a further set of vessels and a long-handled ladle upon it. The gaily-coloured object below has been explained as a 'dumb waiter', intended for bringing up further supplies needed for the banquet; but a better suggestion, which is due to Professor Watson, is considered below. One commentator[105] cites a passage from the *Chao-hun* poem in order to explain the scene as a banquet; and enjoyment of such a scene is regarded as being typical of the luxuries that were available to members of the feudal aristocratic classes to which the deceased belonged. To this suggestion it may be objected that the passage in the *Chao-hun* is deliberately describing a scene that was wont to take place on earth; and this is inconsistent with what is believed here to be the motif and message of the painting.

An Chih-min[106] takes the platform on which the scene rests to symbolize the earth, and believes that the scene portrays the human world of the flesh with which the deceased was embroiled. In this connection he cites a famous passage from the *Huai-nan-tzu*,[107] which writes of heaven as the cover or firmament and earth as the base or supporting fundament. An allusion to this concept may be present in the painting at this point, in conjunction with the lid (no. 1) whose function can be taken to be that of a cover; but the main significance of the tableau seems to be not that of an earthly scene so much as that of a stage reached by the deceased in her journey.

Ways to Paradise

Professor Watson has made the valuable suggestion that the gaily-painted object standing below the innermost table represents the coffin in which the deceased was buried. Certainly the colours, if not the shape of the object, are evocative of one of the coffins that was used for burial; and it could well be that in this object we see the first of several portrayals of the deceased on her journey from earth to paradise.

(6) *The causeway*
This is marked with spiral pattern decoration, and its oblique stance contrasts with all other features of the painting. The two leopards, whose presence has not been explained, face outwards.

(5) *The upper tableau*
This includes a portrait of the deceased. She is shown attended by two male and three female servants, and as befits her age she leans upon a staff. The whole party stand on a white platform, decorated with the patterns that are usually engraved on jade; and the lady herself stands on a slight dais or eminence. Three dazzling pearls or jewels adorn her head-dress, and there is reason to believe that the use of such decorations was privileged and limited to members of the nobility.[108] The identification of the central figure of the tableau with the deceased woman who was buried in the tomb is also suggested by comparison of the dress of the painted figure and the clothing found as part of the funerary furnishings.[109] A number of literary passages testify to the practice of painting portraits of the Han court, but the painting from Ma-wang-tui is probably the oldest surviving example known from China.[110]

The division of the attendants into two groups of two and three invites comparison with the division of the five birds at the apex of the painting, on either side of the central figure there. The two groups of the tableau are shown with different types of head-dress, and are said to comprise three female attendants and two male waiters, who are bearing trays of refreshments or offerings. The scene is comparable with that shown in the upper part of the fresco from Ying-ch'eng-tzu, where again a deceased person is portrayed, accompanied by acolytes, on the last stages of the journey to paradise.[111]

(2) *The bat or bird in flight*
This is sometimes identified with the mythological *Fei-lien*

Shang Chih-t'an[112] alludes to this creature as a bat, and the identification is supported by the enlarged photographs now available. However, the symbolical meaning of the bat as a harbinger of good fortune is by no means clear at this time, and the figure in the painting is not

The painting from tomb no. 1, Ma-wang-tui

necessarily to be associated with the so-called bat-type decoration that is seen in some Han mirrors.[113]

An Chih-min doubts the tentative suggestion that the creature is to be identified as the *Fei-lien*,[114] which is mentioned or alluded to in some of the *Ch'u tz'u* poems such as the *Li-sao*, *T'ien-wen* and *Yüan-yu*.[115] The term also appears as the name of a lodge which was erected at Ch'ang-an in 109 BC,[116] but by the second century AD the expression had become sufficiently obscure to require explanation. Thus Ying Shao (AD 140–206) describes *Fei-lien* as a 'divine creature capable of raising the winds'; and Chin Cho (fourth century AD) explains it as 'possessing a body like a stag, a head like a sparrow, horns, a serpent's tail and the markings of a panther.'[117] The term is apparently not seen in the *Shan-hai-ching*; Hawkes translates it as the 'Wind god'; and the standard note to a passage in the *Huai-nan-tzu* describes the *Fei-lien* as a 'long-haired creature with wings.'[118]

The creature with outstretched wings who is depicted so boldly in the painting hardly corresponds with these descriptions, and no reason has been suggested for including the God of the Winds in the painting. Nor does the creature resemble very closely other objects that have been found elsewhere (e.g. in Korea), and identified as *Fei-lien*.[119] However, the suggestion is not to be ignored, in view of the references in the *Ch'u tz'u* to *Fei-lien* as an outrider, riding behind the wanderer, and as a harbinger deliberately sent to prepare the way for a pilgrim's progress.[120]

While rejecting the identification as *Fei-lien*, An Chih-min suggests two possibilities (i) The creature was inserted by the artist in order to fill a blank space in the painting. This idea is hardly acceptable in view of the meticulous care paid to the composition. (ii) That the feature is associated with the traditional concept of the lid or cover of heaven.

There remains the possibility that the bird is the *Luan huang* or Bird of Heaven, mentioned in the *Li-sao*.[121] In this passage the bird gives prior notification of the arrival of a soul in heaven.

vi. Description of the painting: the upper part

Twelve elements may be discerned in the upper part of the painting, which displays the artist's view of paradise (an asterisk indicates those features which are also seen in the painting found in tomb no. 3):

*16 Two towers, or gateposts, evidently built in two orders that are seen in perspective, and with shaped, tapering heads.
17 A pair of leopards, climbing the gateposts and looking inwards.

18 A pair of male figures, seated between the gateposts, robed and hatted.
19 At the right-hand side: a wingless dragon, coiled in a tree, among whose branches are set eight small red discs. The upper branches enclose (20).
*20 A larger disc, also red, representing the sun, with a two-legged bird or crow shown in profile.
21 At the left-hand side: a winged dragon, above a cloud-scroll pattern; there is a woman seated on the wing, gazing up to (22).
*22 The crescent moon, enclosing a dancing toad and hare. A cloud-scroll pattern passes behind the toad.
23 A pair of prancing horses, between the two dragons. They are mounted by riders, apparently with human bodies, faces of ?deer, and wearing armour. The riders hold ropes which suspend (24).
*24 A bell, which is held as a canopy over the two male figures (18). The bell supports a series of five circular rings on which a flat dish rests; vapours or aromas appear to be arising from the dish.
25 Placed at the climax of the painting, in the centre and flanked by the sun and moon, a woman dressed in a blue robe, and hatless. In place of legs, her body ends in a scarlet serpentine coil, which emerges from the mouth of one of the dragons (19).
26 Two groups of standing birds, on each side of (25), with brown bodies and red beaks.
27 Two birds in flight, hovering below (25), savouring the aromas which arise from the dish (24); the birds have brown bodies and red beaks.

(16), (17) and (18) *The two towers, leopards and male figures*
The portals of paradise are evidently open to admit incoming travellers, provided that they can satisfy the wardens (nos. 17 and 18) that they are qualified to enter. While several passages of literature indicate that these are the portals of heaven or of The Heavens, in this context the supreme denizen of the realm was still conceived as *Ti*, and not as *T'ien*.[122]

In the *Ch'u tz'u* there are references to the gates of heaven and their dual function. In the *Nine Songs* they are opened wide to allow the Lord of the Lives to descend to earth, and the reference is interpreted by Chinese commentators in terms of *Ti*.[123] A second reference is from the *Li-sao*, where, in the course of his journey the pilgrim

'asked Heaven's porter to open up for me;
But he leant across Heaven's gate and eyed me churlishly'.[124]

The painting from tomb no. 1, Ma-wang-tui

The theme here is that of the painting, which shows the two porters or wardens leaning across the gateway. In this context the text refers specifically to *Ti*, which Hawkes has rendered as *Heaven*; and the expression *ch'ang-ho* of the original is explained by Wang I as 'The gates of Heaven'. The same expression occurs elsewhere in the *Ch'u tz'u*,[125] where the pilgrim

> 'bade heaven's gate-keeper open up his doors,
> And he pushed the portals open and looked out at me'.

The subsequent verses of the poem describe the arrival of the pilgrim at the palace of *Ti*, and an almost identical passage is seen in the *Ta-jen fu* of Ssu-ma Hsiang-ju.[126]

It has been tentatively suggested that the two figures should be identified with the Greater and Lesser Lords of the Lives who feature in the *Nine Songs*, i.e. two impersonations of that strong spirit who possessed powers of life and death over mortals.[127] There are passages in texts such as the *Shih-chi*, *Chou-li*, *Li-chi* and, most clearly, the *Feng-su t'ung-i*,[128] which attest the contemporary belief in these spirits and the practice of worship that was directed to them. On the whole this suggestion seems to be unlikely. It would in any event be incorrect to assume that the two figures are those of two Lords of the Lives, one major and one minor, for, as Waley has pointed out, there was only one such figure in Chinese belief. In addition the whole concept of the *Ta-ssu-ming* poem is that of a god descending to earth to determine the length that should be properly assigned to mortals' lives. Such a theme is at variance with that of the painting which is believed to depict the progress of a soul to paradise.

The two leopards who are mounted upon the pillars call to mind a passage in *Chao-hun*. Here again the theme of the poem is in contrast with that of the painting, as it includes a series of invocations which beg a soul not to entrust itself to the dangers of a hazardous journey through the skies, such as the following:[129]

> 'O soul, come back! Climb not to the heaven above.
> For tigers and leopards guard the gates, with jaws ever ready to rend up mortal men, . . .'

One of the two animals that are painted so vividly certainly stands with 'jaws ready to rend up mortal men'; and while the themes of the painting and the poem differ, the inclusion of this descriptive detail is appropriate in each case. The two comparatively small[130] leopards shown here facing inwards may possibly complement the two larger animals that are seen in the middle of the vertical part of the painting, standing on each side of the causeway (No. 6) and facing outwards.

(19) and (20) *The wingless dragon, tree and eight smaller discs or suns; and the one large sun with the two-legged bird*
A number of different interpretations have been offered for these features of the painting. Possibly the artist was drawing eclectically on the rich mythology of his time and giving rein to his brush so as to include different elements for his composition. At the same time, as the literary sources for such mythology are somewhat slender, it may never be possible to match the painting exactly with corresponding textual allusions.

The total number of red discs or suns shown in the painting is nine. However, there are a number of references to the simultaneous existence of ten rather than nine suns; and at least two writers[131] who have wished to associate the painting exactly with this myth have suggested that the missing, or tenth, sun was deliberately left concealed behind the branches of the tree which the other discs surmount. In view of the artist's consummate skill and his habit of making all features clearly explicit, such an explanation is hardly convincing.

These features may be considered under six headings.

(i) There is the story that long, long ago ten suns came out simultaneously, scorching the earth and killing all growing plants and herbs. So Yao ordered I to raise his bow and to shoot; nine of the suns dropped down; and all the birds of the heavens fell to earth to die, shedding their feathers as they fell. This story forms one of the enigmatic subjects of the *T'ien-wen* poem of the *Ch'u tz'u*; it is also related in the *Huai-nan-tzu*.[132]

(ii) According to the *Shan-hai-ching*[133] the Fu-sang tree grew by the side of the valley of the morning,[134] in the east. This was the place where the ten suns were wont to bathe; and thereafter nine of the suns clustered in the lower branches of the tree, while one rose to the top.

The Fu-sang tree is also seen in several passages of the *Ch'u tz'u*. In the *Li-sao*[135] the wanderer,

> '. . . watered my dragon steeds at the Pool of Heaven,
> And tied the reins up to the Fu-sang tree.'

Here the Pool of Heaven is identified as one of the constellations; and Hawkes explains the Fu-sang tree as a 'mythical tree in the far east which the sun climbs up in his rising.' The same allusion is seen in the

The painting from tomb no. 1, Ma-wang-tui

Nine Songs, where the sunrise is heralded by the glance of a ray from Fu-sang,[136]

'There is a glow in the sky; soon he will be rising in the east.
Now on my balcony falls a ray from Fu-sang.
I touch my horses and gently drive.
The night grows pale; now it is broad daylight.'

(iii) The *Ch'u tz'u* also includes a highly discouraging reference to the ten suns, in a vivid passage of the *Chao-hun*.[137] Here the poet begs the soul to return to its old home of the body, for,

'... in the east you cannot abide.
There are giants there a thousand fathoms tall, who seek only for souls to catch,
And ten suns that come out together, melting metal, dissolving stone.
The folk that live there can bear it; but you, soul, would be consumed.
O soul come back! In the east you cannot abide.'

It would be highly inappropriate to associate the prayer of this passage with the object of the painting.

(iv) There is a passage in the *Chuang-tzu*[138] in the contrary sense, i.e. it refers to the beneficial results from the simultaneous appearance of ten suns, as all manner of creation was thereby illuminated.

(v) Perhaps the most significant passage of the *Ch'u tz'u*, which is to be found in the *Yüan-yu*,[139] mentions nine suns, in the expression *chiu yang*. Hawkes renders the passage as follows:

'In the morning I washed my hair in the Valley of the Morning [*T'ang ku*];
In the evening I dried myself on the coasts of heaven [*Chiu yang*].'

In contrast with the theme of the *Chao-hun* poem, of which a passage has just been cited, the poet of the *Yüan-yu* described a celestial pilgrimage which he saw ending triumphantly; for the soul who set out to escape from the toils of a corrupt world succeeded by various endeavours in reaching a state of purity, or the Great Beginning. It is within this context that the wanderer passed through the Valley of the Morning, and it was during this journey that he found himself by the *Chiu yang* or nine suns. Hawkes' rendering of this expression as 'the coasts of heaven' derives from Wang I's notes to the text, and the interpretation corresponds admirably to the stages of a journey which led from earth to paradise, i.e. the cliffs that lay between heaven and earth. It may also be noted that the *Yüan-yu* poem takes the mystic pilgrim through the palace of the supreme power (*Ti*).[140]

(vi) The suggestion[141] that the eight smaller discs are in fact stars and have nothing to do with the myths regarding the sun, or the suns, receives some support from the inclusion of a large number of stars between the sun and the moon in the painting that was found in tomb no. 3.[142] However, the interpretation of the eight as a stylized version of the Dipper seems to be less likely.

It may perhaps be tentatively concluded that the imagery of the one major and eight minor suns is to be associated with *Ti* rather than with a power named heaven. It would seem that the story of I shooting down the nine suns is not appropriate to the theme of the painting, which does not appear to allude to the subsequent death of the birds and their loss of feathers. Similarly the fearsome ten suns of the *Chao-hun* are not of direct relevance to the painting. The artist has perhaps combined the story of the Fu-sang tree in the east with the idea of the *Chiu yang*, which signify the cliff that separates the skies from the earth, and which travellers in search of purity will find on their way to paradise.

The wingless dragon below the Fu-sang tree balances the winged dragon that crouches below the moon on the other side of the painting. A number of literary passages suggest that the dragon may allude to the movement of the sun, conceived sometimes as being achieved by horse and chariot, sometimes by a chariot which was drawn by six or eight dragons. In addition to the passages from the *Li-sao* and the *Nine Songs* that are cited above[143] there is a further reference in the *Chiu-t'an* of Liu Hsiang.[144] This poem dates from over a century after the time of the painting, and some of its allusions may possibly not have been appropriate when the artist was at work. But again we are told of a pilgrim following the path of the sun who sings that he

'tethered my six dragons to the Fu-sang tree'.[145]

Similarly a passage of the second or third century AD refers specifically to the sun who rode in a carriage to which six dragons were harnessed, under the control of Hsi and Ho.[146]

The twin-legged bird which is shown so strikingly in the full disc of the sun also appears in the painting which was found at tomb no. 3, Ma-wang-tui; and in both paintings the crescent moon is shown with her attributes of the toad and the hare. These symbols recur in connection with TLV mirrors and the Queen Mother of the West; they

The painting from tomb no. 1, Ma-wang-tui

are considered separately below, in the light of the literary evidence and their wider implications.[147]

In the two paintings from Ma-wang-tui the distinction between the sun and the moon is obvious at sight, in so far as the one is shown full-face and the other as a crescent. However, in other examples of Han art the two bodies are both shown as full circles, and the presence of the attributes there may have been necessary for purposes of identification. It would seem that, in general, the sun's attribute first appears as a two-legged bird, as in these two paintings; next, it takes the form of a bird seen from above, in flight; finally, during the eastern Han period, we find the attribute of the three-legged bird or crow.

(21) and (22)   *The winged dragon and woman seated on the wing; the crescent moon with toad and hare*

An Chih-min has suggested[148] that the winged dragon, which stands in perfect symmetry with the wingless dragon by the Fu-sang tree, is to be identified with Ying lung, who, as related in the *Shan-hai-ching*, was able to provide an abundant fall of rain in the south.[149] Ying lung is described as a winged dragon in one of the notes to the *Huai-nan-tzu* and in the *Kuang-ya*;[150] but the relevance of this myth to the rest of the painting has yet to be explained. A further reference, in the *Ch'u tz'u*, is similarly concerned with water and the regulation of its supply.[151] Hawkes translates the passage as 'What did the winged dragon trace on the ground?'; he cites the story of the dragon who assisted Yü the Great by tracing lines on the ground to show where he should dig his water-courses. But here again there seems to be no direct connection with the other concepts or allusions of the painting. The symbolism of the dragon who flies below the moon must remain unknown at present.

Sun Tso-yün points out that in general the moon is shown in Han art full-face; his statement that the painting provides a unique view, of a crescent moon, was probably true at the time when Sun was writing (before January 1973); but the discovery of the painting in tomb no. 3 has subsequently provided another example in an almost identical context.[152]

A number of traditions are concerned with the woman who is seated on the dragon's wing and with the toad and hare that are encompassed within the moon's crescent. Possibly a number of elements of Chinese mythology have been fused here by the artist, in so far as each one has a bearing on the attainment of immortality. It is of considerable importance that both the toad and the hare are portrayed in the moon, and not just one of those animals alone. The elements of the myth may be discriminated as follows:

Ways to Paradise

(i) The earliest reference is probably to be found in the *T'ien-wen* poem, where the catechism reads:[153]

'What is the peculiar virtue of the moon, the Brightness of the Night, which causes it to grow once more after its death? What does it advantage it to keep a frog [or hare] in its belly?'[154]

(ii) The *Huai-nan-tzu* refers in at least two passages to the presence of the toad within the moon, and to the illumination cast upon the world by the moon, feeding on the toad.[155]

(iii) A further passage of the *Huai-nan-tzu* carries the story of how I sought the drug of immortality from the Queen Mother of the West; and how Heng O stole the drug and fled therewith to the moon. The standard commentary of the *Huai-nan-tzu* explains that Heng O was the wife of I; she stole the drug from her husband before he had been able to take the requisite dose. According to a later version of the story, which dates from the time of Chang Heng (AD 78–139), having attained a state of immortality, Heng O fled to the moon to be transformed into a toad.[156]

(iv) The toad is specifically credited with the power of conferring immortality in a passage of the *Hsüan-chung-chi*,[157] which reads 'Horns grow on the toad's head, consumption of which brings 1,000 years of life and ability to feed on the Essence of the Mountains.'

(v) The existence of the toad and hare together in the moon is mentioned in a fragment of Liu Hsiang's comments to the Classics and in the anonymous *Ch'un-ch'iu yüan-ming pao*.[158] Similarly Chang Heng identified Heng O with the toad; he also wrote of the moon as being the ancestress of the essences of Yin, which 'being accumulated together are transformed into an animal with the image of a hare.'[159]

(vi) There are also references to a three-legged toad in the moon, complementing the three-legged bird who is the attribute or symbol of the sun.[160]

In iconography the hare and the toad were grouped together from the *Chan-kuo* period onwards.[161] The Han artist who conceived the set of astronomical diagrams for a tomb built near Lo-yang *c.* 50 BC likewise showed both creatures, as did many of his successors in the eastern Han period.[162] Just as some of the murals which depict the Queen Mother of the West display the three-legged bird, so too do they include a toad and a hare; and these two are shown independently of a circular disc. In some of these reliefs the hare is shown pounding his drugs with his pestle and mortar; sometimes the toad dances with glee, holding a strange object in his hands; we may surmise that he is in a state of

The painting from tomb no. 1, Ma-wang-tui

euphoria induced by taking a dose, and near to the state of immortality so greatly desired.[163] Occasionally an artist depicts the moon as a disc with either the hare or the toad by itself.[164] The concept of the toad as an agent for the renewal of the moon may be compared with the story that is seen elsewhere that a toad, by eating the moon, causes its eclipses.[165]

Possibly this part of the painting is to be interpreted as a series of two scenes. In the first we are shown Heng O, still possessed of her mortal coil, but set on her flight to the moon to achieve immortality; and secondly we see Heng O after her transformation, living happily in the moon in the guise of a toad. Fong Chow[166] takes the view that we are looking not at Heng O in the process of transformation, but at the deceased countess herself, on her way to immortality. An alternative suggestion is made below (p. 59) for the depiction of this highly important concept which was crucial to the theme of the painting.

For his treatment of the left-hand side of the upper part of the painting the artist has combined several ideas and drawn on several elements of mythology. The moon takes her rightful place in the heavens, which form the abode of *Ti*; and they form the destination for which all those who yearn for immortality seek. The moon herself, shown somewhat exceptionally as a crescent, may serve as a symbol of immortality, as her regular cycle takes her through birth, death and re-birth. At the same time we are shown how one human being achieved the desired state by consuming the drugs prescribed for the transformation, and the artist was perhaps suggesting means whereby the countess too could, or had, achieved a similar aim. Possibly the figure of Heng O is also designed to recall to the viewer's mind the story of I shooting down the suns, although, as has been seen, there are reasons for doubting whether the eight minor discs on the right-hand side of the painting derive from that story.

It is perhaps questionable whether the image of the toad and the hare carried with it implications of the Queen Mother of the West; for although those attributes accompany the Queen in later examples of Han art; and although she is mentioned in writings of 130 BC or later, there is little to show for certain that she had as yet entered into the Chinese concept of immortality at the time when the painting was made.[167]

(23), (24) and (27) *The horses and riders, the bell and the two birds in flight*
These symbolic elements of the painting seem to be associated together; the riders on the prancing horses suspend the bell, and the bell supports a vessel which attracts the attention of the birds. As yet no satisfactory

Ways to Paradise

explanation has been furnished for the individual elements or the whole complex.

On the basis of two passages in the *Shan-hai-ching* and the *Huai-nan-tzu*, Shang Chih-t'an identifies the two animals as the horses of heaven, who are possibly termed *Ch'eng-huang* or *Fei-huang*.[168] However, there are reasons for doubting this suggestion.

(i) The description of the *Fei-huang* does not include any specific mention of the horses of heaven; the *Shan-hai-ching* writes that 'its form is like that of a fox[169] and it bears horns upon its back.' The animals in the painting scarcely resemble such a beast; and in place of the horns they carry demon riders who are engaged in suspending the bell by means of ropes. These demons have yet to be identified.

(ii) The *Shan-hai-ching* includes a somewhat different description of the *T'ien ma*, as follows:[170]

> 'There are animals there [i.e. on the Ma-ch'eng hills] whose form resembles that of a dog, with black heads, and they take to flight at the sight of human beings; they are called the horses of heaven.'

Such creatures are again somewhat different from those that are depicted in this part of the painting.

(iii) The mythological creatures of the passage which has just been cited are to be distinguished from the Heavenly Horses of the Han period, when they are first mentioned for a date after 120 BC. Whatever the origin of the expression and its application to a special breed of horse that was being imported from central Asia, the spiritual qualities with which they are invested do not appear to have had any concern with P'eng-lai or the paradise that lay beyond.[171]

An Chih-min[172] attempts to explain the bell in terms of a passage in the *Chou-li*, which concerns the use of bells to issue a warning. Cheng Hsüan's note to the passage enlarges on the text by commenting that the bells were rung to warn the population that orders were being given for their compliance. An Chih-min suggests the possibility that the riders on the animals may be identified as the commissioners of heaven who were responsible for the bells. No proof or further evidence may be adduced in support of this suggestion.

As yet the bell and its ribbons, the five multi-coloured globes which surmount it, the flat dish at the summit and the aromas that arise therefrom remain unexplained. Perhaps it may be tentatively suggested, without supporting evidence, that the dish was suspended in this elaborate way in order to catch the sweet dews that descend from heaven and which are known to bring blessings.[173] (For an explanation of the bell in conjunction with the ring and sash of the vertical part of the painting, see p. 140 note 100.)

The painting from tomb no. 1, Ma-wang-tui

The two birds who are seen to be savouring the aroma that arises from the dish are likewise not identified in literature for certain. An Chih-min[174] suggests that they are the wild geese mentioned in the song composed by Liu Pang in the style of Ch'u. He adds that their inclusion in the painting may allude to their ability to fly to great heights; and at the same time it fills in a blank space in the painting.

(25) and (26) *The woman's figure, ending in a serpentine tail, and the two and three birds at the left and right*
This beautiful figure stands at the head of the painting and forms the climax to which the viewer's eye has been inexorably drawn through the many stages of the story. The figure has been identified variously, and in the opinion of the present writer somewhat questionably, as Fu Hsi, Nü Kua or Chu lung.

(i) The identification of the figure with Fu Hsi, who is described in the *Shih-chi* as one of the spirits of heaven or as the ancestor of man, has been suggested by Sun Tso-yün and Shang Chih-t'an.[175] They draw attention to a comparable figure which appears in a relief from Shantung, and which likewise has a human head and human body, ending in a serpent's tail. In addition there is a descriptive label engraved on the relief which identifies that figure as Fu Sheng.[176]

Other evidence, largely of the eastern Han period, incorporates a somewhat later and possibly more fully developed tradition regarding Fu Hsi. He is regularly shown as one of a pair, being linked to Nü Kua; they are said to have human heads and serpentine or dragonish bodies, and they are very often shown holding attributes, such as the circular discs of the sun and the moon, with the bird and the hare, or their characteristic compasses and set-square.[177]

There are reasons for doubting the explanation of this figure as Fu Hsi. As An Chih-min has pointed out, there is no evidence to show that the myth had been formulated as early as the time of the painting.[178] Of equal significance is the contrast between the concept of Fu Hsi as male and the figure of the painting which is clearly female. In addition while Fu Hsi is described in the somewhat later passages as having a human face and serpentine body, the figure in the painting has a human face and a human body, with the serpentine element starting only in place of the legs. This varies from the authentic figures of Fu Hsi of eastern Han art. Apart from the single example which is quoted above, Fu Hsi is regularly shown as one of a pair; his presence in the painting alone, as one of the spirits of heaven or as the acknowledged ancestor of man, does not appear to have a direct bearing on the theme of the painting.

Fu Hsi does not feature in the *Shan-hai-ching*, which describes several creatures as possessing human heads and serpentine bodies.[179] The reference in that work to Nü Kua is of a somewhat different nature; it relates how there were ten spirits called the 'inner organs of Nü Kua; when these had been transformed into spirits they inhabited the fields of Li-kuang.'[180] Of the three references to Fu Hsi in the *Ch'u tz'u* one is to the music which he composed and one to the carpenter's instrument which later became one of his attributes.[181] The third reference is in the *Chiu ssu* of Wang I, dating from the second century AD; here the poet describes a journey into the distance to 'seek advice of the High Lord, Fu Hsi.'[182]

(ii) Two scholars identify the central figure as Nü Kua. Professor Doi[183] describes Nü Kua as the female spirit who created man; she writes that the creation of man itself suggested the idea of deathlessness, and that the artist used the image so as to convey the idea of a deathless world. Some support is forthcoming for this suggestion from a passage in the *T'ien-wen* poem,[184] which reads 'How was Nü Wa's body fashioned? By what means was she raised up, when she mounted on high and became High Lord?' [*Ti*]. Kuo Mo-jo writes of Nü Kua as the female supreme goddess whose presence reflects a matriarchal society; he suggests that it was only later, under the influence of the Confucians, that the male element came to be emphasized in Chinese culture and that Fu Hsi was introduced to partner Nü Kua. While both scholars correctly observe that the figure of the painting is that of a female, their explanations need further support.[185]

(iii) An Chih-min's identification of the figure with Chu Lung was also accepted by Fong Chow.[186] Chu Lung does not figure in Finsterbusch's index, and the identification rests on literary evidence, without the support of other artistic representations.

According to the *Shan-hai-ching*,[187] Chu Lung was a spirit with a human face and snake's body, found on the Chang-wei hills beyond the north-western seas. This spirit was able to control the wind and the rain, and to illuminate the 'Nine Darknesses'. Kuo P'u's comment to this last expression is based partly on a passage in the *Ch'u tz'u*. He explains it as meaning that Chu Lung provided illumination for the north-western part of the heavens, which was not subject to the changes of Yin and Yang.[188] There is possibly a further reference to Chu Lung in the *Ta-chao*.[189]

It is claimed that the figure at the central apex of the painting corresponds with the description of Chu Lung, and that the power exercised by that spirit over the seasons was such that its rightful place was that of an arbiter or lord of the heavens. However, the identification seems somewhat doubtful. The features of the painting do not correspond with those of the texts that are cited; and the figure stands at

The painting from tomb no. 1, Ma-wang-tui

the central part of the painting, with no specific bias towards the north-west; nor is there any suggestion that the figure is fulfilling its function of shedding light where it has been denied from other sources.

It is however possible that the figure derives from an earlier version of the myth which later developed into that of the twin figures of Fu Hsi and Nü Kua. It can hardly be identified with *Ti*, lord of the world who presides over paradise, as there is no suggestion that *Ti* was a female figure or that he possessed a body with serpent's coils in place of legs. There remains one further possibility for which no proof can be adduced, but which would seem to be acceptable in view of the interpretation of the painting as the pilgrim's progress; that the artist depicted a final stage in the journey of the countess, when she has reached her destination, and that we see her in the company of the hosts of heaven, sloughing off her mortal coil as easily as a snake sheds the skins that he discards. It may further be suggested that the two sets of birds[190] that hover around the central figure, two on the left and three on the right, correspond with the two sets of acolytes who attended her in the previous stages of her pilgrimage, and whose presence was in turn matched by the two sets of vessels seen in the lower tableau, of the life within P'eng-lai.

While no direct evidence can be adduced to support this suggestion, it may be noted that there are at least three other works of Han artists, in addition to the painting of tomb no. 3 Ma-wang-tui, which may have been inspired by the same theme of a search for paradise: the fresco from the tomb of Ying-ch'eng-tzu, which shows a postulant arriving in the world of the immortals, in company with his acolyte; the stone relief from Ssu-ch'uan, where we see a man seeking the gift of immortality from the Queen Mother of the West; and the paintings from the tomb of Pu Ch'ien-ch'iu, with the two figures of human beings that end in a serpent's tail.[191] In addition it is suggested below that figures who are seen elsewhere in attendance on the Queen Mother of the West and whose legs have been replaced by a serpentine coil are likewise to be explained as successful seekers of the elixir of immortality.[192]

Chapter Three

TLV mirrors and their significance

Although the TLV marks first appear on types of mirror that were in fashion by 100 BC or earlier, it is only from *c.* 50 BC until AD 100 or 150 that they form the dominant characteristic of Chinese mirrors. TLV mirrors proper may be classified on the basis of the treatment of the TLV pattern itself, the other decorative details and the terms of the long inscriptions that are fashioned around the outer edge. It is suggested below that a sequence may be observed in the content of the inscriptions, which corresponds with changes in the Chinese view of paradise.* The earlier examples refer to the force of Yin and Yang and invoke the blessings that may be imparted by the symbols of the Five Phases; examples of the next distinct stage describe the habits of the immortal beings of another world, with some intermediate examples with elements of both of these types of inscription; finally there are two, and only two, examples in which the Queen Mother of the West is specifically mentioned in connection with the life of the world to come. These examples lead forward to the mirrors of later styles wherein the Queen Mother features more prominently, in high relief. The principal decorative features of the mirrors symbolize two views of the cosmos – one based on Five and one on Twelve – which are neatly reconciled together. The four animals, together with the central knob or boss, represent the cosmos of the theory of the Five Phases; the central square of the mirror, with its twelve divisions, represents the cosmos that is seen in parts of the *Huai-nan-tzu*, and also on the boards used by diviners to determine the position of an individual within the cosmos at a given moment of time. The square of the Twelve is neatly harmonized with the symbols of the Five.

* For select inscriptions, see Appendix Two.

TLV mirrors and their significance

In addition the TLV mirror bears other functions, of which one may be closely related to divination. The diviner's board comprised two discs which could be rotated so as to record observations of an actual situation for the appropriate conclusions to be drawn. The TLV mirror however is fashioned as a single fixed piece, which includes many of the elements that are seen on the board. The mirror in fact presents the two discs fixed rigidly and permanently in the most favourable position of the cosmos, in the hope that the deceased person with whom it was buried would be blissfully situated in that position for eternity. The Ts, Ls and Vs were, as it were, guide-lines, allowing the discs to be placed correctly; this would be doubly favourable, as both cosmological theories had been reconciled therein.

In addition the inscriptions or the decorative details of the mirrors convey explicitly or symbolically the presence of the world to come, where it was hoped that the spirit of the deceased person would enjoy the fruits of paradise. For, above all, the TLV mirrors served to provide a means of communication between the dead and those known realms of the cosmos to which philosophers had been content to restrict their attention.

This study is set out as follows:

i. Earlier studies of mirrors and the new evidence, pp. 62–4
ii. The development of mirrors and their inscriptions in pre-Han and Han times, pp. 64–6
iii. The emergence of the TLV pattern and its place in the sequence of Han mirrors, pp. 66–70
iv. Symbolic features of TLV mirrors, 71–5
v. The diviner's board, its use and features, 75–80
vi. The purpose of the TLV mirror, 80–5

Characteristic features of TLV mirrors are described in Appendix One, which traces the changes that appeared in the pattern and in the formulae of the inscriptions; texts and translations of select inscriptions are given in Appendix Two. Details of diviners' boards are given in Appendix Three, and Appendix Four concerns the distribution and chronological sequence of different types of mirror. The validity of the dates that appear on some inscriptions is discussed in Appendix Five; Appendix Six treats certain features of decoration and the calligraphic styles of the inscriptions. (The system of referring to individual mirrors as, e.g. C 1101, X 9005 etc., follows the classification that is suggested and the list that is given in Appendix One.)

Ways to Paradise

i. Earlier studies of mirrors and the new evidence

Distinguished scholars such as Karlgren and Umehara, Miss Bulling and Komai have achieved highly impressive results during the last three or four decades by analysing the decorative details and inscriptions of Chinese mirrors, and it is thanks largely to their pioneer work that valid criteria may be formulated for classifying these beautiful objects. These scholars have depended on evidence of two sorts; first, the mirrors which are available for visual inspection in the museums and collections of Europe, East Asia and America; and, secondly, the facsimiles that have been printed, either from rubbings or from photographs, in the catalogues that have been compiled from the Ch'ing period onwards.[1] But unfortunately both of these sources of information have usually been subject to an overriding limitation. With a few exceptions it has not been possible to trace the origin of the mirrors or to relate them to particular tombs or sites of excavation. Authentification has likewise been absent for many of the mirrors which were brought to the attention of scholars and art historians during the first half of the twentieth century.

Fortunately the situation has improved basically in recent years. Since 1950 methodical reports of excavations have been published in China almost immediately after the preliminary investigations of newly-found sites has been completed; and both the regular periodicals such as *Wen-wu*, *Kaogu* and *Kao-ku hsüeh-pao*, and the full-scale monographs that treat some of the major sites, carry systematic accounts of the controlled excavation that has taken place. In particular, recent publications have been concerned with evidence of two types; first, that of a few sites which have been studied in considerable detail and which may either be identified as the burial grounds of named individuals or dated within a matter of a decade (e.g. sites such as Shih-chai-shan, or Man-ch'eng); and, secondly, the evidence of groups of graves of a sufficiently homogeneous nature to permit treatment as a single unit and the establishment of a typology (e.g. the 225 graves of Shao-kou, near Lo-yang).

In general the publications that have followed Miss Bulling's major study of Han mirrors of 1960 have served to corroborate and supplement the inferences and conclusions reached in the past. It has also become possible to draw certain finer distinctions than have been justified hitherto. However, two limitations must be stated immediately. In the first place there are very few early mirrors which bear an inscription that identifies the date of manufacture for certain; for as is shown below there are reasons for suspecting nearly all examples that are dated in this way before AD 145.[2] Secondly, as with any subject in

TLV mirrors and their significance

which art forms and fashions are concerned, it would be unreasonable to expect to trace a regular sequence whereby one style of mirror yielded place neatly to its successor and then disappeared. At the most it may be possible to note the signs which indicate the introduction of new styles and to enquire whether they can be related to developments in other fields of Chinese art and intellect at that time.

The following enquiry is directed to the classification and interpretation of TLV mirrors,[3] mainly on the basis of their inscriptions. The changes that may be observed in the content of the inscriptions are studied in relation to changes in other features of style and decor, and related to the intellectual and religious developments of Han China. While a number of scholars (such as Kaplan (1937), Yetts (1939), Yang (1947), Cammann (1948), Komai (1953), Needham and Hayashi (1973, 1), have noted the cosmological significance of the TLV mirrors and discussed their similarity with the patterns to be seen on *Liu-po* boards, gnomon boards and diviners' boards they would probably all agree that they are far from being satisfied that their suggestions are wholly convincing or form a complete answer to the problems that are concerned. In standing on the shoulders of such scholars and using evidence that has been found since their time I would no more claim to be putting forward the final word on the subject. I venture simply to fasten on further aspects of comparison between the TLV mirror patterns and the marks that are seen on diviners' boards, and to attempt a more definite statement of the purpose of the TLV mirrors. I believe that it is possible to discriminate between five major types of TLV mirror and their sub-divisions, and to distinguish those that were actually fashioned in the Han and Hsin dynasties from some of those which, despite such claims, were probably fabricated at a later date.

The enquiry is based on a large number of published facsimiles[4] and direct inspection of a smaller number that may be seen and handled in museums. Where there is no chance of personal examination and we must depend on facsimiles, we can only accept on trust that the examples are authentic – i.e. that they were not specifically manufactured at the whim of a collector. It is also necessary to bear in mind that facsimiles that derive from rubbings or copying may lose some accuracy in the course of transmission. Moreover, while the recent Chinese periodicals and monographs provide rich sources of information regarding the new finds and the circumstances of their discovery; and while they shed a new light on the distribution of the various types in the Han provinces; with some notable exceptions the reproductions that grace those publications are often of a poor quality and do not permit detailed analysis. For this reason it has been thought imprudent to include many examples from these publications in the list that is appended below; however, considerable information from these sources has been included elsewhere where appropriate.[5]

I am grateful to the directors and members of staff of the following museums for permission to examine mirrors in their collections and to reproduce photographs below: the Ashmolean Museum, Oxford; the British Museum; the Fitzwilliam Museum, Cambridge; the Museum of Far Eastern Antiquities, Stockholm; and the Victoria and Albert Museum.

ii. The development of mirrors and their inscriptions in pre-Han and Han times*

Although this enquiry is not primarily concerned with the processes of manufacture, there are a few points to which attention should be drawn.

1. It is possible to use the same mould to make a number of mirrors, and to introduce minor variations in so doing (e.g. in the text of the inscription).[6] However, all the mirrors that are listed below have been treated as individual examples and are believed to be unique.[7]
2. Two examples have been noted (one post-Han) where mirrors have been made from a positive instead of a negative mould.[8]
3. The mirrors were regularly made in slightly concave form, with a resulting weakness that may eventually bring about splits or breakage.[9]
4. The diameters of TLV mirrors, as measured in 89 examples,[10] vary from 5.9 to 23.3 cm, and the great majority measure between 10.5 and 22.1 cm. The Han foot is usually taken as being 23.1 cm, and it would seem that no significant attempt was made to fashion mirrors which were measurable exactly by the Han inch (0.1 feet). Of 89 mirrors, the measurements of 18 approximate to within 0.3 cm of a Han inch.[11]

Bronze mirrors were manufactured in China long before the Han period. They are found in funeral furnishings where they take their place among other valuables and precious vessels of bronze, and their origin may be traced to the Chou period or even earlier.[12] Literary passages which extend from the *Shih-ching* to texts of the *Ch'un-ch'iu*, *Chan-kuo*, Han and post-Han periods testify to the value placed on mirrors both for decorative and prophylactic purposes.[13] Sometimes they were worn on the person, attached to a leather belt. According to a late source they were carried on the back as a protection against

---

* For a list of the mirrors that have been considered and notes on their characteristics, see Appendix One.

TLV mirrors and their significance

Fig. 10. TLV mirror (C 4111); made from a positive mould, with consequent reversals in the decor and characters

spirits or influences that are to be encountered on mountains; and it has been suggested by one writer that the habit of wearing a mirror as part of one's apparel may be compared with the practice of the shamans of the northern peoples.[14] Similarly, mirrors were buried in tombs as a protective device for the deceased, and attention has been drawn to the prevalence of this practice in Japan as well as China. The earliest evidence for the practical use of mirrors by ladies in the arrangement of their toilet is probably to be found in Ku K'ai-chih's famous scroll of the fourth to fifth century.[15]

Inscriptions on the Han mirrors refer to these objects as *ching*; no case has been seen in which the character *chien*, which is used in some early texts, appears on inscriptions. A distinction has been suggested whereby *ching* denotes a mirror made of burnished bronze or iron, of the types that are under study, and *chien* signifies a basin which was filled with water and used for the purposes of reflection.[16]

Karlgren has observed[17] that no inscribed mirrors derive from before the Han period, as the characters of the inscriptions are in small seal or later types of script, but not in earlier types. Miss Bulling[18] has accepted this distinction as a valid criterion for distinguishing pre-Han and Han mirrors, and the examples that have been found since the time when Karlgren and Bulling were writing do not include inscribed mirrors which can definitely be assigned to the pre-Han period. It should however be noted that Liu T'i-chih, who is not over-critical, described no less than eleven mirrors which carry an inscription as Ch'in; these include six TLV mirrors which are described below under type B.[19]

Those scholars who have attempted to classify Chinese mirrors, to set the types in chronological sequence or to associate them with different localities would probably agree that the development of mirror types in the Han period may be discerned in general terms as follows.[20]

(a) *Earlier types*
These are characterized as thin, with slender central bosses and short simple inscriptions. The decorative patterns, in low relief, are geometrical or stylistic, with no natural or animal forms. E.g., see Bulling (1960), Plates 2, 3, 8, 15. They may be exemplified in the types known as Shou-chou and Ts'ao-yeh. (See Plates II, IV.)

(b) *Later types*
Thicker than (a), these have heavy external rims and a more prominent boss in the centre. There are two, and occasionally three, inscriptions; the innermost one is set around a square or circular centre, and a longer one appears in an outer ring. Eventually the outer inscription is set in square blocks, each of four characters, radiating from the centre. The decoration is in high relief and includes representations of divine, human or animal figures and man-made artefacts such as carriages. E.g., see Bulling (1960), Plates 71, 75, 79. (See Plates XXII, XXIV.)

iii. The emergence of the TLV pattern and its place in the sequence of Han mirrors

The origin of the TLV pattern is unknown. But it is possible and indeed necessary to draw a distinction between the TLV marks in their first appearance, where they are imposed on typical decorative designs already evolved, and their symbolical use as a pattern in TLV mirrors

TLV mirrors and their significance

proper, where they form an essential and characteristic element of the design.

TLV marks are first seen on mirrors of earlier styles, such as *Ts'ao-yeh* or *Shou-chou* (see Plates III, V), and it is not impossible that in some cases they were added thereto long after the original manufacture, and after the emergence of the TLV mirror proper with its deep symbolical significance. The TLV pattern reaches fruition in the regular examples which emerge about midway in the whole development of mirrors during the Han period. By the middle of the eastern Han period, perhaps AD 100 to 150, the TLV types had yielded pride of place to other types of mirror; but opinions vary regarding the time when the TLV mirror proper (as opposed to the TLV marks) first appeared. The following distinction is drawn in the scheme of classification that is submitted below (see Appendix One):

(a) Existing types of mirror to which the TLV marks were applied (classified in Appendix One below as types A and B)
(b) Fully-fledged TLV mirrors bearing a regular series of characteristic features (type C and, possibly, some that are listed under D 10)
(c) Mirrors in which some features of the TLV pattern were retained, or misused, for decorative purposes only (type X and, possibly, D 20)

In so far as the attitudes, purposes and training of the various scholars and art historians who have written on this subject have varied, so too have the points that they regard as significant and the criteria that they have adopted for drawing distinctions between types. As a result, there is a measure of overlap rather than identity between the categories suggested and the terminology that is used. However, there is general agreement among scholars such as Karlgren, Miss Bulling, the authors of the report on the Shao-kou graves, Suzuki, Komai and Hayashi, in placing the evolution of TLV mirrors proper during, or towards the end of, the first century BC, and their replacement by mirrors of other styles in the middle of the eastern Han period.[21]

The development of TLV mirrors forms an integral part of the history of Chinese mirrors in general. The marks T L and V first appear on early types of mirror that are exemplified in the *Chan-kuo*, Ch'in and Han periods; the pattern characterizes the sophisticated products of the middle part of the Han period; and it survives to be adopted in some examples that were fashioned as late as the T'ang dynasty. Changes in style of the TLV mirrors are marked by the appearance of different decorative devices and the inscription of different types of formulae. Such variations are to be considered in the light of the intellectual changes evident in China from 100 BC to AD 100. Inferences drawn regarding some of the archaeological sites may be used with some caution as a guide to dating.*

From the simple use of the TLV marks we may trace the production of mature TLV mirrors proper, bearing a deep and complex symbolical significance, to a period of decadence when those symbolic features were utilized simply as decorative devices. In the process the design had been elaborated considerably and standardized in some respects, possibly under the influence of the diviner's board; and it is in types C and D 10 that we shall find evidence of the full ideological significance of the TLV mirror. Types D 20 and X include some examples which can only be regarded as excellent, on aesthetic grounds. But the mirrors of these types were made by designers who seem to have been unaware of the full intention of the symbolism. Some of the examples are highly irregular and were manufactured long after the period of the beautiful products listed in type C. Some of the mirrors listed in sub-type D 20 are closely akin to the irregular examples of type X. The following conclusions may be drawn tentatively from the classification which follows below (Appendix One):

1. There are certain well attested examples of types A and B in tombs that may be dated from about 100 BC.

2. With the exception of types A and B, the outside dates for TLV mirrors may be taken at perhaps 50 BC, when the *Wu hsing* cosmology was winning general acceptance, until perhaps AD 100–150, when the post-TLV types had taken over in popularity. A significant and early example may be seen in C 1101.

3. The inscriptions of some of the best-attested and the most perfect examples refer both to the Hsin dynasty (AD 9–23) and to Han. On balance I believe that such inscriptions were made in the time of eastern rather than western Han.[22]

4. The different varieties of type C emerge at about the beginning of the first century AD, or a little earlier, possibly being preceded by some examples of sub-type D 10. The most likely sequence is for sub-types C 11, C 12 and C 19 to precede C 21–24, whose inscriptions refer specifically to the cosmic situation of mankind. Sub-types C 31 and C 32 are transitional between C 21–24 and C 41–49, whose inscriptions refer specifically to the life of the immortals.† Sub-type C 50, possibly the latest of the regular TLV mirrors, bears features that are seen in the style of mirrors of the second century AD and later, whose popularity

---

* See Appendix Four.
† For select inscriptions, see Appendix Two.

Types of TLV mirrors*

Type	Features	Example
A	*Ts'ao-yeh* pattern mirror, with TLV marks superimposed; earliest datable example from *c.* 100 BC	Plate III
B	*Shou-chou* pattern mirror, with TLV marks superimposed; from *c.* 100 BC	Plate V
C	Regular TLV pattern mirrors, with inscriptions and characteristic features: (i) a central square with a large central boss, an inner inscription and twelve minor bosses, bound by four Ts and eight large bosses; (ii) an inner circle, with Ls, Vs, the four animals (*ssu shen*) and a series of smaller animals; (iii) an outer inscription, set in its own circular band; (iv) bands with degree markings, zigzag divisions and cloud-scroll pattern. There are five main sub-types, depending on the content of the outer inscription, and set here in suggested chronological sequence; outside dating 50 BC to AD 150	
	C 11, C 12, C 13, C 19: inscriptions invoke general blessings†	Plates VI, VII–IX
	C 21, C 22, C 23, C 24: inscriptions refer to the Five Phases, Yin Yang	Plates X, XI
	C 31, C 32: inscriptions include elements of those in sub-types C 2 and C 4	Plate XIII
	C 41, C 42, C 43, C 49: inscriptions allude to the life of the immortals	Plate XV, Figures 10, 13
	C 50: inscriptions allude to the life of the immortals and the Queen Mother of the West	Plate XVI
D	TLV pattern mirrors without outer inscription	
	D 10 with inner inscription; this sub-type may include some of the earliest TLV mirrors proper	Plate XVII
	D 20 without inner inscription	Plate XVIII, Figure 23
X	Irregular types of TLV mirrors, including some believed to be of post-Han make	
	X 10 with specific references to Wang Mang	Plate XIX, Figures 24, 26
	X 20 with incomplete features	Figure 25
	X 90 with pronounced signs of post-Han make	Plate XX

* For details of classification and list of examples, see Appendix One.
† It is possible that C 13 mirrors are to be placed later in the sequence.

ousted that of the TLVs.[23] There may however be some reason to show that some examples of type C 4 are made at an early date.[24] C 13 is probably later.

5. Type C gives place to D 20 and X; and these are accompanied or followed by new fashions in mirrors of a completely new style.

6. The development from types A to X is consistent with the chronological pattern of intellectual change, whereby the theory of the *Wu hsing* was propagated and popularized in the time of Liu Hsiang (79–8 BC) and Wang Mang; followed during the first century AD by a more general credence in the ways to find immortality; and then by the cult of the Queen Mother of the West. While it cannot be said for certain at what particular time the search for elixirs and the worship of the Queen Mother of the West gained a wide following, it is fairly certain that these developments followed the deliberate attempt to foster the theory of *Wu hsing*.

7. The sequence that is suggested above may be matched by changes in decorative detail:

i. Low relief is succeeded by high relief.[25]
ii. It is suggested[26] that some of the TLV mirrors whose inscriptions bear a specific date for the time of Wang Mang are spurious, in the sense that they were not necessarily made at the times stated. If this suspicion is valid, it may be noted that mirrors which are dated by their inscription to a particular year hardly enter into question until after the TLV types have been replaced by other types in popularity.[27]
iii. The regular C types, of the Hsin and Han dynasties, are often decorated with a comparatively large number of animals and birds that are ancillary to the four beasts. There is a tendency for these to yield place to a smaller number of animals. Animals then appear as four pairs (i.e. the four beasts, each with a partner), and eventually as the four beasts only (see Appendix Six).
iv. The mirrors dated from *c*. AD 145 are of very different designs from the TLV types.[28]
v. The cloud scroll that is proper to the C types is in time replaced by decorative patterns of a geometrical type which sometimes incorporates animals or other figures in the design.

8. A final stage may be seen when inscriptions that belong properly to TLV mirrors and their symbols are transferred to post-TLV types, which bear few of the TLV's symbolic characteristics; by now the symbolism has been completely forgotten or ignored.[29]

iv. Symbolic features of TLV mirrors*

A number of scholars have drawn attention to some of the aspects of TLV mirrors. In particular, students of the inscriptions owe a deep debt to Bernhard Karlgren who, as in so many fields of Sinology, was one of the first contributors to apply the critical and scholastic methods of the west to a subject of Chinese studies. As early as 1934 Karlgren presented annotated translations of the inscriptions of 257 mirrors, together with a list of the graphic variants to be found; those texts include a number of inscriptions that appear on the TLV mirrors which are under study here.[30]

At much the same time Sidney Kaplan, who was concerned with the design rather than the inscriptions of the mirrors, observed the similarity of certain features with those of the fragments of a diviner's board that had been found in Lo-lang, Korea.[31] It will be shown below that more recent discoveries now make it possible to pursue this line of enquiry further, and the suggestions that follow in due course are made in full recognition of Kaplan's early initiative.

The earliest description of the features of TLV mirrors to appear in English was probably that of Yetts. This formed part of his account of one of the most perfect of all TLV mirrors, no. 28 in the Cull collection (C 2104). In view of the slender scholastic and archaeological resources that were available at the time when Yetts was writing (before 1939), very great credit is due to him for his imaginative approach and scholastic achievement. He describes the mirror[32] in connection with Han astronomical ideas of the division of the heavens and the designation of certain constellations. He suggests that the central boss of the mirrors signifies[33] 'both the dome of heaven's vault around the celestial pole and also a corresponding central region on earth'; and he describes the symbolical function of the *ssu shen*. He also draws attention to the similarity between the TLV pattern and the marks which appear on *liu-po* boards; and he suggests that the explanation of the TLV pattern is to be found in the lines seen on two surviving examples of Han sun-dials or, more strictly speaking, gnomon chronometer boards.[34]

More recently Hayashi Minao has summarized the views put forward by a number of scholars.[35] He cannot accept the suggestion of Nakayama and Gotō, that the TLV pattern derived from the floral type of decoration seen on mirrors of the middle and later western Han period.[36] He discusses the correspondence seen by some scholars with the gnomon boards,[37] whose function he examines in some detail. Together with Cammann he sees reason to doubt whether the marks formed an

---

* Details of these features are given in Appendix One, pp. 158 f.

integral and essential part of these dials; and he doubts whether the TLV pattern necessarily derives from the same origin. It may perhaps be suggested that the Vs which appear on the dials were made for the practical purpose of setting them correctly.[38]

Yang Lien-sheng, who had been preceded in part by Nakayama and Yetts,[39] drew attention to the correspondence between the TLV pattern and the marks of the *liu-po* boards; he linked this with the depiction of immortals engaged in the game, as may be seen in mirrors decorated in high relief, that were produced towards the end of the eastern Han period.[40] Other scholars who have noted and discussed the similarity of the TLV pattern and the marks on the *liu-po* boards include Mizuno and Lao Kan.[41] Hayashi explains the use of the rods and counters of the game of *liu-po*; and he does not find the theory wholly convincing as an explanation of the pattern.[42] Hayashi also criticizes Lao Kan's comparison of the TLV pattern with the plan of early Chinese buildings, and regards this as untenable.

Cammann[43] considers the TLV mirrors in the context of a lengthy time span extending from the second century BC to the developments of the T'ang period. He takes the view that the latest examples retain the essential characteristic, i.e. the Vs, while other elements may have disappeared; and this view may be exemplified in X 9005, whose inscription is dated at AD 650. In discussing the association of the TLV mirrors with the marks of the *liu-po* boards, Cammann concludes (p. 162) 'In short, the total plan of the mirror gives the impression that someone had placed a circular *pi*, the jade emblem of heaven, on top of a square plan of the earth, like the *liu-po* board, and then cut off the projecting corners of the latter, flush with the curve of the *pi*.' He takes the function of the Vs as that of marking off the boundaries of the four quarters of the world, and the Ts as being the gates of the Middle Kingdom. Cammann explains the Ls as barriers which marked off the swamps that lie at the ends of the earth; and with this explanation he associates the emergence of the Yü or weather bird, and the cycle of rain.

Cammann notes that the prominent central boss of the mirror represents the centre of the universe, or 'omphalos or centre of the world.'[44] In addition he sees an association between the twelve inner bosses and the nine regions of the earth; for nine divisions can be figured by projecting horizontal and vertical lines so as to join the bosses that lie opposite one another in the central square of the mirror. Cammann understands the eight outer bosses as the Pillars of Heaven, and he concludes (p. 165) that the TLV pattern represents the 'Universe as though seen by a Heavenly eye looking down from the palace of the Supreme Emperor through the hole in the dome of the sky.' In

TLV mirrors and their significance

considering the inscriptions of the mirrors, Cammann takes note of the invocations that are exemplified in types C 2 and C 4.

Cammann follows Karlgren in accepting the outside dates of 100 BC to AD 100 as marking the period of currency of the TLV pattern.[45] As has been observed this view requires some modification; and it should be noted that the mirror quoted by Cammann as being representative (D 2015) does not possess the characteristic features of the regular types. While agreeing with Cammann's view that the TLV pattern must be explained in a cosmic context, Hayashi is unable to accept his explanation of the individual features (i.e. the Ts, Ls and Vs) as being satisfactory. Hayashi also rejects as untenable Komai's explanation of the Ts as representing a draftsman's compass and the Ls as representing a set-square.

In her earlier study (1955) Miss Bulling interprets TLV mirrors in two ways; they can be explained in material terms as representing buildings; and they may also be regarded as symbols of the cosmic scheme of the universe. She traces evidence to show that the patterns of early Chinese mirrors were made in imitation of embroidery and stitchwork, and that they thereby represented some of the designs used originally in textiles. She suggests that some types of mirror are representations of umbrellas or canopies, of the type that were used on ritual occasions; and she notes the similarity between the patterns seen in some mirrors and the decoration of the ceilings of buildings or tents. In applying this suggestion to a TLV mirror,[46] which is stated to represent a building and a canopy, Miss Bulling explains the Ts, Ls and Vs in architectural terms as struts, brackets and props. While the boss in the centre symbolizes the *T'ai chi* or Great Ridgepole of the Universe, as well as the central post of the building, the twelve minor bosses are the smaller posts used in construction, and the eight bosses represent posts 'standing like gate-posts in pairs on each side of the square' (p. 34). However, the main purpose of these mirrors is to imitate canopies and umbrellas rather than buildings. Just as umbrellas and canopies attract the presence of benevolent spirits, so too are mirrors regarded as fulfilling the same function (p. 40).

In interpreting TLV mirrors in both celestial and terrestrial terms, Miss Bulling (pp. 42 f.) sees a reflection of the celestial order, with the centre representing the pole star, the palace of the ruler, or, according to another terminology, the cosmic mountain K'un-lun, whose inhabitants include the Queen Mother of the West and the immortal beings. In addition there are symbols of constellations, and the Vs stand for the cosmic mountains at the four corners of the universe. Finally, Miss Bulling suggests that the row or rows of chevrons represent mountain ranges, which stand at the edge of the world and support the base of the vault of the sky; and according to these cosmic terms the bosses are interpreted as being the pillars of the sky. In her later work[47] she elaborates this interpretation:

> Whenever the sawtooth patterns decorate the rim of the mirrors they symbolize cosmic mountains ... believed to surround the sky along the edges of the universe. When three concentric zigzag lines are shown the middle one represents a river meandering between two mountain ranges surrounding the universe.

In commenting on Miss Bulling's writings, Hayashi agrees that considerable importance should be placed on the significance of a cover or canopy to symbolize heaven; and there can be no doubt that the symbolism is designed as an abstraction of heaven and earth. However, he questions the suggestion that the design derives from that of a canopy and cannot accept the interpretation of the Ts and Vs as parts of a building. It may perhaps be added that Miss Bulling's interpretation in cosmic terms is somewhat mixed and does not allow for the development of different ideas during the period in question.

Hayashi himself[48] accepts the suggestion that the TLVs form a symbolic microcosm; and, as may be illustrated from passages in the *Lü shih ch'un-ch'iu* and the *Huai-nan-tzu*, the possession of such a symbol may enable an owner to gain mastery of the world. The elements of the TLV pattern form parts of this microcosm as follows:

i. The four Ts that stand around the square earth are four cardinal points (*ssu chi*). These lie at the extremities of the two cosmic lines or ropes (*sheng*) which cross the universe and hold it together; the Ts comprise a vertical prop which supports an horizontal beam.[49]
ii. The four Vs mark the four corners of the heavens, as described in the *Huai-nan-tzu*.[50]
iii. The four Ls represent devices used by carpenters to set a straight line, i.e. a container for ink, through which a thread is passed and coloured, for use in marking. They thus symbolize the ends of the two cosmic lines (*sheng*), as if they had been drawn with the help of such an instrument.

In general Hayashi's explanation of the TLV pattern does not conflict with the suggestions that will be made below; and his explanation of the Ts and Vs possibly supplements the correspondence with certain features of the diviner's board which will be discussed hereafter. However, Hayashi's view of the Ls is unsatisfactory, as it is not consonant with his explanation of the Ts and the Vs. For, while he takes the latter as

TLV mirrors and their significance

abstractions of cosmic properties, he regards the Ls as being no more than diagrams of man-made instruments used for a practical purpose in the human world. It is somewhat far-fetched to explain such diagrams as symbols of cosmic entitites that are believed to bear a universal significance. In addition, as Hayashi himself states, evidence for the use of inked markers before the T'ang period is anything but certain.[51]

v. The diviner's board, its use and features

Material evidence discovered recently prompts a reconsideration of the suggestion made by Kaplan in 1937, in which he drew attention to the similarity between the TLV pattern and the marks on diviners' boards. The reconstructed example and the fragment of a board which were available to Kaplan may now be supplemented by several other finds and a few references in literature. In addition his suggestion may be considered in the light of some of the characteristic features of TLV mirrors which are absent from the example which he used.[52]

The characteristic shape and features of the diviner's board of Han days may be described as follows:[53] (see Appendix Three)

i. The instrument comprised two discs, one circular and one square. The circle was made so that it could be rotated in relation to the square, either being seated in a well within the square or being attached thereto by a pivot.
ii. The opposite corners of the square disc were linked by two boldly drawn diagonal paths. Parts of these paths were invisible when the instrument was assembled, as they passed beneath the circular disc.
iii. Two straight paths, one horizontal and one vertical, linked the central points of the four sides of the square disc; these paths were likewise partly concealed when the circular disc was in position.
iv. Both the circular and the square discs were bounded by several bands of characters. The number of bands varies in each of the examples, and the series of characters that are inscribed there also vary. In one example, that dates from the Six Dynasties' Period (no. 6 in Appendix Three) one of the bands bears the characters for a set of 36 animals. In one example (no. 5) the outermost rims of both the discs were graduated in degree markings.
v. In four examples (nos. 2, 3, 4 and 5) the seven stars of the Dipper, joined together by a straight line, were inscribed in the central area of the circular disc; the pivot which held the two discs together passed through or near the central star of the constellation (epsilon UMa).

Ways to Paradise

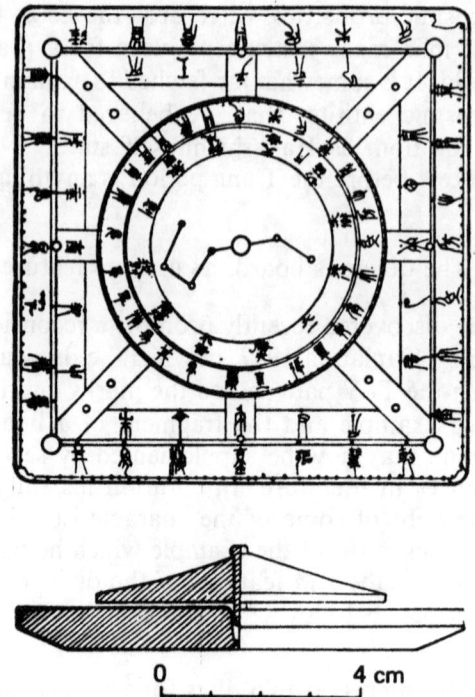

Fig. 11. Diviner's board; from tomb no. 62, Mo-tsui-tzu, Kansu

Several literary passages testify to the practice of divination during the Han period;[54] it may be surmised that in some cases the question for which an inspired answer was required concerned the particular occasion, day or time that would be suitable for a proposed action. A passage of a slightly earlier date,[55] which expresses the views of the so-called legalist school, castigates this practice along with other activities that are likely to lead to the ruin of a state, e.g., the worship of spiritual beings, a faith in the efficacy of divination by means of milfoil or oracle bones, prayer and sacrifice. It would have been in conformity with the principles of the modernist statesmen who served the Han empire during its first century to frown on these activities in the same way;[56] but it could be expected that divination would be regarded as a highly reputable activity by those of a Taoist or quietist persuasion, and by some of the reformist statesmen whose attitude became fashionable from *c.* 70 BC.

A few crucial passages in texts such as the *Huai-nan-tzu*, the *Shih-chi* and the *Han-shu* shed considerable light on the characteristics of the instruments that are under discussion. They are termed *shih*; there

TLV mirrors and their significance

seems to be little doubt that they symbolized the cosmos, with the circular and square discs standing for heaven and earth respectively. The characters of the Twelve Branches that appear on one of the bands of the discs also have a cosmic function; the vertical and horizontal paths link the characters that appear at opposite sides of the square, i.e. *tzu* with *wu* and *mao* with *yu*; and these two paths are the two *sheng*, i.e. the two imaginary ropes or guide lines which bind the cosmos together. There are also four 'hooks' (*kou*) which are situated between the four other pairs of terms that comprise the Twelve Branches; these are the four nodal points (*ssu wei*) of the cosmos, situated at the corners of the square; and they were believed to have been characterized by their own special qualities, e.g., requital for bounties and good deeds in the north-east, etc.[57] The four terminal points of the two ropes are the *ssu chung*, i.e. the four medial points along each one of the four sides of the square.

Towards the beginning of the eastern Han dynasty, Cheng Chung (*fl.* AD 50–70) described the general purpose of the diviner's board (*shih*) as being that of 'comprehending the appointed seasons of heaven and apportioning good and ill fortune.'[58] From earlier passages, in the *Shih-chi* and Ch'u Shao-sun's supplementary additions to that work,[59] we learn that when using his board a diviner had necessarily to regard heaven and earth as his models and to symbolize the four seasons; and he would revolve the circular board (*shih*) and set the square board (*ch'i*) correctly. In addition we have an account of an actual incident in which the boards were used, which comes from Ch'u's additions.[60] The incident occurred in the middle of the night, when the king of Sung required, somewhat urgently, an expert interpretation of a highly perplexing dream.

> 'The operator stood up, adjusting the board with his hands. Raising his eyes to heaven he gazed at the light of the moon; he looked to see where the Dipper was pointing and determined the position where the sun was situated. As auxiliary aids he used a pair of compasses and a set-square, together with weights and scales. Once the four nodal points (*ssu wei*) were fixed and the eight trigrams were facing one another, he looked for the signs of good or evil fortune, and the first to appear was that of the beetle.'[61]

Finally we may quote an incident which is reported to have taken place in AD 23 in the presence of Wang Mang.[62] At the time Wang Mang was witnessing the death throes of his empire; as ever he was anxious to substantiate his claim to be acting in conformity with the revealed way of heaven.

Ways to Paradise

'The astronomer of the court placed the diviner's board (*shih*) before him, and? set the square board for the cyclical position of the sun.[63] Wang Mang turned his mat round in such a way that he was seated in accordance with the direction of the handle of the Dipper.'

From the later *T'ang liu tien*[64] we learn of the existence of three types of diviner's board at that time, including the *Liu jen* board exemplified as no. 6, in Appendix Three. Unfortunately there are no direct statements regarding the method of using the board during the Han period; the following tentative suggestions are based on the evidence of the boards themselves and the literary passages that have been quoted.

1 The operator revolved the circular disc, of heaven, so that its position corresponded with the point apparently reached by the sun in the heavens, as measured from the celestial equator. In this way he was taking heaven as his model.[65] (In practice this action may well have followed the next.)
2 The operator set the square board to correspond with the four cardinal points of the compass; in this way he was taking earth as his model.
3 The handle of the Dipper engraved in the centre of the circular disc indicated the result of divination, by pointing in a particular direction or selecting one of a number of animals.[66]

The importance of the Dipper and its handle stands out clearly in the incident of AD 23; it indicated the appropriate position to be adopted, and Wang Mang regulated his behaviour accordingly. It is possible that the Dipper was intended to play a similar role in example no. 5 of Appendix Three, although there is no display of animals in any of the bands. The importance of the animals as harbingers of good or evil fortune is shown very clearly in the passage cited from the *Shih-chi*, where however the precise significance of the beetle is not revealed. But the passage is supplemented by the presence of the animals carved in relief on board no. 1, and described in 36 characters in no. 6; and it is not impossible that the bands of board no. 4, where the inscription has been effaced, once included a series of terms for the correct selection of an animal by the handle of the Dipper.[67]

It has been shown above that the TLV pattern appeared in the first instance on types of mirror that were being made *c.* 100 BC or perhaps earlier; and it has been suggested that the regular types of TLV mirror, with their full panoply of symbolism, may be dated from the time of Wang Mang or possibly a few decades previously. Without further archaeological evidence or further examples of mirrors of a transitional

TLV mirrors and their significance

style such as C 1101, little can be said of the stages whereby the pattern of types A and B developed into the finished examples of type C. Probably the process accompanied the growth of faith in the *Wu hsing* and the acceptance of that theory's explanation of the cosmos.

The number of diviners' boards available for study is small and can scarcely permit general inferences. However, it is of considerable value to the present enquiry to note that two of the examples, nos. 3 and 5, date from the time of Wang Mang, when some of the best examples of TLV mirror were being fashioned. The possibility that the TLV mirrors and the diviner's boards were related rests in the first instance on the following similarities between the two objects:

Feature	Diviner's board (see Appendix Three)	TLV mirror
Diagonal paths	In nos. 1, 4, 5, 6	Traces may be seen in the pointers within the central square and in the Vs. One irregular example (X 1001) bears full diagonal lines
The two *sheng* and their terminals	The transverse paths in nos. 4, 5; the four 'gates' in no. 1	The four Ts[68]
The four nodal points (*ssu wei*)	The four bosses at the corners, accompanied by four pairs of minor bosses; see nos. 1 and 5	The sets of four or eight bosses
The Twelve Branches	As set in the bands of the square discs, alone or in combination	As set in the inner square, accompanied by the 12 minor bosses
Animals	Set in relief in no. 1; and given in a list of 36 members, no. 6	The four dominant beasts (*ssu shen*), and a host of other creatures
Degree markings	Possibly seen in no. 5	A regular feature

The principal differences between the TLV mirrors and the diviners' boards are:

i. In the board, the square lies outside the circle, whereas in the mirrors the circle encompasses the square, thereby forming a symbol of the universe.[69]

Ways to Paradise

Fig. 12. Diviner's board; from the tomb of Wang Hsü, Lo-lang, Korea, as reconstructed

ii. Whereas the board was designed to allow one of the discs to rotate, the mirror was fashioned as a single piece, which permitted no manipulation or adjustment.

vi. The purpose of the TLV mirror

The diviner's board was made for the practice of divination, in order to ascertain an individual's destiny or, perhaps, the most appropriate time for a proposed action. It is suggested here that the TLV mirrors, which bear some of the features that appear on the boards, were deliberately made as stylized versions of those instruments; that their design exemplified the most favourable position that could be obtained by manipulating the two discs of the diviner's board; and that it was set so

PLATE VIII
TLV mirror (C1902; diameter 16.6 cm).

PLATE IX
TLV mirror (C1903; diameter 13.1 cm).

PLATE X
TLV mirror (C2104; diameter 21 cm); shown by kind courtesy of the present owner.

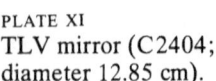

PLATE XI
TLV mirror (C2404; diameter 12.85 cm).

TLV mirrors and their significance

Fig. 13. TLV mirror (C 4312)

as to retain that combination in perpetuity. The designers adapted the pattern of Ts, Ls and Vs which, whatever their origin, appeared on *Ts'ao-yeh* and *Shou-chou* mirrors; and they did so in order to provide the bearer of the mirror, alive or dead, with an assurance that he or she was situated in a correct relationship with the cosmos. The cosmic significance and benediction of the mirror remained valid for ever.[70]

If the TLV mirrors are regarded as being stylized versions of the diviner's board the actual Ts, Ls and Vs may be explained partly as vestigial signs of the lines that appear on those instruments and partly as instructions to set the two dials in their correct and permanent position. The Vs may be regarded as traces of the diagonal paths which appear on the compass boards, and the Ts mark the terminal points of the two cross-lines. The designer of the mirror has obeyed two instruc-

Ways to Paradise

tions; he has set the four Vs so that they point directly to the four corners of the square, where they match up with the floriate lines already there, and almost form the diagonal paths. In this way he has brought the four Ls of the outer dial flush with the cross-bars of the Ts, which stand at the centres of the four sides of the square. Each one of the Ls encloses a symbol whose meaning is clear for all, literate or not, to understand; for they display the four beasts of the four directions, which correspond with four of the Five Phases.

In addition the designer has obeyed a second instruction. He has ensured that each one of the Ls, with its all-important symbol, has been brought alongside the appropriate member of the Twelve Branches that lie within the Inner Square. As a result, the four symbols are situated in their correct places, in conformity with the divisions of the universe that are implied by the Twelve Branches; and the cosmic scheme of the Five has been reconciled with that of the Twelve.

In this connection, attention is due to a few rather exceptional mirrors which are so made that an extra ring has divided the circle of the mirror into two zones; and while the Ts lie within the inner zone, the Vs are situated in the outer zone, carrying the Ls along with them.[71] In these particular examples the designer appears to have divided his mirror into two discs; it is possible to imagine the one being rotated in relation to the other, and the Vs bringing the Ls correctly to their stations. It may also be noted that in the diviner's board the inscriptions run sometimes clockwise and sometimes anti-clockwise, and the combination of bands of inscriptions that are set in opposite directions itself suggests rotation. Possibly the same result may be seen in the mirrors; here the inscriptions read regularly in a clockwise direction; an anti-clockwise direction is suggested by the Ls, whose open side usually faces right.

Reference has been made above (p. 63) to the similarity between the patterns of the TLV mirrors and those of the *liu-po* boards. In one example of a board that has been found recently[72] four circular medallions appear in a way that corresponds with the four bosses, or *ssu wei*, of the mirror, and which is too striking to be ignored. A possible explanation of the overriding similarity between the TLV pattern and the marks of the gaming boards may be that the pattern derived from the diviner's board and was transferred not only to mirrors, but also to other types of board that were used in divining; and they helped the players of *liu-po* to interpret their throw. This matter will be considered in further detail below (see p. 84).

Whether or not the TLV mirrors were connected with the design of the diviner's board, they were certainly deeply involved with the Han view of the cosmos, and they attempted to symbolize that scheme in its

TLV mirrors and their significance

perfection. Although the cosmology in question had owed its formulation to Tung Chung-shu (c. 179–c. 104 BC) it had not gained general acceptance until some decades before the time of Wang Mang. By then the attitude that is described elsewhere as 'Reformist'[73] had come to exercise a dominant influence on religious practice, intellectual outlook and political purposes. Its cosmology was based on the underlying unity of the Triad of heaven, earth and man; it explained the rise and fall of all things, whether of the spirit or of the flesh, of the world of nature or of man, in terms of the succession of the Five Elements or Phases (*Wu hsing*), and the rhythmical workings of Yin and Yang. However, there was one major deficiency in the scheme; it made no provision for the place of a man's soul after death. It showed how one of the major problems that beset the Han mind, that of accommodation with the natural surroundings of the world, could be solved; but it provided no answer to those who asked about the great hereafter.

The TLV mirrors, however, were as much concerned with this second problem as they were with the first. This is clearly evident from those inscriptions which describe the ways of the immortal beings and which refer, in two instances, to the Queen Mother of the West. Concern with the life of the hereafter is seen also in the very situation of the mirrors, and the care taken to provide them as a talisman for travellers into the great unknown; it is also seen in some of the decorative features.

The inscriptions refer to the habits of the immortals and, occasionally, to the way in which they mount the clouds and wander unchecked over the universe.[74] The same theme may be discerned in the feathered or winged men who appear quite regularly along with the animals, and in the scroll of clouds that bounds the world at its rim. The references to the Queen Mother of the West on two inscriptions lead forward to her depiction in the later type of mirrors, fashioned in high relief, which became popular after the TLV type had lost its appeal. In those scenes the Queen Mother is seen enthroned in all her glory with her attributes and acolytes in attendance. (See Plate XXII.)

Both the decorative details and the inscriptions of the TLV mirrors display their all-powerful symbolism; for the mirrors were intended to set a man permanently in his correct relation with the cosmos and to escort him to a life in the hereafter. The circular heavens surrounded the square earth; the central boss of the square could be taken as the axis of the universe;[75] alternatively it can be taken as a symbol of earth, corresponding with the four beasts who symbolize the other members of the *Wu hsing*. The Twelve Branches and twelve bosses symbolize the twelve divisions of the heavens; the four bosses, or four pairs of bosses, symbolize the four nodal points (*ssu wei*). From the all-important passage of the *Shih-chi* that is quoted above we learn that the *ssu wei* must be fixed before the diviner can start to read his answer. In the TLV mirrors these are fixed; the four beasts set the mirror to face the right directions and to conform with the sources of Yin and Yang. The world of the immortals is represented by the presence of mythological figures; and access to their world may be obtained by mounting the clouds.

Some of this symbolism is seen elsewhere, in work which was executed before the *Wu hsing* theory had gained currency; an example may be seen in the painting from Ma-wang-tui, which was finished a good century before the TLV mirrors had reached their final stage.[76] The prominent features of the sun and the moon of the upper part of the painting have their counterpart in the small medallions, bearing images of bird and toad, that are seen in some of the choicest of TLV mirrors. Similarly the figures of the immortals or winged men of the TLV mirrors may be compared with some of the charming, elf-like figures which embellish the coffins of Ma-wang-tui (e.g., see Figure 5).

If it is accepted that the TLV mirror was related to the diviner's board, it must be considered within the context of Han methods of divination and the Han attitude towards the problem of evil. Here a general distinction may be drawn between the augur's answer to the problem of evil, which came to be associated with the basic thought of the *I-ching*, and the metaphysical approach, which was based on the cosmic system of the *Wu hsing*.[77]

The augur's methods were varied. They were based partly on a simple trust in chance, as is exemplified in consultation by means of shells and oracle bones. More sophisticated methods were based on the belief that a random throw of the hand or selection of milfoil would reveal which one of the 64 situations of the *I-ching* was prevailing at a given moment of time; how changes, that were apparently of a violent nature, could be reconciled with the regular order of the universe; or what steps were appropriate to a given situation encountered in daily life. It is also possible that the game of *liu-po*, which depended on the random throw of dice, should be explained as a means of divination. It is of considerable interest to note that the game was played both by immortals and by human beings.[78]

As distinct from these methods, the board with its two discs was designed to ascertain the situation of the cosmos by taking exact measurements in celestial and terrestrial terms. The system on which these measurements depended was that view of heaven and earth which is mentioned in texts such as the *Huai-nan-tzu*. The importance of the TLV mirror lies in its combination of two modes of thought: divination by means of the specialist's board, and the metaphysical view of the world according to the theory of the *Wu hsing*. For the mirrors display

TLV mirrors and their significance

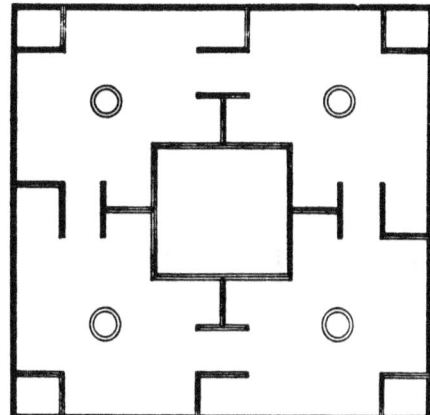

Fig. 14. *Liu-po* board (38 by 36 cm);
from tomb no. 1 Ta-fen-t'ou, Hu-pei

the universe as conceived in the *Huai-nan-tzu*; at the same time they depict the cosmos as conceived by the *Wu hsing*. The two are thus reconciled together. In addition the TLV mirrors possessed one further function. They combine those explanations of the cosmos with a means of achieving life eternal among the immortals. Such a means, if separated from metaphysical speculation, was by no means contradictory to its principles.

Perhaps it may not be too fanciful to discern a measure of continuity in these aspects of Chinese practice. From the board which Wang Mang consulted at a moment of crisis, we may pass to the TLV mirrors, where the circle has been spun and the answer conforms with the truth of the cosmos; thence we may perhaps proceed to the geomancer's compass that is still in use today.[79] These beautiful discs carry inscriptions of the Twelve Branches and the Ten Stems, in the same characteristic combination that is seen on the Han diviner's board; they also display the eight trigrams and the twelve divisions of the heavens; and the 28 mansions are laid out, with an exact apportionment within the 365 and a quarter degrees of the circle. Possibly even the dominant colours of the geomancers' compasses of the last century may be traced back to the diviner's board of Han. One of the boards from Korea (no. 4 in Appendix Three) was decorated in gold, scarlet and black; and the same combination of colours may be seen on the geomancers' compasses of the nineteenth century. It may also be noted that just as the geomancers' compasses regularly carry inscriptions on their reverse sides, so too do two of the six examples of the *shih* that are cited here (nos. 2 and 6 in Appendix Three). Whereas in the Han *shih* the instrument was set by rotating the inner disc against the outer square, in the modern geomancers' compass the direction is found by use of a magnetic needle.

Chapter Four

The Queen Mother of the West

    i. The myth of the seasonal meetings, p. 86
   ii. References to the Queen Mother of the West, from the oracle bones to the *Hou Han-shu*, p. 88
  iii. The deficiencies of Han cosmology and the search for deathlessness, p. 96
  iv. The soteriological movement of 3 BC and early references to the cult of the Queen, p. 98
   v. Iconographical evidence: characteristics in the depictions of the Queen, p. 101
  vi. The Weaver and the Oxherd, p. 112
 vii. The meeting of the Queen Mother of the West and Han Wu ti, p. 115
viii. The cosmological importance of the seasonal meetings, p. 119

i. The myth of the seasonal meetings

In the preceding chapters we have attempted to review some of the intellectual developments of the Han period; and we have taken note of certain philosophical and religious activities evolved to answer contemporary doubts regarding the present, to assure a faith in man's own purpose and authority, and to provide for his well-being in a life to come after death. We have studied a recently found painting and its mythology as evidence of beliefs that were held in the first half of the second century BC; and we have considered the function of certain types of mirror as expressing a synthesis of some of the intellectual concepts and religious beliefs that were current at the beginning of the Christian era. In this chapter we turn to a mythology whose roots stretch back well before the imperial period but which seems to make its first forceful impact on Han iconography from perhaps 100 AD.

    This mythology concerns the regular seasonal meetings of two forces

The Queen Mother of the West

that are needed to maintain the eternal rhythms of the cosmos and which can provide a means of rebirth and immortality. The myth is apparent in diverse guises that have not always been associated together; i.e. the faith in the Queen Mother of the West as a donor of everlasting life and as an arbiter of the cosmos; the portrayal of the Queen's rare meetings with certain favoured temporal rulers; and the story of the rare but essential meetings of two heavenly bodies, the Weaver and the Oxherd. While no precise chronology can possibly be suggested, the myth seems to have affected Chinese art most strongly at a time well after the acceptance of the *Wu hsing*, Yin-Yang theory of the processes of nature. The importance laid on the ancient and well-known stories of the Queen Mother and her partners, on her gift of immortality, and on the meetings of the Weaver and the Oxherd takes its place among a series of answers that sought to fill the deficiencies of Tung Chung-shu's scheme. The myth appears to have gained currency at much about the time when Wang Ch'ung (27–c. 100 AD) was criticizing Tung's scheme on other and entirely different grounds; and while Wang Ch'ung was protesting as a rationalist and a scientist against the enormities attributed to Tung's theories, others of a different bent were seeking to supplement its aridities by a faith placed in the supremacy of certain unseen powers. The Han mind fastened on the myth of the Queen Mother and her partners, or the meetings of the two constellations, as a means of self-assurance and fortification, at a time before the faith of the Buddha had begun to affect the Chinese outlook.

The Queen Mother of the West features in literature and iconography from the *Chan-kuo* period onwards; and while it has long formed the subject of study by a number of distinguished scholars,[1] a re-examination is now justified in view of recently discovered archaeological material. Thanks largely to such evidence it is now becoming possible to re-assess the development of Chinese concepts of immortality and the cosmos during the Han period, and to review the place taken by the myth in Han thought.

The greater part of the evidence dates from the eastern Han period and later, but there are a number of references to the Queen Mother in earlier texts, when the elements of the myth were probably in a less mature stage of evolution. In its final form the myth bears on the maintenance of the cosmic order, the processes of rebirth within the world of nature and the attainment of immortality. The myth was apparently not affected by Buddhist doctrine until quite late.[2] It evolved spontaneously from popular beliefs and cults, rather than being imposed as part of an intellectual policy by an authority; it arose from a view of the cosmos in which man forms but one of several closely linked elements, rather than from a view of the universe in which the ordered organization of man stands as the ultimate goal of human endeavour; and some of the details of the myth bear comparison with parts of Taoist ritual.

At the same time the myth complements rather than conflicts with the Confucian view of the world as this came to be formed during the Han period. It filled one of the obvious deficiencies of that philosophy; and there are signs that here, as elsewhere, the intellectuals of the Confucian persuasion were glad to make use of somewhat strange ideas, if they could thereby enjoin a greater degree of obedience to the authority of the state, or a greater devotion to its purposes.[3]

The myth and cult of the Queen Mother of the West embraced a number of elements and concepts which, being originally of independent origin, were drawn together by perhaps AD 100. In the meantime a short-lived soteriological incident of 3 BC had been inspired by a desire to invoke the Queen's presence and blessing. Later the Queen is pictured as residing at the centre or at the pivotal axis of the cosmos; she is accompanied by attributes that symbolize her power of conferring immortality, some of which may have been taken over from earlier and different beliefs.[4] Still later, but still within the Han period, we find the Queen accompanied by a partner, the King Father of the East, and the image of the two forms a talisman of cosmic bliss that was adopted as a decorative theme for bronze mirrors. The partnership of these two personages invites comparison with another story that likewise derives from early China, that of the rare meetings of the two constellations. Similarities suggest that both of these myths arose within the concept of the annual cycle of birth, decay and rebirth; they may be associated with the two nature festivals of mid-summer and mid-winter.

The following account will attempt to trace the evidence of literature, iconography and historical incident chronologically; and it should be said at the outset that the chapter owes a great debt to the results of Kominami's work.[5] Although most of the artistic evidence cannot be dated precisely, there are general indications of chronological and regional distinctions. If translations of literary passages are readily available elsewhere, they will not necessarily be given here in full; at times it will be necessary to examine particular technical topics at length, by way of a slight digression.

ii. References to the Queen Mother of the West from the oracle bones to the *Hou Han-shu*

The expression *Hsi wang mu* has been identified with the terms *Hsi mu*, of the oracle bone inscriptions, and *Hsi lao*, which appears once in the

The Queen Mother of the West

Huai-nan-tzu.⁶ Dubs has argued that the term must mean 'Mother and Queen [or goddess] in the West', and cites Chavannes and Huber in support.⁷ He quotes the discredited identification of *Hsi wang mu* with the Queen of Sheba, and mentions the possibility that the term is the name of a place or a tribe, together with Pelliot's final conclusion that *Hsi wang mu* was a very ancient mythological figure, feminine from the outset.⁸ Karlgren interprets the expression as the name of a land, used also to denote its ruler, who was not necessarily female; this explanation has been accepted by Bauer, and further support may perhaps be found.⁹ In the following pages, which refer specifically to the place of *Hsi wang mu* in Han thought and religion, the expression will be rendered as Queen Mother of the West; for, by Han times, it is quite clear that we are concerned with an object of ritual or invocation who was conceived primarily as a female personage.

In the passages which will be cited below, we hear first of the Queen as a timeless being who has attained the *Tao*. She is described as a hybrid, semi-human figure, possibly possessing power to control some of the constellations. Soon she is associated with Mount K'un-lun, although she is sometimes said to reside within a cave. Her realm possesses numinous qualities and boasts material pleasures which, together with her own magical powers, are sufficient to attract an earthly ruler to seek meetings or contemplate taking up his abode in her domains. The Queen's powers are such that she can enjoy, or even confer, the gift of deathlessness, and she may be able to disrupt the even operation of the universe.

The earliest references in literature to the Queen Mother of the West is probably to be found in the *Chuang-tzu*. The passage gives the names of a number of personages who had succeeded in attaining the *Tao*, together with their subsequent activities. *Hsi wang mu* is in the company of Fu Hsi, Huang ti and others; on attaining the *Tao*, she took up her seat at *Shao-kuang*, and 'none knows her beginning, none knows her end'. It may be noted that the passage also mentions the attainment of the *Tao* by Yü Ch'iang, whose name has been cited above in connection with the painting from Ma-wang-tui.¹⁰

Altogether four passages of the *Shan-hai-ching* immediately concern the Queen Mother of the West, and before these may be considered, the nature and dating of that work require brief examination. In general, the book may be considered in three parts, of which the first (chapters 1–5, known as the *Wu-tsang-ching*) is of greatest concern here, as it contains material that may be dated some two centuries before the Han period, but may well reflect beliefs current in that time. The second part of the book (chapters 6–9 and 10–13) may be dated some time in western Han,¹¹ and the third from the fourth century AD.¹²

Ways to Paradise

Parts of the book thus reproduce myth that had become enshrined in Han folklore from an earlier age; parts bear an authority which may have influenced Han writers and artists. Of the four passages in question, the first (a) is from the *Wu tsang ching*; the next (b) comes from the second part of the book; and the last two passages (c) and (d) derive from the additions of Kuo P'u (fourth century AD).

(a)[13]

'Three hundred and fifty *li* further west, the place where the Queen Mother of the West resides is termed the "Mountains of Jade". The form of the Queen Mother of the West is human, with the tail of a leopard and the teeth of a tiger. She is skilled at whistling; and over her dishevelled hair she wears the *sheng*. It is she who commands the *li* and the *wu ts'an* of the heavens.'

The features of the leopard's tail and tiger's teeth that are described here may be compared with the depictions of the Queen Mother, seated upon a creature that is formed partly of a dragon and partly of a tiger;[14] an explanation of the *sheng*, a headdress or crown, will follow below.[15]

The terms *li* and *wu ts'an* present some difficulty. Dubs renders the last sentence of the passage as 'She has charge of Heaven's calamities upon the five [types of] crimes'; and he associates the sentiment with the belief that heaven exercised a degree of moral control over mankind. Karlgren cites Maspero's interpretation of the passage[16] to mean that the Queen Mother is the 'goddess of epidemics'; and he suggests that the expression could mean that she directed malignant spirits. However, a totally different interpretation of the two terms *li* and *wu ts'an* is given in Hao I-hsing's note, where they are identified as the names of stars or constellations. This view, which is accepted by Karlgren and Kominami, is of considerable significance.[17]

(b)[18] The following passage refers to an area that lies east of the north-western corner of the space within the four seas:

'On the summit of the mountains of the serpent shamans there is a man who stands facing east, holding a cup; one name for the place is the Mountain of the Turtles. The Queen Mother of the West wears the *sheng*, leaning on a stool.[19] To the south there are the three green birds,[20] who collect food for the Queen Mother of the West, north of the wastes of K'un-lun.'

The depiction of a man, or of men, holding cups occurs in some of the stone reliefs which will be described below.[21] The question of the

The Queen Mother of the West

Fig. 15. Queen Mother of the West; from a stone relief in Shantung

birds, also seen in a passage from the *Wu-tsang* part of the *Shan-hai-ching*, will be considered in Chapter Five.

(c) The reference to K'un-lun in the preceding passage, which dates from before 6 BC, is elaborated in the following citation, which is drawn from the additional part of the *Shan-hai-ching*, appended by Kuo P'u. Dubs has expressed the view that the passage 'undoubtedly contains quite ancient material':[22]

'South of the western lake, by the shores of the flowing sands, behind the Red River and before the Black River there is a great mountain called "The heights of K'un-lun". There are spirits there with human faces and the bodies of tigers, striped and with tails, white in all cases.[23] Below, there are the depths of the Jo River which encircles the spot. Without, there is the mountain of the flaming fire, and when an object is cast therein it is immediately burnt. There is a person who wears a *sheng* on the head, with the teeth of a tiger and the tail of a leopard; she dwells in a cave and is named "Queen Mother of the West". On this mountain there are found all manner of living creatures.'

The statement that the Queen Mother of the West dwells in a cave, in the manner of a deity of the earth, may be contrasted with depictions that show her at the summit of a mountain or a pillar.[24]

(d)[25] A further passage from the latest part of the *Shan-hai-ching* describes the delights that attend a number of mountains, one of which is that of the Queen Mother of the West.[26] The mountains possess certain numinous qualities, and some of them are the homes of shamans. The text lists the material pleasures of life on the mountain of the Queen Mother of the West, the land of abundance, whose delights include the consumption of phoenix eggs and honey-dew.

This passage carries implications that do not appear in the other citations from the *Shan-hai-ching*. For whereas they are concerned with the attributes of the Queen, the last passage describes the joys of her realm, which are indeed to be found mentioned in other works of Chinese literature. According to other sources the magical nature and quality of those delights were such as to tempt at least one temporal ruler to forswear the cares of government and to renounce his honourable status and position. This famous story concerns the journey of Mu, king of Chou, to the far west and his readiness to forget the need to return to his homeland; the story becomes embellished with more detail the longer that it is developed. Possibly a connection may be drawn between the pleasures that are envisaged here and which lead to a happy oblivion of the cares of the world with another concept, as yet unseen, with which the Queen Mother of the West came to be associated; this is the idea or hope of a state of deathlessness, or of a life spent in the realm of the immortal beings. The story may be traced in a number of passages.

The earliest reference is probably to be found in the somewhat dubious 'Bamboo Annals' (*Chu-shu chi-nien*), and the following version is that of Wang Kuo-wei's reconstructed text, as corrected by Fan Hsiang-yung.[27]

'In the thirteenth year the king set out on a journey west, as far as the place where the green birds lie at rest. In the seventeenth year[28] the king set out on a journey to the west; he reached the heights of K'un-lun and was received by the Queen Mother of the West. The Queen Mother of the West detained him, saying "There are birds ... mankind". The Queen Mother of the West came to the king's court and was received as a visitor in the Chao Palace.'

Part of the interest of this passage lies in the statement of the return visit which the Queen paid to the king; the significance will appear later in connection with the myth of the meeting of the two constellations and the accounts of Han Wu ti's entertainment of the Queen Mother.

A far longer and more elaborate version of the story is to be found in the *Mu t'ien tzu chuan*, whose textual history is likewise subject to considerable doubt.[29] Possibly some of the imagery and the details of the ceremonial that are described are taken from the formal accounts of procedure at the courts of the kings of Chou; or they may reflect the practices of the *Chan-kuo* period.

It will be seen from the translations that the passage relates how the king of Chou made a formal presentation to the Queen of precious gifts and symbolic valuables such as jade and silk. The courtesies included an exchange of songs composed in each other's honour; the

Queen's song referred to her own territorial dominions and, above all, to the possibility that the king would be able to avoid death, and that he would be paying a return visit. This the king promised to do, once he had been back to set his own realm in order; in a much later addendum to the passage, which is included in Kuo P'u's citation, the Queen promises the king that he will attain immortality and that she will become his spouse.[30]

It is also of interest to note that the king is said to have planted a sophora tree (*huai*) before leaving the Queen's realm; and the many beasts that are said to have inhabited her domain include, not only the tiger and leopard with whom we are familiar, but also magpies. Reference will be made below to the association of the Queen Mother with K'un-lun as the centre of the cosmos, and to the central tree that acts as a pivot.[31] Magpies play a role in the myth of the Weaver and the Oxherd.[32]

Allusions to these concepts of the Queen Mother are to be seen conspicuously in well-known writings, such as those of T'ao Ch'ien.[33] The story appears with somewhat different details twice in the *Shih-chi*.[34] According to this source, King Mu appointed Tsao-fu to be his charioteer and drove westward on a journey of inspection; and being received in due course by the Queen Mother of the West he was so delighted that he forgot to return to his own land. It may also be noted that there is a reference to the Queen, and probably an allusion to the story, in one of the poems of Yang Hsiung (53 BC–AD 18).[35]

The *Lieh-tzu*'s account of the story occurs within the context of a search for material pleasures and the illusions that a magician is deemed capable of bringing about.[36] The text gives no details of the Queen's attributes or powers, but includes an entirely new concept in which moral criteria are involved. The passage is translated as follows by Graham:

'Then he was the guest of the Western Queen Mother who gave a banquet for him on Jasper Lake. The Western Queen Mother sang for the King, who sang in answer; but the words of his song were melancholy. He looked westward at Mount Yen, where the sun goes down after its daily journey of ten thousand miles. Then he sighed and said: "Alas! I, who am King, have neglected virtue for pleasure. Will not future generations look back and blame me for my errors?"'[37]

The only passage cited so far which mentions the idea of deathlessness is that of the *Mu t'ien tzu chuan*. The concept is next seen in literature of the western Han period, i.e. in the writings of Ssu-ma Hsiang-ju and in the *Huai-nan-tzu*.

Ways to Paradise

Ssu-ma Hsiang-ju refers to the Queen Mother in his *Ta-jen fu*, which was composed and submitted to the throne as a voluntary act between 130 and 120 BC.[38] The following translation is that of Hervouet:

'Aujourd'hui de mes yeux, j'aperçois Si-wang-mou.
Sur ses cheveux blancs tout brillants elle porte un bijou[39] mais vit [dans une grotte;
heureusement elle a le corbeau à trois pattes qui lui sert de messager.
S'il faut vivre d'une telle vie et ne jamais mourir, survivre à dix mille [générations ne sera pas source de joie.'

This passage includes descriptive details that have been seen already, e.g., in the *Shan-hai-ching*. Deathlessness is regarded as a property of the Queen Mother, but there is no specific reference to her powers of conferring such a gift upon others; indeed this idea has so far only appeared in the much later addendum of Kuo P'u to the *Mu t'ien tzu chuan*; and it is to be noted that the idea of living for ever is anything but a cause of envy on the part of the Superman, the hero of Ssu-ma Hsiang-ju's poem. It may also be noted that, as in one of the passages cited above from the latest part of the *Shan-hai-ching*, the Queen is envisaged as living in a cave.

One attribute which is ascribed to the Queen in this text has not been seen elsewhere, i.e. the three-footed crow. Comparison is immediately invited with the three birds who are stated in the *Shan-hai-ching* to collect food for the Queen Mother. There is some controversy whether there are really two concepts here or whether some of the text is corrupt; the question will be considered below.[40]

Of the three references to the Queen Mother of the West in the *Huai-nan-tzu*, two are of particular significance. One possibly constitutes the first direct allusion to the Queen's powers of conferring the means to attain deathlessness; in another there appears to be a close connection between the Queen Mother and the maintenance of the cosmic order.

The first reference relates the well-known story of the theft of the drug of immortality.[41]

'We may compare I's request for the drug of deathlessness from the Queen Mother of the West and Heng O's theft and flight with it to the moon. He was saddened by the loss, having no means of replacing the drug. Why so? Because he did not understand whence the drug of deathlessness originated.'

The point of the comparison lies in actions which are doomed to defeat their own objectives, such as the administrative methods advocated by Shen Pu-hai, Han Fei and Shang Yang.[42]

The Queen Mother of the West

The second passage[43] refers not to *Hsi Wang Mu*, but to *Hsi Lao* (*Mu*), the old person of the west; the text makes the identification clear. It is related that in certain circumstances the Old Lady of the West snaps her headdress (*sheng*) and the 'Divine Yellow' sighs. These melancholy events occur in a whole list of the calamities which affect the cosmos and the world of nature when the *tao* is lost. The Queen Mother's destruction of her attribute has been interpreted as a symbolic rupture of the cosmic order for whose maintenance she is responsible. Further reference to this aspect of the Queen Mother's powers will follow in due course below.[44]

The third reference occurs in the *Huai-nan-tzu*'s fascinating account of the universe and its divisions.[45] In the description of the strange, mythical, outlying countries and the peoples who are to be found outside China's borders, the Queen Mother is said to exist on the edge of the flowing sands. The general context is that of the lands in the west, where K'un-lun has already featured, and the passage continues, in Major's translation:[46]

'The Music People [or "Happy People"] and the Na-lü People live on an island in the Weak Water in K'un-lun. Three Dangers Mt. is to the west of the Music People . . .'

The passage does not include any reference to the characteristic attributes or the powers of the Queen Mother; and it is possible that the term *Hsi wang mu* should be interpreted here not as a personal name but as a topographical term.[47] It may also be of some importance to note that the Queen Mother is directly associated not with K'un-lun but with the 'edge of the flowing sands'.

The passage from the *Chu-shu chi-nien* which is cited above[48] refers to a visit which the Queen Mother of the West is said to have paid to a Chinese monarch. Elsewhere in that text, and in several other works, the visit is transferred somewhat anachronistically to no less a person than the sovereign Shun;[49] and in the *Hsün-tzu* another of the Confucian heroes, Yü the Great, is said to have studied with the Queen Mother.[50]

The most significant passage in the *Shih-chi* and *Han-shu* regarding the Queen Mother of the West occurs in the account of the Western Regions, and reads as follows:[51]

'It is said: "The leaders of An-hsi [i.e. Arsacid Persia] have learnt by hearsay that in T'iao-chih there is the Weak Water and the Queen Mother of the West; but they have all the same never seen them".'

The corresponding passage in the *Han-shu* adds to this: 'If you travel by water westward for some hundred days you draw near the place where the sun sets.'

The significance of the passage lies in its negative characteristics. In a text whose original form may date from *c.* 90 BC or earlier, knowledge of the Queen Mother of the West derived from hearsay; there was no firm supporting evidence; and there was no attempt at a precise definition, in geographical terms, of the place of residence of the Queen. For a more direct association between K'un-lun and the Queen, we must wait for the 'original' notes appended to the list of administrative units that formed the Han empire in AD 1–2, which is now incorporated as Chapter 28 of the *Han-shu*. The note is appended to the entry for Lin-ch'iang prefecture, in the commandery of Chin-ch'eng:[52]

'To the north-west and beyond the defence lines, there is the stone chamber of the Queen Mother of the West, the Lake of the Immortals and the Salt Lake ... to the west there is the Hsü ti Pool, the Weak Water and the shrine of Mount K'un-lun.'

A reference in a similar context in the *Hou Han-shu* is little more informative:[53]

'West of that land [i.e. Ta Ch'in] are the Weak Water and the flowing sands, close to the residence of the Queen Mother of the West and near the point where the sun sets.'

iii. The deficiencies of Han cosmology and the search for deathlessness

From the work of Han sculptors and engravers we know that by the eastern Han period the Queen Mother of the West was playing an important part in Chinese religious beliefs. The cult had acquired characteristics that may not be found in the earlier evidence cited hitherto; it followed a number of philosophical and religious experiments found to be ineffective, but whose developments must now be considered.

By the early decades of the first century BC Tung Chung-shu's cosmological system, based partly on the earlier theories of Tsou Yen, was being accepted as orthodox; it was to be sponsored by a number of leading statesmen; and from perhaps 50 BC or so it was beginning to make its mark on Han iconography. However, the system was gravely weakened by two major deficiencies; it provided no answer to the question of man's destiny after death; and it encompassed no direct

PLATE XII
TLV mirror (detail of C3101); Crown copyright, Victoria and Albert Museum. The small medallion at the top right corner of the inner square shows the 'bird in the sun'.

PLATE XIII
TLV mirror (C3101; diameter 20.6 cm); Crown copyright, Victoria and Albert Museum.

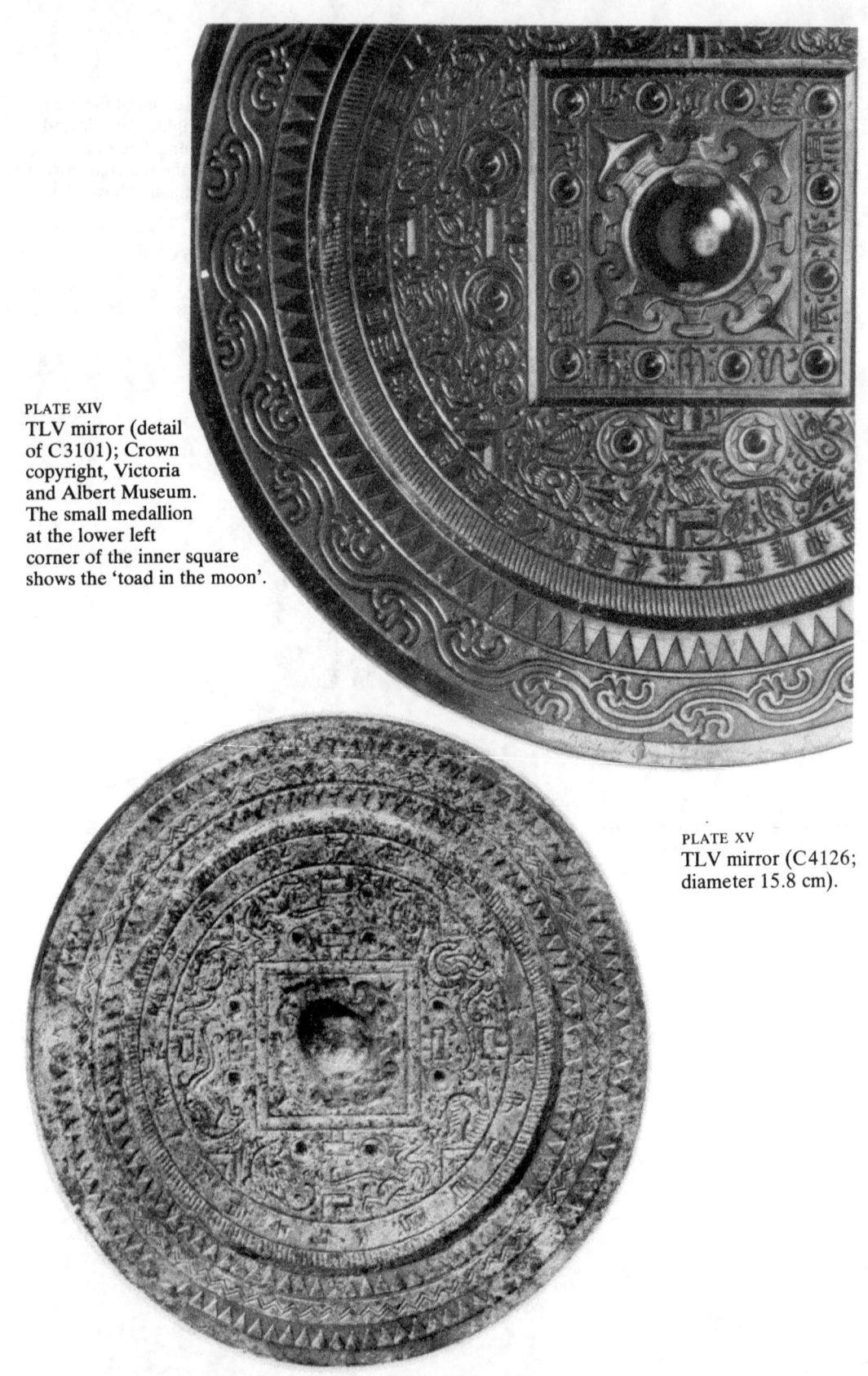

PLATE XIV
TLV mirror (detail of C3101); Crown copyright, Victoria and Albert Museum. The small medallion at the lower left corner of the inner square shows the 'toad in the moon'.

PLATE XV
TLV mirror (C4126; diameter 15.8 cm).

The Queen Mother of the West

means of contact or physical access between the three realms of heaven, earth and man.

Attempts had been made to fill these gaps in the time of Wu ti. Emperors and others had sought the way to paradise by way of the east, through the intermediacy of P'eng-lai, as is exemplified in the painting from Ma-wang-tui. In addition the court of Wu ti had been open to the blandishments and promises of the magicians or *fang-shih*, but their claims had been finally discredited by 108 BC. The failure of the *fang-shih* to procure immortality was accompanied by a certain amount of devotion to the Power of Yellow, or the Yellow Emperor, who, it was hoped, could show the way to such felicity;[54] but, as yet, there does not appear to have been any endeavour to solve the problem of deathlessness by an appeal to the Queen Mother of the West.

Possibly the failure of the magicians to satisfy Wu ti's hopes may have led him to seek a path to immortality by way of the west rather than the east, where they had failed so miserably to substantiate their claims; but as yet the concept was by no means clearly expressed. One of the nineteen hymns that were sung at ceremonies of state and whose text is included in the histories refers specifically to the horses of heaven; and the psalmist expresses the wish to ride upon them, so as to reach K'un-lun.[55] Now, while the significance of K'un-lun as a fairy land of of the west will indeed be considered below, it should be noted that the hymn in question refers solely to the *Ch'ang-ho*, i.e. the gate of the palace of *Ti*. There is as yet no reference to a paradise over which the Queen Mother of the West presides.

Attempts to communicate with heaven may be seen in Wu ti's construction of a terrace or eminence for the purpose, the *T'ung-t'ien-t'ai*,[56] in about 110 BC, and in the ceremony conducted at the summit of Mount T'ai in that year. As yet, however, there was no specific worship of heaven that was conducted by the emperor. Indeed, it was just at this time that steps were being taken to emphasize and intensify the state's devotion to other objects of worship, the Five Powers, or *Ti*, the Grand Unity and the Earth Queen.[57]

It is possible that the myth of the Queen Mother of the West was developed during the first centuries BC and AD, partly as a means of filling the two deficiencies in the cosmology of the day; the Queen's powers and intervention were sought as a means of acquiring immortality, when other means had been seen to fail; and her situation came to be regarded as a means of communicating with heaven. It may also be noticed that it was just from this time onwards, i.e. *c.* 100 BC that Chinese eyes were being directed towards the west for an entirely different purpose. This purpose may, nonetheless, have suggested a new road towards the sacred; for explorers, merchants, and officials were

Ways to Paradise

now actively engaged in opening up the routes which Chang Ch'ien had pioneered; they were establishing contacts with the far west, where the realm of K'un-lun was thought to lie.

The imperial cults of the Han dynasty underwent a radical transformation from 31 BC, when heaven was adopted as the supreme object of worship. However, as has been the case with other 'Reformations', the changes that were introduced then were by no means accepted wholeheartedly; practice reverted, or was changed again, on several occasions.[58] Shortly before the next incident to be considered here, which took place in 3 BC, the imperial cults had once again been restored to their earlier objects of worship, and the Five *Ti*, the Grand Unity and the Earth Queen were again being worshipped at Yung, Kan-ch'üan and Fen-yin.

iv. The soteriological movement of 3 BC and early references to the cult of the Queen

The incident may be described as a soteriological movement in which the powers of the Queen Mother were invoked; it took place in the first month of the fourth year of Chien-p'ing, i.e. in February to March 3 BC. There are three accounts of the event in the *Han-shu*, and in the translations which follow below the supplementary information provided by the commentaries has been utilized. As is usual in the *Han-shu*, the passage in the imperial annals, which follows immediately, is the least detailed.[59]

> '[Chien-p'ing], fourth year, spring. There was a severe drought [in the first month: February to March]. In the area east of the passes, the people were exchanging tokens in preparation for the advent of the Queen Mother of the West. They passed through the commanderies and kingdoms, moving west to within the passes and reaching the capital city. In addition persons were assembling to worship the Queen Mother of the West, sometimes carrying fire to the roof-tops by night, beating drums, shouting and frightening one another.'

The second account of the incident is included in the treatise on movements in the heavens, with one of which it is closely linked.[60] This association need occasion no surprise, as it illustrates the application of Tung Chung-shu's theory of the cosmos; a strange phenomenon in the heavens was being matched by a comparable occurrence in the world of man.

> 'On the day *ting-wei* in the first month of the first year of Chien-p'ing,

The Queen Mother of the West

in the reign of Ai ti [i.e. 4 March 6 BC], at the fourth hour a white emanation filled the skies. It was as broad as a bolt of fabric and over 100 feet long, moving in a south-westerly direction with a roar like thunder, and remaining for about one divison of time.[61] It was named the Hound of Heaven, and it was repeatedly said that failure to obey its commands would result in an outbreak of [hydrophobia?] and the outburst of songs of anger.

In the first, second and third months of the fourth year of that period (February to May, 3 BC) the people were in a state of high excitement, frightening one another with a clamour and an uproar. People were running around hither and thither, exchanging tokens, preparing for the royal advent and worshipping the Queen Mother of the West. In addition it was said that the straight-eyed folk were due to come.'[62]

The third account is included in the chapters on strange phenomena:[63]

'In the first month of the fourth year of Chien-p'ing, the population were running around in a state of alarm, each person carrying a manikin of straw or hemp. People exchanged these emblems with one another, saying that they were carrying out the advent procession. Large numbers of persons, amounting to thousands, met in this way on the roadsides, some with dishevelled hair or going barefoot. Some of them broke down the barriers of gates by night; some clambered over walls to make their way into [houses]; some harnessed teams of horses to carriages and rode at full gallop, setting up relay stations so as to convey the tokens. They passed through 26 commanderies and kingdoms, until they reached the capital city.

That summer the people came together in meetings in the capital city and in the commanderies and kingdoms. In the village settlements, the lanes and paths across the fields they held services[64] and set up gaming boards for a lucky throw;[65] and they sang and danced in worship of the Queen Mother of the West. They also passed round a written message, saying "The Mother tells the people that those who wear this talisman will not die; and let those who do not believe Her words look below the pivots on their gates, and there will be white hairs there to show that this is true."

By the autumn these practices had abated. This was the time when the emperor's grandmother, the dowager empress Fu, was behaving arrogantly and taking an active part in the government.'

The *Han-shu* incorporates the comments that were offered on this occasion by Tu Yeh;[66] these include the statement that *Hsi wang mu* is the appellation of a female, and that chess playing is an activity of males.

Apart from its intrinsic interest there are a number of significant details in the accounts of this short-lived movement. It started in the first month of the year; this period, and in particular the seventh day of the first month, will feature below in the myth of the meetings of certain personalities. According to Wang Hsien-ch'ien[67] the advent processions were of the type that were practised until quite recently, by way of preparation for the progress of an emperor; they may have started as a means of clearing the roads for his presence. That the movement included elements of a religious excitement seems clear from some of the details, e.g., the beating of drums, the raising of fire, song and dance. Possibly the carriage of manikins may be associated with similar activities that took place at some of the seasonal festivals, as will be observed below.[68] Above all there are two features of the movement which relate to the subsequent aspects of the cult of the Queen Mother and the search for immortality: her promise of deathlessness to believers; and the place taken by games of chance in some Han iconography.

Curiously enough there is a further reference to the Queen Mother in a story which, while dating from a much later text, is likewise placed in the time of Ai ti or slightly earlier.[69] The story concerns Yang Pao, a scholar who lived as a recluse in the time of that emperor and his successor. At the age of nine, he once reached the northern side of the Hua-yin Mountains, when he saw a golden sparrow which had been savaged by owls; the fledgling had fallen to the foot of a tree, where it was being cruelly treated by crickets and ants. Yang Pao took the bird home and kept it in a cage made of fabric. He fed it on golden flowers only, and after about a hundred days it began to grow down and feathers, and then flew away.

That night a boy clad in yellow garments came to Yang Pao and greeted him twice. 'I am the messenger of the Queen Mother of the West', he said; 'in your loving kindness you helped and saved me from suffering, and I am truly grateful for the relief that you gave me.' He then gave Yang Pao four rings, of white jade, with the promise that his sons and grandsons would all be men of a pure heart and that they would rise to become the highest statesmen in the land.

As far as I am aware the next reference to the worship of the Queen Mother that is to be found in the Standard Histories concerns a considerably later period of time, in the middle of the fourth century. Here, the initiative derived not from a spontaneous popular movement, but from the patriotic instincts of a senior official; and the action that was proposed was directed towards the happiness and safety of the dynasty.

The Queen Mother of the West

It may be noted that at this time the cult was apparently limited to parts of north-western China.

In AD 345 Ma Chi, governor of Chiu-ch'üan commandery, submitted a memorial to his superior officer. He wrote that the southern hills of Chiu-ch'üan formed the core of K'un-lun; this was the place which was concerned in the story of the visit paid by Mu, king of Chou, to the Queen Mother of the West, and his ecstatic happiness, to the point of forgetting to return home. Ma Chi observed that there was a stone chamber, a hall of jade and other beautiful objects on the mountain, as if it were the palace of a god; he suggested that it would be fitting to found a shrine there to the Queen Mother of the West, as a means of providing the dynasty with the blessing of eternal felicity. The history adds, tersely, that Ma Chi's advice was adopted.[70] We are left to speculate on the real motives behind the decision.

v. Iconographical evidence: characteristics in the depictions of the Queen

Sources which reveal the extent and development of popular religion in Han China are scarce, and there is no means of determining how far the movement of 3 BC should be regarded as an isolated event. As yet there is nothing to show that the cult of the Queen Mother had affected formal aspects of Han religious practice, or that she was being regularly invoked as a means of procuring immortality on behalf of a dear deceased relative. Indeed, at this time the characteristic talisman which was buried with the dead of the upper classes was the TLV mirror, fast becoming fashionable. It has been suggested above that these mirrors evolved as a means of filling some of the deficiencies of Tung Chung-shu's philosophy; of linking that system with the path that led to immortality; and of fixing the dead in the most felicitous circumstances of the cosmos. The cult of the Queen Mother seems to have become popular at a somewhat later stage; but it may likewise be regarded as fufilling the same function, on a mythological rather than a philosophical basis.

At the time of the movement of 3 BC no certain evidence can be adduced from TLV mirrors or other works of art to show that the Queen Mother of the West was exercising a powerful influence on the Han intellect or emotions. The single example of a TLV mirror which bears the date of AD 10 together with an image of the Queen Mother can hardly be accepted as authentic;[71] and the two TLV mirrors whose inscriptions mention her name are, it is suggested below, of a later date and development.[72]

Fortunately there is a considerable body of iconographical evidence

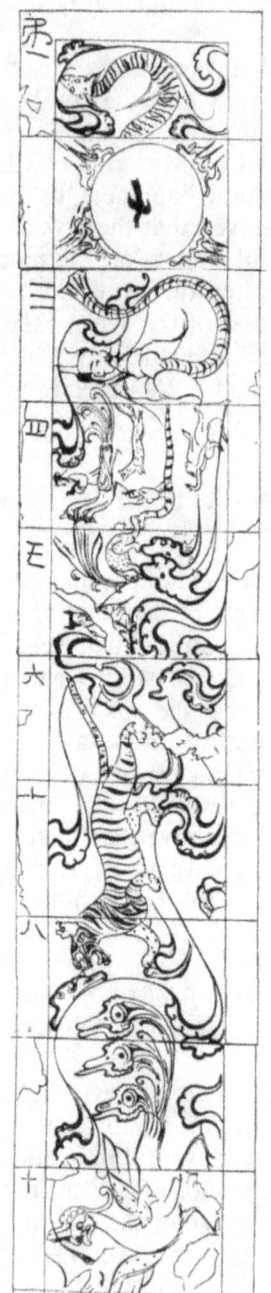

Fig. 16. Roof-paintings from the tomb of Pu Ch'ien-ch'iu, Lo-yang (see note 95 to Chapter Two)

The Queen Mother of the West

to supplement the literary sources. In some cases a figure bears a caption which identifies it as the Queen Mother; more frequently the Queen can be recognized by the characteristic headdress, and then by other attributes who regularly attend her. While precise dating is not possible, the evidence tends to support the supposition that it was only from the end of the first century AD or even later that the Queen Mother's appeal was sufficiently strong to require her presence on sacred works of art.[73] She appears in dated mirrors, either in the inscription or by way of depiction, from 160 onwards, and possibly in one instance in 105.[74] There are low-relief sculptures from east China (Shantung) and decorated bricks from the west (Ssu-ch'uan) which, though undated, are probably from the eastern Han period; there are a few uniquely dated objects such as the jade screen of Ho-pei, of 174, and, possibly, the painted lacquer box from Wang-tu, of 182;[75] finally there are the richly carved stones from I-nan which can hardly be earlier than 250 and may well be dated a few decades later.[76]

Some of the characteristic attributes which appear on these works of art correspond with the descriptions of literature; others invest her with the power of enjoying and conferring immortality; and some proclaim that her correct situation lies at the centre of the universe, whence she may control the rhythm of the cosmos. These characteristics will be considered as follows:

1. The *sheng*
2. The dragon and the tiger
3. The hare
4. The toad
5. The three-legged bird
6. The armed guardian
7. The suppliants
8. The nine-tailed fox
9. The game of *liu-po*
10. The cosmic tree or pillar, and K'un-lun

1. The sheng

Of all the attributes attached to the Queen Mother of the West, the *sheng*, or characteristic headdress, is perhaps the most important, in so far as the literary and artistic evidence for this feature combines to prove the identification of certain figures as the Queen. As the *sheng* symbolizes the character and perhaps the powers of the Queen; and as the use of the *sheng* is limited to the Queen, and occasionally her consort, the term is translated here as 'crown'.

A number of the references to the Queen that are cited above state that on her head she wears the *sheng*; and in a later, and perhaps more fanciful, passage, this appears as a 'sevenfold crown'.[77] From the reliefs of the Wu Liang shrines, a mirror of the T'ang period and a find from

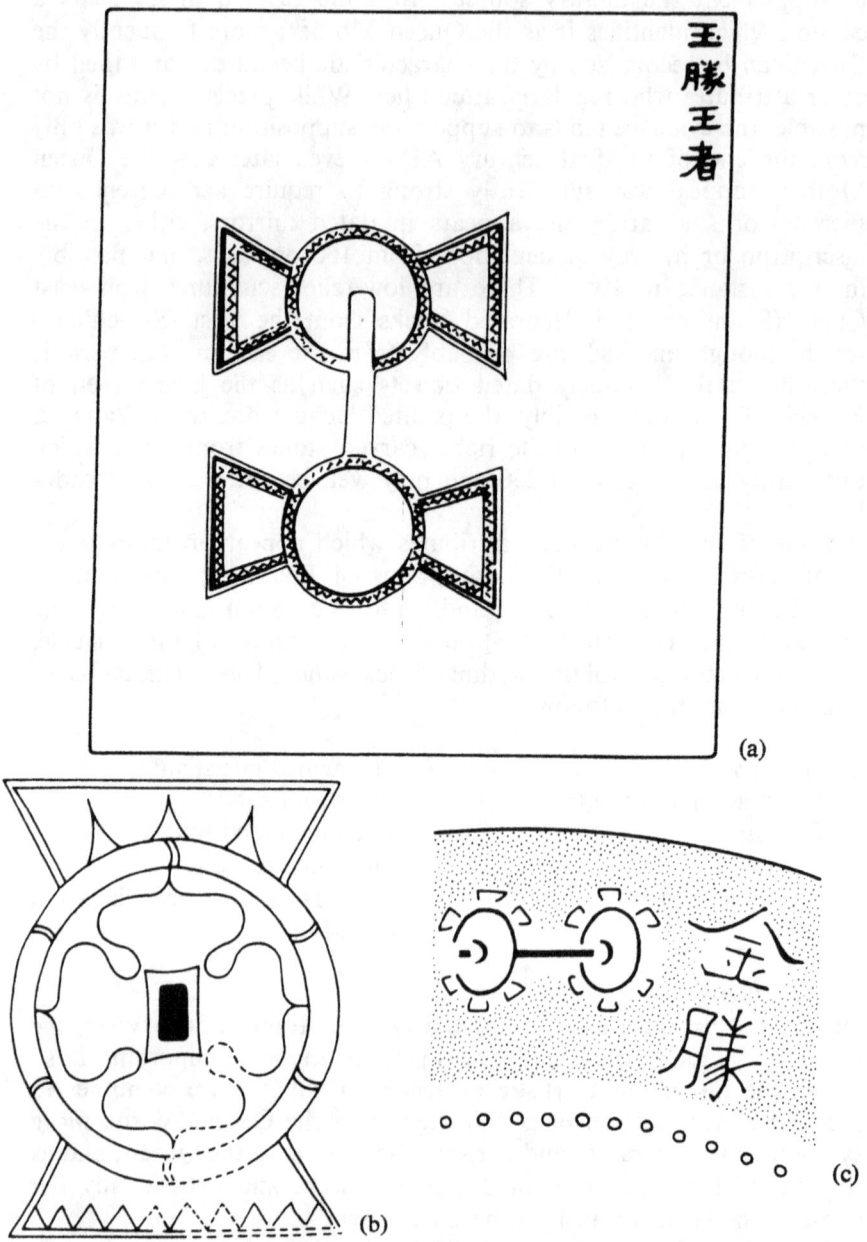

Fig. 17. The *sheng*, or Queen Mother's crown; (a) detail from the Wu Liang shrines, Shantung; (b) characteristic disc, of jade, found at Daedong kang, Korea; (c) detail from a mirror of the T'ang dynasty (National Museum, Kyoto)

The Queen Mother of the West

Korea, the *sheng* may be identified as a pair of discs that are linked by a straight rod.[78] In the latest of these examples the discs are circular, but in the earlier instances they are characteristically shaped as a circle that is held between two triangular parts, the whole being made of a single piece of jade. A female figure wearing this type of headdress is sometimes described in an inscription as the Queen Mother of the West;[79] and this type of headdress or crown recurs regularly in the representations of that personage.

While the term *sheng* has traditionally been interpreted to mean an ornamental headdress,[80] there is reason to associate it with the process of weaving, and even to suggest that it may be traced to the shape of the spools that were thus used.[81] In this connection it may be noted that while, in nearly all cases, the *sheng* appears in the stylized form that is described above, on one particular relief the headdress of the Queen is somewhat different; it appears to consist of two spools joined by a horizontal rod; and to each of the spools there appears to be attached a twirl of thread.[82] The significance of associating the Queen Mother of the West with the process of weaving will be considered below.

The *sheng* forms a characteristic attribute which makes possible the identification of certain figures as the Queen Mother of the West; and from this initial premise other details may also be identified as attributes. In some of the later representations the *sheng* also appears as the headdress of the Queen's partner, the King Father of the East; and in some of these instances identification is possible owing to the presence of descriptive labels.[83] Perhaps one of the most interesting depictions is to be seen in the jade screen from Ho-pei[84] which consists of two tableaux, of the Queen Mother of the West and the King Father of the East respectively. Both figures wear the *sheng*; and the two upright sides of the screen are each formed of a pair of discs, of a type that is seen regularly at the ends of the Queen's crown. In the TLV mirror which is inscribed for AD 10 and whose authenticity has been called into question, only part of the *sheng* seems to have been depicted.[85] In some very late examples the Queen Mother is shown not with the *sheng* but with another type of headdress, the *kuo*, and sometimes with a pair of earrings.[86]

2. The dragon and the tiger

In a few instances the Queen Mother is depicted seated upon a dragon and a tiger,[87] or upon a single creature comprising parts of these two animals.[88] The two animals are themselves associated with Yang and Yin, and their linkage may express the idea of omnipotence and continuity that is achieved by the fusion of the two forces.[89] The feature recalls the description of the Queen as possessing the 'tail of a leopard and the teeth of a tiger.'[90]

3. The hare
The hare is seen busily engaged in striking a drum or mortar, in an occupation that has been identified as that of pounding the drug of immortality. Sometimes there is a pair of these charming animals, and in one relief a team of three is shown at different stages of the work.[91] In one example the hare is presenting the branch of a herb or plant, which presumably possesses magical properties.[92]

It will be recalled that the hare appears within the crescent moon in the paintings found at Ma-wang-tui. The wider implications and the significance of the hare in connection with immortality are considered in Chapter Five below.

4. The toad
The concept of the toad in the moon and its association with immortality have been considered above.[93] In the portrayals of the Queen Mother of the West the toad is sometimes shown dancing with glee, and sometimes holding a strange object or a pair of objects above his head.[94] Possibly a clue to the identification of these objects may be seen in the relief from the Wu Liang shrines,[95] where the toad is holding the vessel in which two hares are energetically pounding their drug. Similarly in the painting from tomb no. 1, Ma-wang-tui, the hare, toad and object are so placed that they may conceivably be representing the same scene.

5. The three-legged bird
This appears regularly in Han iconography in two ways; as an attendant of the Queen Mother of the West, and within a circular disc, symbolizing the sun. The subject is considered separately in Chapter Five below.[96]

6. The armed guardian
This figure appears only rarely, and he is shown carrying a halberd.[97] He has been identified as *Ta-hsing-po*, who is mentioned in a passage of the *Shan-hai-ching*,[98] and he may be compared with other armed guardians who are seen elsewhere in different contexts (e.g., the frescoes of Ying-ch'eng-tzu, or some of the tombs from Ssu-ch'uan).[99]

7. The suppliants
These are figures of persons who have come to pay homage to the Queen Mother in the hope of acquiring the elixir of immortality. They are seen in various forms:

(i) In the brick from Ssu-ch'uan (Plate I), there is a prostrate figure

The Queen Mother of the West

Fig. 18. Queen Mother of the West; from a stone relief from T'eng hsien, Shantung

carrying a wand or tablet, possibly denoting his status as that of an official. The pair of figures seated opposite the suppliant have been explained as being the attendants of the Queen Mother, and it is possible that they are interviewing the suppliant on her behalf. This figure may be compared with a somewhat different representation of a suppliant, who is shown in successive postures until he eventually reaches paradise; in one of these postures he is prostrate.[100]

(ii) In two reliefs from Shan-tung[101] a pair of cup-bearing men attend at each side of the Queen Mother of the West. While the purpose of the cups cannot be determined for certain, it is possible that the suppliants are proffering them in order to receive a potion of the elixir. In the relief from T'eng-hsien the cups are in fact partially inverted, and the legs of the two suppliants have been transformed into a serpentine coil. It is tempting to suggest that in this relief, the suppliants have 'drunk their cup a round or two before' and have already embarked

107

on the road of transformation into immortals. Such an explanation would be consistent with the suggestion that is offered above for the central figure who stands at the apex of the painting from Ma-wang-tui.[102] The presence of a cup-bearing man or men near the Queen Mother is mentioned in a passage from the *Shan-hai-ching* that is cited above.[103]

(iii) The reliefs from Tz'u-yün, Chia-hsiang and elsewhere[104] portray men who are in a similar posture of supplication, and who are evidently offering herbs to the Queen Mother. By analogy with the hare who appears holding such a spray, it may be suggested that they are likewise holding parts of the immortal or magical herbs, in the hope that they may be compounded into the elixir.

8. The nine-tailed fox

Perhaps the most splendid example of this animal, whose tail divides into nine branches, appears in the brick from Hsin-fan, Ssu-ch'uan.[105] He is seen elsewhere fairly frequently, e.g., in the jade screen from Ho-pei and in other reliefs,[106] and on a bronze wine goblet; here the artist has portrayed a world of delights in which the Queen Mother is receiving tribute from a whole host of animals and immortals.[107] Sometimes the tail divides into less than the full complement of nine branches;[108] sometimes the fox is shown holding a baton or a sword.[109]

The nine-tailed fox is shown in other contexts without a direct association with the Queen Mother of the West. These include the decorative band of a bronze wine warmer which is dated in 26 BC,[110] and a relief from Sui-ning (Kiangsu).[111] In the latter example he is accompanied by symbols of auspicious omen, and there is good reason to identify the nine-tailed fox as just such a creature. According to one passage, Yü the Great once saw a white nine-tailed fox, who appeared to him as a good omen, in the course of his inspired labours.[112] The animal features along with a white hare, a white deer, white tiger and three-legged bird in the highly auspicious portents reported for c. AD 85–88;[113] and his characteristic qualities are explained in a passage from the *Po-hu-t'ung*.[114] The nine-tailed fox is also known in Japanese mythology, being identified as Hua Yang, consort of Pan Tsu.[115] In the *Shan-hai-ching* the four-footed, nine-tailed fox is said to come from the land of Ch'ing-ch'iu.[116]

Elsewhere the number nine is associated with other aspects of paradise. The *Huai-nan-tzu* refers to the Nine Heavens[117] and there is a reference to the nine walls of K'un-lun in the *T'ien-wen* poem.[118] At a much later period there are references to the lighting of a nine-branched lamp at the meetings which are said to have taken place between the Queen Mother of the West and Han Wu ti; such lamps were used in Taoist ritual during the *Nan-pei-ch'ao* period.[119]

Fig. 19. Queen Mother of the West, a wheelwright at work, and other scenes; from a relief from Chia-hsiang, Shantung

Ways to Paradise

Finally attention must be drawn to a complementary figure of Han iconography who appears in a similar context. This is the monster who bears nine heads, seen mainly on reliefs from Shantung.[120] Sometimes this creature appears without any apparent association with the Queen Mother,[121] sometimes among the rarities and delights of the world of K'un-lun.[122] Sometimes he appears in the company of the King Father of the East and his attendants, e.g., on a stone which is paired with one that shows the Queen Mother of the West.[123] This nine-headed monster has been variously identified as Jen Huang or Mr Liu, the minister who served Kung Kung, but these suggestions seem to be unlikely. The animal can surely be taken to represent K'ai-ming, who is mentioned in the *Shan-hai-ching* as a guardian of K'un-lun.[124]

9. The game of liu-po

One of the accounts of the incident which took place in 3 BC mentions that gaming boards were set up as one of the popular activities prior to the advent of the Queen Mother of the West; and reference has been made above to the possible use of the *liu-po* board as a means of divination.[125] While there is no direct link in iconography between the game and the Queen Mother, it is of interest to recall that immortals are shown playing it in the decorative features of some Han mirrors and bricks.[126]

10. The cosmic tree or pillar, and K'un-lun

In a few instances the Queen Mother of the West is shown situated at the summit of a cosmic tree or pillar. In a damaged and slightly obscure brick from Ch'eng-tu[127] she is seated upon her throne of the dragon and tiger, attended by some of her servants; and the throne surmounts a tree. A far clearer representation, however, appears on one of the carved stones of I-nan, where the Queen upon her pillar is matched by a corresponding stone showing the King of the East upon his.[128] Hayashi cites the [*Hai-nei*] *shih-chou-chi*[129] in connection with the shape of these pillars, whose narrow base tapers outwards so as to form a broad platform at the top. Ascent to the top is apparently not possible for ordinary mortal beings; and it may be suggested that the pillar represents the *Shao-kuang* where, according to the *Chuang-tzu*, the Queen resided.[130] The two attendants (i.e. hares for the Queen Mother and immortals for the King)[131] are likewise situated at the top of the pillars; together the three pillars arise from a single base, whose zigzag decorative lines are probably intended to symbolize a mountain. Perhaps it is too fanciful to suggest that the three pillars and the base are intended to form the character *shan*.[132]

It has been suggested that the design of a lacquered bowl from

Lo-lang, Korea, dated c. AD 69 shows the Queen Mother wearing the *sheng* together with one other immortal,[133] situated at the top of a tree. However, this identification seems to be unlikely; the headdress of the female figure is not of the type now known to be that of the *sheng*; and none of the usual attributes of the Queen are present.

The concept of the cosmic tree which forms the centre of the world may be traced in Chinese literature from the *Chan-kuo* period, in various guises.[134] Sometimes it appears as a single tree, such as the Fu-sang or the Jo-mu; later it is known as the beautiful tree whose growth stems from a pair of trunks, the Mu-lien-li.[135] At times the tree is conceived as connecting the three worlds of heaven, earth and the Yellow Springs; and as such it may be compared with the ladder by means of which Fu Hsi and his sister ascended to heaven.[136] As the Fu-sang, the concept embraces the tree up which the sun climbs and descends, once daily. In one instance it is described as a giant peach-tree growing on the top of T'ao-tu Mountain. It is possible that a late western Han pottery model from Ho-nan may be identified as this tree;[137] the nine branches of the model recall the concept of the nine heavens and the use of the nine-branched lamp.[138] It may be noted that peaches feature as a symbol of the gift of immortality in some of the passages which are cited below in connection with the meeting of the Queen Mother of the West and Wu ti.

The universal appearance of the cosmic tree in symbolism has been noted frequently enough and requires no elaboration here.[139] In a late passage from the *Shen-i-ching*, which will be cited below (see p. 125) the concept appears as a copper column which grows from the top of Mount K'un-lun, thereby linking the concept of the tree with that of K'un-lun as the centre of the world.

There are many references in Han literature to the magical qualities and delightful properties of K'un-lun. A number of passages refer to the Queen Mother of the West as living in close proximity. In addition, the name K'un-lun was twice adopted by Han Wu ti for symbolical reasons, once to name the region of the source of the Yellow River, and once to denote part of the edifice of the Ming-t'ang.[140] Possibly the depictions of the Queen Mother of the West seated upon a mountain or at the summit of a tree are to be interpreted as the realm of K'un-lun, but such an identification would be firmer were there contemporary literary evidence.[141] It is perhaps more likely that the realm of K'un-lun is shown, with the Queen Mother enthroned in all her glory, on the sides of a wine goblet that seems to be of a comparatively late date.[142] This scene may be contrasted with a similar tableau that appears on the bronze wine-warmer whose inscription dates it at 26 BC. The world of animals that is portrayed there includes the auspicious nine-tailed

Ways to Paradise

fox and at least one hare; he, however, is not engaged in pounding the drug of immortality; and there is no sign of the presence of the Queen Mother of the West.[143]

vi. The Weaver and the Oxherd

The suggestion that the Queen Mother of the West became invested with powers to control the destiny of the cosmos derives, initially, from a passage that has been cited from the *Huai-nan-tzu* and from her depiction at the central pivot of the universe. The idea that she could affect cosmic rhythms and changes acquires some support from a second myth which must now be considered, in view of certain similarities. This is the story of the rare meeting of two constellations, male and female; and this myth in its turn may be related to the later tale of the meeting between the Queen Mother of the West and Han Wu ti.

The Weaver and the Oxherd (or more properly draught ox) may be identified as the Chinese names of two constellations lying on opposite sides of the Milky Way, and corresponding to some of the stars of Vega and Altair;[144] the Oxherd is sometimes termed the River's Drum (*Ho ku*). The characteristic shape of the two constellations, i.e. the Weaver as a triangle and the Oxherd as a straight line, each consisting of three stars, may be seen in at least one Han stone relief, whose date is at present subject to controversy.[145]

The earliest reference to the two constellations is perhaps to be seen in the following passage from the *Book of Songs* (Waley's translation):[146]

> 'In Heaven there is a River Han
> Looking down upon us so bright.
> By it sits the Weaving Lady astride her stool,
> Seven times a day she rolls up her sleeves.
> But though seven times she rolls her sleeves
> She never makes wrap or skirt.
> Bright shines that Draught Ox,
> But can't be used for yoking to a cart.'

The interpretation of the poem is subject to considerable difficulty, and none of the traditional explanations are entirely satisfactory. Karlgren translates the passage as follows:

> '... in the heavens there is the (celestial) Han (the Milky Way), it looks down and is bright; (slanting) triangular is the Weaving Lady, during one day (-and-night) she is seven times removed (i.e. from one "mansion" to another in the firmament). Although she is seven times

The Queen Mother of the West

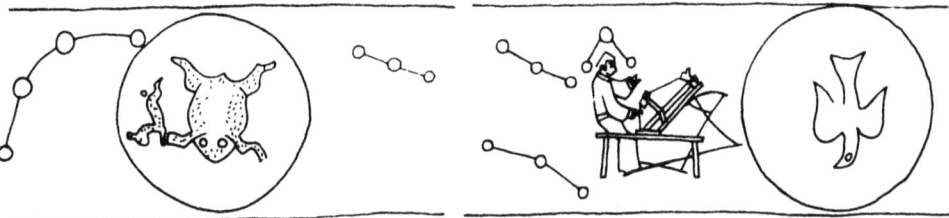

Fig. 20. The constellations of the Weaver and the Oxherd; from a relief in the Hsiao-t'ang-shan shrines, Shantung

removed, she does not achieve any interwoven pattern; brilliant is the Draught Ox, but one does not yoke it to any carriage;'[147] ...

Despite the difficulties of exact interpretation it seems that the poem refers to the failure of the two constellations, as personalities. The Weaver is unable to complete her apportioned work; and the Oxherd, or Draught Ox, may not be used to harness a carriage. It may be noted that in this passage the journey is to be undertaken by the male rather than the female partner.

Opinions vary considerably regarding the meaning of the enigmatic term *ch'i hsiang*, rendered above as 'seven times she rolls up her sleeves' (Waley) and 'she is seven times removed' (Karlgren). Kominami[148] suggests that *hsiang* is a term that was concerned with the process of weaving, and that the symbolic appearance of seven may be associated with the references to the seventh day of the seventh month which appear in the later versions of the story.[149] The basic meaning of the character *hsiang* seems to be to unloosen clothing.[150]

The next reference occurs considerably later, in one of the Nineteen Old Poems of the Han period.[151] Here again there is an explicit reference to the failure to complete a spinning task; and the implication is that, for this reason, the two personalities of the constellations were unable to meet; the translation that follows is that of Waley:

> 'Far away twinkles the Herd-boy star;
> Brightly shines the Lady of the Han River.
> Slender, slender she plies her white fingers;
> Click, click go the wheels of her spinning loom.
> At the end of the day she has not finished her task;
> Her bitter tears fall like streaming rain.
> The Han River runs shallow and clear;
> Set between them, how short a space!
> But the river water will not let them pass,
> Gazing at each other but never able to speak.'

Ways to Paradise

While the date of the foregoing citation cannot be precisely ascertained, the next passage, which is cited from the *Ssu-min yüeh-ling* of Ts'ui Shih,[152] can be placed in the middle of the second century AD; and by now the story has become attached to the seventh day of the seventh month:

'On the seventh day of the seventh month, the copies of the scriptures are put out to dry in the sun; wine, preserves and the fruits of the season are set out; fragrant powders are scattered on the matting, and prayers are offered to the Drum of the River and the Weaving Maid. It is said that the spirits of these two stars are due to meet; all those who keep watch that night harbour their own desires. Some say that you may see an effusion, shining brightly, pure white, in the middle of the Milky Way, just like the waves of an earthly river, shimmering with lights that reflect the five colours. This is taken as the answering token, and if anyone who sees it bows down and prays, his wish will be granted when three years have passed.'[153]

A fragment that may derive from the latter part of the second century ascribes the meeting to the night of the seventh day, when the Weaving Maid is due to cross the river with the help of a bridge formed by magpies. Possibly this is the first specific indication that the journey, which will bring about the meeting of the two, is being undertaken by the female partner.[154]

By the sixth century the myth appears with greater detail and some explicit features. The summer festival of the seventh day of the seventh month is an occasion not only for the meeting of the two constellations, but also of prayer for technical skills by those who are engaged in the task of weaving.[155] According to one source, of the mid-sixth century,[156] it was popularly believed that the two partners were married on that night; but as the second of the following two passages will show, such a union was only temporary. It was deemed suitable so long as the Weaving Maid continued with her work; once she ignored such responsibilities the partnership was interrupted, to be renewed only once annually. It may be noted that here again it is the female partner who undertakes the annual journey for the meeting.[157]

1. 'On the seventh day of the seventh month it is the night of the meeting of the Oxherd and the Weaving Maid. That evening the women of the household reel their finest silk yarn and thread their seven holed needles, sometimes making their needles of gold, silver or copper. They set out tables and mats in the house with wine, preserves, gourds and fruit, and with these they pray for skill. If a

The Queen Mother of the West

      spider spins his web upon a gourd this is taken as the answering token that their prayers will be granted.

2. East of the River of Heaven was the Weaving Maid, daughter of the God of Heaven. Year by year she toiled at her loom and shuttle, weaving the cloth of Heaven, embroidered with a pattern of clouds. The God of Heaven took pity on her lonely state and promised that he would match her with the Oxherd swain from the west side of the river. But once the two were married the Weaving Maid abandoned her work of weaving. The God of Heaven grew angry; he charged her with neglect and commanded her to cross back to where she belonged on the east side of the river; and now only once a year does she cross the river to meet her swain, on the night of the seventh day of the seventh month.'

In another version of the story, after the marriage the oxherd is driven away by the God of Heaven to the constellation Ying-shih, as he has failed to repay the sum of 20,000 cash (coins) which he borrowed for the wedding.[158] This differs from the usually accepted traditional story, which follows the version of the *Ching Ch'u sui-shih-chi* that is given above.

In discussing the myth of the meeting of the two constellations on the night of the seventh day of the seventh month, Izushi draws attention[159] to the widely known concept that the Milky Way forms the home to which the souls of the dead repair; this is found, for example, in Greece, Finland, Lithuania and Mexico. In this manner the Milky Way forms a bridge which connects the worlds of earth and man with another realm; if it could be demonstrated that this concept was entertained in China, it would go far towards supplementing the weaknesses that are inherent in Tung Chung-shu's system. Izushi cites a variety of ideas which attempt to explain the origin of the story.[160] He suggests that the attachment of the story to the seventh day of the seventh month was a later accretion, due to the influence of *Wu hsing* thought.[161] Izushi also believes that originally the story of the meeting was quite separate from the custom of praying for skills which is evidenced in the passages that are cited above.

vii. The meeting of the Queen Mother of the West and Han Wu ti

It will be recalled that the passage cited above (p. 90) from the earliest part of the *Shan-hai-ching* possibly refers to the Queen Mother's control of certain constellations; and attention has been paid to the function of one of her attributes, the *sheng*, as a symbol of weaving. Comparison is immediately suggested with the story of the two constellations, one of whom is engaged in weaving; and just as some of the accounts of the Queen Mother of the West are concerned with her rare meeting with a Chinese monarch, so too is the story of the two constellations concerned with a meeting of the two partners, contrived rarely and with some difficulty. These hints are inadequate to prove an essential link between the two stories, but further evidence may be seen in a somewhat later tale in which the Queen Mother is involved. This is the story of the meeting of the Queen Mother and Han Wu ti (reigned 141–87 BC). It first appears in a text that may date from the third century AD; and it can probably be assumed that the readers to whom it was addressed were familiar with the accounts of Wu ti's preoccupation with immortality and his attempts to procure the elixir.[162]

The following passages show that the story has some elements in common with the evidence already considered. The meeting occurs on the seventh day of the seventh month, and it is the female partner who undertakes the journey. Again we encounter three birds, and we read of a preparation for the Queen's advent. While the style of the tale is much more elaborate than that of the others, there is a more explicit concern with deathlessness and the means of its attainment than has been seen hitherto.

The earliest accounts are those of the *Po-wu-chih*, a miscellany which is attributed to Chang Hua (late third century), and the *Han Wu ku-shih*. This latter text has been ascribed to Pan Ku, but it may be regarded as a composition of the third century or later – possibly as late as the sixth century.[163]

1. The following passage is from *Po-wu-chih*:[164]

'Han Wu ti loved the ways of the immortal beings and he used to worship famous mountains and great lakes so as to seek the ways of those holy ones. Once upon a time the Queen Mother of the West sent her messenger riding upon a white stag to tell the emperor that she was coming; so he furnished the Hall of the Nine Flowery Delights with curtains[165] to await her visit. On the seventh day of the seventh month, at the seventh division of the clock, the Queen Mother arrived at the west side of the hall, riding in her carriage of purple clouds. Being on the south [*sic*] side she faced east;[166] on her head she carried the seven-fold energies of new growth, pulsating like clouds. Three green birds, as large as crows, waited in attendance at her side; and at the given moment the lamp of nine lights was set up.

The emperor was on the east side, facing west. The Queen Mother produced seven peaches, the size of pellets; five she gave to the

The Queen Mother of the West

emperor, two she ate herself. When the emperor had eaten his fruit he straightway laid the pips in front of his knees. "What shall you do with the peach stones you have taken?" asked the Queen. "The peaches are so sweet and excellent that I should like to plant them" replied the emperor. With a smile the Queen Mother told him that the peach trees would bear fruit only once in every 3,000 years.

It was only the emperor who sat facing the Queen Mother; none of those in attendance upon him were allowed to draw nigh.'

The passage continues with the story of Tung-fang Shuo's attempt to steal the peaches.

2. A more detailed account is given in one of the versions of the *Han Wu ku-shih*,[167] which actually goes so far as to name the seventh day of the seventh month as Wu ti's birthday:

'The Queen Mother sent her messenger to tell the emperor that she would be visiting him on the seventh day of the seventh month. When the appointed day came, the emperor swept the inner parts of the palace and lit the lamp of the nine decorated branches. On the seventh day of the seventh month he kept vigil in the hall of the Reception of Flowery Delights. At the exact hour of midday he suddenly saw that there were green birds arriving from the west and roosting in front of the hall[168] . . .

That night, at the seventh division of the clock, there was not a cloud in the sky; it was dark, as if one might hear the sound of thunder, and stretching to the edge of the heavens there was a purple glow. By and by the Queen Mother arrived. She rode in a purple carriage, with the daughters of jade riding on each side; she wore the sevenfold crown upon her head; the sandals on her feet were black and glistening, embellished with the design of a phoenix; and the energies of new growth were like a cloud. There were two green birds, like crows, attending on either side of the Mother. When she alighted from her carriage the emperor greeted her and bowed down, and invited her to be seated. He asked for the drug of deathlessness, and the Queen said "Of the drugs of long, long ago, there were those such as the Purple Honey of the Blossoms of the centre, the Scarlet honey of the Mountains of the clouds, or the Golden juice of the fluid of jade[169] . . . But the emperor harbours his desires and will not let them go, and there are many things for which his heart still yearns; he may not yet attain the drug of deathlessness."

Then the Queen drew out seven peaches; two she ate herself and five she gave to the emperor . . .[170] She stayed with him until the fifth watch, and although she discussed matters of this world, she was not willing to talk of ghosts or spirits; and with a rustle she disappeared...¹⁷¹

Once she had gone the emperor was saddened for a long time.'

The longest and most elaborate account of the story is that of the *Han Wu-ti nei-chuan*, which is probably to be dated in the sixth century.¹⁷² As a full translation of this fascinating text is easily available, it is sufficient here to note a few points of special interest.

1. The visit of the Queen Mother is said to have taken place in the year 110 BC, which was a highly significant year in the history of the state cults of Han. Recently a number of steps had been taken to reaffirm the importance that the state attached to worshipping the Five Powers of the cosmos, the Grand Unity and the Earth Queen. The ceremonies that were performed at Mount T'ai in 110 BC were addressed principally to the Power of Yellow, or Huang ti, now being associated with the idea of immortality. These developments were taking place at a time when the faith that had been placed in the powers of the intermediaries was fast ebbing owing to their failure to substantiate their claims.¹⁷³

2. While the figure of Tung-fang Shuo, Wu ti's courtier who attained the state of immortality, appears in several accounts of the incident, the mention of Tung Chung-shu seems to be unique to this version. Whereas Tung-fang Shuo could very reasonably have been portrayed as showing concern or taking part in activities of the type that are described, the philosopher Tung Chung-shu was hardly the man to have been moved by their appeal.

3. The suggestion in the *Han Wu-ti nei-chuan* that the Han emperor was prepared to scorn the honours of this world in preference for seeking the way of bliss in the other world calls to mind immediately some of the passages which relate the encounter between the Queen Mother and Mu king of Chou.

4. As part of the preparatory ceremonies, the emperor had the lamp of the nine lights lit, as is related with somewhat different phraseology in the other passages that have been cited; this is reminiscent of the nine-branched lamp that was used in some of the Taoist ceremonies of the *Nan-pei-ch'ao* period.¹⁷⁴ In addition, Wu ti provided refreshments in the form of jujubes from the Jade Gate and wine made from grapes. It will be recalled that jujubes are mentioned in some of the inscriptions of TLV mirrors as the food that is consumed by immortals; and the Jade Gate was one of the points of access to China from the far west.¹⁷⁵ The use of the grape was introduced to China by way of the Silk Roads from *c*. 100 BC.¹⁷⁶

5. In this version of the story the Queen Mother is said to be wearing,

The Queen Mother of the West

not the *sheng*, but *T'ai-chen ch'en ying chih kuan* or 'la mitre des Très Purs Enfants de l'Aurore' (Schipper, p. 73). In the *Han Wu ku-shih* this appears as the *ch'i sheng* or sevenfold crown, and in the *Po-wu-chih* as *ch'i chung ch'ing ch'i*, 'des vapeurs bleues qui s'accumulaient en sept couches successives' (Schipper, p. 5). It is somewhat tempting to associate the *ch'i sheng* and its various alternates with the enigmatic *ch'i hsiang* that appears in the passage of the *Shih-ching* regarding the Weaving Maid and the Oxherd.[177]

viii. The cosmological importance of the seasonal meetings

There may be reason to suggest that the stories and characteristics of the main figures who have been involved so far, the Queen Mother of the West and Mu king of Chou, the two constellations, and the Queen Mother and Han Wu ti, form part of a much larger and more important myth. This myth saw the continuity of the universe as depending on two annual meetings that took place in summer and winter. It was celebrated, or even re-enacted, in the two festivals that took place on the seventh days of the first and seventh months so as to mark the progress of the annual cycle.

From a sixth-century text of which parts have already been cited we learn of activities that took place on the seventh day of the first month:[178]

> 'The seventh day of the first month is the day of Man. Seven varieties of herb are used to brew soup; figured silks are cut and gold foil is engraved to form human manikins which are attached to a screen or carried as ornaments? on each side of the head? People likewise fashion decorated *sheng* as presents for each other; and they climb up on high to recite poetry.'

The passage calls to mind the exchange of tokens reported as one of the features of the religious cult that was intended to honour the Queen Mother of the West in 3 BC. The appearance of the *sheng*, worn where the Queen wore her own headdress, is surely significant. While the reference to the screen leaves much to the imagination, we are reminded of the beautiful screen of jade carved in the form of the Queen Mother of the West with some of her attributes.[179] Although the purpose of the screen is not certain, it can probably be assumed with safety that it bore a religious or ritual function.

It is possible that this passage refers to practices that date from long before the sixth century and that were concerned with the Queen Mother. The Sui commentator Tu Kung-chan writes:

'The decorated *sheng* originated in the Chin dynasty. According to the *Tien-chieh* of Li, wife of Chia Ch'ung [217–283], they were shaped like the golden *sheng* of charms. In addition they depicted the visit paid by the Queen Mother of the West, wearing her *sheng*, to Wu ti, in the Hall of the Reception of Flowery Delights, on the seventh day of the first month.'[180]

Tu's citation is from a text written during the third century, and it is of considerable significance that in this passage the meeting between the Queen Mother and Wu ti is ascribed to the first rather than to the seventh month. Kominami[181] traces the stress laid on the seventh days of the first and the seventh months in folklore. From early Japanese practice he suggests that the importance of the seventh day of the month lay partly in its function as marking the phases of the moon; and he links the two festivals of the first and seventh months with the progress of the agricultural year. Finally, it may be noted that in at least one passage the movements of the Weaving Maid are also associated with both of the months that are in question:[182]

'The three stars of the Weaving Maid lie east of the Market of Heaven... they may be seen in the eastern quarter regularly on the sixth and seventh days of the seventh month and the first month...'

It is suggested then that a connection may be discerned between three elements: the myth of the Queen Mother of the West, with her characteristic headgear and powers of immortality; the story of the rare meetings of the Weaving Maid and the Oxherd; and the accounts of the meetings of the Queen Mother and Han Wu ti. It is further suggested that these elements are bound up together with the two annual festivals that marked the cycle of seasonal change, and that the Queen Mother was conceived as possessing the power to renew the cosmic cycle, as it were by weaving a web of continuity and rebirth. The association of these various elements together receives support from several other considerations.

There are several passages which link the Queen Mother with sericulture. In one it is related that Tung-fang Shuo observed the Queen Mother picking from mulberry trees by the shores of the White Lake;[183] elsewhere the decorated *sheng* forms part of the headdress worn by imperial ladies during their ceremonial practice of sericulture.[184] Moreover, in addition to the exchange of *sheng* as presents on the day of the Man's festival (the seventh day of the first month), we hear later of sacrifices which were rendered to the shuttle on the other operative date, the seventh day of the seventh month.[185]

A further significant detail may be seen in the recurring presence of

The Queen Mother of the West

a bird or birds in the various stories that have been under consideration. Birds attend the Queen Mother from some of the earliest references; birds form a bridge for the journey that the Weaving Maid pays to the Oxherd; and in a citation that will appear below the Queen Mother journeys on a bird to meet, not Han Wu ti, but the King Father of the East.[186]

In recent times two versions of the myth of the two constellations have been current in China.[187] According to one, the Weaving Maid was the grand-daughter of the Queen Mother of the West. While she was living on earth, she became the bride of the Oxherd, but once this fact became known to the Queen Mother, the Weaving Maid was transported to the heavens. The Queen Mother drew a line with a hairpin; this line became the Milky Way which separates the two constellations; and it is only once a year that they are permitted to meet.[188]

The final aspects of the myth may be seen both in literature and iconography. The implication that the Queen Mother of the West possesses the function of spinning the web of the cosmos is already present in one of the passages of the *Huai-nan-tzu*, where the destruction of her crown constitutes one of the signs of universal catastrophe.[189] But maintenance of cosmic harmony and of the cosmic cycles is seen in the union of the two forces at stated intervals, and this union is symbolized in the meeting of the two constellations. It also comes to be symbolized in another meeting, that of the Queen Mother of the West and the King Father of the East.

In the case of the other meetings (i.e. that of the two constellations and that of the Queen Mother and Han Wu ti) it is the female partner who undertakes the journey. In this latest instance it is usually the King of the East who travels to visit the Queen of the West; i.e. the male spirit of the sun, of the east, visits the female spirit of the moon, of the west. Parallels to this myth may be found in many parts of the world;[190] the renewal of the cosmic cycle in this way relates very closely to the renewal of life rather than the acceptance of death. In China this is seen in the search for deathlessness that was undertaken by Han Wu ti, and in the provision of tokens of immortality in graves.

The two figures of the Queen and the King appear together in iconography of the second century AD and later; very often the two are shown with the same or corresponding attributes. An excellent example may be seen in the jade screen from Ho-pei, which is dated at AD 174.[191] Here the two figures are seen without any indication of the journey that ends in their meeting, but this is seen very clearly in stone reliefs that derive from both the eastern and the western traditions of Han art, in Shensi and Shantung.[192]

Ways to Paradise

Most striking of all are the representations of the figures with an indication of their cosmic function, as may be seen in the decor of a jade pillow from Wang-tu, Shantung (dated AD 182), and in some of the sculptures from I-nan. The jade pillow from Wang-tu[193] is so shaped that it is clear that the Queen of the West and the King of the East together hold the cosmos in their keeping. In the sculptures from I-nan,[194] probably to be dated after the Han period, the two figures are shown conspicuously at the summit of mountains or the tops of vertical pillars, unattainable to ordinary mortals; from those heights they may direct their influence on the cycles of the universe. Like the Queen Mother, the King of the East is shown wearing the *sheng*. While the Queen is attended by a pair of drug-pounding hares, the King has at his side two winged immortals who are similarly engaged; these have been identified as Ch'ih Sung and Wang Ch'iao.[195]

The Queen and the King appear together on a number of mirrors, of high relief, of the later Han period and afterwards, with genuinely dated examples from AD 160. Sometimes the two figures are simply mentioned in the inscriptions, where they are invoked as examples of longevity, and the terms of the inscriptions are highly reminiscent of those found on TLV mirrors. Other examples carry a depiction of the two partners.[196]

The mirrors which are decorated with the images of these two personages bear a symbolic value which is no less important than that of the TLV mirrors. The same intellectual purpose persisted, i.e. that of providing a perfect cosmic situation wherein the deceased person could endure, in the hope of a life eternal. It has been suggested above how the TLV mirrors fulfilled this function in relation to the contemporary metaphysic, and how they supplemented the deficiencies of that metaphysic. By the middle of the second century AD, TLV mirrors were giving place to other types, which were embellished more lavishly and with less attention to the formalism of orthodox cosmology. The mirrors appearing from that time onwards with their specific references to the Queen Mother of the West and the King Father of the East carried a message for the deceased that was of no smaller import than that of earlier types. Their design symbolized that all-important meeting, achieved rarely and with some difficulty, whereby the cosmic rhythms are renewed and an individual can hope to achieve a life of perpetual delight, in the manner of King Mu of Chou or Han wu ti.

Both these types of talisman lay beyond the influence of Buddhism which was now beginning to affect China.[197] For the Buddhist ideas of life, death and rebirth were utterly different from the hopes that were entertained within the Taoist scheme of early Chinese thought. In Buddhism, a further stage of existence could be attained through self-

The Queen Mother of the West

Fig. 21. Queen Mother of the West and King Father of the East; from sculptures in a tomb at I-nan, Shantung, ?third century AD. Both the Queen and the King are shown wearing the crown. The pair of pounding hares is matched by a pair of human figures, and all four are winged

improvement and enlightenment; in Taoism, eternal bliss was attained through disciplines, formulae or ceremonies. In addition the Buddhist preference for cremation rather than interment tended to eliminate opportunities for the burial of mirrors as a talisman for the dead. It may be noted that, by the Wei and T'ang periods, when Buddhism had really taken a hold on the Chinese heart and mind, entirely new fashions had been introduced for bronze mirrors; by then they had become vehicles for artistry, which was certainly exquisite enough, but which lacked symbolical significance of a religious type (e.g., see Plate XXV).

The results of the foregoing enquiry may be summarized as follows. The ideas and symbols which have been discussed hitherto appear in the first instance independently; with the passage of time they become associated together as parts of a single mythology; and in the process they were elaborated and stylized.

The earliest texts describe the Queen Mother of the West with certain characteristics of dress and location; in the latest depictions she appears as Queen of the Universe, holding court, attended by her faithful servants and giving audience to a suppliant. There is a hint in the *Huai-nan-tzu* that she could wield powers over the cosmos; some centuries later she is described, together with the King Father of the East, as 'creator of heaven and earth, moulder of all things that are created, mistress acknowledged by all those who ascend to heaven or descend to earth...'[198]

K'un-lun, which was described in the *Chan-kuo* poems of the *Ch'u tz'u* as a land of delights, was invested with mystical properties of a cosmic nature in the *Huai-nan-tzu*. By the reign of Han Wu ti, the name had acquired a magical quality; by the time of Liu Hsiang (74–8 BC) it was being hailed as a home of immortal beings; and it is only in comparatively late texts that there is a specific association between K'un-lun and the Queen Mother.[199] From the early stories of the meetings of the Queen with Mu, king of Chou and of the two constellations, we advance to the tales of two meetings, either between the Queen and Han Wu ti, or between the Queen and her own partner, the King Father of the East.

The earliest references which associate the Queen Mother with immortality are those of the *Huai-nan-tzu* and Ssu-ma Hsiang-ju. In Ssu-ma Hsiang-ju's poem immortality is regarded as anything but an object of yearning. But the artists whose *chefs d'oeuvre* were designed to satisfy religious urges of the eastern Han period were glad to depict suppliants praying to the Queen for this great gift of felicity. The work of those artists also reveals a new use of ancient symbolism. The two-legged bird who symbolized the sun, or the three birds said to have sought provisions for the Queen Mother of the West, have often become the three-legged bird who stands at her side. The hare, known from long before both in China and elsewhere as the symbol of the moon, has become an animal with a mission and a responsibility; she prepares the elixir for the Queen to dispense to her suppliant; and the nine-tailed fox, known first as a symbol of good omen, has become another of the Queen's regular courtiers.

During the course of these changes other developments had occurred. By about 100 BC the metaphysical theory of Tung Chung-shu had been formulated on the basis of earlier ideas of the *Chan-kuo* period. At the same time various ways were being envisaged of seeking a state of immortality, either by way of P'eng-lai or with the help of magicians

The Queen Mother of the West

or intermediaries; and such methods had become discredited. But the faith in Tung Chung-shu's system held firm for many decades to come. After the short-lived popular movement of 3 BC, Tung's system was represented in material form, in the design of the eastern Han's capital city of Lo-yang, and in the TLV mirrors of those days.

From perhaps c. AD 100 there emerged a stronger and more lively concept of the Queen Mother of the West than hitherto. This concept does not appear to have derived from a popular movement, and it is evidenced in the officially inspired writings and works of art of the upper classes. By now the Queen was conceived as possessing energies with which to keep the rhythm of the cosmos moving, in the same way as a spinning maid must be kept to work continuously at her loom; the Queen was also being invoked as a power who could confer immortality. While these powers were ascribed to the Queen Mother herself, there also developed a further belief; they became operative in the rebirth of the natural cycle, achieved by the union of the two cosmic forces. Such a union had perhaps been enacted in the twice-yearly festivals of the seventh days of the seventh and the first months, and it may lie behind the earlier tales of the rare meetings of various sets of partners. In iconography, the Queen is shown exercising those powers by her situation at the summit of a mountain, i.e. K'un-lun, or at the head of the tree or pillar of the cosmos.

These ideas, together with the stylized attributes of the Queen Mother, are seen in literature and art from the second century AD onwards. At much the same time there developed the dual symbol of the Queen Mother of the West and the King Father of the East, who were likewise destined to meet on rare occasions. The portrayal of these two figures formed a powerful talisman which could, it was hoped, set a deceased person in a correct relationship with the cosmos, such that he or she could partake of all its blessings; those blessings included the power of rebirth in another world.

This discussion of the Queen Mother of the West will conclude with the citation of a passage of a somewhat late date, which alludes to a number of the features that have been described above, and which illustrates the myth in its most highly developed form.[200]

> 'On K'un-lun there rests a copper pillar whose heights reach unto the very heavens; it is named the Pillar of Heaven. It is three thousand *li* wide in girth and it curls around like unto a crooked knife. Below there are the meandering houses, the establishments of the nine courts of the immortal beings. Above there is the great bird whose name is "Seldom seen"; he faces south; he stretches his left wing to cover the Prince of the East; and he stretches his right wing to cover the

Ways to Paradise

Queen Mother of the West. On the back of the bird there is a small plot that has no feathers and that is one myriad and nine thousand *li* large. Once each year the Queen Mother of the West climbs upon the wing to go unto the Prince of the East . . .

. . . An inscription that is engraved for the bird says: "The bird 'Seldom seen' flashes brightly in emerald and scarlet hues; he sings not neither does he eat; in the east he covers the Prince of the East, in the west he covers the Queen Mother of the West. When the Queen Mother desires to go east, she climbs upon the bird and herself makes her passage. Yin and Yang are then partnered together, and only when the twain do meet is their work fully accomplished".'

Chapter Five

The bird in the sun and the hare in the moon

Circlets shaped like the sun and the moon and bearing within them the imprint of a bird, a hare or a toad have appeared in connection with each of the three subjects studied in the foregoing chapters. They are seen most boldly in the painting from Ma-wang-tui, and most exquisitely in the miniature medallions on some of the TLV mirrors. In the depictions of the Queen Mother of the West, the three animal symbols appear regularly, either in circlets or independently, rendering active service to their mistress. The symbols of the bird and the hare are worthy of separate treatment in view of their repeated appearance both in early and later Chinese iconography and in other mythologies. In addition the complexities that attend the Chinese rendering of the bird in the sun require fuller examination.

As far as may be ascertained the adoption of the toad as a symbol of the moon is peculiar to China, and there are no immediate parallels to the story that the moon's power of illumination derived from feeding on the animal.[1] The appearance of the 'Hare in the Moon' as a symbol of regeneration and illumination has been regarded as an archetype whose roots lie deeply behind the conscious mind of man. As will be shown immediately a link between the flight of a bird and the movement of the sun is by no means unique to China.

The Egyptian depiction of the sun-god Ra with the head of a hawk has been explained as deriving from the concept of the sun moving across the sky in the manner of a bird's flight.[2] In the *Rg-veda* the sun is described as a bird in various terms; in California there is a tradition that the sun and the moon were brought into being by a hawk who carried and dropped two globules of fire in the skies;[3] in Jewish mythology we hear of the bird who ran before the sun bearing a message written in golden letters.[4]

Some of these accounts portray the sun and the bird as two separable beings and there is no immediate reason given to account for the presence of the bird within the sun as there is (outside China) to account for the presence of the hare within the moon (see p. 132 below). It has been suggested that the Chinese idea of the presence of a bird or crow within the sun may be traced to early man's observation of sun-spots, which can be seen by eye with an unexpectedly high degree of frequency.[5]

In the Chinese tradition a distinction must be drawn between the portrayal of a bird as a symbol of the sun and the story of the three birds who provided the Queen Mother of the West with her needs; as will be seen, both of these ideas merge with, or develop into that of a three-legged bird or crow.

Perhaps the earliest reference to the subject is to be found in a fragment that is attributed to Kan Te, the astronomer of the fourth century BC; it is of interest to note that even at this early stage the concept of a three-legged bird makes its appearance, albeit in terms which cannot be wholly understood. The passage reads:

> 'Since the cock has three feet and the crow has two feet, the cock dwells within the sun and the essence of the crow becomes a star which controls the orbit of the Grand Yang [*T'ai-yang*].'[6]

In a somewhat later, but still relatively early, passage the *Huai-nan-tzu* refers to the presence of the *chün wu*, the crouched crow, in the sun and that of the toad in the moon.[7] Still later, the final part of the *Shan-hai-ching* refers to the Fu-[sang] tree and declares that 'as one sun dawns, so does another set, each being carried on its way by a crow.'[8]

In the meantime a number of passages refer to a three-legged bird or crow and its magical or prophylactic qualities. A statement that a three-legged bird lives in the sun and that a hare and toad live in the moon is included in the fragmentary notes to the Five Classics that are attributed to Liu Hsiang (79–8 BC);[9] there is also a reference in Ch'u Shao-sun's additions to the *Shih-chi*.[10] A work ascribed, probably incorrectly, to Kuo Hsien (*c*. 26 BC to *c*. AD 55) relates that Tung-Fang Shuo had told Wu ti of the three-legged bird which was wont to descend to earth in order to consume certain herbs which prevented the onset of old age;[11] and the idea duly appears in the writings of Chang Heng (AD 78–139).[12] By the time of the standard commentary of the *Huai-nan-tzu*[13] the concept of the three-legged crow had become firmly established; for it is used to explain the somewhat enigmatic *chün* of the passage from that work which is mentioned above. Other references may be seen in texts such as the *Ch'un-ch'iu yüan-ming-pao*[14] or Kuo P'u's notes to the *Shan-hai-ching*.[15]

The bird in the sun and the hare in the moon

Perhaps the most telling evidence, which fortunately enough is datable, comes from the *Tung-kuan Han-chi*. Among the phenomena of good fortune reported for the age of Chang ti (reigned AD 76–88) there is included the flocking of three-legged birds at P'ei, in AD 85, and the birth of a three-legged crow in Tai commandery in the next year. The creatures also feature in the summary of the portents that were observed for the reign.[16] Wang Ch'ung's counter-arguments of protest form telling evidence for the currency of the belief in the animals that inhabited the sun and the moon.[17]

Izushi cites the passage from the *Ch'un-ch'iu yüan-ming-pao* as bearing a significance on the origin or meaning of the concept of the three-legged bird. The passage reads:[18]

'The allotted number of Yang arises from one and is formed by three; as a result there is the three-legged crow in the sun.'

Izushi suggests that while the tale of the crow in the sun was of early origin, the further detail that it possessed three legs was a later addition, which developed from the Yin Yang philosophy as a means of identifying the sun with Yang. Izushi adduces other instances in which the number three is significant in this way, and his suggestion is consistent with the assumption that Yin Yang *Wu hsing* theories began to affect Han art and iconography from not earlier than *c.* 50 BC.

Beginning with the paintings from Ma-wang-tui, the appearance of the bird in the sun may be traced in a number of examples of Han art. Very often the bird is displayed in flight, as seen from above, e.g., in the series of astronomical designs on the roof of a tomb near Lo-yang of *c.* 50 BC,[19] and in the small medallions that are incorporated in the more choice mirrors of about Wang Mang's time.[20] The same posture was adopted for the bird in some works of the eastern Han period, e.g., the murals of the Kuo family shrine[21] of the first century AD, and a bronze sword hilt found at Yang-kuan-ssu, Nan-yang.[22] The three-legged bird duly appears in the whole host of imagery painted on the walls of a tomb near Ho-lin-ko-erh, dating in the second half of the second century AD.[24]

A striking representation of the sun and his attribute is to be seen in a stone relief from T'ung-shan, Kiangsu, which is dated at the end of eastern Han; unfortunately the published facsimile is insufficiently clear to determine whether the bird has two or three legs;[25] a two-legged bird is clearly visible in an engraving from Ssu-ch'uan.[26] Miss Bulling writes that the three-legged bird appears among the 'amazing array of animals on the main zone of TLV and other mirrors.'[27] It may also be noted that a form of the bird appears as an emblem of the sun in Japan

Ways to Paradise

Fig. 22. Queen Mother of the West; from a relief from Shantung

being 'depicted on the banners set up in front of the Imperial Palace on state occasions.'[28]

The passage from the twelfth chapter of the *Shan-hai-ching* that is cited above[29] refers to the three green, grey or black (*ch'ing*) birds who collect food for the Queen Mother of the West. These birds have been identified by Hao I-hsing with the three birds mentioned in the following passage from the earlier part of the *Shan-hai-ching*:[30]

> '220 *li* further west is the place which is called the Mountains of the Three Dangers, where the Three Green Birds live.'[31]

In yet a further passage, this time from the final part of the *Shan-hai-ching*,[32] we read that:

> 'there are three green birds, with red heads and black eyes. One is named Great Pelican, one is named Small Pelican, and one is named Green Bird.'

These birds feature among the delights that constituted the dream world of the Queen Mother of the West. It is of interest to note a coincidence, in passing, whereby some of the birds painted at Ma-wang-tui are depicted with red heads and black eyes.

In the next stage of the story the three birds have been transformed into a three-legged bird or crow who serves the Queen Mother. This is seen first in a passage of Ssu-ma Hsiang-ju's *Ta-jen fu* that is cited above (composed after the period 130–120 BC).[33] It also appears, much later, in a note written by Kuo P'u, as a comment to the text of the *Shan-hai-ching*.[34] It should however be noted that some scholars reject the text of the *Ta-jen fu*, as being erroneous, and believe that it should be corrected so as to read 'three birds' rather than 'three-legged bird (or crow)';[35] grounds for such emendation, other than a desire to find rational uniformity, seem to be slender.

In iconography, the Queen Mother of the West is portrayed, as has

The bird in the sun and the hare in the moon

been shown above, with the three-legged bird, the hare and the toad taking their regular places among her attributes. In addition the Queen is sometimes shown in a heavenly context, where there are also two medallions, embellished with the bird and the hare or toad respectively.[36] The symbols are here fulfilling two functions; they place the Queen in the company of the heavenly bodies; and they provide her with servants to procure the elixir of immortality.

From a consideration of the foregoing textual and artistic evidence it seems that independent origins can be traced for the emergence of the bird as a symbol of the sun; for the evaluation of a three-legged bird as an auspicious omen; and for the tale of the three birds who served the Queen Mother of the West with her needs. In the conflation of these themes a three-legged bird – first seen in a text of the fourth century BC – came to be portrayed in several different contexts.

The image of the hare in the moon is seen in Chinese art from the time of the painting at Ma-wang-tui at least. As has been seen above the hare is at times accompanied by the toad; and the hare is also seen as one of the regular attendants of the Queen Mother of the West, pounding the drug of immortality with an energy and verve that would do credit to any sorcerer's apprentice. In this respect the iconography is remarkably consistent, with the hare sometimes appearing twice, or even three times within the same tableau, and always being engaged in the same occupation. At least one of these scenes is reminiscent of other tableaux that appear on Han reliefs from Shantung, where teams of individuals are portrayed working at a corporate task such as that of an iron-foundry or a wheel-wright's shop.[37]

The presence of the hare is of particular interest in view of the widespread appearance of the animal as a symbol elsewhere. He is seen in a variety of cultures extending from those of Classical Greece to Ireland, and embracing those of Buddhist India, North America, Egypt, Europe, China and Japan. The recurrence of certain characteristic features has been examined in a masterly study by Layard, whose recognition of the archetypal qualities of the hare deserves the highest respect and admiration.[38]

The hare takes his place occasionally rather than regularly in the paintings that adorn early man's cave dwellings. Such paintings, emblazoned in the very womb of mother earth, serve to display the ambivalent nature of man's relation with the animals; his admiration for their qualities and splendours, and his dependence on their immolation for his own survival. The link that is forged in this way between man, mother earth and the animals who inhabit her, serves partly as a means of ensuring a successful hunt by man for his prey and thus his continued survival on earth.

131

Ways to Paradise

The hare possesses a number of features, characteristics and habits which single him out from other creatures and make him a particular object of surprise, awe and veneration. He is alone among animals to be marked by a visible split lip. As distinct from the young of other animals, the leveret is born fully furred and with wide-open eyes; to rear her young the doe deliberately carries each one to a separate form, where it will be nourished and brought up in safety, thanks to its mother's constant care and industry. The prolific fertility of the hare arises, as is now known, from its peculiar and probably unique capacity for super-foetation, i.e. the 'fertilization of an already pregnant female which causes the simultaneous development of eggs of two different ovarian cycles within the ovarian tract.'[39] While it is only recently that these physiological facts have been established to the satisfaction of scientists, writers of the ancient world such as Aristotle, Hippocrates and Pliny had more than a vague inkling of the hare's capacities in this respect. The belief that the male, in addition to the female, is capable of giving birth was accepted by Sir Thomas Browne,[40] anxious as he was to establish the facts of nature; other citations testify to a belief in the androgynous nature of the animal.[41]

The highly-strung nature of the hare is seen in the animal's sudden fits and starts, its melancholia and unheralded leaps. Countrymen are well aware of the hare's peculiar behaviour in the face of fire, when it seems to return to the smoke and flames rather than to seek an escape therefrom, even at the cost of suffering scorching. In the world of the twentieth century hares stand out as one of nature's jokers, congregating on airfields, and even challenging aircraft to a contest of speed.

The moon is univerally adopted as a symbol of the processes of birth, death and re-birth, thereby bringing comfort and assurance to man during the long winters of his discontent.[42] As will be shown immediately there is likewise a universal association between the hare and the moon, and various suggestions have been made to account for his selection for this role.[43] Unlike other animals, the hare is fond of appearing on moon-lit nights; traditionally, albeit incorrectly, it was believed that the hare's period of gestation lasted for one month; and the seemingly mad behaviour of the animal may have suggested that it had been moon-struck. Just as the moon brings light from the darkness, as the single great luminary, appearing and disappearing suddenly for no obvious reason, so too has it been observed that the hare behaves suddenly, irrationally and intuitively, as if lit by an inner illumination.

The Buddhist tradition of India tells of the hare practising the ideal of selfless immolation for the sake of others.[44] By way of reward the animal was translated to a life of eternity in the moon; from the moon the hare illuminates mankind, and his image may always be recognized

The bird in the sun and the hare in the moon

there. Folk tales from both India and Africa relate to the wisdom of the hare, his deviousness and his capacity for tricks; and Africa has its own version of how the skin of the hare came to be flung up to lie upon the face of the moon. The connection between the hare and the moon recurs in ancient Egypt, where it may be traced to Osiris. A number of Egyptian deities are depicted with a hare's head; and the hare forms the basis of the hieroglyphic sign *un*, used to denote the idea of *being*. In North America the hare is seen as a symbol of the light shining in the darkness, like the moon; the great hare of the Algonquin was believed to control the world, possessing the power of creating sun and moon; and the same people credited the hare with the invention of picture-writing. In Europe various beliefs and customs link the hare with the seasonal festivals of the two equinoxes, such as the story of the hare which lays the Easter eggs, or the hunting of the hare in Ireland, at the end of the harvest. In Europe too the hare featured as a sacrificial animal; as in Classical Greece, it was believed that it slept with its eyes open.

There is no specific account in Chinese literature which explains the presence of the hare in the moon; indeed, the question that is put in the *T'ien-wen* poem of the *Ch'u tz'u* shows that the animal formed a fit subject for a riddle.[45] The story of the hare in the moon is said to have reached Japan in the wake of Buddhism;[46] however, as we know from Chinese art that the idea was prevalent in China long before Buddhism reached either China or Japan, the story could conceivably have reached Japan at an earlier stage. Later it was assimilated to the tale of the white hare of Inaba which is recounted in the *Kojiki*.[47]

Some of these characteristics recur in the part played by the hare in China. The association with the moon may be illustrated not only in iconography, but also in certain linguistic expressions, such as *T'u-p'o*, *Po-t'u* or *Yü-t'u*, which are used to denote the moon. Possibly the clear and prominent treatment of the animal's eyes in the painting from Ma-wang-tui,[48] and the use of the expression *ming shih*, 'Clear sight', to denote the animal[49] may be related to the observation that he sleeps with his eyes open. But whereas in Europe the appearance of a hare was sometimes thought to presage a calamity, such as the outbreak of fire, in China the red, white and black hares were each regarded as an auspicious portent that foretold the coming of a just and prosperous era.[50] The overall identity of the symbolism with that of other cultures remains predominant. There could be no clearer link between the hare and the cycle of birth, death and re-birth, than the image of the animal pounding the drug of immortality under the benevolent gaze and supervision of the Queen Mother of the West.

Notes to Chapter One

1. For the relationship between religious, intellectual and political changes and their association with dynastic incidents, and the use of the terms *Modernist* and *Reformist*, see Loewe (1974, 1).
2. I.e. the *Chiu chang suan shu*, possibly produced in the first place during the reign of Chao ti or Hsüan ti; see Needham, vol. 3, pp. 24 f.
3. For astronomical instruments and the development of calendar, see Maspero (1950), pp. 15 f.; Needham, vol. 3 *passim*; Sivin, and Eberhard (1970).
4. See WW 1973. 12, pp. 18, 23 and Plates 1–4. This evidence follows that of the manuscripts and paintings from Ma-wang-tui, which are dated considerably earlier (see WW 1974.9, p. 43; WW 1975.6, pp. 1, 6, 14, 16). For the corpus of recently found material, see Loewe (1977).
5. E.g. see the magnificent opening passage in HNT 8. The problems of the HNT include the extent to which that work is based on earlier material, and how far authorship of different parts of the work can be discriminated; see Major, chapters I, II. Major's work is one of the few attempts to treat this text to critical scholastic examination.
6. I.e. the empress Tou, mother of Ching ti; see HS 97A.7a *et seq*.
7. See chapter Three, p. 74: Chan, pp. 305 f.; Major, pp. 19 f.; Bodde (1961), p. 387.
8. Other passages on this theme may be seen in YTL (29) p. 209, and HS 72.13a *et seq*.
9. The *I-ching* was the only one of the books which were later chosen to form the canon that had been exempted from the Ch'in proscription. The present text of the work includes a motley of accretions and comments, much of which may well date from the second century BC. For techniques of divination, see chapter Three below, pp. 76 f.
10. I am indebted to Nathan Sivin for valuable discussion and clarification of these and other matters, and it is thanks to his suggestion that I have adopted the term 'Five Phases' for *Wu hsing* (see also John S. Major, 'A note on the translation of two technical terms in Chinese science: *Wu-hsing* and *Hsiu*', in *Early China*, 2 Fall 1976, pp. 1–3). While the main arguments of the Han Confucian school are too well known to require annotation, translations of some of the more important primary material will be found in Chan, pp. 271 f., and de Bary, pp. 160 f.; see also HS 27A, introductory passage.
11. A list of the phenomena which occurred during the western Han period is given in HS 26, 27. The subject has been treated by a number of writers, e.g. H. Bielenstein, 'An Interpretation of the Portents in the *Ts'ien Han shu*' (BMFEA, XXII (1950), pp. 127 f.); W. Eberhard, 'The Political Function of Astronomy and Astronomers in Han China' (in J. Fairbank, *Chinese Thought and Institutions*, Chicago, 1957, pp. 33 f.), and Eberhard (1970), pp. 11 f. See also Dubs' appendixes on eclipses, in HFHD.
12. See Loewe (1974, 1), chapter Five.
13. Possibly the earliest known examples are (i) in the paintings of the tomb of Pu Ch'ien-ch'iu (see note 95 to chapter Two below); and (ii) the pediment of a tomb now in Lo-yang dated *c*. 50 BC (see KKHP 1964, 2, pp. 107 f., *Wen-wu ching-hua* no. 3, Peking 1964, pp. 2 f.). Here three of the animals associated with the Five Phases are clearly visible, but the fourth side of the screen is unfortunately somewhat obscure.
14. For a passage in the *Shu-ching* which concerns the rupture of communications between heaven and earth, see B. Karlgren, *The Book of Documents* (reprinted from BMFEA XXII), p. 74; *Lieh-tzu* 5.1b (Graham, p. 96); and Maspero (1924), p. 94. For a very similar theme, where the rupture of one of the supports results in imbalance, see Maspero (1950), vol. 1, p. 23; Needham, vol. 3, p. 214; HNT 3.1b, 2a; *Lun-heng*, 11, pp. 473 f. (Forke, vol. I, pp. 250 f.)

Notes to Chapter One

15. For the prevalence of divination see HNT 8.1b, and note 54 to chapter Three below. For the various principles and methods of divination, see pp. 76 f., SC chapters 127, 128.
16. See *Tso chuan* 21 (Duke Chao 7th year; J. Legge, *The Chinese Classics*, 1872, vol. V, Part II, p. 618; S. Couvreur, *La Chronique de la principauté de Lòu* (Paris, 1951), vol. iii, p. 141), and *Lun-heng* 21.894 (Forke, vol. I, p. 209). The meaning of the original passage is by no means clear, as is testified by the comments to the text. The account that is given here is based on the statement of the *Chien* commentary, which cites the *I-ching* in support. Liebenthal, p. 333, cites a passage from the *Li-chi* (Couvreur, pp. 289 f.). Recent writers on the Chinese view of death and the nature of man include Maspero (1950), vol. I, pp. 24 f., 49 f.; Needham, vol. 5, part 2, pp. 85 f.; Granet (Freedman), pp. 80 f. See also Pokora, pp. 76 f., for a fragment from Huan T'an.
17. See Needham, vol. 5, part 2, pp. 84–5.
18. See Maspero (1950), vol. I, p. 28, which also alludes to the custom of ensuring that the eyes of the corpse are closed and the mouth open; Liebenthal, p. 341, who cites Mou tzu, *Li-huo-lun* (Hung-ming-chi, SPTK ed., I.8b; translated by Pelliot in *T'oung Pao*, 19 (1920), pp. 301 f.); Hawkes, p. 101; Higuchi, p. 74; and note 59 to chapter Two below. For the use of jades and bells in ceremonies that were designed to invoke the souls of the deceased Son of Heaven or of ancestors, see Hayashi (1973, 2), pp. 9 f.
19. See Hawkes, pp. 101–103.
20. *Ch'u tz'u* 9.3a; Hawkes, p. 104.
21. For various interpretations, see Shang, p. 43, Higuchi, p. 81; for the view of the painting of an escort of the soul to heaven, see MWT (Report), p. 43, Bulling (1974); for the view that it is an attempt to recall the soul to earth, see Doi, p. 87, Hayashi (1973, 2), p. 10. See also note 100 to chapter Two below.
22. Maspero (1950), vol. I, p. 28.
23. E.g. for Huo Kuang, in HS 68, 11b and Keng Ping, in HHS 19 (biog. 9), 12a; see also HHS 10A, 19a, and other references cited in KK 1972.1, p. 28, note 8, and in Higuchi, p. 191. Prescriptions for the style of the jade-suits, varying in accordance with the rank of the deceased person are given in HHS (tr.), 6.2a and 10b.
24. See Maspero (1950), vol. I, p. 53 and Yü Ying-shih for the search for the immortality of the material body. For a second instance of the successful preservation of a corpse from decomposition, see WW 1975.9, pp. 1 f.
25. These inscriptions may have been made previously, on articles which had been used in daily life. Alternatively they may appear on burial goods which were made specially for the purpose. In each case the object of the inscription was to ensure that ownership was beyond dispute.
26. *Lun-heng*, 23, p. 958 (Forke, vol. II, p. 369).
27. For a building constructed for religious purposes south of Ch'ang-an, see fig. 1, and KK 1963.9, pp. 501 and figs. 20, 21.
28. For this subject see Yü Ying-shih; for the transitional nature of the paradise of the west in the time of Wu ti, see chapter Two, note 171 below.
29. The *Yüan-yu* poem of Liu Hsiang (Hawkes, p. 167) is perhaps one of the earliest visions of a journey to the paradise of the west. The poem is to be distinguished from the earlier poem of that title (Hawkes, p. 81; see also note 38 to chapter Four below). For the search for the paradise of the east, see pp. 34 f.
30. For these two attitudes see Loewe (1974, 1).
31. *Lun-heng*, 20, pp. 869 f. (Forke, vol. 1, pp. 191 f.).
32. HHS, 59 (biog. 49), 11b *et seq.*, translated in von Zach, pp. 217 f.
33. HHS, 59 (biog. 49), 15a; for the terms P'eng-lai etc., see chapter Two.
34. HHS, 59 (biog. 49), 20b.

Notes to Chapter Two

1. See Loewe (1974, 1), p. 197.
2. The most important poems in the *Ch'u tz'u*, for purposes of the present enquiry are (1) *Ta-ssu-ming* and *Shao-ssu-ming* (Hawkes, pp. 35 and 39 f., Waley (1955), pp. 37 f.); Hawkes believes that they were written not long after the time of Ch'ü Yüan (fourth century BC). (2) *T'ien-wen* (Hawkes, pp. 45 f.). Hawkes dates this in the fourth century BC and considers its various interpretations as (a) questions put to a painting, (b) a ritual catechism and (c) a set of riddles. The evidence of the painting possibly lends some support to (a) (e.g., see Hawkes, p. 47 nos. 17–18, and Doi 86 for a question which could very reasonably have been put to the painting that is under study). (3) *Yüan-yu*; see note 38 to chapter Four below; (4) *Chao-hun* (Hawkes, p. 101, dated *c*. 241 BC; and (5) *Ta-chao* (Hawkes, p. 109, dated *c*. 208 BC).
3. HS 18.1b; HS 40.18a; HS 97A.5a.
4. HS 13.15a,b and 26b; HFHD, vol. 1, p. 103.
5. HS 14.15b.
6. The commandery of Kuei-yang was detached and brought under the central government, perhaps in 144 BC; and in 111 this large territory was divided into the two commanderies of Kuei-yang and Ling-ling; see HS 28A (3).46a and 56a, and Ch'üan Tsu-wang's notes to those passages; for a map, see Loewe (1967), vol. 1, pp. 178 f., and Loewe (1974, 2), pp. 72–3.
7. I.e. *Ch'eng-hsiang*, renamed *Hsiang* in 145 BC; for the use of this term in reference to the central government of the empire, see Hulsewé (1955), p. 14; for the kingdoms, see Loewe (1974, 1), p. 311; and see HS 14.3a, HS 19A.26a,b, and HS 38.10b for the complement of officials in the kingdoms and their status.
8. E.g., Chia I (in HS 14.3b) and Ch'ao Ts'o (HS 49.22a).
9. It is possible that popularity was courted by an attempt, or claim, to alleviate the rigours of the Ch'in penal code, although the Han measures remained stern enough. The institution of the kings and nobles (*hou*) was brought about for a number of reasons, due partly to administrative needs and partly as a means of securing the loyalties of Liu Pang's supporters.
10. See Loewe (1974, 2), pp. 69 and 324 note 5.
11. See MWT (report), p. 1, fig. 1 and Plate 1.
12. For a preliminary report on tombs nos. 2 and 3, see WW 1974.7. pp. 39 f.
13. Dated in Wen ti's time 180–157 BC (WW 1963.2, pp. 13 f.); for similar tombs, sometimes less elaborate, of an earlier date, see WW 1957.9, pp. 21 f. (at Hsin-yang; dated in the *Chan-kuo* period); WW 1974.2, pp. 36 f. (at Tzu-tan-k'u, near Ch'ang-sha; dated in the middle part of the *Chan-kuo* period); see also KKHP 1957.1, p. 93 and KKHP 1957.2, p. 85.
14. MWT (Report), figs. 3–4, Plates 2–4.
15. For the system of multiple coffins in Han usage, see Shih Wei; see Anon (3) for identification of the wood that was used; MWT (Report), figs. 6–16; and Yü Sheng-wu for the decor of the coffins. Parts of the outsize timber constructions of some of these tombs have been re-assembled and are available for inspection in the Provincial Museum of Hu-nan, Ch'ang-sha.
16. MWT (Report), plates 5–7, 26 and figs. 17–28 (figs. 22–26 are at the end of vol. 1).
17. Cf. the motif of clouds and mythological creatures on TLV mirrors (see pp. 160–61). For the decor of the coffins, see MWT (Report), Plates 24–57; for the mythological creatures, see Sun (2).

Notes to Chapter Two

18. The full array is best seen in MWT (Report), figs. 22–26, and they may be compared with the device at Sha-tzu-t'ang (WW 1963.2, frontispiece and Plates 2, 3). The arrangement may be contrasted with that of the pediment at Lo-yang (see note 13 to chapter One, above).
19. See MWT (Report), Plates 8–23, figs. 36, 37.
20. For the cases used for packing and the sealing, see MWT (Report), figs. 99–102 and Plates 209–228.
21. See MWT (Report), figs. 39–66, Plates 78–153, and Chang Hung-yüan.
22. See MWT (Report), figs. 67–89 and Plates 154–97, and Kao.
23. See MWT (Report), figs. 90–3 and Plates 198–203.
24. See Loewe (1967) vol. 1, p. 47 and p. 141, note 90. The precise purpose of these figures and those found at Ma-wang-tui is not known; it is possible that they were not intended to be averters of evil, as suggested in MWT (Report), p. 100, but as crude figures of attendants. For some support to the suggestion that they were included as objects of worship, see Waley (1955), p. 39; and a passage in the *Lun-heng*, cited from *Shan-hai-ching*, regarding Mount Tu-shuo (*Lun-heng* 22, p. 937, Forke, vol. 1, p. 243), Chow, p. 8.
25. See MWT (Report), figs. 94–8 and Plates 204–7.
26. See MWT (Report), Plates 229–34.
27. See MWT (Report), figs. 107–9 and Plates 235–51.
28. See MWT (Report), Plates 252–3
29. See MWT (Report), fig. 110 and Plates 226–7, 254–5. For other examples of replica coins, see Ch'ang-sha, pp. 80 f., and note 38 below.
30. See MWT (Report), fig. 111 and Plate 178; the mirror is of P'an-ch'ih type (type no. 1 in the scheme published in Shao-kou; see Appendix Four below).
31. See MWT (Report), fig. 112 and Plate 256.
32. See MWT (Report), fig. 36 nos. 53–7 and Plate 270–92.
33. See Wu-wei, Plates 1–5.
34. Indications on a few strips (e.g., nos. 195, 221, 251) of intermediate spaces left within a column of writing may suggest that inscription took place after the strips had been bound together as a single document.
35. E.g., nos. 140, 263, 304 etc.: cf. some of the strips in document TD 7 in Loewe (1967), vol. 1, Plate 8.
36. E.g., at Yang-t'ien-hu, Hsin-yang and Wang-shan (see Loewe (1967), vol. 1, p. 7 and p. 129 notes 24, 25); for tomb no. 3, Ma-wang-tui, see WW 1974.7, pp. 43 f. For other examples see Loewe (1977), pp. 105–6.
37. I.e., the half *liang* (one liang = 24 *shu*).
38. Cf. another find of replica coins at the western Han tomb of Sha-tzu-t'ang; there was a total of 18 pieces, including 10 *Ying-ch'eng* coins and 8 *Pan-liang* of which some were of the large, Ch'in, model and some of the smaller, Han type (WW 1963.2, p. 18, fig. 7 nos. 5–7 and p. 23).
39. See MWT (Report), p. 156, note 5.
40. See SC 19.4 and HS 16.61a; textual differences between the two versions are noted in the comments to those passages.
41. For reduction in rank as a means of redemption from punishment, see Hulsewé (1955), pp. 205 f.
42. See HS 19B.12b.
43. *Feng-ch'ang*, later *T'ai-ch'ang*.
44. HS 4.8b and HS 4.11a (HFHD, vol. 1, pp. 240, 246).
45. For the situation of Chiang-hsia, see Loewe (1967), vol. 1, pp. 178 f.
46. See MWT (Report), pp. 157–8, and Ch'en Chih. Miyazaki has argued that the tomb should be identified as that of one of the consorts of the kings of Ch'ang-sha, in view of the extravagance displayed in the style of burial. He believes the scale of 1,000 funerary objects to be excessive for the burial of a noble's relative but suitable for that of one of the kings; in support he cites the burial of 1,200 objects at the tomb of the king of Chung-shan, at Man-ch'eng. Miyazaki also notes that the nobility of Tai depended for its income on the emoluments of no more than 700 households; and he believes that so small an estate could not run to the magnificence displayed in tomb no. 1.

He suggests that the tomb should be identified as that of the queen of the first or, more likely, the second king of Ch'ang-sha (the first king reigned for six months only, in 202 BC; his successor held the throne until 194 BC). If this suggestion is to be accepted, it is again necessary to assume that the consort survived until the issue of the new coins in 175 BC.
47. See the preliminary report in WW 1974.7, pp. 39 f.
48. See MWT (Report), p. 129 (item 441–18), fig. 86 and Plate 179; for the reading, see Chow, p. 21, note 5.
49. The body had been dressed in twenty layers of shrouds, carefully secured by nine bands in order to retain rigidity; see MWT (Report), figs. 29–35 and Plates 62–70. The purpose of preserving the corpse intact was presumably to encourage the *p'o* to stay there or, alternatively, to provide it with a home to which it could return after wandering elsewhere. See Needham. vol. 5 part 2, p. 303. The intact corpse of a male was recently found in tomb no. 168, Feng-huang-shan, Chiang-ling (Hu-pei province) dated in 167 BC (see WW 1975.9, pp. 1 f., and Loewe (1977), p. 127.
50. See HS 13.15a,b; *San-kuo-chih* 28 (*Chung-hua shu-chü* edition, Peking 1959), p. 771, note by P'ei Sung-chih, citing Kuo Sung's *Shih-yü*; WW 1972.9, p. 47, note 8.
51. 22 of these were bound together, 11 were loose; see MWT (Report), Plate 58; for the qualities of peachwood, see Bodde (1975), pp. 132 f., and Hulsewé (review of that book, in *T'oung Pao* LXIV (1978), p. 129).
52. See *Hsi Han po-hua*, p. 1; An, p. 43; MWT (Summary), p. 6.
53. See SC 28.69 (MH, vol. III, p. 493); HS 25A.33b and notes thereto; HHS (tr.) 6.4b; Sun (1), p. 54; for more recent practices, see WW 1977.11, p. 26.
54. See MWT (Report), Plate 286, nos. 244–5; Shang, p. 43.
55. See WW 1974.7, p. 42 and Plates 2 and 5; *China Pictorial* 1974.11, p. 40. It is also possible that remnants of a banner found elsewhere had been buried to fill the same role as the two paintings from Ma-wang-tui; see WW 1972.12, p. 10, for an item included in tomb no. 49, Mo-tsui-tzu (dated 126–167).
56. Two paintings have been found since the discoveries of Ma-wang-tui: (a) from the *Chan-kuo* period, at Tzu-tan-k'u, near Ch'ang-sha; see WW 1973.7, p. 3, WW 1974.2, p. 36, and *Ch'ang-sha Ch'u mu po-hua* (Peking 1973); (b) from the Han period, at Lin-i, Shan-tung; see fig. 6, and WW 1977.11, pp. 24 f. and 28 f.
57. See chapter One above, pp. 11 f.
58. See Waley (1955), pp. 37 f., 100 f., and Hawkes, pp. 35 f.
59. See Doi, p. 87, and chapter One, note 18 above.
60. See Shang, p. 43; Sun (1), p. 54; MWT (Report), p. 43.
61. See Plate XXVIII.
62. See Plate I.
63. See An Chih-min p. 43; MWT (Summary), p. 7; *Hsi Han po-hua* first page.
64. See Sun (1), p. 54.
65. See Chow, pp. 11–12; and Shang, p. 46, for the view that the painting had been influenced by Yin Yang *Wu hsing* thought.
66. For the orders of 'Mutual Conquest' and 'Mutual Production', see Needham, vol. 3, pp. 253 f., and Loewe (1974, 1), pp. 281, 302 f.
67. For the interpretation of the painting in terms of P'eng-lai, see Shang, p. 44; for other representations of P'eng-lai, see Laufer (1909), p. 192.
68. See SC 6.40 and 65 and SC 28.24, 72 and 77 (MH, vol II, pp. 152, 190 and vol. III, pp. 436–7, 498, 504) for searches for P'eng-lai that were undertaken by rulers of the *Chan-kuo* period, the first Ch'in Emperor and Han Wu ti, and for references to similar activities by the Yellow Emperor.
69. See SC 28.47 (MH, vol. III, p. 465). For the cult of immortality by means of the Eastern Route, by the First Ch'in emperor, see YTL (29), p. 208.
70. For the relationship between alchemy, aurifiction, aurifaction and macrobiotics, see Needham, vol. V, part 2, pp. 8 f.
71. For the belief in the consumption of jujubes or dates by immortals, see inscriptions on mirrors, of the type exemplified in Appendix Two below, for sub-type C 41, and in sub-types C 42, C 43.

Notes to Chapter Two

72. SC 28.57 (MH, vol. III, p. 478) and HS 25A.27a. For An Ch'i's role as an intermediary, from the Yellow Emperor, see SC 28.64 (MH, vol. III, p. 486). Luan Ta also claimed to have seen Hsien Men, an immortal whom the first Ch'in emperor had tried to contact (SC 28.21 and 23, MH, vol. III, pp. 432, 436 and SC 6.45, MH, vol II, p. 165).
73. SC 28.64, 80 f. (MH, vol. III, pp. 514 f. For sweet dew, see SC 28.53 (MH, vol. III, p. 471) and note 173 below.
74. *Kan lu* was adopted as a regnal title for periods beginning in 53 BC, AD 256, 359 and 926. For a figure of the portent, see engravings on the Han stele of AD 171, known as *Hsi Hsia sung* (*Shoseki meihin sōkan* collection II, no. 28, Tokyo, 1960); for the concept within a Buddhist framework, see Loewe (1966), p. 232.
75. See *Lieh-tzu* 5.2a (Graham, p. 97).
76. As alluded to by Shang, in WW 1972.9, p. 44.
77. See *Wen-hua*, pp. 8-10 for bronze vessels, from Man-ch'eng; MWT (Summary), Plate 8 and MWT (Report), Plates 157, 158 for lacquer vessels; and Shao-kou Plates 1, 2 for pottery vessels with flat lids, decorated in polychrome.
78. See An Chih-min, p. 47; *Hsi Han po-hua* second page.
79. For representations of this union, see Cheng (1957), Plates IV (9) and V (10); Finsterbusch, nos. 127, 137, 150; WW 1975.8, p. 63, fig. 1; and a funerary brick preserved in the Museum of Far Eastern Antiquities, Stockholm (*Ars Asiatica* VII, Paris and Brussels 1925, p. 74, no. 582 and Plate XLIII). The use of a ring, or series of rings, to join two interlaced dragons appears to have become a fashionable device; see, e.g., reliefs from a tomb at Shih-li-p'u, dated 167-189 (see fig. 8, and KK 1966.2, p. 73, fig. 7). There are also a number of examples, principally from the eastern Han period, where a ring and junction of straight lines has been used as a regular pattern to form a framework around a tableau.
80. See H. Hansford, *Chinese Carved Jades* (London 1968), Plates 25, 26; Hayashi (1969), pp. 273 f., *Wen-hua*, Plate 26; Rawson and Ayers, pp. 43 f.; see also note 100 below.
81. See MWT (Report), Plate 36. The device was emblazoned in scarlet and gold at the end of one of the coffins. It is also seen, without the suspended sash, in western Han tomb no. 1, Sha-tzu-t'ang, where it links the necks of two cranes (see Plate XXVI). A striking example of the device is seen at Shih-li-p'u (Kiangsu), where the coils of a pair of dragons are interlaced so as to form two rings (see fig. 16).
82. *Lieh-tzu* 5.2a, Graham, p. 97.
83. SHC 17.3b; a shorter reference, with slightly different detail, will be found in SHC 8.5a. For the dating of the various parts of the *Shan-hai-ching*, see chapter Four, p. 148, n. 11, 12.
84. For a reference to 'bird-turtles' in the T'ien-wen poem, see *Ch'u tz'u* 3.4b, Hawkes, p. 48.
85. See WW 1972.6, pp. 44-8 for Han stone reliefs from Shan-tung, whose subject has been associated with acupuncture; and WW 1973.4, p. 54 for decorated bricks of the eastern Chin period found near Chen-chiang. See also Loewe 1978 p. 111.
86. See Chow, p. 11, Shang, p. 44; and SHC 1.10b, 2.5a for further references to a human headed bird.
87. See SHC 9.4b. The passage does not appear to be included in the extant *Mo-tzu*. In the note to *Ch'u tz'u* 5.7a,b, the figure of 90 years replaces that of 19 years.
88. See HS 25B.22a.
89. *Ch'u tz'u* 5.7a, Hawkes, p. 84; for the connection between Kou Mang and the east, see Wang I's notes to the passage.
90. SHC 16.4b. For spirits of the mountains with human faces and birds' bodies, see SHC 5.6a, 5.27b, 14.4b and 16.4b; for the subject of hybrid forms in Chinese art, see Loewe (1978).
91. Shang, p. 44.
92. *Hsi Han po-hua*, second page; MWT (Report), pp. 42-3; see also Hou ching-lang 'La sculpture des Ts'in' (*Arts Asiatiques*, XXXIII, 1977, pp. 144-8).
93. *Ch'u t'zu* 3.4b, Hawkes, p. 48.
94. An Chih-min, p. 49.
95. The mural from Chi-an is reproduced in An Chih-min, p. 49 as fig. 4. The reference is to SHC 16.8a, where rebirth is achieved by Chuan Hsü; the passage also mentions

Ways to Paradise

the transformation of serpents into fish. The same ideas occur in HNT 4.13b (Major, p. 75) and the standard commentary to that passage.

Possibly a further example of a giant appears in the paintings in the recently discovered tomb of Pu Ch'ien-ch'iu near Lo-yang (see fig. 16), which has been dated tentatively, but by no means certainly, between 86 and 49 BC. (See WW 1977.6, pp. 1 f, 13 f. and 17 f.) However, in a somewhat speculative article, Sun Tso-yün identifies the figure as that of an exorcist (see Sun (3), pp. 17–18). The remarkable series of paintings in the tomb may perhaps be interpreted in the same sense as that of the painting under consideration here, as conveying the souls of the deceased persons to paradise. The tomb included the bodies of two persons, one male and one female, and it is possible that two figures of the painting, with human heads and serpentine tails, fulfil the same function as the central single figure at the apex of the painting from Ma-wang-tui (see pp. 57 f. above). The paintings of the tomb of Pu Ch'ien-ch'iu also include other examples of items that are considered in this volume, i.e. (i) Circular medallions of the sun and the moon, with their symbols of the bird and toad, together with the cassia tree. (ii) Four animals symbolizing four of the Five Phases; three of these are of the regular form known frequently from later iconography, (see pp. 160 f. below); the fourth is of an unusual type, being a hybrid creature with a sheep's head, snake or tiger's tail, and wings, and being accompanied by a second hybrid; these two together take the place that is usually occupied by the snake and tortoise of the north. (iii) The Queen Mother of the West, with a headdress that may be an early form of the Queen's crown (see pp. 103 f. above, for the *sheng*), and a number of the attendants who usually accompany her (i.e. two human acolytes, one mounted on a serpent and one on a three-headed bird; a hare; a fox with a tail of nine branches; and a dancing toad; for these attributes, see pp. 105 f.).

96. See Plate XXVI.
97. An Chih-min, p. 47.
98. See *Chou-li* 12.8a, Biot, vol. II, p. 540. For the problems of authorship and dating of the *Chou-li* and the *K'ao-kung-chi* chapter, see Biot, vol. II, p. 456; Nagasawa Kikuya (translated by P. Eugen Feifel, *Geschichte der Chinesischen Literatur*, Darmstadt, 1959, p. 108); Chang Hsin-cheng, vol. I, pp. 342 f.; Needham, vol. I, p. 111 and note (d) on that page ('The *Chou Li* is almost certainly a Han compilation, though it may well contain many fragments of earlier writings'); and Cho-yun Hsu, *Ancient China in Transition*, Stanford, 1965, p. 210, note 76 ('The *Chou Li* is a large well organised book that contains a great many fascinating though often impractical ideas. According to one theory it was written by an anonymous scholar of the *Chan-kuo* period to describe a utopia governed by a gigantic bureaucracy . . . However, further research concerning the nature of the *Chou Li* is still needed'). For the evidence that the *K'ao-kung-chi* was added as a supplement to replace part of the book, see Karlgren (1931), pp. 3 f.
99. An Chih-min, p. 47. The explanation depends on the passage of the *Chou-li* (see note 98 above), but it is perhaps questionable whether this should be applied to an artistic production of the type of the painting that is under study, and which is redolent of the romantic qualities of the traditions of south China. In addition, the jade ring is seen elsewhere at Ma-wang-tui, e.g., on one of the ends of the coffins (see Plate XXVII); see also Finsterbusch nos. 94, 96. In this context the function of the jade ring may be explained differently (see under feature 4, p. 40 above). Finally, the frame which is in question in the *Chou li* is essentially rectangular, while the characteristic of this part of the painting is circular.
100. For the interpretation of the object as a *huang*, see MWT (Report), p. 42; Hayashi (1973, 2), pp. 9 f.; Rawson and Ayers, p. 43; Higuchi, p. 77. I am indebted to Mrs Rawson for a personal communication on the subject, which is also treated in Hayashi (1973, 3). Hayashi cites archaeological evidence for associating the bell, ring, ribbon and pendant (*heng*) together; he quotes literary evidence to show that jade rings and other objects were used as instruments to invoke spirits to earth, and that ribbons were intended to lend support to the spirits. In connection with the custom of invoking the *hun* to return to earth, he observes that bells were used to recall the souls of ancestors (Hayashi (1971), pp. 49–50). For the bell, see pp. 55–6.

Notes to Chapter Two

101. *Hsi Han po-hua* second page; An Chih-min, pp. 47, 48; Shang, p. 44.
102. At the time of writing this aspect of alchemy has not yet been described in Needham's studies.
103. MWT (Report), p. 42.
104. *Lieh-tzu* 5.2a, Graham, p. 97.
105. *Hsi Han po-hua*, second page.
106. An Chih-min 47.
107. HNT 1.1a.
108. See HHS (treatise) 30.17a.
109. See MWT (Report), p. 42.
110. See An Chih-min, p. 48, Doi, p. 86; HS 54.23a and HS 68.19a.
111. See MWT (Report), pp. 42 f.
112. Shang, p. 44.
113. See WW 1961.1, p. 64, no. 14; KK 1963.8, p. 426 and fig. 5 (Item M 14.11); Bulling (1960), p. 60; KKHP 1965.1, p. 150 (Items 4.1 and 11.42) and p. 148, fig. 35.3.
114. An Chih-min, p. 47; *Hsi Han po-hua*, second page; see also Karlgren (1946), pp. 317 f.
115. *Ch'u tz'u* 1.22a, 3.13b, 5.7b (Hawkes, pp. 28, 51, 85).
116. HS 6.26b (HFHD, vol. 2, p. 90).
117. HS 6.26b, notes.
118. HNT 2.12a.
119. See KK 1960.6, p. 30.
120. See the references given in note 115 above and *Ch'u tz'u* 8.14b and 16.29a (Hawkes, pp. 100, 168).
121. *Ch'u tz'u* 1.22a (Hawkes, p. 28).
122. At the time of the painting, *Ti* still held pride of place in the worship that formed part of the state cults of Han, being inherited from Ch'in. It was not until considerably later that *T'ien* featured in a prominent way in the state cults (see Loewe (1974, 1, chapter 5).
123. *Ch'u tz'u* 2.12a,b; Hawkes, pp. 39 f.; Waley (1955), p. 37.
124. *Ch'u tz'u* 1.23a (Hawkes, p. 29).
125. *Ch'u tz'u* 5.6a (Hawkes, p. 84); for the date of this poem (*Yüan yu*), and its relationship to Ssu-ma Hsiang-ju's *Ta-jen fu*, see chapter Four, note 38 below.
126. See Hervouet (1964), p. 293, note 3.
127. An Chih-min, p. 45; see *Ch'u tz'u* 2.12a, *et seq.*, Hawkes, pp. 39 f., Waley (1955), pp. 37 f.; for the Lords of the Lives or 'Directors of Destiny', see p. 33 above.
128. See SC 27.9, where *ssu-ming* is the name of one of the stars; *Chou-li* 5.10b (Biot, vol. I, p. 420); *Li-chi* 14.3a (Couvreur, vol. II, p. 266); *Feng-su t'ung-i* 8.9b, 10a, for the later custom of worshipping *ssu-ming* by means of manikins (Waley (1955), p. 39).
129. *Ch'u tz'u* 9.4b (Hawkes, p. 105).
130. Their size should be compared with that of the two human wardens.
131. An Chih-min, p. 46 and Sun (1), p. 54.
132. See *Ch'u tz'u* 3.9b (Hawkes, p. 49); HNT 8.7b. For an account of the stories of the nine or ten suns and parallels in other mythologies, see Erkes, pp. 33 f,, Karlgren (1946), pp. 267 f.; for the myth see Bodde (1961), pp. 394 f.
133. SHC 9.3a; see also 14.5a.
134. I.e. *t'ang ku*; for this rendering see (v) (p. 51 above).
135. *Ch'u tz'u* 1.21b (Hawkes, p. 28).
136. *Ch'u tz'u* 2.16a, Waley (1955), p. 45. Waley, whose version is given here, comments on the Fu-sang tree 'The "propped-up mulberry tree", the place where the sun rises'. For a different interpretation of the poem, see Hawkes, p. 41. For other references to Fu-sang in the *Ch'u tz'u*, see Hawkes, pp. 137, 168.
137. *Ch'u tz'u* 9.2b (Hawkes, p. 104).
138. *Chuang-tzu* 2.37b.
139. *Ch'u tz'u* 5.5a,b; Hawkes, p. 83.
140. *Ch'u tz'u* 5.6b; Hawkes, p. 84. For the interpretation of the expression *chiu yang* to mean the sun, see HHS 49 (biog. 39), 12a.
141. Lo K'un, pp. 48–9.

142. See WW 1974.7, p. 42 and Plate 5.
143. *Ch'u tz'u* 1.20a (Hawkes, p. 28); *Ch'u tz'u* 2.16a (Waley (1955), p. 45).
144. *Ch'u tz'u* 16; see Hawkes, pp. 150 f.
145. *Ch'u tz'u* 16.28a,b; Hawkes, pp. 167–8.
146. See the note of the standard commentary to HNT, as cited in *T'ai-ping yü-lan* 3.5a (see An Chih-min, p. 46).
147. See chapter Five below; Chavannes (1893), pp. 80 f.; Laufer (1911), p. 21.
148. An Chih-min, p. 47.
149. *Shan-hai-ching* 14.6a.
150. HNT 6.11b; *Kuang-ya* 10.134 (*Ts'ung-shu chi-ch'eng* edition).
151. *Ch'u tz'u* (*T'ien wen*) 3.5b (Hawkes, p. 48).
152. Sun (1), p. 55. In the painting from Chin-ch'üeh-shan, Lin-i, Shan-tung, the moon is shown full-face.
153. *Ch'u tz'u* 3.4a (Hawkes, p. 47).
154. The text reads *hare*; for the rendering *frog*, as in Hawkes, see Wen I-to's comments, as cited in Sun (1), p. 55.
155. HNT 7.3a and HNT 17.2a.
156. HNT 6.16b; HHS (treatise) 10.3a.
157. Cited in *T'ai-p'ing-yü-lan* 949.1b.
158. See *Wu ching t'ung-i*, in *Yü-han Shan-fang chi-i-shu* 52 (3).1a; and *T'ai-p'ing-yü-lan* 4.7b.
159. Chang Heng, *Ling hsien*, as cited in the notes to HHS (tr.) 10.3b.
160. See Eberhard (1942) 2, p. 198.
161. See Sun (1), p. 55 for a reference to a mural of the *Chan-kuo* period.
162. See KKHP 1964.2, Plate 3.7; for examples in eastern Han, see An Chih-min, p. 53, note 11.
163. See Plate I, for a relief from Ssu-ch'uan, and fig. 19 where the toad grasps a canopy in his hands.
164. See Finsterbusch no. 161, and Cheng (1957), fig. 10 (also shown in Loewe (1968), p. 117, fig. 39). For representations of the toad alone in eastern Han, in Korea and in the T'ang period, see An Chih-min, pp. 46–7 and p. 53, notes 12–14.
165. HNT 17.2a; for the occurrence of the story in Annam, see Maspero (1924), p. 40.
166. See Chow, p. 13.
167. For the concept of the Queen Mother of the West in early literature, see chapter Four below; see note 95 above for her depiction in a tomb that may possibly be dated in western Han.
168. SHC 7.4b; HNT 6.10a.
169. For the alternative reading *ch'i* (type of horse) in place of *hu* (fox), see Hao I-hsing's note to SHC 7.4b.
170. SHC 3.12a.
171. The balance of the literary and historical evidence suggests that the term *T'ien ma* was hardly used before the middle of Han Wu ti's reign, i.e. *c.* 110 BC; and that while the *T'ien ma* may have been conceived as possessing a spiritual significance, as guides who lead a soul to the abode of the gods in the skies, or to K'un-lun, they were not associated specifically with the power of *T'ien*, conceived as a deity.

The term *T'ien ma* appears in one of the nineteen hymns of state whose text is included in the Standard Histories (see HS 22.26a *et seq.*; MH, vol. III, pp. 620–1; Waley (1955a); Yü Ying-shih, p. 96; Loewe (1974, 1), p. 199). The *Shih-chi* carries a very short summary of the hymn (SC 24.7); in the full text, the reference to *T'ien ma* is linked with events that occurred in 120 BC or later (i.e. the appearance of a horse at the Wo-wei river, in 120 BC, and the negotiations for the receipt of horses of special quality from Ta Yüan, shortly before 104 BC).

The theme of the hymn in question is that the *T'ien ma* will carry the emperor to the homes of the blessed, which are termed once as K'un-lun, and once as Ch'ang-ho, i.e. the gate of the abode of *Ti*, who is invoked in another of the hymns (HS 22.21a; MH, vol. III, p. 614). The supreme being who is mentioned in the hymn is *T'ai-i*, the Grand Unity, whose worship had been inaugurated by Wu ti in 113 BC (see Loewe (1974, 1),

Notes to Chapter Two

p. 169). Elsewhere there is a reference to P'eng-lai (HS 22.32b; MH, vol. III, p. 628).

It would seem that *T'ien ma* appears in the hymns at a time of transition in Chinese belief. The paradise to which Wu ti aspires is connected with K'un-lun, which was conceived as existing in the west and as being distinct from P'eng-lai in the east; the *T'ien ma* who come from the west will take Wu ti back to their home; but as yet that home is not identified as the paradise over which the Lord *T'ien*, let alone the Queen Mother of the West, presides.

The Chinese appreciation of the special horses from central Asia and their attempts to acquire some of the animals are described in HS 61.6b and HS 61.8b, with reference to a time shortly before Li Kuang-li's campaign of 104–101 BC. Probably the two portions of the text which concern the incident have been separated during the course of transmission, and the text should be reconstructed so that they may be read consecutively. For the textual problems of HS 61, see Hulsewé (1975).

172. An Chih-min, p. 45; *Chou-li* 1.23b; Biot, vol. I, p. 57.
173. It is difficult to trace the origin or development of the concept of the dew of heaven with its magical properties. See note 74 above for its adoption in regnal titles from 53 BC onwards, and for its appearance on a stele of AD 171. Early references to sweet dew, as a good omen, are to be seen in the *Lü shih ch'un-ch'iu* (SPPY ed. 1.8b) and HNT 8.1b. The intention of catching the dew was the motive for Wu ti's erection of a copper column a little later (see HS 25A.25a). See also *Ch'un-ch'iu fan-lu* 13.9b. For an early reference, see *Tao-te ching* 32.
174. An Chih-min, p. 45.
175. Sun (1), p. 55; Shang, p. 45.
176. Sun (1), pp. 55 and 61, note 6; for the inscription, which may be doubtful, see Shan-tung, p. 105, fig. 203.
177. For literary references, see Sun (1), p. 55, Shang, p. 45. For representations of Fu Hsi and Nü Kua, see Finsterbusch nos. 101–2, 106, 137, 150, 158, 161 and 167 (from Ssu-ch'uan) and nos. 274–5, 282 (from Shantung). More recently found examples may be seen in WW 1973.6, p. 30 (figs. 22, 23) and WW 1975.8, p. 63, fig. 1.
178. See An Chih-min, pp. 45 and 52, note 3.
179. See MWT (Report), p. 41; SHC 7.3b; 13.1b; 17.7a,b.
180. SHC 16.1a.
181. *Ch'u tz'u* 10.5a and 14.3b (Hawkes, pp. 111 and 137).
182. *Ch'u tz'u* 17.6a (Hawkes, p. 173).
183. Doi, p. 88.
184. *Ch'u tz'u* 3.15a (Hawkes, p. 51).
185. Kuo Mo-jo, pp. 3 f. It is questionable whether literary evidence can be found to show how strongly the myth of Nü Kua was being accepted at the time when the painting was created; see Bodde (1961), pp. 386 f.
186. An Chih-min, p. 45; *Hsi Han po-hua*, first page; Chow, p. 12.
187. SHC 17.7a.
188. SHC 17.7b, Kuo's note *ad loc.*, and *Ch'u tz'u* 3.7a (Hawkes, p. 49).
189. See *Ch'u tz'u* 10.3a (Hawkes, p. 110); SHC 8.1a; HNT 4.13b (Major, p. 75).
190. Shang (p. 45) identifies the birds, whether standing or flying, and irrespective of whether they are beside the central figure or savouring the dish, as phoenix, i.e. the attendant messengers of the lord of heaven, who welcome and conduct souls to heaven; see *Ch'u tz'u* 1.22a,b (Hawkes, pp. 28–9). This explanation is somewhat loose and unrefined. An Chih-min (An, p. 45) takes the five standing birds as cranes; he cites the *Shih-ching* (Waley (1937), p. 314, Karlgren (1950), p. 126) for a reference to the cry of cranes which was heard in heaven; and HNT 17.16a,b for a description of cranes as being birds of very long life. An also cites the evidence of post Han literature and of eastern Han tomb decorations; the explanation is not wholly convincing
191. See note 95 above. See also Hulsewé (1965), pp. 86–9 for the suggestion that the inclusion of a copy of the *Mu T'ien-tzu chuan* in the tomb which was discovered *c.* 280 was intended as a means of escorting the deceased to the next world.
192. See p. 107.

143

Notes to Chapter Three

1. See, e.g., Feng, Liu and Lo.
2. See Appendix Five.
3. Chinese and Japanese writers refer to these as *Kuei-chü ching, Fang-ko kuei-chü ching,* or *Ssu-shen ching* (*Kiku kyō, Hōkaku kiku kyō, Shijin kyō*).
4. A list of the sources used is given in Appendix One.
5. E.g., see Appendix Four below.
6. See Bulling (1960), p. 14 and Umehara (1943), pp. 145 f.
7. C 1205* is shown twice in Liu 16.72a,b as if two specimens were in existence; similarly, C 4304 is shown in Liu 15.89a,b. In addition there are a number of mirrors which are listed in Appendix One below whose diameter is of the same size and which could conceivably have derived from the same mould; however, other differences are such that this would appear to have been impossible. See (i) C 2103, C 2202, C 2203, C 4102 and C 4108, where the diameter is 18.3 cm (8 Han inches); (ii) D 1004, D 1009, X 2014 and X 9003, where the diameter is 16.4 cm (7.2 Han inches); and (iii) B 0006, D 2001, D 2009, D 2019 and X 2005, where the diameter is 11.5 cm (5 Han inches).
8. See the note to C 4111 in Appendix One.
9. See Cheng (1957), p. 178.
10. Information is not available for the other examples which are listed in Appendix One.
11. I.e.:

mirrors	Han inches	cm
X 2013	4	9.2
D 2001, D 2009, X 2005	5	11.5
D 2008, D 2012	6	13.8
D 2010, X 1008		13.9
C 2308		16.0
D 2006, X 2011	7	16.1
C 4201		16.2
C 2103, C 2202, C 2203, C 4102, C 4108		18.3
None	8	18.4
C 3101		20.6
None	9	20.7

12. See Cheng (1963), Plates 33–35 etc., for mirrors in the Chou period; and Watson (1963), p. 62 and (1972), pp. 81 f., for the development of mirrors from the earliest times until Han.
13. For these passages, see Karlgren (1934), pp. 12 f., and Komai, pp. 7 f. For the prophylactic powers and properties of mirrors, see *Pao-p'u-tzu nei p'ien* 17.1b (SPPY), as cited in Needham, vol. 5, part III, p. 106.
14. See Komai, p. 9; Eliade (1964), pp. 153 f.; Blacker, p. 106.
15. The scroll shows a mirror in use, being attached to an upright pole (see reproductions of the scroll in Komai, p. 16, fig. 3; Hu-nan, fig. 1; T'ang, fig. 68; Lo-lang (Harada), p. 53, fig. 23). For a different use of the boss and loop, during use, see note 7 to Appendix One. For a pottery figure described as that of a woman holding a mirror, which was found in a tomb near Ch'eng-tu of the eastern Han period, see KKHP 1958.1, p. 98 and Plate 6.4.

* The system of referring to mirrors follows the classification that is suggested and the list that is given in Appendix One.

PLATE XVI
TLV mirror (C5002; diameter 15.3 cm).

PLATE XVII
TLV mirror (D1007; diameter 14.2 cm).

PLATE XVIII
TLV mirror (D 2009; diameter 11.5 cm).

PLATE XIX
TLV mirror (X 1004; diameter 15.8 cm); dated in the inscription, probably anachronistically, at AD 10.

Notes to Chapter Three

16. For this distinction, see Karlgren (1934), p. 13 and Komai, pp. 7 f.
17. Karlgren (1941), pp. 16 f.
18. Bulling (1960), p. 16.
19. See Liu 15.1a *et seq.*, and B 0002 in Appendix One below.
20. For clear and representative sets of facsimiles of mirrors, of types dating from the *Chan-kuo* to the T'ang and Sung periods, see Chekiang, Hu-nan, Lo-yang (mirrors) Shensi, Ssu-ch'uan (mirrors) and T'ang, together with its supplement. Recent articles concerning the classification and dating of mirrors and their inscriptions have appeared as follows: KK 1955.6, pp. 56 f. (a general survey of mirrors); WW 1957.8, pp. 28 f. (the development of decoration on mirrors); KK 1958.1, pp. 88 f. (*Chan-kuo* mirrors from Ch'ang-sha); WW 1963.2, pp. 25 f. (corrections to the renderings of inscriptions as given in Shensi, Ssu-ch'uan (mirrors), Chekiang, Hu-nan and Shao-kou); KK 1963.9, pp. 516 f. (plain mirrors from the pre-imperial period). For a comparison of Han mirrors with other genres of Han art, see Nishimura.
21. A summary of these views and of the classification adopted in Shao-kou is included in Appendix Four.
22. See p. 174 note 25 to Appendix One.
23. See C 5002, whose details lend some support to the view that sub-type C 50 is late and somewhat decadent.
24. See C 4208, which has a coin of Wang Mang's style embedded in the design. Possibly this may be taken as evidence that the mirror was made in Wang Mang's time. However, there are grounds for believing that indications of manufacture of this period were sometimes included deliberately as a means of anachronism; see p. 170 below.
25. See Umehara (1943), Plates 11, 17 for examples of high relief mirrors dated 159, 167. There do not appear to be any mirrors of this type with earlier dates.
26. See under Type X and X 1004, X 1005 in Appendix One below; and pp. 170 f., 186 f.
27. See Appendix Five.
28. See Umehara (1943), Plates 8 *et seq.*
29. E.g., Liu 15.44b and Feng 34a.
30. See also KK 1958.9, pp. 84 f. for a table of abbreviated characters and variants seen on Han and *Liu-ch'ao* mirrors, together with the texts of 46 select inscriptions; for explanatory notes on select inscriptions, see WW 1962.2, pp. 25 f.
31. See Kaplan; Lo-lang (Harada) and Lo-lang (Painted basket).
32. Yetts, pp. 116 f.
33. Yetts, p. 120.
34. See Yetts, pp. 151, 155, figs. 39, 40; Needham, vol. 3, pp. 305 f., and figs. 128-9, 132. Facsimiles of the dial are also given in Lao Kan *Chü-yen Han-chien k'ao-cheng* (Taipei, 1960), pp. 72-3; Komai, p. 120, fig. 20; Hayashi (1973, 1), pp. 4–5, figs. 3, 4a,b; and Loewe (1968), p. 102, fig. 33.
35. Hayashi (1973, 1), pp. 2 f.
36. See the pioneer work by Nakayama; and Gotō, pp. 92 f.
37. This suggestion was probably first made by Liu Fu; see Yetts and Needham, *loc. cit.*
38. See Cammann (1948), pp. 159–60. For the use of these dials see Needham, vol. 3, pp. 302 f.; figs. 131 and 132 illustrate how later examples of these instruments had to be set in two planes for correct operation. For the importance attached to setting other instruments correctly, e.g., diviner's boards, see the passages cited on pp. 76 f. above.
39. Yang (1947) and Yang (1952); Nakayama, p. 471.
40. E.g., Yang (1947), Plate I; Needham, vol 3, fig. 130. For other references, and stone-cut representations of immortals playing *liu-po*, see Finsterbusch, vol. 1, p. 223, s.v., *Liu-po-Spiel*; KK 1957.4, Plates 3 f.; KK 1964.2, p. 90; WW 1972.12, Plate 5.3; KKHP 1965.1, Plate V.4 (Item 73.1); Hayashi (1974), Plate 30; see also note 78 below.
41. Hayashi (1973, 1), p. 57, note 11 refers to Mizuno (a work which has not been available for consultation) and Lao Kan in CYYY 35 (1964), pp. 15-30.
42. Probably the fullest account of the game is to be found in Komai (pp. 106 f.), who draws on literary and archaeological evidence to describe the nature of the game, its currency

Ways to Paradise

in Han times and previously, and the addictions of the immortals to the sport. The game was current from the *Chan-kuo* until the *Liu Ch'ao* period.

43. Cammann (1948).
44. Cammann (1948), p. 162 and (1950), p. 107. For the concept of the centre of the world, see chapter Four, p. 111.
45. Cammann (1950), p. 107.
46. See Bulling (1955), p. 33, fig. 12. This example would be classified here under sub-type D 10, with the peculiarity that the inner inscription is set so as to be read in a column (for the normal arrangement, see p. 159).
47. Bulling (1960), p. 63.
48. Hayashi (1973, 1), p. 10.
49. For the story of the rupture of these supports, see note 14 to chapter One above. For the *ssu chi*, and the 'ropes', see p. 74.
50. See Hayashi (1973, 1), p. 11.
51. See WW 1960.6, p. 14, fig. 3 for an example of one of these carpenter's instruments, from a post-Han tomb in Sinkiang.
52. Kaplan, Plate XI, fig. a. This example has no outer inscription, inner inscription or set of twelve bosses.
53. In addition to the references given in Appendix Three below, see WW 1963.4, p. 11.
54. See note 15 to chapter One above. For the complement of officials engaged in divination and similar practices who were subordinate to the *T'ai-ch'ang*, see HS 19A.6b, 7a. For the prevalence of the practice, see HS 4.2a,b (HFHD, vol. 1, p. 225); HS 96B.18a,b; YTL (29) 204; Loewe (1974, 1), p. 122; Wu-wei, pp. 136 f. See also SC 127.14 (Ch'u Shao-sun's addition to the *Shih-chi*), for an incident in which the object of divination was to ascertain whether a specified day would be auspicious for contracting a marriage; and HS 30.72a for an entry for *Hsien Men shih fa*, a manual for the use of the diviner's board, in 20 *chüan*. For a general study, see Ngo.
55. *Han-fei-tzu* 15.1a.
56. For the modernists' attitude, see Loewe (1974, 1).
57. For these terms see HNT 3.11a, Ch'en, p. 135 and Hayashi (1973, 1), pp. 11 f. The concept of the heavens in the *Huai-nan-tzu*, chapter 3, comprises two ideas. (i) They are divided into the *chiu yeh*, or nine zones, of which eight form a periphery around the central, ninth part (see also *Ch'u tz'u* 3.3a, Hawkes, p. 47 for the concept of the Nine Divisions of the Heavens). (ii) The heavens also comprise the *liu fu*, or six orders, or six departments, which consist of the twelve divisions *tzu*, *ch'ou* etc. For an account of early Chinese ideas of cosmology, see Needham, vol. 3, pp. 210 f., and vol. 5, part 2, pp. 77 f., and Needham 'The cosmology of early China', in Blacker and Loewe (*ed.*) *Ancient Cosmologies* (London, 1975), pp. 87 f.
58. Comment to *Chou li* 6.43a (Biot, vol. II, p. 108), Ch'en, p. 132, HFHD, vol. 3, p. 463.
59. SC 127.7 and 128.31; see the note by the *So-yin* commentator to the first passage.
60. SC 128.13. There may also be a reference to a diviner's board in one of the fragments ascribed to Shen Pu-hai; see note 63 below.
61. *Chieh ch'ung*. This expression is seen in texts which include (i) *Ta Tai Li-chi* 13.9a (with the reading *chia chih* in place of *chieh*); (ii) *Lü shih ch'un-ch'iu* (SPPY) 7.2b; (iii) HNT 16.22a; (iv) HNT 5.11a; (v) HNT 5.17a; (vi) HHS (tr.) 13.8 b. Passages (ii) and (iv) are identical.

In the *Lü shih ch'un-ch'iu*, the appearance of *chieh ch'ung* and the consequent destruction of the crops are said to be the direct result of a governor's defiance of the natural rhythm of the cosmos, by ordering actions that were appropriate to winter to be taken during a different season. Similarly in (v) the appearance of the creatures and the subsequent natural calamity was also regarded as being due to ordering inappropriate actions to be taken during the winter. In the standard commentary to passage (ii), *chieh ch'ung* are defined as creatures like turtles. However, the character of creatures who can form potential destroyers of the crops is more consonant with the explanation of *chieh ch'ung* that is attributed to Cheng Hsüan in a note to passage (vi). Here they are defined as *yüan* (young locusts), *chung* (grasshoppers, or locusts), *t'iao* (cicadas) or *ch'an* (cicadas); these are said to be borne in fire and to lie hidden during the autumn.

Notes to Chapter Three

In the passage of the *Shih-chi* that is under consideration here, *chieh ch'ung* appears as an omen during the process of divination. It is significant that the lists of animals and creatures arrayed round one of the diviner's boards (see Appendix Three) includes the terms *piao* (chrysalis) and *ch'an* (cicada) – the latter being specified in Cheng Hsüan's examples of the term.

62. HS 99C.27a (HFHD, vol. 3, p. 463).
63. *Jih shih chia mou*. The meaning of this expression is doubtful, and the rendering is based on the tentative emendation of *mou* to *ch'i*. Some support may perhaps be lent to the emendation by consideration of one of the fragments of Shen Pu-hai (see Creel (1974), p. 354, where, in a difficult passage, there is a choice between the readings *chi* and *mou*; possibly both of these are incorrect, being in place of an original *ch'i*); see also a somewhat enigmatic passage in SC 28.58 (MH, vol. III, p. 479).
64. *Ta T'ang liu tien* 14.60a (*Wen-hai ch'u-pan she*, Taipei 1962).
65. For measurement from the equator rather than the ecliptic, see Needham, vol. 3, pp. 229 f. It is possible that the operator of the diviner's board fixed his circular disc by aligning the extra characters *wu*, or *wu* and *chi*, that are seen out of sequence in some of the bands (e.g., see Appendix Three, no. 5, and notes (c) and (e)) so as to point to the appropriate one of the twenty-eight mansions where the sun was situated.
66. It is not possible to see from the facsimiles whether the Dipper had been replaced by another device in examples 1 and 6 of Appendix Three.
67. In this connection it is worth noting the allusion in the *Wu hsing ta i* of Hsiao Chi (Sui dynasty) to the use of 36 animals in the course of divination. See note (h) to Appendix Three below. A further reference to the role played by animal figures in divination may probably be seen in a description of the steps taken by the king of Wei in AD 220 to determine whether he should accept the imperial mandate. It is reported that, in the course of divination, he 'retained the turtle'; this result evidently encouraged the king to assume the title of emperor. See the passage from the lost *Hsien ti chuan*, cited in note 3, *San-kuo-chih* 2 (*Chung-hua shu-chü* punctuated edition, Peking 1959, p. 75).
68. See Cammann (1948), p. 163.
69. This symbol is also seen in the design of a building constructed for a religious function south of Ch'ang-an (see KKHP 1959.2, p. 45 and KK 1963.9, p. 501); it is also seen in the use of Han coins impressed into clay for decorative purposes in Han tombs. See fig. 1.
70. For the use of mirrors in daily life, see pp. 65 and 144 note 15 above. There is no means of ascertaining whether TLV types were used in daily life along with other types.
71. These examples are C 1101 (see p. 159 below); C 4308; C 4309; C 4312; and D 2022. See Plate VI and fig. 13.
72. WW 1973.9, pp. 26 and 34, figs. 38, 39. The markings were painted in red lacquer on a white background. The board was found at Yün-meng, Hu-pei, in a site that is dated in early western Han.
73. See Loewe (1974, 1), pp. 11 f.
74. E.g., see the inscriptions on C 3201 etc. in Appendix Two.
75. As in Bulling (1955), p. 34; for the theme of the centre of the universe, see chapter Four, p. 111.
76. See chapter Two above and fig. 7.
77. For the problem of evil, see chapter One above, pp. 2 f.
78. For the prevalence of divination, see note 15 to chapter One above, and note 54 above; for *liu-po* boards, see notes 40–2 above. SC 106.5 carries an account of a game that was played between the imperial heir apparent and the son of the king of Wu, in which the imperial heir apparent murdered his opponent by striking him with the gaming board. Possibly the importance of the incident and the significance of the outrage will be better understood if it is supposed that the two contestants were actually playing the game as a means of ascertaining their future in dynastic terms, by means of divination.
79. Examples may be seen in Taiwan and Hong Kong; for a detailed explanation of these instruments, see Needham, vol. 4, part 1, pp. 293 f., figs. 338, 340. For the association of the diviner's board and the magnetic compass, see Needham, vol. 3, Plate LXXX.

Notes to Chapter Four

1. See Chavannes in MH, vol. II, pp. 6–7; Erkes; Dubs (1942); Yü Ying-shih; Kominami.
2. The earliest literary reference to the Queen Mother is probably to be seen in the passage from the *Chuang-tzu* that is cited above (see p. 89). The Buddhist idea of the abandonment of desire enters into the subject in a passage from the *Han Wu ku-shih* which is cited below, and which is variously dated from the third to the sixth centuries (see p. 117 and p. 154 note 163).
3. See pp. 92 f. above for the connection between the Queen and one of the kings of Chou, and p. 95 for links between the Queen and Yü the Great.
4. E.g. the toad and the hare; see pp. 53 f. above and chapter Five.
5. See I. Kominami's excellent and well-illustrated article in *Tōhō gakuhō* 1974.
6. For the references in the oracle bone inscriptions, see Ch'en Meng-chia, as cited by Kominami, p. 75, note 11. For the *Huai-nan-tzu*, see p. 95.
7. Dubs (1942), p. 222, note 2; MH, vol. II, p. 8.
8. See Pelliot in *T'oung Pao* 27 (1930), p. 392. Yüan (p. 195) regards the question of the sex of Hsi Wang mu as undecided.
9. Karlgren (1946), pp. 270 f.; Bauer, pp. 142–3. Karlgren suggests that the character *mu* 'mother' is a short form for *mu* 'acre'. Some support for the interpretation of the term as a geographical expression may perhaps be found in a passage from the *Huai-nan tzu* (4.13a) that is cited on p. 95.
10. *Chuang-tzu* 6.11a, Dubs (1942), p. 223. For the suggestion that certain types of hill censer were modelled on the idea of *Shao-kuang*, see Dubs (1959), p. 261; for the suggestion that *Shao-kuang* is represented, somewhat differently, on the sculptures of I-nan, see p. 110. For Yü-ch'iang, see chapter Two, pp. 40 f. above.
11. For the *Shan-hai-ching*, see Karlgren (1946), pp. 204 f.; Maspero (1965), p. 507, note 1; Hulsewé (1965), p. 87 and the works cited there. For editions of the *Shan-hai-ching*, see Maspero (1924), p. 2.

    The *Wu-tsang-ching* (chapters 1–5) is regarded by Mänchen-Helfen (followed by Hulsewé) as being the oldest part of the work, being written towards the end of the fourth century BC. Karlgren, however, regards the whole book as a 'product of the Han era, in parts not even of early Han'; he observes that while these five chapters include some genuine elements of folklore of the Han period, some elements were 'invented by the author in the interests of completeness and parallelism'; and he adds that it is impossible to determine what proportion of the work really corresponds to living folklore of the Han period.

    Chapters 1–5 were edited by Liu Hsiang (79–8 BC), and it was left to his son, Liu Hsin, to publish the text. This was achieved in 6 BC, together with the second part of the book (chapters 6–9, the *Hai-wai-ching*, and chapters 10–13 the *Hai-nei-ching*, with an appended treatise on rivers). This part was written in the Han period, revealing a degree of geographical knowledge that could not have been available previously. Maspero dates the treatise on rivers that follows chapter 13 to the end of the second and beginning of the first century BC.
12. The third part of the *Shan-hai-ching* (chapters 14–17: *Ta-mang-ching* and chapter 18, again entitled *Hai-nei-ching*) consists of additions appended by Kuo P'u, the compiler and commentator of the fourth century AD whose notes cover the whole of the text. These notes are followed, in most standard editions, by the commentary of Hao I-hsing (1757–1825).

Notes to Chapter Four

13. SHC 2.19a; Dubs (1942), p. 224; Kominami, pp. 42 and 76, note 22; Karlgren (1946), pp. 271–2.
14. See Plate I.
15. For the *sheng*, see pp. 103 f.
16. Maspero (1924), pp. 35, 88–9; see also Yüan, p. 195.
17. See also Dubs (1959), p. 260 for the interpretation of *wu ts'an* as a comet. For the importance of the astronomical interpretation, see pp. 112 f.
18. SHC 12.1a; Dubs (1942), p. 225; Kominami, pp. 42 and 76, note 22.
19. I omit the character *chang*, which is regarded as an interpolation.
20. For the subject of the three birds, see chapter Five below; *ch'ing* is variously rendered green, blue, grey or black. (Some of the birds in the painting from Ma-wang-tui are depicted with grey bodies.)
21. See figs. 15, 18.
22. SHC 16.5b; Dubs (1942), p. 226; Kominami, pp. 42 and 76, note 22.
23. Dubs renders '... with stripes and a tail, both of which are [spotted with] white'. Hao I-hsing (1757–1825) identifies these creatures with Lu wu (see note 124 below).
24. For the concept of the cave as Mother Earth and as the home of a deity, see Evans and Thomson, p. 105, Eliade (1957), pp. 155 f.
25. SHC 16.3a; Dubs (1942), p. 231.
26. This involves a slight emendation of the text so as to accord with the reading given in T'ai-p'ing yü-lan 928.6a.
27. The original strips which carried this text were found *c*. 280, but by the Sung period the text had disappeared. Scholars of the Ch'ing period doubted the validity of a subsequent version, which was ascribed to Shen Yüeh. In 1917, Wang Kuo-wei published a reconstruction of those parts that he believed to be authentic, on the basis of the earlier work of Chu Yu-tseng. This version was thought to be by no means free of error, and it was corrected and supplemented by Fan Hsiang-yung in 1956. See Hulsewé, in *Historians of China and Japan* (ed. Beasley and Pulleyblank, Oxford University Press, 1961), p. 33, note 13; Fan, pp. 1–4; Creel (1970), pp. 483 f. For the passage quoted here, see Fan, p. 27; Karlgren (1946), p. 271; Dubs (1942), p. 226; and the text of the *Chu-shu chi-nien* in the *Basic Sinological Series*, p. 45.
28. I.e. 985 or 946 BC; see Dubs (1942), p. 226, note 14.
29. SPTK edition 2.14b and 3.1a; Cheng (1933), pp. 138 f.; Dubs (1942), p. 227; Karlgren (1946), p. 270; Bauer, p. 143. Dubs (*ibid.*, p. 229, note 18) accepts a date of before 299 BC for the text. For a later and even more elaborate description of the delights of the Queen Mother of the West and her realm, see *Hsi wang mu chuan* 1.1a (*Shuo-fu* ed.) dated by Bauer (p. 251) in the fourth or fifth centuries, attributed to Huan Lin (Han period).
30. Dubs (1942), p. 227, note 17.
31. See pp. 110 f.
32. See a fragment ascribed to the *Feng-su t'ung-i* (pp. 114 and 153 note 154).
33. See Hightower, pp. 229 f.
34. SC 43.4, 5 (MH, vol. V, pp. 9–10); and SC 5.6 (MH, vol. II, pp. 6 f.); Dubs (1942), p. 229.
35. HS 87A.17a; Dubs (1942), p. 233.
36. The text was compiled perhaps *c*. AD 300, including some material that may be considerably older. *Lieh-tzu* 3.2a; Graham, p. 64; Dubs (1942), p. 229.
37. Dubs' interpretation of the passage varies somewhat. He renders the final part as follows: 'Alas! If I were not so full of virtue, I could have yielded to her pleasures. But later generations would after my death have criticized me for it, [saying that] I had done wrong!'
38. SC 117.88; HS 57B.17b; Karlgren (1946), p. 272; Dubs (1942), p. 232; Hervouet (1972), p. 200. See Hervouet (1964), pp. 288 f. for the circumstances in which this *fu* was composed. The similarity between the poem and *Yüan-yu*, in the *Ch'u tz'u*, and the relationship between the two works, has formed the subject of enquiry by a number of scholars. Hervouet (1964), pp. 288 f. takes the view that *Yüan-yu* was not composed before the Han period; Hawkes (p. 81) believes that it was later than the *Ta-jen fu* and drew upon

it extensively ('I think the date of its [i.e. *Yüan-yu*'s] composition is probably not much earlier than the beginning of the first century BC.'). Kuo Mo-jo (as quoted by Hervouet, p. 291, note 5) believes that both poems were written by Ssu-ma Hsiang-ju, but this view is rejected by Hervouet in common with most other writers. Hervouet's view is that *Yüan-yu* dates from the early days of Han, and that it was Ssu-ma Hsiang-ju who was the imitator.

39. I.e. *sheng* (see pp. 103 f.).
40. See chapter Five.
41. HNT 6.16b; Dubs (1942), p. 232; Karlgren (1946), p. 272.
42. For the relationship of the thought of these three legalists, see Creel (1974).
43. HNT 6.13a; Dubs (1942), p. 232.
44. See pp. 119 f.
45. HNT 4.13a (Major, p. 75).
46. Major, p. 75.
47. See p. 89 above.
48. See p. 92 above.
49. The *Chu-shu chi-nien* (*Basic Sinological Series*, p. 6; Dubs (1942), p. 230), carries the statement that the Queen Mother came to pay court to Shun. This is elaborated in the *Ta Tai li chi* 11.7b (see Dubs (1942), p. 230) and the *Shang-shu ta-chuan*, as cited by Meng K'ang (lived *c*. 180–260), where it is said that the Queen Mother presented Shun with valuable gifts (see notes to HS 21A.3a,b).
50. *Hsün-tzu* 19.3b; Dubs (1942), p. 230. The passage is rendered by Dubs: 'Yao studied with Yin-shou, Shun studied with Wu-cheng Jao, and Yü studied with the Mother Queen of the West'.
51. SC 123.13; HS 96A.28b; Dubs (1942), p. 234. For the authenticity and relationship of the *Shih-chi* and *Han-shu*, see Hulsewé (1975), pp. 83 f. The name T'iao-chih has been identified with a number of places; probably the most acceptable theory is that the name is a version of Taoke, at the mouth of the river Granis (the modern Hilla), near Būshehr (Bushire) in the Persian Gulf (see Hulsewé *China in Central Asia*, Leiden 1979, pp. 113 n. 255, 114 and 224 n. 849).
52. HS 28B (1) 10a,b. Ching-ch'eng commandery included parts of the modern provinces of Kan-su and Ch'ing-hai, with the prefecture of Lin-ch'iang placed probably to the east of the Koko Nor.
53. HHS 88 (biog. 78). 14a. In contrast with this passage, see HHS 2.17a and HHS (tr.) 23.34a, where K'un-lun appears as a more specific geographical term.
54. HS 25A.35a; Loewe (1974, 1), pp. 184, 303.
55. For the horses of heaven, see note 171 to chapter Two above.
56. HS 25B.1b, 2a.
57. See Loewe (1974, 1), pp. 28 f., 167 f.
58. HS 11.6b; HFHD, vol. 3, p. 33; Loewe (1974, 1), p. 176.
59. HS 11.6b; HFHD, vol. 3, p. 33; Dubs (1942), p. 235.
60. HS 26.59a; Dubs *ibid*.
61. I.e. one of the seven or eight parts into which each of the twelve hours of the Han day and night were divided, corresponding to some 15–20 minutes; see Loewe (1967), vol. 1, p. 160, note 91.
62. For the straight-eyed men, whose physical abnormality marked them out as strange creatures who foreboded no good, see SHC 12.3a and 17.7b, and *Ch'u tz'u* 10.2b (Hawkes, p. 110). Possibly two are shown, in menacing attitudes, on one of the reliefs of the Wu Liang shrines (Hayashi (1974), pp. 263–4; fig. 17, third register).
63. HS 27C (A) 22a; Dubs (1942), p. 235; Kominami, p. 73.
64. The character *chi* is omitted in some editions of the *Han-shu*.
65. The terms used to describe gaming boards are discussed in Mizuno, which has not been available for consultation.
66. For Tu Yeh's biography, see HS 85.19a *et seq*.; for his views on religious practice, see HS 25B.17b.
67. Lived 1842–1918; see his note to HS 11.6b.
68. See pp. 119 f.

Notes to Chapter Four

69. From the *Hsü Ch'i hsieh-chi* of Wu Chün (469–520) as cited in Li Hsien's notes to HHS 54 (biog. 44).1b. For other references in folklore to the theme of the grateful animal who rewards his benefactor, see Thompson B 350–B 399 (B 375.3 and B 375.31 concern birds who are duly grateful for their release).
70. *Chin-shu* (*Po-na-pen* ed.) 86.27b. The commandery of Chiu-ch'üan had been founded (probably in 104 BC) in the area between *c.* 95 and 100 degrees east, and 38 and 42 degrees north.
71. X 1004.
72. I.e. the two mirrors of sub-type C 50; for her depiction in a tomb that may be of western Han date, see note 95 to chapter Two. See Appendix One.
73. See Hayashi (1974), p. 240, for the opinion that the faith in the Queen Mother of the West flourished during the eastern Han period.
74. For the authenticity of early dated mirrors, see Appendix Five. For mirrors which refer to the Queen Mother and are dated in AD 160, 167, 167, 189, 281 and 283, see Umehara (1943), nos. 12, 16, 17, 24 (Han) and nos. 9 and 14 (Six Dynasties). For inscriptions in other mirrors which mention the Queen Mother and the King Father of the East, see Karlgren (1934), nos. 117, 140, 143, 152, 157, 174, 222, 228, 248 etc.
75. See Plate XXIII and note 191 below, and Plate XXI.
76. Hayashi (1973, 1), figs. 28-32 identifies several pairs of figures as the Queen Mother of the West and the King Father of the East, on a number of high relief mirrors which presumably date from the last decades of eastern Han or possibly later. These figures are not accompanied by the attributes which are described here, and for this reason the identification may be brought into question. Alternatively, it can perhaps be maintained that it is correct, and that with the passage of time the two figures have lost their chracteristic attributes which were regarded as essential in an earlier age. It should however be noted that the figures identified on fig. 32 (Hayashi *ibid.* p. 38) are situated incorrectly, being in inverse positions in relation to the four animals.

Chavannes (1913), p. 80 identifies a scene in the Hsiao-t'ang shan shrine as one of the Queen Mother; in this connection the date of the shrine may be of crucial importance. With a *terminus ad quem* of AD 129 (as fixed by one of the inscriptions), interpretations and dating of this memorial have varied considerably; see Soper, who suggests that the shrine records the history and fate of Wang Chang, who was put to death in 24 BC.
77. See the passage from the Han Wu ku-shih, cited on p. 117.
78. For the appearance of the *sheng* in a tomb dated AD 398, see WW 1973.4, p. 57, fig. 14.
79. See Kominami, p. 44, fig. 6.
80. E.g. by Yen Shih-ku (581–645), in a note to HS 57B.18a.
81. See Kominami, p. 47.
82. See Plate I.
83. See Kominami, figs. 27, 28.
84. Plate XXIII; see note 191 below.
85. I.e. X 1004.
86. Hayashi (1974), pp. 250, 284 and Plates 13, 31.
87. See Hayashi (1974), Plate 31, for a relief from the Wu Liang shrines; Kominami, fig. 25, for a brick from near Ch'eng-tu; Finsterbusch, nos. 131, 132, 142; Lo-lang (Harada), pp. 42 f.
88. See Plate I.
89. For representations of the union of Yin and Yang, see chapter Two, p. 40 above and note 79 to chapter Two.
90. See the passages from the *Shan-hai-ching* that are cited on pp. 90–1.
91. See fig. 15. Chavannes (1913), vol. I, no. 1237, Plate DXV, p. 264 shows a rubbing of a relief of the Queen Mother of the West from an unknown source, which likewise includes two double-headed creatures, as yet unexplained.
92. See Plate I.
93. See chapter Two, pp. 52 f. above.
94. See Plate I and figs. 16, 19, and Hayashi (1974), Plate 21.
95. Hayashi (1974), Plate 32.
96. The bird does not appear in the later carvings, of I-nan. Examples of the bird may be

151

seen in TLV mirror D 2004 (fig. 23), and in an early eastern Han relief from T'ang-ho, Ho-nan (WW 1973.6, pp. 31, 35, 40, figs. 3, 19). For the depiction of a three-headed bird, see note 95 to chapter Two above.
97. See Plates I, XXII.
98. SHC 12.1a; see Yü Hao-liang in KK 1957.4, p. 108.
99. See Plate XXVIII, and Finsterbusch, nos. 5, 7.
100. See Plate XXVIII.
101. See figs. 15, 18.
102. See chapter Two above, pp. 57 and 139 and note 95 for the two similar figures, in the paintings of the tomb of Pu Ch'ien-ch'iu (fig. 16).
103. SHC 12.1a, as cited on p. 90 above.
104. See figs. 15, 19.
105. See Plate I.
106. See Plate XXIII, figs. 16, 19.
107. I.e. a gilt bronze vessel in the Avery Brundage collection, M. H. de Young Memorial Museum, San Francisco. See Hayashi (1974), pp. 248 f., and Plate 12; and the catalogue which accompanied the exhibition of the Brundage collection, entitled 'The fascination of Asian Arts' (Osaka, Tokyo, Fukuoka and Takaoka, April to August 1970), pp. 20–1.
108. See figs. 22, and Hayashi, *ibid.*, plate 21.
109. See fig. 19.
110. Watson (1973), p. 111, no. 175; part of the design has been reproduced on the dust jacket of *Historical Relics Unearthed in New China*, Peking 1972.
111. Hayashi (*ibid.*), Plate 43.
112. *Wu Yüeh ch'un-ch'iu* 6.4a.
113. *Tung-kuan Han-chi* (SPPY ed.) 2.4b. This work was compiled by a number of hands writing throughout the later Han dynasty (see Bielenstein, p. 10).
114. *Po-hu-t'ung* 5.2b, Tjan, vol. 1, pp. 241 f. The animal is listed among a number of lucky omens, and is explained as follows in 5.3a (Tjan, vol. 1, p. 242): 'What is the Nine-tailed Fox? When a fox dies it turns its head towards the hill [where it was born]; it does not forget its [place of] origin. It means that in comfort a man must never lose sight of calamities [impending]. Why must [this fox appear] with nine tails? When the nine concubines [of the King each] receive their proper places, his sons and grandsons will enjoy abundant peace. Why [is the emphasis laid] upon the tail? It is to indicate that his posterity shall be numerous.'
115. See K. Nozaki, *Kitsune Japan's fox of mystery, romance and humor*, Tokyo 1961 (Hokuseido Press), p. 112, for an account of Tamamo-no-mae; and see T. Hitomi, *Densetsu sesshōseki* (Tokyo, 1971) for an account of the subject in Japan.
116. SHC 9.2a. See also SHC 1.3b, 4a; 4.5b and 14.3b for animals like a sheep or fox with nine tails.
117. I.e. the *chiu yeh* of the heavens; see chapter Three above, note 57. See HNT 6.12 and Major, p. 17.
118. *Ch'u tz'u* 3.6b; Hawkes, p. 49.
119. See the passages cited from the *Po-wu-chih, Han Wu ku-shih* and *Han Wu-ti nei-chuan* cited on pp. 116–18 below.
120. See WW 1974.12, pp. 82 f., for a total of twelve examples.
121. Hayashi (1974), Plate 6.
122. Hayashi (1974), p. 288 and Plate 35.
123. WW 1974.12, p. 82, no. 2.
124. Hao I-hsing's note to SHC 16.5b interprets the animal-human spirit mentioned there as Lu wu, which has nine tails. Morohashi (41708.102) curiously illustrates the term with a nine-headed man-tiger monster, i.e. K'ai-ming (SHC 11.3a, 4b); for the 'Great Nine-headed serpent' of the *Ch'u tz'u*, see chapter One, p. 12 above, and SHC 17.4a. See also KK 1966.2, p. 74, fig. 8.1.
125. See chapter Three above, pp. 72, 82, 84, and 147 n. 78.
126. See chapter Three, notes 40, 41, 42 and 78.
127. Finsterbusch, no 17 and Kominami, p. 66, fig. 25; see also Finsterbusch, nos. 411, 416, 417 etc.

Notes to Chapter Four

128. See fig. 21.
129. Hayashi (1974), p. 231. Authorship of the [*Hai-nei*] *shih chou chi* has been ascribed to Tung-fang Shuo, but it is to be dated after the *Han Wu ti nei-chuan* (see note 172 below); see Chang Hsin-cheng, p. 1042.
130. See pp. 89 and 148 note 10 for a different concept of *Shao-kuang*.
131. For the identification of these two immortals, see pp. 122 and 155 note 195 below.
132. For another depiction of the Queen Mother on top of a chain of mountains, see Finsterbusch, no. 999.
133. Lo-lang (Harada), p. 42 and Plates LVII, LVIII; Kominami, p. 53, fig. 11 and p. 54.
134. Kominami, pp. 51 f. traces the references to and concept of the Chien-mu, T'ao-tu shan, Fu-sang, Jo-mu and Mu-lien-li, in texts such as the *Shan-hai-ching*, *Lü shih ch'un-ch'iu*, *Ch'u tz'u* and *Huai-nan-tzu*; see also Major, p. 44.
135. This is best seen on the reverse side of the *Hsi Hsia sung* stele of AD 171 (*Shoseki meihin sōkan* collection II, no. 28, Tokyo, 1960), together with symbols of good fortune such as the golden dragon, the white deer. For a representation, see Hayashi (1974), Plate 45, Laufer (1911), pp. 6 f.
136. See Yüan, pp. 47–8.
137. WW 1973.1, p. 1 and WW 1973.2, pp. 51 (fig. 8) and 52.
138. For the nine heavens and the nine-branched lamp, see p. 108 above.
139. See Eliade (1954), pp. 12 f.; Eliade (1957), pp. 63 f.; Eliade (1961), pp. 42 f.; Schwabe, pp. 294 f.; and Butterworth.
140. SC 28.82 (MH, vol. III, p. 511); SC 123.29; HS 25B.3a; HS 61.8a.
141. In the *Yüan-yu* poem of Liu Hsiang (79–8 BC; see *Ch'u tz'u* 16.27b *et seq.*, Hawkes, pp. 167 f.) the poet ascends K'un-lun and musters the immortals; there is a conspicuous absence of references to the Queen Mother of the West; for similar, negative evidence, see pp. 99 and 150 and note 55 above.
142. See note 107 above.
143. See note 110 above.
144. Strictly speaking the term *oxherd* is incorrect, as early Chinese practice was for boys to tend single animals rather than a herd. The constellations are termed *Chih-nü* and *Ch'ien-niu*; see Schlegel, pp. 184, 196; Bushell, vol. I, p. 38 and figs. 13, 14; Izushi, pp. 118–19, 124; Kominami, p. 34; Needham, vol. 3, p. 282 and fig. 102.
145. Kominami, p. 34; for the dating of the Hsiao-shan t'ang shrine, see note 76 above.
146. The citation is from the poem *Ta tung* (*Hsiao ya*); Waley (1937), p. 319; Karlgren (1950), p. 155. For comments on the place of the myth in the context of the *Shih-ching* and its beliefs, see Granet (Freedman), pp. 54 f.
147. I have omitted the note given in Karlgren's version; see also Karlgren (1944), p. 123.
148. Kominami, p. 35.
149. E.g., see the citation from the *Han Wu ku-shih*, pp. 117 f.
150. See Chou Fa-kao, *Chin-wen ku-lin* (Hong Kong, 1974), 10 (8), no 1130.
151. Waley (1946), p. 60; Diény, pp. 26–7, 105; Kominami, p. 36.
152. For this work see P. Ebrey, 'Estate and Family management in the Later Han as seen in Monthly Instructions for the Four Classes of People' (*Journal of the Economic and Social History of the Orient*, vol. XVII/part II, May 1974, pp. 173–205). See also Shih Sheng-han, *Ssu-min yüeh-ling chiao-chu* (Peking 1965), p. 58; Christine Herzer, *Das Szu-min Yüeh-ling des Ts'ui Shih* (Hamburg, 1963), p. 86.
153. It has been suggested that part of this passage has been introduced into the text from the *Feng-t'u-chi* of Chou Ch'u (western Chin period); see Kominami, pp. 36 and 75, note 6.
154. Fan Ning, p. 425, Kominami, pp. 36 and 75, note 7. The fragment is ascribed to the *Feng-su-t'ung* of Ying Shao (c. AD 140–206), but it has been suggested that it too may have derived from the *Feng-t'u-chi* of Chou Ch'u; for a reference to magpies, see p. 93 above. See also Fan Ning, p. 422 for reference to the subject by Ts'ai Yung (132–192) and Ts'ao Chih (192–232).
155. Kominami compares the prayer for skills in Liu Tsung-yüan's essay *Ch'i-ch'iao wen* (annotated collected works of Liu Tsung-yüan, SPTK edition, 18.1a *et seq.*).
156. From the *Hsü Ch'i hsieh-chi* of Wu Chün (469–520), as cited in *T'ai-p'ing yü-lan*

31.9a, and *I-wen lei-chü* 4, p. 76 (*I-wen lei-chü*, with Wang Shao-ying's annotation, reprinted Peking, 1965).
157. Both passages are ascribed to the *Ching Ch'u sui-shih-chi*, by Tsung Lin (Liang dynasty). For the first passage, see *T'ai-p'ing yü-lan* 31.7b. The second passage is ascribed to the work by a number of authorities quoted by Kominami (p. 75, note 9), who, however, points out that it is not included in extant versions.
158. This version is cited from the *Jih-wei-shu*, in *T'ai-p'ing yü-lan* 31.8a. According to another version of the story, the penalty imposed on the couple for the neglect of their work was a restriction of their meetings to one occasion every seven days. However, the crow who had been entrusted with the delivery of this command to the two partners gave the message erroneously, to the effect that a meeting would be permitted only once annually, on the seventh day of the seventh month. See Ching Wen, 'Lu-an chuan-shuo', in *Pei-ching ta-hsüeh yen-chiu-so kuo-hsüeh-men chou-k'an* no. 10, 1925 (as cited in Kominami, p. 75, note 11; the text has not been available to the present writer).
159. Izushi, p.115.
160. Izushi, pp. 120 f.
161. Izushi, p. 128.
162. I.e. as related in the *Shih-chi* and *Han-shu* (see chapter Two, pp. 37 and 138 note 68). For the suggestion that during the period c. AD 100–400 the text of the *Han-shu* was available while that of the *Shih-chi* was not, see Hulsewé (1975), p. 87.
163. See Schipper, p. 9, Kominami, p. 39, Chang Hsin-cheng, pp. 659–60.
164. Kominami, pp. 38 and 75, note 14; Schipper, p. 5. For the question of the authenticity and validity of the *Po-wu-chih*, see Chang Hsin-cheng, pp. 1049 f.
165. Schipper renders as 'un dais'.
166. Alternatively, according to Schipper (p. 5) the Queen Mother arrived at the south-west side of the hall and faced east.
167. I.e. in the *Ku hsiao-shuo kou-ch'en* (Lu Hsün's collected works, Shanghai 1938, vol. 8, p. 463). The text does not appear to be included in other prints of the work.
168. The passage omitted in the translation relates how the emperor consulted Tung-fang Shuo on the question of how he should best prepare for the visit. He was told to purify the palace; and he lit the choicest types of incense, which possessed prophylactic powers, in order to do so.
169. The text lists some other drugs, by name.
170. The omission describes Wu ti's desire to plant the pips, as in the passage from the *Po-wu-chih*, with the Queen adding that the pips are not to be planted in the earth beneath.
171. There is a reference to Tung-fang Shuo, ending with the Queen's injunction to Wu ti to treat him handsomely.
172. See Chang Hsin-cheng, pp. 660–1, Schipper, pp. 3–20. Schipper expresses a slight preference for dating the text in the second rather than the first half of the century (p. 19). For a summary of the passage in question, see Hightower, p. 232.
173. See Loewe (1974, 1), pp. 82, 199.
174. See Kominami, p. 40.
175. See Loewe (1967), vol. 1, pp. 50 and 142, note 3.
176. HS 96A.38a.
177. See pp. 112–13.
178. I.e. the *Ching Ch'u sui-shih-chi*, in *Pao-yen-t'ang pi chi* (*Kuang chi*), f.2b; Kominami, pp. 44 and 77, note 25.
179. See Plate XXIII.
180. See Tu Kung-chan's note, as cited in Kominami, p. 44.
181. Kominami, p. 45.
182. The passage comes from the *Hsing ching*, attributed to Kan Te and Shih Shen (*Ts'ung-shu chi-ch'eng* ed. 3.65). For Kan Te, see chapter Five, p. 128 above. The 'Market of Heaven' is an alternative name for the constellation *Fang* (see Schlegel, p. 117).
183. See *Pieh-kuo tung ming chi* 1.2a (Han Wei ts'ung-shu, 1592 ed., reproduced photographically Shanghai, 1925). This work is falsely ascribed to Kuo Hsien (c. 26 BC to c.

Notes to Chapter Four

AD 55); it is probably to be dated in the Six Dynasties' Period (see Chang Hsin-cheng, pp. 1042–3).
184. HHS (tr.) 30.18a.
185. *Hsin T'ang-shu* 48.16b, 17a (R. des Rotours, *Traité des Fonctionnaires et Traité de l'armée*, Leiden 1947, vol. I, p. 472).
186. See pp. 125–26.
187. See Kominami, pp. 41 and 76, notes 19, 20.
188. Kominami, p. 41.
189. See p. 95 above.
190. Kominami, p. 58; see also Eliade (1957), pp. 172 f. for cosmic hierogamies and androgyny, and Eliade (1958), p. 180 for the association between the moon and weaving.
191. See Plate XXIII. WW 1973.11, p. 11 curiously identifies the two scenes incorrectly, i.e. the upper tableau as showing the King Father of the East, and the lower tableau as showing the Queen Mother of the West. As the upper tableau includes the nine-tailed fox and the hare, there can be little doubt that it portrays the Queen Mother of the West.
192. See fig. 22, and Finsterbusch, no. 403.
193. See Plate XXI. Wang-tu (1959), p. 11, and figs. 30, 31, 37.
194. See fig. 21.
195. See Hayashi (1974), pp. 231–2, fig. 2 (p. 232) and Plates 2, 30; Yü Ying-shih, pp. 92, 107; Hawkes, p. 116; Pokora, pp. 231, 245. See also above, pp. 110, 148 note 10, and 153 note 130.
196. For dated mirrors whose inscriptions invoke the Queen and the King, see note 74 above. (The example for AD 189 is also shown in Bulling (1960), Plate 65). On Umehara (1943), nos. 12, 17 the Queen Mother may be depicted in relief. For undated mirrors, see Liu 15.41b, 43b, 54b and Feng 11a, 24a; for Umehara (1943), no. 6, which is dated in AD 105, see Appendix Five.
197. Signs of Buddhist influence on the treatment of the subject of the Queen Mother may perhaps be detected in the ideal of freedom from earthly desire and in the part played by peaches in the story.
198. The citation is from the *Hsüan-tsung hsiang-chuan* 1.6b of Hung Ying-ming (c. 1602; illustrated edition 1915). This text purports to incorporate supplementary chapters of the *Lieh hsien chuan*, which is ascribed to Liu Hsiang, but is dated variously in the *San kuo* and *Liu-ch'ao* periods; see Chang Hsin-cheng, pp. 1229 f.
199. For allusions and references in the *Ch'u tz'u*, see *Li-sao* (*Ch'u tz'u* 1.20b, Hawkes, pp. 28–9; 1.34b, Hawkes, pp. 33–4; *Chiu ko* (dated shortly after the time of Ch'ü Yüan) 2.18b, Hawkes, p. 42, Waley (1955), p. 47; *T'ien-wen* 3.6a (Hawkes, p. 49). The most elaborate account of K'un-lun in the Huai-nan-tzu is seen in chapter Four, which may be described in Eliade's terms as 'mythic geography' (Eliade 1961, p. 39); see HNT 4.2b et seq., Major, pp. 39 f. For Wu ti's adoption of the name K'un-lun for the site of the source of the Yellow River, see SC 123.29 and HS 61.8a, and Hulsewé (1975) for the relationship of these two texts. For the use of the name for part of the complex of the Ming t'ang, see SC 28.82, MH, vol. III, p. 511; HS 25B.3a. For Liu Hsiang's reference, see *Ch'u tz'u* 16.27b, Hawkes, p. 167. For an early passage which discusses the Queen Mother's residence in close proximity to K'un-lun, see *Shan-hai-ching*, as cited on pp. 90–1 above.
200. The passage is cited in the *Shui-ching-chu* 1.20a, as from the *Shen-i-ching*. The *Shui-ching-chu* is ascribed to Li Tao-yüan (died 527). The *Shen-i-ching* is attributed to Tung-fang Shuo, with a commentary ascribed to Chang Hua, of the Chin dynasty; but it is thought to be a later production, of the Six Dynasties Period (see Chang Hsin-cheng, p. 1041).

Notes to Chapter Five

1. See chapter Two, pp. 50, 53 f. above. For stories of the frog in the moon elsewhere, see Thompson A 751.3, A 751.3.1.
2. See Frazer, pp. 557 f., 566; Olcott, pp. 58 f., 292; Izushi, p. 75.
3. Izushi, p. 76.
4. See Thompson B 7.3.
5. Izushi, p. 77. For the early observation of sun-spots in China, see Needham, vol. 3, p. 436; for the observation of sun-spots by eye, see P. Lancaster Brown, *Astronomy in Colour* (London, 1972), p. 44.
6. See Schlegel, p. 124, Yetts, p. 139.
7. HNT 7.3a.
8. SHC 14.5a,b. A passage in the earliest part of the *Shan-hai-ching* (1.8b) describes a bird whose body is that of a wild duck (*chiao*), with a white head, three feet (alternatively hands) and a human face, termed *Ch'ü-ju*.
9. *Wu ching t'ung-i*; see *Yü-han-shan-fang chi-i shu* 52.3a; Soymié, p. 296.
10. SC 128.28.
11. *Pieh-kuo T'ung-ming-chi* 4.1a (*Han Wei ts'ung-shu*). The work is probably of the Six Dynasties period (see note 183 to chapter Four above).
12. See the *Ling hsien* of Chang Heng, as cited in Liu Chao's note to HHS (tr.) 10.3a.
13. See the note to the passage in HNT 7.3a. For the authorship and date of the commentary (probably completed by *c*. 212) see Major, p. 2.
14. See *T'ai-p'ing yü-lan* 3.3a.
15. SHC 14.5b.
16. See note 113 to chapter Four above.
17. *Lun-heng* 11, pp. 503 f.; Forke, vol. I, pp. 268 f.
18. *T'ai-p'ing yü-lan* 3.3a; Izushi, p. 78. The passage may be compared with part of the *Ling hsien* of Chang Heng (see note 12 above).
19. See KKHP 1964.2, Plates 2(3) and 3(1).
20. See p. 160, and Plates XII, XIV.
21. See WW 1961.4–5, pp. 44 f. and 50, fig. 2.
22. KKHP 1963.1, p. 137, fig. 26 and Plate 4.22.
23. Finsterbusch, no. 91.
24. WW 1974.1, p. 12.
25. KK 1957.4, pp. 33 f. and Plate 15. For further examples in which it is not clear whether the bird has two or three legs, see Rudolph and Wen, 58, 59.
26. Finsterbusch, no. 101.
27. Bulling (1960), p. 64.
28. See W. G. Aston, *Shinto* (*The Way of the Gods*), London, 1905, p. 136.
29. See chapter Four, p. 90.
30. SHC 2.22a; Dubs (1942), p. 225.
31. For references to the San wei Mountains in the *Book of Documents*, see Dubs (1942), p. 225, note 9. For T'ao Ch'ien's reference to the three birds and the three mountains, see Hightower, p. 236.
32. SHC 16.3a; Dubs (1942), p. 231; see chapter Four, p. 91, passage (d).
33. See Hervouet (1964), p. 313 and (1972), p. 200. For the *Ta-jen fu*, see note 38 to chapter Four above.
34. SHC 12.1a. Hao I-hsing's note refers to a citation from the *Yü-ti-t'u*, quoted by the *Cheng-i* commentary to the *Shih-chi*.

Notes to Chapter Five

35. E.g., see Dubs (1942), p. 232, notes 35, 36, and the statements of opinion by Chang I (lived *c.* 227–232) in notes to SC 117.88 and HS 57B.18a. The text of the poem that is given in HS 57B.17b reads 'three-legged crow', which Shen Ch'in-han (1775–1831), thought to be erroneous. However, Hervouet (1972), p. 200 retains the reading *san tsu wu* in his translation, observing that there is other textual evidence to be borne in mind.
36. See Finsterbusch no. 403; for a three-headed bird in attendance on the Queen, see fig. 16.
37. See fig. 19, which shows the Queen Mother in the upper tableau and a wheelwright's shop in the lower tableau. For a representation of an iron-foundry, see Loewe (1968), p. 190, fig. 88 (based on WW 1959.5, pp. 43–4, and *China Reconstructs*, vol. 6 (no. 2), 1957, p. 10).
38. Layard's pioneer work may be supplemented for various non-European cultures by essays in *La Lune Mythes et Rites* (Sources Orientales, 5, Paris 1962). For a clear exposition of the concept of the archetype and the place of the myth, see Evans and Thomson, pp. 103 f.; for the nature and habits of the hare, see the same volume, pp. 18 f. In the following summary I rely heavily on Layard and Evans and Thomson, to which readers in general are referred for precise references.
39. See Von S. Bloch and others, 'Beobachten zur Superfetation beim Feldhasen' (*Zeitschrift für Jagdwissenschaft*, Hamburg, 1967), as cited by Evans and Thomson, p. 24.
40. *Pseudodoxia Epidemica*, London 1646, Book Three, chapter 17.
41. E.g., see the delightful quotation from Edward Topsell, cited by Evans and Thomson, pp. 24–5.
42. See Izushi, p. 85.
43. See Evans and Thomson, pp. 111 f.; Thompson A 2216.3 for the motif of the moon splitting the hare's lip; K 1716 for the hare acting as the ambassador of the moon; and Schwabe, p. 328.
44. For details of these and other traditions, see Layard, pp. 100 f., Thompson A 751.2, A 759.4.
45. See chapter Two, p. 54 above.
46. See Sieffert, p. 331.
47. See Donald L. Philippi, *Kojiki* (Princeton, and Tokyo, 1969), pp. 93 f.
48. For the deep-set eyes of the hare, as emphasized in other mythologies, see Thompson, A 2239.1, A 2332.4.1.
49. This expression is used in the context of sacrificial animals; see *Li chi* 1.25a (Couvreur, vol. I, p. 101). For the clear sight of the hare, see Thompson A 2461.1.
50. *Sic* Layard, p. 129, citing Mayers, pp. 234–5 and Nott, pp. 86–7. See Granet (1926), p. 534 and Soymié, p. 298 for various beliefs, e.g., that the hare conceives by gazing at the moon (in the *Po-wu-chih*, according to Mayers); that the hare becomes pregnant by licking the fur of the male; or that the hare brings forth its young orally.

Appendix one*

Classification and list of TLV mirrors
(A) Proposed scheme of classification of TLV mirrors
(B) List of TLV mirrors under reference

(A) Proposed scheme of classification of TLV mirrors

Type A
Ts'ao-yeh mirrors incorporating the TLV marks.[1] A 0002 is perhaps the earliest datable example, from the Shih-chai-shan site of c. 100 BC. The TLV lines often cut across the existing pattern, which may include four bosses. Diagonal lines or pointers radiate from the four corners of the central square, which includes a short inscription; this is usually cut in 'squared' characters,[2] and conveys a prayer for felicity. The inscriptions are read sometimes in a column, sometimes in a horizontal line; they may run in a clockwise or an anti-clockwise direction.

Type B
Shou-chou type mirrors incorporating the TLV marks.[3] Very often the straight lines of the TLV pattern cut across the curvilinear flow of the Shou-chou design, and the circular centre is replaced by a square from which the Ts sprout. There are no bosses on this type, other than the one at the centre. In addition to the examples listed below, Liu (15.1a–2a) shows six others which he describes as Ch'in. These mirrors bear an inscription (in Lesser Seal script) that is identical with that of B 0002, being a prayer for blessings, set clockwise around the central square, and read in a column. B 0001 carries a second inscription, which is set clockwise around the outer rim. In B 0003 a four-character inscription lies across the head of one of the Ts.

Type C
This is the regular, fully-developed type of TLV mirror, subdivided into five sub-types. Apart from a few exceptions, which will be discussed

* Footnotes, see pp. 173 f.

Appendix one – Classification and list of TLV mirrors

immediately, the TLV marks are independent from other elements of the design, and even act as separators dividing those elements from each other and thus emphasizing their symbolical significance.

The two exceptions in which the TLV lines cut across, or are superimposed on, other elements of the design are C 1101 and C 5002. C 1101 was found in a grave near Ch'ang-sha that has been dated in the latter part of the western Han period. Its decorative scheme is in many respects similar to that of mirrors in type B, and it may be regarded as being in a transitional stage between type B and type C proper.

C 1101 also bears a further, highly interesting feature, of an inner ring which separates the centre and the Ts from an outer circle, which encompasses the Vs and the Ls. The possible significance of this feature as marking the influence of the diviners' board on the design of TLV mirrors is discussed above.[4] The inclusion of the extra ring which separates the mirror into zones is comparatively rare, being seen in C 4308, C 4309, C 4312 and D 2022; but in these examples the TLV lines do not interfere with the background pattern, as is the case with C 1101.

C 5002, the other example where the TLV pattern interrupts other elements of the design, bears a number of irregular features, and there are reasons for regarding it as a late example.[5]

The following features which are regularly seen in the mirrors of Type C have been chosen for description here in view of their symbolical significance.[6] I leave it to art historians to fasten on other characteristics as possessing equal importance in tracing the development of the decoration of TLV types of mirror.

1. A square centre, surrounding a large central boss or loop through which a tape or cord was passed, for use either in handling the mirror or for attachment to a stand.[7] Four floriate markers surround the boss, pointing to the four corners of the square. This feature survives on types of mirror that are later than TLV.

2. An inner inscription, regularly in seal script, of the twelve characters in the series of the Twelve Branches. The characters are set in a line rather than a column; they face the outside, in a clockwise direction, and the first one of the series is placed at the 'northern' point of the square (for a definition of the 'northern' point, see under 6 (c) below).

3. Twelve small bosses, set at the corners of the square and intermediately between the characters of (2).[8]

4. Four Ts set centrally on each side of the square, corresponding with the four cardinal characters *tzu, mao, wu, yu* of the inner inscription.

5. Eight large bosses, set in pairs around the corners of the square.

6. The inner circle, which includes the principal decorative and symbolical features:

(a) The four Ls set so that the horizontal bars lie immediately flush with the cross-bars of the Ts. The Ls are open to the right side.
(b) The four Vs set to point directly to the four corners of the square.
(c) The four animal symbols of four of the five phases or directions, i.e. the *ssu shen* or four beasts, lying to the right of the Ls. The upright bars of the Ts, which are placed centrally on the sides of the square, mark the four cardinal points of the compass; the *ssu shen* serve to define those points as north (snake and tortoise), east (dragon), south (bird) and west (tiger); there is some evidence to show that these animals were sometimes given prominence by gilding.[9]

While the *ssu shen* are not seen on types of mirror that were evolved before the TLV type, they are sometimes incorporated in the design of post-TLV types.[10] In a few instances the dragon and tiger carry at their heads small circular medallions which are engraved with the figures of a bird and toad respectively, as symbols of the sun and moon. This choice and exquisite detail is seen in six examples of sub-type C 21, one of sub-type C 23, one of sub-type C 31, and three of C 41.[11]

(d) A series of smaller animals, birds, spiritual or mythological creatures, including a rider, a winged man, and a unicorn sheep.[12]

7. An outer inscription, in *li-shu*, set in a clockwise direction to be read in a column. The starting position of the inscription is often marked by a device such as a quincunx, or a group of three or four dots, and very occasionally by a decorative device such as a bird.[13] This position is always set at one of the eight points of the compass, and there is a marked preference for the north-east and north, and against the east, west and north-west.[14] The text of the inscriptions is usually derived from set formulae, which are composed in rhyming lines of seven, and less frequently of six, characters; and these lines are sometimes followed by short prayers for blessings. The length of the inscriptions varies considerably, depending on the number of the component parts of the formulae which are included; in the examples shown in Appendix One they range from 8 to 63 characters. Possibly the optimum length was 52 characters, as seen in C 1201 and C 1202, as this figure roughly relates to the number of degrees of the Han circle.[15] Some of the inscriptions are incomplete, breaking off in the middle of a line; some are marked by errors such as the omission of a character, which may be crucial to the sense, or by reversing the order of two characters.[16] Classification of the fomulae used permits the subdivision of type C as shown below into sub-types C 11 to C 50.

8. A band with a large number (i.e. over 250) of degree markings,

PLATE XX
TLV mirror (X 9003; diameter 16.4 cm).

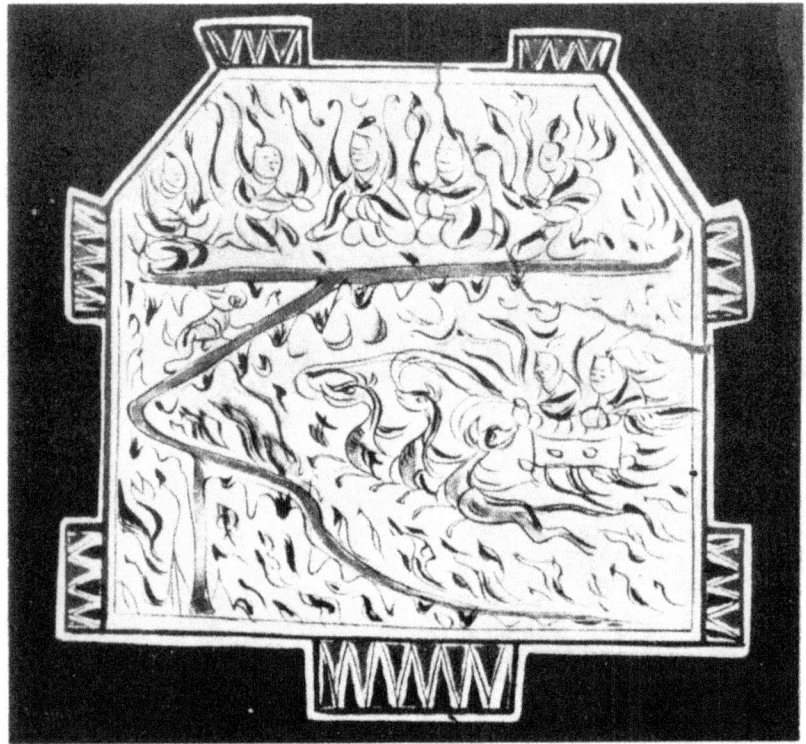

PLATE XXI
End of pillow shaped object from tomb no. 2, Wang-tu, Ho-pei, possibly showing the Queen Mother of the West; dated AD 182; 11.6 by 11.2 cm.

PLATE XXII
Mirror in high relief, showing the Queen Mother of the West and her partner; diameter 18.5 cm; Crown copyright, Victoria and Albert Museum.

PLATE XXIII
Screen, of jade, showing the Queen Mother of the West in the upper register, and the King Father of the East in the lower register; 16.5 by 15.3 cm; dated after AD 174.

Appendix one – Classification and list of TLV mirrors

which are set sometimes regularly so as to point to the centre of the mirror, sometimes obliquely and parallel with each other. These markings are seen in other types of mirror than TLV, both from the earlier and later stages of development.

9. A band marked with chevron or zigzag divisions. It remains open to question whether the degree markings and/or the chevron divisions bore a decorative, symbolical or functional purpose:

(a) Decorative: these features appear in types of mirror whose symbolism is not characterized by the features of TLV mirrors and where there would be no need for the functional purpose that is suggested under (c) below. It is therefore possible that the bands are solely decorative.
(b) Symbolical: Miss Bulling believes that the chevrons represented mountains, sometimes with a river running between two ranges.[17] It may also be asked whether the degree markings or the chevrons are an attempt to represent the divisions of the circle or of the 28 lunar mansions of the heavens.[18]
(c) Functional: it may be suggested that the marks are a device which enabled the designer to space his elements in the mirror, and, more particularly, the characters in the inscription. However, faulty spacing in some of the inscriptions may be cited as reasons against this suggestion.[19]

10. An outermost band, decorated with a cloud-scroll pattern. This is frequently replaced by two further sets of chevron divisions. On some mirrors which are believed to be of a later date than the regular TLV types, it is replaced by a decorative band of a geometrical or stylized pattern, which sometimes includes figures of animals, or the imprint of coins.

Three main stages may be traced in the classification of type C TLV mirrors, following the content and formulae of the inscriptions:

(a) C 11, C 12 and C 19: the inscriptions express prayers for happiness, couched in terms of temporal values (for C 13 see pp. 164 f.).
(b) C 21, C 22, C 23 and C 24: the inscriptions include specific references to the scheme of the cosmos, as explained according to the theory of *Wu hsing*.
(d) C 41, C 42, C 43 and C 49: the inscriptions allude to the life of the immortals and their habits.

Ways to Paradise

In general there is a clear distinction between the formulae which appear in these different sub-types. However, due allowance must be made for (c), where the elements of one formula are coupled with those of another, later stage; and (e) for the inclusion in a few inscriptions of an element that is seen more regularly in the types of mirror which displaced the TLV in popularity. Two further stages must therefore be distinguished:

(c) C 31 and C 32: these are intermediate sub-types, where the inscriptions refer both to the scheme of the cosmos and to the life of the immortals. Examples are comparatively rare.
(e) C 50: the formulae are of the type used in (d); but they also include a reference to the Queen Mother of the West. Only two examples have so far been recorded.

For the following reasons the sequence of stages and types that is suggested above is believed to be generally true in chronological terms.

It may well be held that the most pure and original types of TLV mirror are those wherein the symbolism is implicit, and where no need has been felt to explain its features to the uninitiated. For this reason there may be grounds for believing that some examples of sub-type D 10, which carry no outer inscription, were the earliest of the TLV mirrors proper to appear.[20] It would also seem that, of the C sub-types, C 11, C 12 and C 19 should be regarded as being the earliest. (Reasons why C 13 should be put at a later stage are suggested below; see p. 165.) For while many of the inscriptions of those sub-types invoke a blessing and even refer to the Five Phases, they do not specify how the decoration of the mirror serves to satisfy those powers. The inscriptions of the sub-types of C 2, however, refer explicitly and specifically to the symbols seen on the mirror, i.e. the *ssu shen*, with their protective qualities, and their conformity with the rhythm of Yin and Yang.

In this sense the mirrors of sub-types C 2 may be regarded as the earliest forms of debasement, as compared with C 1, in so far as they spell out the message that was implicit, and the symbolism has lost its instantaneous, compulsive power. The mirrors of sub-types C 2 refer to the cosmic scheme that was formulated by Tung Chung-shu (*c*. 179–*c*. 104 BC) and others; but it was only from *c*. 50 BC that it was promoted as part of the orthodox faith of the state; and such sponsorship was subject to a new measure of enthusiasm under Wang Mang (reigned AD 9–23).

There is considerable evidence to show how the cult of immortality was practised before then, for example under the direct encouragement of the first Ch'in emperor and later by Han Wu ti (reigned 141–87 BC).

Appendix one – Classification and list of TLV mirrors

However, at about the time when the *Wu hsing* theories were being formulated by Tung Chung-shu there had occurred a series of incidents in which the cult had been discredited, and the *fang-shih* who had promised successful results had been dismissed and punished. Possibly as a result of their failure a new impetus was added to the religious cults of state,[21] and there seems to have been less conspicuous emphasis than previously on the means of acquiring deathlessness. Probably we must wait until the first century AD before the search for immortality received a new measure of enthusiasm and support. It is thus likely, on ideological grounds, that the C 4 sub-types of TLV mirrors, which describe this aspect of the cosmic situation, are to be dated after the sub-types of C 2. This conclusion gains some support from internal, archaeological and artistic evidence, as follows:

(i) Mirrors of types C 1 and C 2 refer specifically to the Hsin dynasty; no examples of C 4 do so.
(ii) While C 1 mirrors are found in graves dated in western Han, no C 4 mirrors may be said to do so for certain: C 4 type mirrors are found regularly in graves that may be dated in mid eastern Han or later.
(iii) There are more perfect examples, stylistically, in types C 1 and C 2 than in type C 4; and more examples of debased types in C 4 than in C 1 and C 2.[22]

The references to the Queen Mother of the West in mirrors of type C 5 are a preview of a feature that became more pronounced in mirrors of the later styles, that followed the TLV. These are the mirrors fashioned in deep relief, in which human and animal figures and sometimes artefacts such as carriages are delicately modelled; and they sometimes retain the square centre of the TLV types.[23] There are mirrors of this type which invoke the blessing of the Queen Mother of the West in one of two ways; they either depict the Queen, together with her partner Tung Wang Fu, in person; alternatively their presence is mentioned in the inscription.[24]

The examples of C 5 may be regarded as transitional, in the sense that their ideology is moving from the earlier concept of immortality to the cult of the Queen Mother of the West. A further interesting example of a TLV mirror in this connection is classified below in type D 20, as it bears no inscription (D 2004). This mirror may likewise be regarded as transitional; the decoration has been changed radically in such a way that the symbolism of the *ssu shen* has been eliminated and replaced by that of the Queen Mother of the West and her attributes.

Notes on the sub-types of type C follow.

Ways to Paradise

Fig. 23. TLV mirror (D 2004). The usual symbols of TLV mirrors are replaced by various types of decoration, including the Queen Mother of the West with some, but not all, of her attributes

C 11, C 12, C 13 and C 19
Except for two examples in C 13, which, as may be seen, is somewhat different from the other sub-types, the inscriptions do not refer to Yin and Yang or to the presence of the four beasts, and they are concerned with temporal blessings only. In this sense the inscriptions follow directly from the tradition of those seen on mirrors of types that preceded TLV; but whereas in the earlier types the inscriptions were short, in the mirrors under consideration the sentiments are expressed at greater length, in rhyming lines of seven characters. Some of the allusions, e.g., to the illumination given by the sun and the moon, recall the terms of inscriptions seen on earlier mirrors; in two cases (C 1101, C 1102) they refer to the Five Phases as a source from which the qualities

Appendix one – Classification and list of TLV mirrors

or blessings of the mirror were derived. At least five examples (C 1202, C 1203, C 1204, C 1205 and C 1207) refer specifically to the Hsin, and one (C 1206) to the Han dynasty. The inscriptions bear the following characteristics:

C 11 References to the *Wu hsing*

C 12 The formula mentions the submission of foreign tribes. Karlgren's view, that this dates from the start of the first century BC has been rejected by Miss Bulling; to the present writer it seems more likely that the formula conformed with the political situation in the time of Wang Mang.[25]

C 13 The formula alludes to the origin of poems with seven characters to the line, and includes three other elements, i.e.:
  i. Manufacture of the mirror
  ii. Prayers for blessings
  iii. The beneficent influence of the dragon and tiger.[26]

There are reasons for believing that mirrors of sub-type C 13 may be late. There are no examples which bear the full symbolism that is seen in other mirrors of type C (e.g., none of the six examples have a regular centre with an inner inscription of the Twelve Branches), and the style of the calligraphy is marked by a deliberate archaism, such as is seen on later types.[27] As against the six examples that are listed under C 13, there is a disproportionately high number of mirrors with this type of inscription that must be classified elsewhere. These include three examples listed under type X,[28] where the TLV marks are incomplete and the mirrors must be regarded as being irregular; and there are at least two mirrors, which are not of TLV type and which carry marks of later styles, but whose inscriptions are of the type under discussion.[29] Finally, the references to the dragon and tiger that are seen on C 1303 and C 1304 are not of the usual type that is exemplified in mirrors of type C 2; they bear the marks of somewhat haphazard and unskilful imitation of earlier practice.

C 19 Miscellaneous

C 21, C 22, C 23, C 24
In these sub-types the inscriptions spell out the symbolic significance of some of the features of the design; for reasons that are suggested above they may be regarded as deriving from a later stage than the inscriptions of C 11 and C 12. The formulae, which are framed in rhyming lines of seven characters, refer to the presence of the dragon and tiger in their appropriate cosmic situations and the function of the bird and the warrior in maintaining conformity with the demands of Yin Yang. The formula, which includes some or all of the following elements, is also seen on mirrors of the late, post-TLV, types.[30]

Ways to Paradise

  i. The existence of supplies of copper
  ii. The manufacture and inscription on the mirror
  iii. The presence of the *ssu shen* and their protective qualities
  iv. Prayers for blessings

The inscriptions of C 21 refer to the Hsin, those of C 22 to the Han dynasty; and it seems likely that the latter are of eastern rather than western Han make. It has been suggested above that C 12, whose inscriptions do not explain the symbolism, precede C 21 and C 22 which do so explicitly; and it has been further suggested that the inscriptions of type C which refer to Han do not date before Wang Mang.[31] In addition C 21 includes several examples whose design includes the rare feature of the medallions which are set at the heads of the dragon and the tiger, whereas no examples of C 22 have yet been noticed which carry this delicate mark of the high point reached in the design. It may also be seen that there are more signs of irregularity in the mirrors of C 22 than of C 21, with the exception of the omission of a character in the inscriptions of three examples (C 2102, C 2105, C 2106).[32] It would seem that C 21, where the symbolism is fuller and the execution more correct, preceded C 22, and that the inscriptions of the latter are therefore more likely to refer to the eastern than the western Han dynasty. It may be remarked that C 2104 is one of the most beautiful of the TLV mirrors inspected.

C 23 inscriptions are distinguished in that, while bearing no reference to the Hsin or the Han dynasty, they name the *Shang-fang* as the maker, as do examples in some other sub-types: the *Shang-fang* was the title of the agency of government, which, being subordinate to the Superintendent of the Lesser Treasury (*Shao-fu*), was responsible for the manufacture of articles and the employment of craftsmen for the benefit of the imperial palace.[33] The inscriptions of type C 24 do not refer to the Hsin or Han dynasty and they do not name the *Shang-fang* as the maker.

C 31, C 32
The inscriptions, in rhyming lines of seven characters, refer both to the *ssu-shen* and presence of Yin Yang, as in the sub-types of C 2, and also to the existence of the immortal beings, as in the sub-types of C 4 (see below). They include all or some of the following elements:

  i. The name of the maker of the mirror
  ii. The manufacture of the mirror
  iii. The presence of the *ssu shen* and their protective qualities
  iv. Prayers for blessings

Appendix one – Classification and list of TLV mirrors

v. The existence of the immortal beings and their habits

In C 31 the references to the *ssu shen* precede those to the immortals, and may include the full details that are seen in the inscriptions of type C 2, element (iii). Several examples were made by the *Shang-fang*, including a most excellent example of all mirrors, C 3101, which even bears the circlets at the heads of the dragon and tiger. In type C 32 the references to the *ssu shen* follow those to the immortals, which include details seen in the formula of sub-types C 41, C 42, element (iii). The makers include the *Shang-fang* and the Wang family.[34]

C 41, C 42, C 43, C 49
There are excellent examples of mirrors in this class, such as C 4102 or C 4103. A somewhat inferior example (C 4108) is from a site which is dated in the middle eastern Han period, on archaeological grounds,[35] and there are a number of examples with marks of late decadence. The inscriptions refer to the immortal beings, their obliviousness of old-age, and their habits such as the consumption of elixirs, including dates or jujubes.[36] The formulae used in C 41 and C 42 are almost identical, but distinct from that of C 43; and while the inscriptions of C 41 and C 42 are in rhyming lines of seven characters,[37] those of C 43 are in lines of six characters; and the inscriptions in sub-type C 49 are somewhat idiosyncratic. The makers of the mirrors are named in C 41 but not in C 42. The elements of the inscriptions are as follows:
In C 41, C 42
 i. The name of the maker of the mirror (in C 41 only)
 ii. The manufacture of the mirror
 iii. The existence of the immortal beings and their habits
 iv. Prayers for blessings
In C 43
 i. The sight of the immortals, and their habits, on mountains
 ii. The use of the dragon and clouds as a vehicle for ascent
 iii. Prayers for blessings
There are a number of signs of decadence in the mirrors of C 43, on the grounds of decor; and it may also be suggested that the explicit reference to the use of the clouds as a means of mounting to the land of the immortals is a further sign, in so far as the designer thought it necessary to spell out the meaning of the symbol (i.e. the cloud-scroll). In three examples[38] the inscription has been transferred from its normal position to an inner ring, which thereby separates the mirror into two zones, and divides the Ts from the Ls and Vs. This interesting feature also appears in C 1101 and D 2022, and invites comparison with the

arrangement of the diviners' board.[39] C 43 is a unique sub-type in bearing inscriptions that were composed in lines of six characters.

C 50

In the two examples of this sub-type the inscriptions refer to the immortal beings and their elixirs, as in sub-types 41 etc.; but they also mention the Queen Mother of the West. Of the two examples, C 5001 has the unique feature whereby the outer and inner inscriptions both start in the west.[40] In the other example there are a number of signs of late debasement, and the absence of the *ssu shen* leaves the starting point of the inscription undefined. These are probably the earliest references to the Queen Mother of the West to be seen in the inscriptions on mirrors.[41]

Type D

The mirrors in this type were made without an outer inscription. Those of D 10 have the usual inner inscription and, with the possible exception of D 1009, retain the symbolic features in a regular way. The mirrors which are listed under D 20, however, bear no inner inscription; they often lack the characteristic features such as the *ssu shen*, or the eight plus twelve bosses; and in a number of cases they bear four bosses, or nine plus eight bosses. There are several cases where it seems that a decorative rather than a symbolical motive accounts for the inclusion of some of the TLV features.

It has been suggested above (p. 162) that some of the mirrors of sub-type D 10, where the symbolism is sufficiently regular and strong to preclude the need for an explanation, may have preceded those of type C, whose inscriptions are intended to make its meaning explicit. The inner inscription, i.e. the terms of the Twelve Branches, is itself included for symbolical purposes and its presence need not invalidate this suggestion. It may also be suggested that the mirrors of D 20, where the characteristic features have become weakened or abandoned, followed at a later stage, at a time when the symbolism had lost its efficacy. However, there may be reasons to doubt this suggestion:

i. Miss Bulling[42] regards D 2001 as belonging to the formative stage of the TLV mirrors.
ii. Hayashi regards a mirror which he illustrates, and which would be classed in D 20, as being an archetypal example of the regular TLV mirrors.[43]
iii. A type D 20 mirror is shown in the report from Shao-kou, as item 111.44. According to the report, grave 111 is dated in period III, i.e. late western Han and Wang Mang.[44]

Appendix one – Classification and list of TLV mirrors

Attention must also be paid to the bosses of these mirrors. With one exception (D 1009) the mirrors in type D 10 bear the regular complement of 12 inner and 8 outer bosses. The exception bears 9 inner and 8 outer bosses, and this combination is also seen in some of the mirrors of type D 20. No explanation has yet been offered to account for this choice of numbers.

Seven mirrors that are listed in D 20 bear four outer bosses only;[45] and it is suggested above that these may represent the four nodal points of the cosmos.[46] However, four bosses are seen in other types and the number cannot be adopted as a criterion for setting different types of mirror in sequence. Four bosses appear both on some mirrors made before the regular TLV types had emerged, and on some highly irregular examples believed to derive from a subsequent stage.[47]

One possible reason for according a late dating to some of the mirrors classified in D 10 and D 20 may be seen in the replacement of the cloud-scroll by a patterned scroll whose style tends to appear on mirrors that are later than TLV (e.g., see Bulling (1960), Plates 50, 54–6, 59, 65, 67, 68, 71).

Type X
The design of these mirrors is marred by irregularities of a serious and conspicuous nature, such that they betray an ignorance, or possibly a rejection, of the main features of the symbolism that is characteristic of the TLV mirrors of type C. The irregularities include:

   i. The substitution of a circular for a square centre
  ii. The omission of the Ts, Ls or Vs
 iii. The Ls are placed to face to the left rather than to the right side
  iv. The four beasts are set in positions relative to each other that do not match the correct points of the compass
   v. The four beasts are relegated to the outer rim
  vi. The inscription reads in an anti-clockwise direction
 vii. The inscription is set so as to be read in a horizontal line from the outside, instead of being placed in a column

It may also be noted that in a number of examples the normal *li-shu* has been replaced by an ornate or archaised form of script.

In many cases the differences from the regular norm are such that the structure of the TLV mirror has been jeopardized; in others (e.g., D 2004) the changes have not been so radical. In a number of cases the distinction has not been clear-cut or certain, and the classification adopted below is, in the last resort, arbitrary.[48] The type is sub-divided here as follows:

Ways to Paradise

X 10
Mirrors with specific reference or allusion to Wang Mang, either in the inscription or in the decoration. (Consideration of this feature follows below.)

X 20
Mirrors where the TLV features are not complete. The inscription of one example is reminiscent of the formula that appears frequently in mirrors of types later than TLV.[49]

X 90
Other mirrors, with pronounced signs of late manufacture, including one that is described as Wei, and others dated AD 136 or later.

The association of certain mirrors with Wang Mang was contrived, authentically or not, by references in the inscription to the Hsin dynasty; by the incorporation of coins of Wang Mang's minting within the decoration; or by specific dating (in the inscription) to a year of his rule as emperor. In one case (X 1007) coins appear on a mirror whose inscription mentions the Han dynasty. Attention is due to the validity of exact dating on mirrors; to the possible reasons for forging a link with Wang Mang; and to the use of Wang Mang's coins for decorative purposes.

Only five of the total number of TLV mirrors examined are dated to a specific year. These include X 2008, at AD 263 and X 9005 at AD 650, and there is no reason to doubt that the mirrors were made in those years, in deliberate imitation of earlier TLV mirrors. The third case (X 9001) is dated Yung-ho first year, i.e. AD 136 or 345, etc.; and it has been suggested by Umehara that the inscription with this date may have been added subsequently to the original manufacture. The remaining two, which are dated at AD 10 and 15 respectively (X 1004, X 1005) are suspect owing to other details that are given in the list below; and it may be added that the years in question were those of a period which witnessed the production of some of the finest examples of TLV mirror, in which the attention to the symbolism was all but faultless.

Only two other Han mirrors bear a date before AD 64, and they may be suspect;[50] it is perhaps not too radical a departure to suggest that the specification of the dates AD 10 and 15 on the two mirrors in question (X 1004, X 1005) was due to deliberate anachronism of a type which betrays its origin.

If it is accepted that these mirrors were fabricated at a later date and that an earlier date was deliberately included in the inscription, the most likely period for such activities would perhaps have been in the

Appendix one – Classification and list of TLV mirrors

Fig. 24. TLV mirror (X 1007)

Sung or Ch'ing dynasties, in order to satisfy the enthusiasm of collectors and antiquarians. Fabricators might well have believed that, by engraving a date of Wang Mang's period upon their handiwork, they were stamping it with the marks of what were thought at the time to be the earliest inscribed mirrors of China. Such a misapprehension and deception could well have arisen from the habit of directing attention to some of the beautiful mirrors of sub-type C 21, without realizing that other types of mirror had been inscribed previously.[51] In such a way fabricators may have attempted to fashion examples which were to be passed off as rarities for the collectors' market.

It may be asked whether the implantation of coins of Wang Mang's mint in the decoration, as in X 1002 and X 1007, was likewise a deliberate device designed to suggest that the mirror was made at an

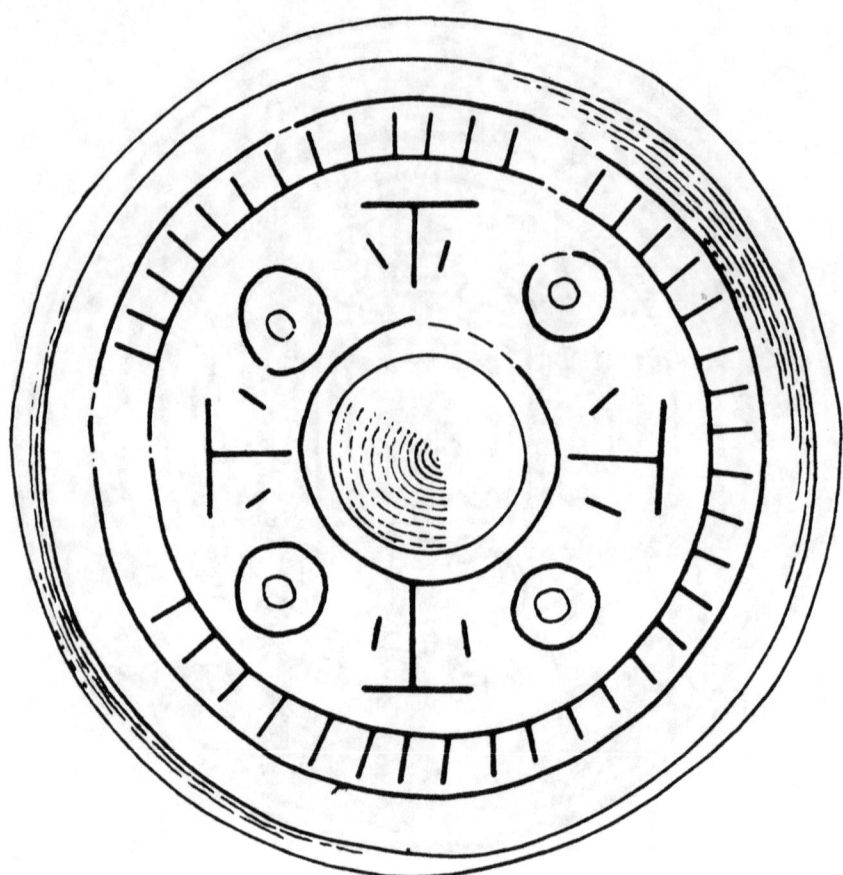

Fig. 25. TLV mirror (X 2010: diameter 5.9 cm). One of the crudest examples of TLV mirrors known

early date. Such a suspicion gains some support from the irregularity attached to the specification of dates of Wang Mang's era in at least one other mirror (see Appendix Five); and it may also be noted that X 1007 is inconsistent, as the inscription mentions the Han dynasty's possession of supplies of copper, while the decor includes two of Wang Mang's coins. However there may be reasons for rejecting such suspicions as groundless. C 4208, which is decorated with one Wang Mang coin, is otherwise not subject to question; and there are many examples of the use of both the standard Han coin and Wang Mang's money for decorative purposes during the eastern Han period. From such evidence it would seem that Wang Mang's coins were not banned after his time as being inappropriate for the restored Han dynasty.[52]

It must remain open to question whether coins were included in this

Appendix one – Classification and list of TLV mirrors

way for their symbolical meaning, as an image of the cosmos – i.e. the circular heavens, enclosing the square earth. It may also be asked whether some designers included them in place of the earlier circlets with the bird and toad which had been inserted so charmingly at the heads of the dragon and tiger.

Notes to Appendix one (A)

1. For examples of Ts'ao-yeh type mirrors see Plate II; Bulling (1960), Plates 14, 15 and Karlgren (1941), Plates 76, 77.
2. For the different types of script on mirrors, see Appendix Six.
3. For Shou-chou type mirrors, see Plate IV; Bulling (1960), Plates 8–11, Karlgren (1941), Plates 21, 43, 51.
4. See pp. 75 f.
5. See under sub-type C 50, and the entry for C 5002 below.
6. Most of these features are seen in two splendid examples of mirrors, C 2104 and C 3101 (Plates X, XII–XIV).
7. See Chavannes (1893), p. 21 and Plate V, and Komai, pp. 15–16 and fig. 2, for a scene on the reliefs of the Wu Liang shrine in which a mirror is held by the hand. For a yet earlier arrangement, whereby a mirror was fitted with three rings placed symmetrically at the outer edge, see WW 1972.5, Plate I; *Historical Relics Unearthed in New China* (Peking 1972), p. 76; and KK 1973.2, p. 82, Plate 12.1.
8. In a few cases there is a somewhat different arrangement of the bosses from that described as features (3) and (5); see under type D below. For the interpretation of the bosses as symbols of the cosmos, see pp. 69 f. According to another interpretation (Cheng (1957), pp. 176 f.), the two sets of bosses represent the sons and grandsons whose existence is the subject of prayer in a number of inscriptions on mirrors. This is illustrated in respect of a mirror that is probably later than the TLV types. It is not impossible that the bosses first appeared as symbols of the cosmos, and that when their significance had been forgotten they were used to allude to the number of sons and grandsons desired.
9. For the origin of these four animals and their symbolic use, see Komai, pp. 96 f., and Hayashi (1973, 1), pp. 15 f. For a predecessor form to the snake and tortoise, see note 95 to chapter Two above; for gilding, see Bulling, p. 61, and examples shown in Moriya (colour plates nos. 1, 2) and Shao-kou (Plate 43.1, Item 59B.10).
10. E.g., see Lo-yang (Mirrors), no. 31.
11. For other contexts in which these attributes appear and their wider significance, see chapter Two, pp. 50 f., and chapter Five.
12. For a consideration of these animals, see Karlgren (1946), p. 261; Bulling (1960), pp. 64 f.; and Hayashi (1973, 1), pp. 19 f.
13. For the presence of a bird, see C 1205; for a decorative device, see C 2203.
14. Out of a total of 90 examples, 37 begin in the north-east; 15 in the north; and 13 in the south-west. For the value and importance of the north-east, see Bodde (1975), pp. 46, 128.
15. The Han circle was divided into 365 and a quarter degrees; $7 \times 52 = 364$. Possibly there may be a similar significance in the inscription of 182 marks at the edge of the square dial of one of the diviner's boards (see no. 5 in Appendix Three). The short length of eight characters in the inscription of mirror C 1903 is clearly exceptional. The longest inscription seen, of 63 characters, appears on C 2102 (for text, see Appendix Two).
16. E.g., in C 2307 the negative *pu* is omitted; in X 9005 the two characters *chu chüeh* (scarlet bird) are reversed. For the omission of the character *wu* (warrior) in several instances, see note 32 below.

Ways to Paradise

17. Bulling (1960), p. 63.
18. For a further suggestion, that border patterns fulfil a protective function, see Waley (1933), p. 138.
19. E.g., see C 1207, and C 3202, C 3203, where the inscriptions are incomplete.
20. See p. 168. It should be noted that some examples of sub-type D 10 are manifestly late (see the irregularities noted in the entries given in the list below).
21. For the promotion of new cults of state and the reaction against the *fang-shih* at about this time, see Loewe (1974, 1), chapter Five.
22. For the possibility that one mirror of this type (C 4208) may have been made at the time of Wang Mang, see note 24 to chapter Three above.
23. See Bulling (1960), Plates 54, 55, 70.
24. For high relief mirrors which depict these figures, see Bulling (1960), Plates 67, 71; Loewe (1968), p. 111, fig. 36; Cheng (1957), Plate II, fig. 4; for a reference to the Queen Mother in an inscription, see Bulling (1960), Plate 65; and for both a depiction and a reference in the inscription, see Bulling (1960), Plate 68 and Komai, Plate 8.3. See also Liu 15.43a,b and 15.44a for late style mirrors made by Mr Yüan, which depict or refer to the Queen Mother; for a mirror whose inscription specifies the date AD 105, see Appendix Five (g) below. Tung Wang Fu is also known as Tung Wang Kung.
25. The question whether the references in inscriptions to Han should be dated to the western or the eastern Han dynasty has been discussed by Karlgren (1941), pp. 19 f., and Bulling (1960), pp. 36 f. These references appear in formulae which, in other mirrors, specify the Hsin dynasty, in identical terms.

Karlgren points to the political and social instability of Wang Mang's time; he argues that as an innovation of this type would have been most unlikely then, the formula derives from earlier practice, which was later adopted, without change, during Wang Mang's dynasty. He further suggests that the specific reference to the submission of the barbarians could only have originated during the time of Han Wu ti (141–87 BC) and Chao ti (87–74 BC); and he suggests that the use of the formula with a specific mention of Hsin in place of Han was due to the conventional acceptance of existing practice.

Miss Bulling disagrees with this conclusion. She believes that the inscriptions should be interpreted not in terms of political developments, but in terms of rites and sacrifices. She concludes (p. 38) 'This type of inscription does not occur on early western Han mirrors nor on any which can, with any degree of certainty, be attributed to the earliest part of the first century BC. But it is very common on eastern Han mirrors. Its beginnings may not ante-date Wang Mang's lifetime by more than a few decades, gaining increasing popularity during the end of the first century BC and the time of Wang Mang's rule.'

The present writer would venture to go even further in respect of the inscriptions on mirrors of sub-type C 12, five examples of which refer to Hsin and one to Han. There would seem to be no archaeological evidence to shown that mirrors of this type were found in graves which can be dated in the time of Wu ti or Chao ti; and it is in any event to be noted that, after the great successes of the earlier part of Wu ti's reign (i.e. up to 108 BC) a policy of retrenchment and even withdrawal was introduced (see Loewe (1974, 1), chapter Seven; and Loewe (1974.2). Furthermore, in the time of Wu ti and even Chao ti the *Wu hsing* theory had not gained universal acceptance, and it would perhaps be too early to expect a general devotion to the powers of the *ssu shen* which appears on these mirrors.

However, there was every reason why Wang Mang should encourage the promotion of new artistic and philosophical developments if they could be used to secure intellectual authority for his regime. The period of Wang Mang's rule is perhaps the only time (except for the very short period of Chu Po's ascendancy; see Loewe (1974, 1), pp. 260 f.) when the two essential concomitants could be seen concurrently, i.e.: (i) a faith in the *wu hsing* and their cosmology; and (ii) a policy of military expansion, as evidenced in the campaigns initiated under Wang Mang in AD 11 and AD 21. Wang Mang's time is therefore more likely to have seen the start of these formulae, and their inscription on this type of mirror, than that of Wu ti or Chao ti. In these particular cases the term Han may therefore be taken, tentatively, to refer to eastern Han, being followed conventionally after Wang Mang's demise.

Appendix one – Classification and list of TLV mirrors

If this argument is acceptable for inscriptions which mention the Han dynasty in connection with the submission of foreign tribes, it may possibly be applicable to other references in inscriptions, e.g., those which mention the dynasty's possession of supplies of copper, as in sub-type C 22. However, it must be borne in mind that there is considerable evidence to show how formulae used in inscriptions need not necessarily derive from the time of manufacture, and that the ones in question need not essentially be associated with contemporary victories. The same formula is seen on mirrors of a very late style, as exemplified in Liu 15.51a,b, and, probably, in Liu 15.36a; 40b; 41a,b; 47a; 48b; 49b; 50a.

26. Element (iii) is seen in two examples only (C 1303 and C 1304); for an irregular example see X 2003. For inscriptions of this type, see Karlgren (1934), nos. 139, 144, 145, 243 etc.; for the form of the first character *ch'i* (seven) see Loewe (1967), vol. II, pp. 105, 361.
27. For calligraphic styles, see Appendix Six.
28. I.e., X 2003, X 2006, X 2007.
29. Liu 15.65b and 15.66a (two examples).
30. See Liu 15.28b, and the late style of mirrors made by Mr Yüan (Liu 15.44b). Mr Yüan was also responsible for mirrors whose inscriptions refer to the Queen Mother of the West (Liu 15.44a). See also a mirror made by Mr T'ien (Liu 15.45b). For a mirror of late style, with deep relief and a foliate border in which the images of four coins have been incorporated, see Liu 15.29b.
31. See note 25 above.
32. It is noticeable that it is the same character, *wu*, which is omitted in each case, and this is also missing in C 2203. While it is doubtful whether the omission was due to ideological reasons, it may be asked whether it was brought about by exact imitation of a faulty original. For other errors in inscriptions, see note 16 above.
33. For the *shang-fang*, see HS 19A.16a,b; for the *Shao-fu* see Loewe (1974, 1), p. 310. For the division of the *shang-fang* into three sections and the evidence of this division in inscriptions, see Komai, pp. 28 f., Bulling (1960), p. 45 and Watson (1972), p. 92.
34. In the majority of cases in which the inscription of a mirror names a person or authority initially, this is designated as the *Shang-fang*, but there are a few cases in sub-types C 32 and C 41 where others, such as the Wang family, T'ai shan or T'ai yin are so mentioned. In types of mirror other than TLV, a number of other names will be found, e.g., Lung, Meng, Yüan, T'ien, Chang, Liu and Tsou (see Liu 15.36b *et seq*.). Karlgren's belief (Karlgren (1934), pp. 36 f., and the translations of inscriptions that are included in that work) that these are the names of the actual makers of the mirrors is partly borne out by the numerous references to the *Shang-fang* as the manufacturer. Miss Bulling however (1960, pp. 46 f.), believes that the names refer to the families who ordered the mirrors to be made, and that many of those which were inscribed 'Wang' were made for the benefit of Wang Mang's family.
35. See Lo-yang (Mirrors), Appendix, p. 8, s.v. no. 83.
36. For references to the consumption of dates or jujubes by immortals, see the story of An Ch'i, as cited above in connection with the painting from Ma-wang-tui (see chapter Two, p. 37).
37. It may be noted that in a number of inscriptions *hai* (Karlgren (GSR) 947x χməg/χâi) rhymes with *hao* (ibid. 1044a χôg/χâu), *tao* (ibid. 1048a d'ôg/d'âu), *lao* (ibid. 1055a lôg/lâu) etc.
38. C 4308, C 4309, C 4312.
39. See pp. 75 f., 204 f., Figs. 11, 12.
40. Only two other examples have been seen where the outer inscription starts in the west (C 3203 and C 4107). No examples have been seen where the inner inscription starts in the west.
41. For depictions of the Queen Mother of the West in mirrors, see note 24 above, pp. 122, 151 n. 76 below, and X 1004. (The inscription of the latter example dates the mirror at AD 10, but the present writer believes it to be of later manufacture.)
42. Bulling (1960), p. 38.
43. See Hayashi (1973, 1), pp. 14, 15 and fig. 13. This mirror bears a rare, and possibly

unique feature, of an outer inscription of eight characters which are enclosed within the Ls and the Vs.
44. See Shao-kou, p. 175 and fig. 71.6.
45. Another example is seen in Hayashi (1973, 1). fig. 13.
46. I.e. the *ssu-wei* (see p. 77).
47. See A 0001, A 0002, A 0004 and C 1101; and X 1007, X 2003, X 2005, X 2007, X 2009 and X 2020. There are also four bosses alone on C 1901; a set of four is combined with a set of seven, eight, nine or twelve on C 2201, C 2404, X 1001, X 1004 and X 2004.
48. E.g., C 1902, C 1903, C 4116 and D 1009 are classified accordingly, despite considerable irregularities; whereas examples of the contrary case are seen in X 1005 and X 1009.
49. I.e. X 2001, whose inscription may be compared with the expression *wei chih san kung*. KK 1966.2, p. 91 cites the appearance of a mirror bearing that inscription as a reason for dating a tomb in the Three Kingdoms period. See KK 1966.5, pp. 248 f. for a mirror with that inscription that was found in a tomb dated to late eastern Han; see also KK 1974.2, pp. 89 f., and Appendix Four below.
50. For mirrors dated in a specific year, see Appendix Five.
51. I.e. those types of mirror which had emerged prior to the TLV mirror; see types 1–5 in Shao-kou, pp. 160 f. and in Appendix Four below. For fabrication in imitation of earlier styles, see Umehara (1943), pp. 145 f., and H. Suzuki in Moriya, p. 39, fig. 2.
52. Wang Mang coins are seen in tombs of the eastern Han period, such as Shao-kou nos. 147, 1017, 1033, 1038. For the decorative use of standard Han coins in a bell, see Feng 43a; see Feng 43b for the use of coins in a mirror not of TLV type. See also below, under D 1008, and KKHP 1965.1, pp. 149 (fig. 36.6), 150 (Item 8.68).

(B) List of TLV mirrors under reference

The following list has been drawn up according to the classification that is suggested above. The notes draw attention to some of the significant features that have been discussed and to variations from a norm. An index of the sources which have been used follows below (pp. 189–91).

Further examples of TLV mirrors may be found, sometimes without fully detailed information, in many of the numbers of *Kaogu* and *Wen wu*, and in monographs such as *Fu-chai*, Chekiang, Hu-nan, Lo-yang (mirrors), Shensi, Ssu-ch'uan (mirrors) or T'ang.

With the following exceptions, the abbreviations used in the list follow those that are given on pp. 230–39.

B	Bulling (1960) plate no.
BM	British Museum
Fitz	Fitzwilliam Museum
M	Moriya plate no.
M (colour)	Moriya colour plate no.
V & A	Victoria and Albert Museum

An asterisk * follows the numbers of those mirrors whose inscription is treated in Appendix Two (e.g., A 0001). Where known, the diameter of the mirror, in centimetres, is given in parenthesis below the reference number.

Appendix one – Classification and list of TLV mirrors

A 0001* (13.2)	The inscription is anti-clockwise.	B 13
A 0002 (15.4)	From a tomb dated *c*. 100 BC.	Shih-chai-shan, pp. 70, 72 (fig. 3), Pl. 45.3 (item M 13.8)
A 0003		Liu 15.98a
A 0004*		Liu 16.30a
A 0005 (13.5)	See Plate III.	V & A M.1-1931
B 0001 (19)		B 9
B 0002*		B 10; see Liu 15.1a to 2a for six mirrors, possibly with identical details
B 0003 (18.5)	The inscription reads from right to left.	B 11
B 0004		B 12
B 0005 (10.8)		BM 1950, 11-17, 230
B 0006 (11.5)	The inscription is identical with that on B 0002. See Plate V.	BM 1932, 12-15, 1
C 1101* (18.7)	From a tomb near Ch'ang-sha, dated in the latter part of western Han. The inscription, which is set intermediately (see C 4308), starts at one of the Ts (the position is undetermined); for the appearance of the *ssu shen*, see Watson (1972), p. 93; see also Bulling (1960), pp. 41-2. See Plate VI.	B, p. 39 (fig. C); Ch'ang-sha, p. 116, Pl. 68 (item 211.20); Uchino, p. 532
C 1102	One character is omitted in the third line of the inscription, which starts in the east.	Liu 15.93b
C 1201* (22.1)	Circlets, at the heads of the dragon and the tiger, are both embossed with the figure of a toad. See Plate VII.	M 34
C 1202	One character (*jen*) is omitted in the second line of the inscription.	B, p. 48 (fig. E); Lo 2.23a
C 1203 (18.8)	A decorative device follows the inscription.	M 5
C 1204		Liu 16.70b
C 1205	A standing bird follows the inscription.	Liu 16.72a,b (the two mirrors shown are apparently identical)
C 1206 (20.5)		M 35
C 1207 (20.3)	The inscription starts just north of east; the spacing is erratic towards the end.	Shensi, no. 49

C 1202, C 1203, C 1204, C 1205 and C 1207 are dated according to the inscription in the Hsin, and C 1206 in the Han dynasty. Makers of the mirrors are named as follows:

Ways to Paradise

C 1201	the *shang-fang*
C 1202, C 1203, C 1204 and C 1205	Wang
C 1206	Ch'iang
C 1207	Tu

C 1301	Of the eight creatures included in the decor, one is a dragon.	Feng 24b
C 1302*	The cloud-scroll is replaced by a patterned scroll; inscription in ornate *li-shu*.	Liu 15.65a (foot)
C 1303	The eight creatures in the decor include one dragon and one tiger; the cloud-scroll is replaced by a patterned scroll.	Liu 15.66b (head)
C 1304 (16.6)	There are eight bosses within the square, set in a circle. The eight decorative animals include a bird, dragon, tiger and unicorn sheep. The inscription is set irregularly and engraved inaccurately, starting in the south-east.	M 18
C 1305 (15.7)	One of the *ssu shen* is set on the wrong side of the L. The inscription starts in the north-west.	M 17
C 1306 (14.2)	The cloud-scroll is replaced by a patterned scroll; the Ls and Vs interrupt the band of the inscription.	BM 1973, 7-26, 54

In C 1301 to C 1306, the inscriptions are in 'ornate *li-shu*' (see Appendix Six); with the exception of C 1304 there are no sets of bosses within the centre. The *ssu shen* appear in full only in C 1305, where one is set incorrectly.

C 1901 (18.9)	There is no outer inscription; an inner inscription, in 'squared' characters, includes elements that are seen elsewhere in the outer inscription. Of the *ssu shen*, the scarlet bird appears at the left of the L.	M 9
C 1902 (16.6)	The content of the outer inscription, in 'squared' characters, is idiosyncratic, starting in the south-west. There is a second band of degree markings placed inside the inscription band. There is no inner inscription. See Plate VIII.	M 8
C 1903 (13.1)	There is no inner inscription. The Ls and Vs cut across the band of the outer inscription; this is in 'ornate *li-shu*', and consists of eight characters only, copied incorrectly from inscriptions of other sub-types. Possibly to be regarded as a late example in which the designer has copied parts of the features of sub-type C 4. See Plate IX.	M 46
C 1904	A band of chevron divisions is set outside the decorative scroll in which animals have been incorporated. The inscription starts in the south-west and refers to the Hsin dynasty and	Feng 41b

Appendix one – Classification and list of TLV mirrors

its silver, which was not used as the primary metal in the manufacture of mirrors (for the use of the term *yin* as an epithet, see Komai, p. 35).

C 2101 (20.5)		M 4; Shodō Pl. 32, pp. 172 f.
C 2102* (22)		B 35
C 2103 (18.3)		M (colour) 3
C 2104 (21)	See Plate X.	Yetts Pl. XXXI (Cull 28)
C 2105 (17.1)		M 3
C 2106 (15.1)	The cloud-scroll is replaced by two sets of chevron bands. The tomb is dated in early eastern Han, on archaeological evidence (see the register at the end of Lo-yang (mirrors)).	Lo-yang (mirrors) 78
C 2107	This inscription is somewhat abbreviated and incomplete.	Feng 42a
C 2108		Cammann (1950), fig. 2

There are circlets at the heads of the dragon and tiger, embossed with a bird and a toad, in C 2101, C 2102, C 2103, C 2104, C 2108 and possibly C 2105. The inscriptions of all eight examples mention the Hsin dynasty; in C 2105, C 2106 and C 2107 the inscription starts in the south-west; the *Shang-fang* is named as the maker of C 2102, C 2103, C 2104 and C 2108. The character *wu* is omitted in the inscriptions of C 2102, C 2105 and C 2106. C 2102 and C 2108 carry the longest inscriptions seen on TLV mirrors.

C 2201	There is no inner inscription; the central boss is surrounded by a snake or dragon (*cf.* X 2014)	B, p. 57 (fig. H)
C 2202 (18.3)	The inner inscription, starting in the south-east, reads in an anti-clockwise direction, the characters being set to be read in a column. There are three small bosses set within the Vs, and others irregularly. The tortoise and snake are set to the left of the T; one character is omitted in the second line of the inscription.	B 42
C 2203* (18.3)	The *ssu shen* are greatly reduced in size and prominence. The outer inscription, starting in the south-east, is a poor attempt at four rhyming lines, in one of which the character *wu* is omitted. The second line omits two characters. There is a decorative device before the start of the inscription.	M 6
C 2204 (16.7)	There are no *ssu shen*; the outer inscription is incomplete and poor.	M 7

Ways to Paradise

C 2205	There is no inner inscription; the outer inscription refers to eight sons and nine grand-grand sons.	Liu 15.21b (foot)
C 2206	The inscription refers to eight sons and nine grandsons.	Feng 32a
C 2207	There is no inner inscription. The outer inscription, starting in the south, is incomplete.	Feng 32b
C 2208	There is no inner inscription; eight inner bosses are set in a circle. The tiger, tortoise, snake, and bird are placed incorrectly; the dragon has been replaced by another animal.	Feng 33a

The inscriptions of all eight examples mention the Han dynasty. In C 2203 the cloud-scroll has been replaced by two sets of chevron marks; in C 2202, C 2206 and C 2208 there is a stylized decorative scroll, incorporating a tiger or other animals.

C 2301	The inscription starts in the north.	Liu 15.29a
C 2302		Liu 15.31b
C 2303		Liu 15.32b (head)
C 2304		Liu 15.32b (foot)
C 2305	The inscription starts in the east.	Liu 15.33a
C 2306	The inscription starts in the north-west.	Liu 15.33b (head)
C 2307	The inscription is preceded by a small decorative device; the character *pu* has been omitted.	Feng 7a
C 2308 (16)		M 25
C 2309 (13.5)		M 26
C 2310 (20.5)	There are circlets embossed with a bird and toad at the heads of the dragon and tiger.	BM 1947, 7–12, 334

In all cases the *Shang-fang* is specified as the maker; there is no inner inscription in C 2304, C 2306, C 2307, and C 2309. The cloud-scroll is replaced by two sets of chevron marks in C 2303, C 2305 and C 2306.

C 2401	The inscription starts in the south-west.	Feng 34b
C 2402* (21.2)	The inscription starts in the north-west; the bird, dragon and tiger are set to the left of the Ls.	Liu 15.63b
C 2403	The inscription starts in the south-west; the bird, tiger and tortoise and snake are set to the left of the Ls.	M 24
C 2404 (12.85)	The inner inscription is a short blessing, of eight characters, and eight bosses are spaced in a circle round the central boss. The outer inscription in squared characters is placed in the outermost circle, i.e. the position usually taken by a cloud-scroll; it is divided by a dragon and a tiger, and is read horizontally, from right to left. In the decorative circle there are four animals only, including two	M 15

Appendix one – Classification and list of TLV mirrors

tigers, spaced along the whole length of each side of the inner square. See Plate XI.

C 3101 (20.6)	There are circlets, with bird and toad, at the heads of the dragon and tiger; one character (*ju*) is omitted in the inscription. See Plates XII–XIV.	V & A M 16–1935; Shodō p. 18 (fig. 24); Liu 15.32a
C 3102 (18.9)	Circlets, as in C 3101.	M 27
C 3103	The final character of the sixth line of the inscription does not rhyme.	Liu 15.31a
C 3104	The inscription starts in the north, and refers to Han and to eight sons and nine grandsons. A geometrically patterned scroll replaces the cloud-scroll.	Liu 15.21b (head)

In C 3101, C 3102 and C 3103 the maker is specified as the *Shang-fang*.

C 3201*	The inscription specifies the *Shang-fang* as the maker, and omits one character. A decorative device follows the inscription.	Liu 15.33b (foot)
C 3202	The inscription starts in the north-west and is incomplete. Two sets of chevrons markings replace the cloud-scroll. Wang is specified as the maker.	Liu 15.48a (foot) and 15.48b
C 3203	The inscription starts in the west and is incomplete.	Liu 15.83a
C 3204	The inscription starts in the south-west.	Liu 15.83b
C 4101 (20.2)	One character is omitted in the fourth line of the inscription.	M 31
C 4102* (18.3)		M 28
C 4103 (22.7)		M 29
C 4104 (19.8)	From a tomb dated, on archaeological grounds, in the middle part of eastern Han (see the register at the end of Lo-yang mirrors))	Lo-yang (mirrors) 84
C 4105 (20)	From a tomb dated in eastern Han, after AD 40 (see Shao-kou, pp. 175, 225, and register at the end of the volume).	Shao-kou (item 1023.1), pp. 166, 168, fig. 73.2 and Pl. 44.1
C 4106		Liu 15.22a
C 4107		Feng 5a
C 4108 (18.3)	The inscription is incomplete; from a tomb dated on archaeological grounds in the middle part of eastern Han.	Lo-yang (mirrors) 83
C 4109	In place of the *ssu shen* there are four pairs of birds.	Liu 15.22b
C 4110	Apparently there are no *ssu shen*; the initial line of the inscription is repeated in the band where the degree markings usually appear.	Liu 15.23a

Ways to Paradise

C 4111	The snake and tortoise, bird and dragon are recognizable, the tiger is questionable. The mirror was apparently made from a positive mould, with resultant reversals; *cf.* a mirror shown in Feng 48b, dated AD 291. See fig. 10.	Feng 4a
C 4112	The facsimile is very unclear, and many details are not recognizable.	Liu 15.23b
C 4113	The inscription is incomplete.	Liu 15.24a
C 4114	The inscription is incomplete.	Feng 3b
C 4115	The facsimile is unclear, with many details not recognizable.	Liu 15.24b (head)
C 4116	There are no animals other than the *ssu shen*; the Ls face to the left; the inscription reads in an anti-clockwise direction. This example should possibly be classified under X.	Liu 15.24b (foot)
C 4117	In place of the *ssu shen* there are four pairs of birds facing each other. The characters of an inner inscription have been replaced by sets of three parallel lines. The outer inscription is incomplete.	Liu 15.27a (head)
C 4118	The inscription is incomplete.	Liu 15.27a (foot)
C 4119	The inscription is incomplete.	Feng 4b
C 4120 (15.8)	An inner inscription has been replaced as in C 4117; the outer inscription is incomplete.	M 32
C 4121		Liu 15.47b
C 4122		Liu 15.48a (head)
C 4123 (19.6)	From the tomb of Wang Kuang, Lo-lang (item 134)	Lo-lang (Wang Kuang), pp. 40–1; Pl. LXXVIII
C 4124		Liu 15.57b
C 4125	Of the *ssu shen*, the tortoise appears without a snake; the dragon and tiger are replaced by birds.	Liu 15.58a
C 4126 (15.8)	See Plate XV.	M 36
C 4127 (15.7)		BM 1973, 7–26, 53

There is no inner inscription in C 4107, C 4110, C 4117, C 4119, C 4120, C 4122, C 4125 and C 4126. Circlets, with bird and toad, appear on C 4101, C 4102 and C 4103. The positions from which the outer inscriptions start are somewhat unusual, i.e. in the north, C 4101, C 4103, C 4104, C 4105, C 4108, C 4114, C 4115, C 4120, C 4124, C 4125 and C 4126; in the east, C 4112, C 4113; in the south, C 4111; in the south-west, C 4121; in the west, C 4107; and in the north-west, C 4102 and C 4116. Makers of the mirrors are specified as follows: the *Shang-fang* C 4101 to C 4120, and C 4127; T'ai shan C 4123, C 4124 and C 4125; T'ai yin (T'ai shih, according to Moriya, p. 33) C 4126; Wang C 4121, C 4122. The cloud-scroll is replaced by a double line of chevrons in C 4108–C 4120 and C 4122–C 4126.

C 4201 (16.2)	M 21

Appendix one – Classification and list of TLV mirrors

C 4202 (14.3)	The tortoise is not accompanied by a snake; the inscription is incomplete.	M 22
C 4203	The red bird is incorrectly situated.	Liu 15.85a (head)
C 4204	The *ssu shen* are irregular	Liu 15.85a (foot)
C 4205	Details are difficult to distinguish; the final character of inscription is unread, presumably *pao*.	Liu 15.85b (head)
C 4206	The *ssu shen* and other animals are replaced by a total of four animals, including two ?? tigers set along the full length of each side of the square. The inscription is incomplete.	Liu 15.85b (head); Feng 8b
C 4207		Feng 8a
C 4208	A coin, of the type issued by Wang Mang, is included in the design at the eastern T.	Feng 7b
C 4209	There are eight animals altogether, which do not include the *ssu shen*. A patterned scroll, including animals, replaces the cloud-scroll.	B 42a

There are no inner inscriptions on C 4202–C 4206. The cloud-scroll is replaced by a double band of chevrons in C 4202, C 4203, C 4204 and C 4205. The inscriptions begin in the north-west on C 4202 and C 4203; the south-west on C 4204; the south on C 4208.

C 4301 (18.9)		M 19
C 4302 (14.1)		M 20
C 4303 (18.7)	Dated by Umehara at the end of western Han, but thought to be later.	Shodō Pl. 30, p. 171
C 4304	The *ssu shen* are placed to the left of the Ls	Liu 15.89a,b
C 4305	The cloud-scroll is replaced by a double band of chevrons; the inscription is identical with that of C 4304. Eight animals altogether, details unclear.	Liu 15.90a (head)
C 4306	There are eight animals altogether, details unclear.	Liu 15.90a (foot)
C 4307	The final character is omitted in the inscription.	Liu 15.90b (foot)
C 4308	The text of the inscription is identical with that of C 4307; it is placed in an intermediate ring which separates the centre and the Ts from the Ls and Vs (*cf.* C 1101)	Liu 15.93a
C 4309	The tortoise is unaccompanied by a snake; dragon and tiger are placed incorrectly; inscription placed intermediately, as in C 4308; cloud-scroll replaced by a decorative scroll which incorporates a tiger.	Liu 15.90b (head)
C 4310		Feng 9b
C 4311*		Feng 9a
C 4312	The inscription is placed intermediately, as in C 4308. See fig. 13.	Feng 10b

C 4313	The eight outer bosses are placed in quatrefoil rather than circular medallions. The inscription includes the usual elements, but in an unusual order.	Feng 10a

There is no inner inscription in C 4302, C 4305–C 4309. Outer inscriptions start in the south-east (C 4301, C 4307), south (C 4303, C 4311) and south-west (C 4302, C 4308, C 4312 and C 4313).

C 4901 (16.3)	The inner inscription is of four characters only; eight inner bosses are set in a circle. The outer inscription, in ornate *li-shu*, starts in the south-east.	M 23
C 4902 (18)	From a tomb dated from AD 40; the cloud-scroll is replaced by two sets of chevrons.	Shao-kou (item 21.34), pp. 166–8, fig. 73.1 and Pl. 43.3
C 5001* (20.9)	The only mirror seen where both the inner and the outer inscription start in the west. The maker is specified as the *Shang-fang*.	M 30
C 5002 (15.3)	There are no *ssu shen* or other animals; the Ls and the Vs cut across the band of the inscription, which is in ornate *li-shu*. The order of the lines of the inscription is illogical; there are references to the habits of the immortals but no mention of their presence. See Plate XVI.	M 47 Shodō Pl. 34, p. 171
D 1001 (17)	The inner inscription, starting in the south, is set in a column; cloud-scroll replaced by two chevron bands.	B 36
D 1002		B 41
D 1003 (23.3)	An extra decorative circle appears in the position usually occupied by the outer inscription. With a diameter of 23.3 cm, this is the largest TLV mirror examined.	M 37
D 1004 (16.4)		M 38
D 1005 (21.1)		M 42
D 1006 (16.6)	The cloud-scroll is replaced by a patterned scroll.	M 43
D 1007 (14.2)	The cloud-scroll is replaced by a patterned scroll. See Plate XVII.	M 44
D 1008	One *wu-shu* coin is included in the inner circle.	Feng 2a
D 1009 (16.4)	The inner inscription, of four characters only, starts in the north-east and reads anti-clockwise; inner bosses are set in a circle.	M 39
D 1010 (18.6)	The outer inscription is replaced by a decorative band; four minor bosses are set intermediately at the heads of the Vs.	BM 1973, 7–26, 55

Appendix one – Classification and list of TLV mirrors

D 2001 (11.5)	The *ssu shen* appear in an outer decorative band, outside the Ts, Ls and Vs.	M (colour) 1; B 29
D 2002	Straight decorative lines link the Vs.	B 37
D 2003	The cloud-scroll is replaced by a decorative band.	B 38
D 2004	Decorations include a figure of the Queen Mother of the West, with hare, three-legged bird; an archer; animals, etc. See fig. 23.	B 39
D 2005 (14.4)	The snake and tortoise are separated into two distinct units; the bird appears twice, once on each side of the L; dragon and tiger are accompanied by a single mythological creature.	M 10
D 2006 (16.1)	Straight decorative bands link the Vs; a decorative band replaces the cloud-scroll.	M 11
D 2007 (11.7)	The cloud-scroll is replaced by two sets of chevron bands.	M 12
D 2008 (13.8)	The cloud-scroll is replaced by a patterned scroll.	M 13
D 2009 (11.5)	The *ssu shen* are aligned over and around each T; the cloud-scroll is replaced by a decorative scroll which incorporates three animals. See Plate XVIII.	M 14
D 2010 (13.9)		M 40
D 2011 (15.6)	The *ssu shen* are erratic; the cloud-scroll is replaced by a decorative scroll.	M 41
D 2012 (13.8)	The cloud-scroll is replaced by a decorative scroll.	M 45
D 2013 (15.6)	The cloud-scroll is replaced by chevron bands.	M 48
D 2014 (10.9)	The cloud-scroll is replaced by chevron bands.	M 49
D 2015		Cammann (1948), fig. 1, from the Freer Gallery, Washington
D 2016 (11.3)	The scarlet bird is possibly not correct.	BM 1936, 11-18, 97
D 2017 (10.5)		V & A M. 268-1956
D 2018 (11.2)	The tortoise and snake are replaced by an animal.	V & A M. 271-1956
D 2019 (11.5)		V & A M. 4-1931
D 2020 (11.8)	There are four pairs of animals altogether, including a tortoise, reduplicated, without the snake; the dragon and tiger are set to the left of the Ls; the bird is reduplicated. There are two extra bands of chevron.	V & A M. 17-1935
D 2021	The snake and tortoise are set to the left of the L.	Kaplan, Pl. IX

Ways to Paradise

D 2022 (10.1)	An inner ring separates the Ts from the Ls and Vs; there are no animals or bosses. From a site which includes artefacts dating from the *Chan-kuo* period to Han.	KK 1965.8, pp. 377, 380 (fig. 6.1), 382

The *ssu shen* do not appear on D 2002, D 2003, D 2004, D 2006, D 2013, D 2014, D 2019, and D 2022. There is a cloud-scroll in D 2010, D 2015 and D 2019 only.

X 1001 (16.6)	The central area is circular, including nine bosses set in a circle, and being linked with the four Vs by four diagonal paths. The four paths each bear short inscriptions, of three characters. Dragon and tiger are placed incorrectly in relation to the other two animals. There are marked signs of gilding the *ssu shen*. The cloud-scroll is replaced by a patterned scroll which incorporates a tiger; there is an extra band of chevron decoration outside the scroll. The outer inscription refers to the Hsin dynasty.	M (colour) 2
X 1002	An inner inscription, in archaised script, carries text of a type usually seen in outer inscriptions. There are no inner bosses; four pointers are set, within the square, pointing inaccurately at the middle positions of the four sides. There are no *ssu shen*, and no Vs. A decorative band (geometric pattern) replaces an outer inscription. A chevron band is replaced by a ring of dots. In place of a cloud-scroll, there is a patterned scroll incorporating animals and three coins of Wang Mang's minting (AD 8.)	B p.54 (fig. G)
X 1003 (11.8)	No inner inscription, inner bosses or Vs. A pair of animals is centred on each of the Ls and Ts, including a dragon, bird, unicorn sheep, and, in one instance a decorative device. The outer inscription, in ornate *li-shu*, is incomplete, mentioning the Hsin dynasty; two bands of chevron decoration replace the cloud-scroll.	M 2
X 1004 (15.8)	There is a circular centre, including seven bosses and an inscription of ? three characters; there are no Ls and no *ssu shen*. The decor comprises a variety of creatures, including a poor representation of the Queen Mother of the West, with only one side of the *sheng*, and the hare. The outer inscription, in archaised style, reads anti-clockwise. It specifies the year Shih chien kuo 2 (i.e. AD 10), refers to the Hsin dynasty and the construction of the Pi-yung building (actually ordered	Liu 16.65b; B p. 50 (fig. F); Shodō, Pl. 29, pp. 16, 171; Umehara (1943) no. 2, pp. 7 f., Pl. 2

Appendix one – Classification and list of TLV mirrors

	in AD 5). There is no cloud-scroll, the outer inscription taking its place. See note 6 to Appendix Four, below. See Plate XIX.	
X 1005	The bird and tiger are shown at the left of the Ls. The outer inscription, starting in the east, in ornate *li-shu*, specifies the year AD 15; the cloud-scroll is replaced by a patterned scroll. See Figure 26.	Umehara (1943), no. 3, pp. 9 f., Pl. 1
X 1006*	No inner inscription, inner bosses, *ssu shen*, Ls or Vs. The outer inscription, in ornate *li-shu*, mentions the Hsin dynasty, and refers to the construction of the *Pi-yung* and the *Ming-t'ang*. The cloud-scroll is replaced by a patterned scroll.	Shodō, Pl. 33, pp. 16, 172
X 1007	No inner inscription, *ssu shen* or Vs. Two coins, of Wang Mang mint, are included in the decor. The inscription is in ornate *li-shu*, mentioning Han; the chevron division is replaced by a ring of dots, partly incorporated into a decorative scroll in place of the cloud-scroll. See fig. 24.	Liu 16.70a
X 1008 (13.9)	No inner inscription, inner bosses; the dragon and the tortoise are misplaced; the outer inscription is in ornate *li-shu*, incomplete, mentioning the Hsin dynasty; the cloud-scroll is replaced by a decorative scroll.	Fitz. O. 201-1946
X 1009 (14.7)	The inner inscription is of four characters only; there are no bosses; the tiger and bird are placed incorrectly. The outer inscription starts in the north-west and mentions the Hsin dynasty; the first two characters of the third line are in reverse order. There is an inner set of chevrons around the central boss.	M 1
X 2001 (18.5)	The central boss is circular, with an inner inscription of eight characters, to be read in anti-clockwise direction. There are no Vs, and the Ls face to the left; the *ssu shen* are in incorrect order. There is a decorative band set inside the degree markings; the cloud-scroll is replaced by chevrons, wave pattern.	B 43
X 2002	No inner inscription, inner or outer bosses, *ssu shen* or Vs; the outer inscription is in archaised style.	Liu 15.63a
X 2003	No inner inscription, inner bosses, *ssu shen* or Vs; the outer inscription is in archaised style.	Liu 15.66b (foot)
X 2004	The *ssu shen* are erratic; there are no Vs or outer inscription; a decorative scroll replaces the cloud-scroll.	B 40

X 2005 (11.5)	No inner or outer inscription, inner bosses or Ls. The *ssu shen*, in incorrect order, are aligned along the length of the sides of the square, without other animals; no cloud-scroll or decorative scroll.	M 16
X 2006*	No inner inscription, inner bosses, *ssu shen* or Ls; the outer inscription is in archaised style; the cloud-scroll is replaced by two bands of chevron.	Liu 15.65b (foot)
X 2007	No inner inscription, inner bosses, Ls or Vs; the dragon and tiger are incorrectly placed; the outer inscription is in archaised style.	Liu 15.65a (head)
X 2008	The inner inscription, in *li-shu*, reads anti-clockwise, specifies the maker as the *Shang-fang*, and dates manufacture, uniquely, to a specific day (7th day of the 8th month of Ching-yüan 4th year, i.e. in AD 263). The centre is circular; there are no Ls, Vs or *ssu shen*. A decorative scroll is set inside the degree markings.	Umehara (1943), Wei no. 8, pp. 53 f., Pl. 23.2
X 2009 (8)	There is a circular centre, with no inner bosses, inscriptions or *ssu shen*, Ls or Vs; from a tomb dated in early eastern Han (see the register appended to Lo-yang (mirrors)).	Lo-yang (mirrors) 80
X 2010 (5.9)	This is a very crude example, with a diameter of 5.9 cm only; the only features present are four Ts; from a tomb dated in early or middle eastern Han. See fig. 25.	Lo-yang (mirrors) 82
X 2011 (16.1)	There are no inscriptions, *ssu shen*, the Ts have no vertical lines; the cloud-scroll is replaced by a patterned scroll.	BM 1973, 7-26, 56
X 2012 (14.5)	No inner inscription, *ssu shen*; the Ts have no vertical lines; the cloud-scroll is replaced by two bands of chevron; the outer inscription specifies the *Shang-fang* as the maker.	BM 1926, 11-17, 1
X 2013 (9.2)	The only features present are the four Ts; from a tomb in Kuang-tung, dated in the middle or later part of eastern Han.	KK 1964.9, pp. 456-7 (item 4.8) and fig. 6
X 2014 (16.4)	The central boss is surrounded by a snake or dragon (*cf.* C 2201); there are no inner bosses, *ssu shen* or outer inscription; TLVs incomplete.	BM 1936, 11-18, 268
X 2015 (9)	With a diameter of 9 cm, this is one of the smallest mirrors examined. There are no inner bosses, inner or outer inscriptions; the snake and tortoise are surmounted by a rectangular stamp bearing an inscription which is illegible; no cloud-scroll, Ls or Vs.	V & A M 279-1956
X 9001	No inner inscription or bosses; the *ssu shen* are set along the whole length of each side of	Umehara (1943), suppl. no. 3, pp. 150 f.,

Appendix one – Classification and list of TLV mirrors

	the square. The inscription, in ornate *li-shu*, starts in the east, and dates manufacture, by Kuang wu, to the first month of the first year of Yung-ho (i.e. AD 136, 345, 416, 433 or 935). See Umehara (1943), p. 151 for decorative details, and the conclusion that the inscription was added subsequently to manufacture.	Pl. 70.2
X 9002	There are inner and outer inscriptions (with idiosyncratic text) starting in the north-east; *ssu shen*, of which the dragon and the tiger are placed incorrectly; and a cloud-scroll. The mirror is dated by Feng in Wei (Three Kingdoms).	Feng 48a
X 9003 (16.4)	Of the *ssu shen*, the tiger and dragon are hardly distinguishable. The twelve branches of the inner inscription are in incorrect order; the Ls face to the left; the outer inscription is anti-clockwise, starting in the south and specifying the *Shang-fang* as the maker; in ornate *li-shu*. See Plate XX.	M 33
X 9004	There are three inscriptions. (1) The innermost, set in a circle around the central boss; in squared style. (2) Intermediate, in *li-shu*, set around the square in a column. (3) The outermost, in ornate *li-shu*, set between two bands of chevron. For the inscriptions, see notes in Liu.	Liu 15.82a
X 9005	There are *ssu shen* and Vs, without Ls or Ts; outer inscription only, in seal character, specifying the date as AD 650.	Suzuki. H., in Moriya, p. 3, fig. 3

List of sources of the foregoing mirrors

British Museum			Bulling (1960)		
1926 11–17 1	X 2012		Figure: C	C 1101	
1932 12–15 1	B 0006		E	C 1202	
1936 11–18 97	D 2016		F	X 1004	
1936 11–18 268	X 2014		G	X 1002	
1947 7–12 334	C 2310		H	C 2201	
1950 11–17 230	B 0005		Plate: 9	B 0001	
1973 7–26 53	C 4127		10	B 0002	
1973 7–26 54	C 1306		11	B 0003	
1973 7–26 55	D 1010		12	B 0004	
1973 7–26 56	X 2011		13	A 0001	

Ways to Paradise

29	D 2001	*Kaogu*	
35	C 2102	1964.9, pp. 456-7	
36	D 1001		X 2013
37	D 2002	1965.8, pp. 377 f.	
38	D 2003		D 2022
39	D 2004		
40	X 2004	Kaplan	
41	D 1002	Plate XI	D 2021
42	C 2202		
42a	C 4209		
43	X 2001	Liu 15	
		21b head	C 3104
Cammann (1948)		21b foot	C 2205
Figure 1	D 2015	22a	C 4106
		22b	C 4109
Cammann (1950)		23a	C 4110
Figure 2	C 2108	23b	C 4112
		24a	C 4113
Ch'ang-sha		24b head	C 4115
211.20	C 1101	24b foot	C 4116
		27a head	C 4117
Cull		27a foot	C 4118
28 (Yetts Pl. XXXI) C 2104		29a	C 2301
		31a	C 3103
Feng		31b	C 2302
2a	D 1008	32a	C 3101
3b	C 4114	32b head	C 2303
4a	C 4111	32b foot	C 2304
4b	C 4119	33a	C 2305
5a	C 4107	33b head	C 2306
7a	C 2307	33b foot	C 3201
7b	C 4208	47b	C 4121
8a	C 4207	48a head	C 4122
8b	C 4206	48a foot	C 3202
9a	C 4311	57b	C 4124
9b	C 4310	58a	C 4125
10a	C 4313	63a	X 2002
10b	C 4312	63b	C 2402
24b	C 1301	65a head	X 2007
32a	C 2206	65a foot	C 1302
32b	C 2207	65b	X 2006
33a	C 2208	66b head	C 1303
34b	C 2401	66b foot	X 2003
41b	C 1904	82a	X 9004
42a	C 2107	83a	C 3203
48a	X 9002	83b	C 3204
		85a head	C 4203
Fitzwilliam Museum		85a foot	C 4204
o.201–1946	X 1008	85b head	C 4205
		85b foot	C 4206
Freer Gallery		89a	C 4304
See Cammann (1948)		89b	C 4304

Appendix one – Classification and list of TLV mirrors

90a head	C 4305	7	C 2204	46	C 1903
90a foot	C 4306	8	C 1902	47	C 5002
90b head	C 4309	9	C 1901	48	D 2013
90b foot	C 4307	10	D 2005	49	D 2014
93a	C 4308	11	D 2006	Figure 3	X 9005
93b	C 1102	12	D 2007		
98a	A 0003	13	D 2008	Shao-kou	
		14	D 2009	21.34	C 4902
Liu 16		15	C 2404	1023.1	C 4105
30a	A 0004	16	X 2005		
65b	X 1004	17	C 1305	Shensi	
70a	X 1007	18	C 1304	49	C 1207
70b	C 1204	19	C 4301		
72a	C 1205	20	C 4302	Shih-chai-shan	
72b	C 1205	21	C 4201	M 13.8	A 0002
		22	C 4202		
Lo		23	C 4901	Shodō	
II 23a	C 1202	24	C 2403	Figure 24	C 3101
		25	C 2308	Plate: 29	X 1004
Lo-lang (Wang Kuang)		26	C 2309	30	C 4303
Pl. LXXVIII C 4123		27	C 3102	32	C 2101
		28	C 4102	33	X 1006
Lo-yang (mirrors)		29	C 4103	34	C 5002
78	C 2106	30	C 5001		
80	X 2009	31	C 4101	Umehara (1943)*	
82	X 2010	32	C 4120	Han no. 2	X 1004
83	C 4108	33	X 9003	Han no. 3	X 1005
84	C 4104	34	C 1201	Wei no. 8	X 2008
		35	C 1206	Suppl. no. 3	X 9001
Moriya		36	C 4126		
Colour 1	D 2001	37	D 1003	V & A	
Colour 2	X 1001	38	D 1004	M 16–1935	C 3101
Colour 3	C 2103	39	D 1009	M 1–1931	A 0005
1	X 1009	40	D 2010	M 4–1931	D 2019
2	X 1003	41	D 2011	M 17–1935	D 2020
3	C 2105	42	D 1005	M 268–1956	D 2017
4	C 2101	43	D 1006	M 271–1956	D 2018
5	C 1203	44	D 1007	M 279–1956	X 2015
6	C 2203	45	D 2012		

* For other mirrors described in this volume, see Appendix Five below.

Appendix two

Select inscriptions of TLV mirrors

A 0001
Constant joy without end. For long may we not forget one another.

A 0004
As we see the light of the sun, so may we for long not forget one another.

B 0002
Great joy, glory and wealth, and may you find your heart's desire. A thousand autumns, ten thousand seasons be yours, with the years of your life prolonged for ever and a day.

C 1101
The holy saints made this mirror; it takes its power from the Five Phases, its life from the peace of nature's order . . . with its inscription and decoration. Its light reflects the sun and the moon, its substance is pure and adamant. With the mirror you may gaze at ideal beauty and avert all that is evil. In the central land may there be great peace; may your children and your grandchildren prosper more and more. The perfect fortune of the Golden Lower Mantle[1] brings the strength of the unbroken thread.

---

[1] See *Chou i*, 1.6b; R. Wilhelm, *The I Ching or Book of Changes*, London, 1951, pp. 15, 391.

Appendix two – Select inscriptions of TLV mirrors

A 0001

常樂未央長毋相忘

A 0004

見日之光長毋相忘

B 0002

大樂貴富得所好

千秋萬歲延年益壽

光象日月其質清剛

以視玉容兮辟不羊

中國大寧子孫益昌

黃常元吉有紀剛

C 1101

聖人之作鏡兮取氣於五行

生於道康兮□有文章

Ways to Paradise

C 1201
The *Shang-fang* made this mirror. The strange peoples of the four regions submit; great is the blessing of the dynasty and its people are at rest. The foreign barbarians are destroyed and the state of the world restored. May wind and rain come in their due season without excess, and may the five crops of the field grow ripe. May your place in office bring lustre and renown, with material earnest of services rendered. Long may you preserve your two parents, and may your children and grandchildren gather strength. May this be handed down as a message to posterity, with joy that knows no end. Long life, wealth and glory.

C 1302
The beginning of the lines of seven words has its own unbroken rule. Tin and copper are refined and the dross expelled. Long may you preserve your two parents, and may profit come to your grandchildren and children.

Appendix two – Select inscriptions of TLV mirrors

C 1201

尚方作鏡四夷服
多賀國家人民息
胡虜殄滅天下復
風雨時節五穀孰
官位尊顯蒙祿食
長保二親子孫力
傳告後世樂無亟
壽富貴

C 1302

朱言之始自有紀
湅冶錫銅去其宰
長葆二親利孫子

Ways to Paradise

C 2102

The *Shang-fang* made this mirror to avert all harm. The fine copper which the Hsin dynasty possesses and which is drawn from Tan-yang has been refined and mixed with silver and tin, and the mirror is pure and bright. Skilled craftsmen have engraved it [i.e. the mould], forming its inscription and decoration. The dragon on the left and the tiger on the right forfend all evil; the scarlet bird and the black . . .[1] accord with Yin and Yang. May children and grandchildren be provided for you in full number, and may you be present at the centre.[2] Long may you preserve your two parents, and may you have joy, wealth and prosperity. Long life be yours, excelling that of metal and stone, as is fit for nobleman or king.

[1] The character *wu* (warrior) should be supplied.
[2] For this expression, see Cammann (1953), pp. 202–3.

C 2203

The fine copper which the Han dynasty possesses and which is drawn from Tan-yang has been mixed with . . .[1] and the mirror is pure and bright. The dragon on the left and the tiger on the right keep the four quarters in order; the scarlet bird and the black . . .[2] accord with Yin and Yang. May your household . . .

[1] Two characters omitted.
[2] The character *wu* should be supplied.

Appendix two – Select inscriptions of TLV mirrors

C 2102

尚方作竟大毋傷
新有善銅出丹陽
湅治銀錫清而明
巧工刻之成文章
左龍右虎辟不羊
朱鳥玄　順陰陽
子孫備具居中央
長保二親樂富昌
壽敝金石如侯王兮

C 2203

漢有善銅出丹陽
和以錫且明
左龍右虎掌三彭
朱爵玄　順陰陽
家

C 2402

Chü-hsü[1], king of antlers, brings delight each day, and by the light of this mirror are formed the thoughts of joy. Upon it are the dragon and the tiger and the four seasons in their due order. Long may you preserve your two parents, may you have joy without trouble. May your children and grandchildren live in obedience and content; may your household enjoy riches and prosperity. As with heaven, so may there be no end, and may you receive great happiness.

[1] For a beast named the *Chü-hsü*, or the *Ch'iung-ch'iung chü-hsü*, see *Shan-hai-ching*, 8.4b, 5a and note, and *Shuo-yüan* 6.1b. For the appearance of the antlered head in protector figures, see Salmony, and Loewe (1978) p. 108.

C 3201

An excellent mirror from the *Shang-fang*, truly very fine. Upon it . . .[1] immortal beings, oblivious of old age. When they thirst they drink from the springs of jade, when they hunger they feed on jujubes. They roam at large throughout the world, wandering between the four oceans. The dragon on the left and the tiger on the right forfend [evil] and protect the Way. Long life be yours, like that of metal or stone, and may you be protector of the land.

[1] The character *yu* has been omitted in the inscription.

C 4102

The *Shang-fang* made this mirror and truly it is very fine. Upon it are immortal beings oblivious of old age. When they thirst they drink from the springs of jade, when they hunger they feed on jujubes. They roam at large throughout the world, wandering between the four oceans. They rove at will on the well-known hills plucking the Herb of Life. Long life be yours, like that of metal or stone, and may you be protector of the land; eternal joy without end, as is fit for nobleman or king.

C 2402

角王巨虛日有憙
昭此明鏡成快意
上有龍虎三時置
渴次玉泉飢食棗
浮浮天下敖三海
徘徊名山采之草

C 3201

尚方佳竟真大好
上有仙人不知老
渴次玉泉汎食棗
浮浮天下敖三海
長保二親樂毋事
子孫順息家富熾
左龍右虎辟保道
壽如金石為國保

C 4102

上有仙人不知老
予天毋極受大福
壽如金石之國保
長樂未央宜侯王 [sic.]

Ways to Paradise

C 4311

If you climb Mount T'ai, you may see the immortal beings. They feed on the purest jade, they drink from the springs of manna. They yoke the scaly dragons to their carriage, they mount the floating clouds. The white tiger leads them . . . . . they ascend straight to heaven. May you receive a never ending span, long life that lasts for ten thousand years, with a fit place in office and safety for your children and grandchildren.

C 5001

The *Shang-fang* made this mirror and truly it is very fine. Upon it are immortal beings oblivious of old age. When they thirst they drink from the springs of jade, when they hunger they feed on jujubes. They rove at will on the hills of the gods, plucking the Herb of Life. Long life be yours, longer than that of metal, stone, the Queen Mother of the West.

Appendix two – Select inscriptions of TLV mirrors

C 4311

上大山見仙人
食玉英飲澧泉
駕交龍乘浮雲
白虎引兮直上天
受長命壽萬年
宜官秩保子孫

C 5001

尚方作竟真大好
上有仙人不知老
渴次玉泉飢食棗
俳佪神山采芝草
壽敝金石西王母

Ways to Paradise

X 1006

The following translation of this exceedingly difficult inscription is that of Karlgren (1934), p. 34.

The New Dynasty has erected a Pi-yung and built a Ming-t'ang; may you be illustrious[1] among promoted scholars and take place among princes and kings; generals and ministers . . .; ten thousand huts of students are in the North; may you have joy without end.

[1] Karlgren accepts the reading *lieh* as being correct, in place of the actual *jan*; see Shodō, Plate 33 and p. 172.

X 2006

The unbroken rule of the seven words starts from the mirror. Long may you preserve your two parents, and may profit come to your grandchildren and children. The mirror expels all that is evil and it is suitable for [sale?].

Appendix two – Select inscriptions of TLV mirrors

X 1006

新興辟雍建明堂
然于舉士列侯王
將軍令尹民所行
諸生萬舍在北方
樂未央

X 2006

未言之紀從竟始
長葆二親利孫子
辟去不羊宜市古

Appendix three

The Diviner's board*

The following table shows details of the examples of these instruments found either in whole or in fragments.
For further information, see Ch'en (1965) pp. 132 f.

NUMBER, MATERIAL	PIVOT	DIPPER	BANDS OF CIRCULAR DISC (from inwards)			
			1	2	3	4
1 Bronze	None	None	None	None	None	None
2 Ivory	✓	✓	the twelve *shen* (b)	combination of the ten stems and Twelve Branches	the 28 mansions	None
3 Lacquered wood	✓	✓	the twelve *shen* anti-clockwise	Combination of the ten stems and Twelve Branches, totalling 24 signs (c) clockwise	the 28 mansions anti-clockwise	None
4 Lacquered wood	✓	✓	the twelve *shen* anti-clockwise	as in no. 3	Unknown (d)	Unknown (d)
5 Lacquered wood	✓	✓	the twelve *shen*; one extra character *wu*, interpolated; anti-clockwise	the 28 mansions anti-clockwise	None	None
6 Bronze	✓	None	the twelve *shen* anti-clockwise	12 Branches and 10 stems, as in no. 5 band (I); clockwise (a)	the 28 mansions anti-clockwise	None

* Reports of a seventh example of these boards, discovered at a site in An-hui province which is dated in 165 BC, were published while these pages were in the press; see WW 1978.8, pp. 12 f., and KK 1978.5, pp. 334 f. and 338f.

NUMBER, MATERIAL	BANDS OF SQUARE DISC (from inwards) I	II	III	IV	OTHER DETAILS	SITE OF DISCOVERY, DETAILS OF DATING	REFERENCES
1 Bronze	8 of the ten stems, omitting *wu*, *chi*; clockwise (k)	the 12 Branches, with intermediate animals in relief; clockwise	the 28 mansions anti-clockwise	None	In Band (III) the 4 characters *tzu*, *mao*, *wu*, *yu* are set within decorative gates. Diagonal paths bear inscriptions,(a) Four major bosses, at the corners, are set within pairs of minor bosses	described by Ch'en Meng-chia as western Han	KKHP 1965.2, pp. 132 f., and Plate II; Lo-lang (Harada), p. 61, fig. 27. Now preserved in the Historical Museum of China
2 Ivory	?	?	?	?	Inscription on reverse side, reading *T'ien kang*	found in Shan-si	KKHP *ibid.*, p. 133. Now preserved in the Museum of the Former Imperial Palace, Peking
3 Lacquered wood	?	?	?	?	Fragments of the circular disc only were found; details follow the analogy with no. 4	found in Korea; cannot pre-date AD 9	KKHP *ibid.*, p. 134; Lo-lang (Painted Basket), p. 97, Plate CVII and English text, p. 23
4 Lacquered wood	8 of the ten stems, omitting *wu*, *chi*; eight trigrams set intermediately; clockwise	the 12 Branches, clockwise	Unknown	the 28 mansions; anti-clockwise	Found damaged; details follow Harada's reconstruction, a golden background, with lines, the 7 stars and inset of the square in scarlet; characters and 8 trigrams in black. There are diagonal paths, and horizontal, vertical paths cut short at the limits of the square	found in Korea; cannot pre-date AD 68	KKHP *ibid.*, p. 134; Lo-lang (Harada), p. 60, Plate CXII and English text, p. 40; WW 1958.7, p. 21; Kaplan, fig. C
5 Lacquered wood	the Twelve Branches and ten stems totalling 20 terms; (e) clockwise	28 mansions; anti-clockwise	None	None	Diagonal paths, a horizontal and vertical path; four major bosses at the corner; two on the diagonals; minor bosses. About 150 degree marks on edge of circular disc; 182 at edge of square disc (f)	from tomb no. 62, Mo-tsui-tzu, Wu-wei; cannot pre-date 8 BC	WW 1972.12, pp. 14, 15, 21 and Plate V
6 Bronze	as in no. 5 band (i)	28 mansions; anti-clockwise	36 animals clockwise (h)	None	Two passages from the *Shih-ching* inscribed on reverse side of square disc; four diagonal paths, inscribed (i)	Six Dynasties period. This instrument has also been termed the *Liu jen* board	KKHP *ibid.*, p. 134; WW 1958.7, p. 20 and Plate II; now in the Shanghai Museum

Notes to Appendix three

(a) The inscriptions are as follows:

(1) at the north-east 己鬼門

(2) at the south-east 戊地門

(3) at the south-west 己人門

(4) at the north-west 戊天門

(b) I.e. twelve terms used as designators for the twelve 'leaders of the months' (see WW 1958.7, p. 20), but apparently not for the twelve Jovian stations, for which see Needham, vol. 3, p. 243. See Bodde (1975), pp. 81 f. for a valuable study of these terms and their relationship to various other series of twelve expressions.

(c) The series of 24 terms is made up as follows: (1) The Twelve Branches are set out in regular sequence. (2) Between each one of the Twelve Branches there is one of Ten Stems; of the ten, *wu* and *chi* (i.e. the two that are omitted in other series; see note (e)) appear here twice, being placed out of sequence, but regularly, i.e.:

子	丑	寅	卯	辰	巳	午	未	申	酉	戌	亥
1	3	5	7	9	11	13	15	17	19	21	23

癸		甲	乙		丙	丁		庚	辛		壬
2		6	8		12	14		18	20		24

	戊			己			戊			己	
	4			10			16			22	

(d) Traces of characters, unread, were found on the blank bands and the diagonals.

(e) The twelve branches and ten stems (omitting *wu* and *chi*) are combined systematically in the following order:

子癸丑寅甲卯己辰巳丙午丁未申
庚酉辛戌亥壬

This same order is retained in modern (i.e. nineteenth century) geomancers' compass boards, with the insertion of the characters for four of the trigrams (as seen in note (i) below).

Appendix three – The diviner's board

(f) WW 1972.12, p. 17 observes that the 182 degree marks of the square disc represent the 365 and a quarter degrees of the Han circle.

(g) It is not possible to determine the total number of terms for certain. The combination is identical with that of band (I) in board no. 5, with the addition of at least two other characters (艮, and one other, illegible).

(h) See WW 1958.7, p. 20. The thirty-six animals of band (III) correspond very largely to the thirty-six that are listed in chapter five of the *Wu-hsing ta-i* of Hsiao Chi, of the Sui dynasty (see *Wu-hsing ta-i* 5, *Ts'ung-shu chi-ch'eng*, ed. p. 122). This text explains that three animals were adopted for each of the Twelve Branches, so as to correspond with the division of each day into its three phases of dawn, noon and dusk. Parts of band (III) of board no. 6 are worn or defective, and there are some points of variance from the list given in the *Wu-hsing ta-i*. The following readings are suggested tentatively for the board, where the characters are set nine to each of the four sides:

West			South			East			North		
25	狚	Tan wolf	16	蠈	P'iao chrysalis	7	狪	Fu (see note)	34	豕	Shih swine
26	猨	Yüan monkey	17	蟬	Ch'an cicada	8	狸	Li wild cat?	35	□	
27	猴	Hou ape	18	虵	She serpent	9	虎	Hu tiger	36	猪	Chu pig
28	鴙	Chih pheasant	19	鹿	Lu deer	10	猬	Wei hedgehog	1	蝦	Hsia frog (see note)
29	鷄	Chi cock	20	馬	Ma horse	11	兔	T'u hare	2	鼠	Shu rat
30	烏	Wu crow	21	獐	Chang stag	12	貉	Ho badger	3	鷰	Yen swallow
31	狗	Kou dog	22	羊	Yang sheep	13	龍	Lung dragon	4	牛	Niu bull
32	猍	? ?	23	□		14	鯨	Ching leviathan	5	□	
33	狼	Lang wolf	24	鴈	Yen goose	15	魚	Yü fish	6	□	

Notes
1 I take this as a variant for 蝦 (see Karlgren (GSR) 33 i and 36).
7 This is described as an animal resembling a sheep, with four ears, no tail, and the eyes set in the back.

Ways to Paradise

(i) The four inscriptions read as follows (*cf.* note (a) above):

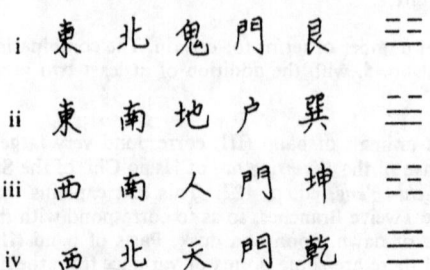

(k) The exceptional treatment given to the two terms *wu* and *chi* is somewhat puzzling. At times the terms are omitted from the series (band (I) in boards nos. 1, 4, 5 and 6; and band 2 in no. 6). They are duplicated in band 2 of boards nos. 3 and 4; and they are given prominence in no. 1. See Ch'en (1965), pp. 136 f.; and Loewe (1974,1), p. 230, note 63, for the use of terms to designate one, or possibly two, military officials (*hsiao-wei*).

PLATE XXIV
Mirror in high relief, with the inscription arranged in rectangular blocks; diameter 11.7 cm; Crown copyright, British Museum.

PLATE XXV
Mirror of late style, from the Sui period, with decorative devices only; diameter 20.2 cm; Crown copyright, British Museum.

PLATE XXVI
Decorated ends of a coffin in tomb no. 1, Sha-tzu-t'ang, Ch'ang-sha; approximately 1 by 1 metre. Devices such as the ring, sash, bell may be compared with details of the painting from tomb no. 1 Ma-wang-tui.

Appendix four*

Types of mirrors and their distribution

(A) The graves of Shao-kou and their evidence for dating
   (i) Classification
   (ii) Distribution
(B) Supplementary evidence
   (i) Mirrors of types earlier than TLV
   (ii) TLV mirrors
   (iii) TLV mirrors of irregular types
   (iv) Mirrors of types that were probably concurrent with TLV
   (v) Mirrors of types which emerged after TLV
   (vi) Mirrors with an inscription of the type *Wei chih san kung*
   (vii) TLV mirrors found in Japan

In his highly detailed study of pre-Han and Han mirrors, Karlgren[1] pays full attention to the development of decoration and to changes of calligraphic style. He assigns five of the categories which he isolates to the Han period (categories F, H, J, K and L); his category F includes some mirrors which bear the TLV pattern and which are classified here as type B. Karlgren dates his categories F, H, J and K to the second century BC; he dates category L, which comprises TLV mirrors of the regular, fully developed types that are classified here as type C, to between *c*. 100 BC and AD 100.[2]

Miss Bulling distinguishes between different types of Han mirror on the grounds of decorative detail, the arrangement of the inscriptions, and the formulae used in the inscriptions; and in general she follows the criteria and terminology used by a number of Chinese and Japanese scholars. The TLV marks first appear on types which she describes as Shou-chou and Ts'ao-yeh; of these, the Shou-chou mirrors (without the TLV pattern) were probably in vogue during the second century BC; Ts'ao-yeh may have evolved, as yet without the TLV marks, from perhaps 100 BC.[3]

Miss Bulling takes the view that a Shou-chou mirror which bears

* For notes, see pp. 214–15.

the TLV marks (B 0001) dates from the third quarter of the second century BC.[4] She ascribes one of the earliest mirrors which bears regular TLV features (C 1101) to between the end of Wu ti's reign (87 BC) and the last quarter of the first century BC. This highly significant and possibly unique example is of a transitional form, which should be placed intermediately between the appearance of the TLV marks on Shou-chou and Ts'ao-yeh types, and before the emergence of the regular TLV mirrors. Miss Bulling treats this example together with another mirror (D 2001)) as being some of the earliest TLV mirrors that are known. Possibly this second example (D 2001) should be placed considerably later.[5]

In considering the dates of some of the later mirrors Miss Bulling accepts the evidence of two inscriptions which appear on X 1004 and X 1005, as being valid. These inscriptions refer to the years AD 10 and AD 15, and they have not been brought into question by experts such as Umehara or Suzuki. Nevertheless I venture, with the greatest respect and diffidence, and without the benefit of personal inspection of the two mirrors, to suspect their authenticity.[6] At the other end of the scale, Miss Bulling suggests that one TLV mirror may date from the *San-kuo* or *Nan-pei-ch'ao* periods. Probably most scholars would agree with her conclusion that 'From about the middle of the eastern Han period onward interest shifted to other types of mirrors although the TLV mirrors were still produced in considerable numbers.'[7]

Perhaps the most elaborate of all schemes of classification of Han mirrors is to be seen in the special report on the group of 225 graves found at Shao-kou, near Lo-yang.

This report distinguishes between fourteen types of mirror altogether and suggests their relative sequence in time.[8] The TLV mirrors take their place as the sixth type, and they are sub-divided in the report into three sub-types, as follows (see Shao-kou, pp. 165 and 174):

(i) With full features of a central boss, four or eight nipples, the four beasts, other animals and inscriptions.[9] The earliest examples are believed to be before Wang Mang; the type was at its most popular stage during Wang Mang's time and lasted until the middle of the eastern Han period.
(ii) With decorative patterns replacing the four beasts and other animals. These are dated in Wang Mang's time or early eastern Han.
(iii) Greatly simplified designs, wherein the Ts, Ls and Vs are not always complete. These are dated from early to mid eastern Han.

H. Suzuki takes the view that the TLV marks emerged in the earliest stages, without the characteristic features such as the four beasts, on

Appendix four – Types of mirrors and their distribution

Fig. 26. TLV mirror (X 1005), dated in the inscription, probably anachronistically, at AD 15

the Shou-chou mirrors of the Ch'in or early western Han periods;[10] but perhaps some further indications are necessary before so early a date can be accepted. Komai and Hayashi[11] believe that the regular TLV mirrors, in their complete form, became current from the end of western Han or the time of Wang Mang, and the conclusions reached here do not differ markedly from these results. While the marks are certainly known from c. 100 BC, some fifty years may have elapsed before they appeared dressed in the full symbolism of the 'Five Phases' as an explanation of the cosmos. By the time of Wang Mang the type reached full fruition; although it gave place to other types of decoration by c. AD 100 or 150, irregular examples were still being made; elements of the pattern were sometimes incorporated in mirrors which were designed up to 500 years later.

(A) The graves of Shao-kou and their evidence for dating

The archaeological excavations that have been conducted in a highly methodical fashion since 1949 have added very considerably to our knowledge of Han China, and the results that have been reported since 1972 have been particularly fruitful. It is now possible to reach more definite and more precise conclusions regarding many problems that have been hitherto unsolved and to correlate material with literary evidences. Artefacts of many types may now be classified in sequences, on the basis of criteria such as the constructional methods used for graves or the style and decor of their contents. In addition, more precise dating is sometimes possible for particular sites elsewhere with the help of the inscriptions found on the walls of a tomb or on some of the artefacts; and several graves have been identified as the resting places of persons known to history.

These studies have been considerably refined and consolidated by the examination of several groups of graves, of which perhaps the most important is that of the 225 graves of Shao-kou, near Lo-yang.[12] The monograph that was published by the *Academy of Sciences* in 1959 gives a full account of the different types of grave and their construction; it considers the different distribution of various types of artefact among the graves; and it classifies a number of types of funeral furnishing, such as utilities of pottery, bronze, iron and lead; coins; or luxuries and treasures of lacquer, gold, silver and jade. These studies have made it possible to establish a fully consistent schema for dating the graves of the site, mainly on a relative basis; and tentative suggestions for an absolute chronology, within broad limits, are included in the report.

However, the schema laid out in the report is subject to certain limitations and cannot be applied universally to the many different and widely scattered sites of Han China. For the graves of this cemetery, numerous as they are, do not include examples of all products of the Han artists and craftsmen. In addition due allowance should be made for regional variation. Shao-kou lies close to Lo-yang, an important, centrally placed city in western Han, and the capital city of eastern Han. It cannot be expected that the same dating pattern will apply, either in relative or precise terms, to all the sites that lie scattered in the far-flung provinces of the Han empire. In some cases it may have taken a very long time for styles to reach the country districts from the capital and its cultural centre, while, owing to chance, the more up-to-date fashions may have spread very quickly in other regions. There may be areas where the arrival of a new style of artefact was delayed,

Appendix four – Types of mirrors and their distribution

while the intermediate, experimental stages did not reach the area in question and are not represented there. By contrast, allowance must be made for the evolution and spread of styles created to suit local conditions in the outlying provinces, which may not necessarily be seen in the metropolitan or other regions.

The report on the graves of Shao-kou cannot do full justice to all the types of TLV mirror exemplified above, as these are not all present at the site; and the report is not concerned with the differences noted in the types of inscription, the symbolism or its importance. Similarly a more detailed classification is necessary for certain other types of Han mirror, e.g., the late styles, decorated in high relief, with human and animal figures; these are hardly represented in the finds from the Shao-kou site.

As in other parts of the world, so in China ancient objects, treasures or heirlooms were at times buried for decades, or even centuries, after the time of manufacture. For this reason the presence of Han mirrors in a grave may sometimes be deceptive, or valueless for the purposes of identification or dating. Valid conclusions must depend on the consistency of a large body of evidence.[13]

A total of 118 bronze and 8 iron mirrors[14] were found distributed in 95 of the 225 graves of the Shao-kou sites; over half of these bear inscriptions. The great majority of the mirrors had been placed inside the coffins, and there are signs that some care had been paid to their exact situation.[15] Some of the mirrors, which had been housed in lacquer containers, had been placed outside the coffins, at no great distance away; and there were signs that some of those that had been placed inside the coffins had been wrapped in silken bags.[16] Occasionally there were traces of cords or fabrics in the loops of the central bosses.[17] Mirrors appear among the funerary furnishings for both sexes; in general one was buried for each individual.

The Shao-kou report classifies the mirrors found at those sites in 14 types, which do not correspond exactly with the types or terms adopted by other scholars. The schema of the Shao-kou report runs from the early *Shou-chou* (or *P'an-ch'ih*) types, to the late Han mirrors in high relief. TLV (*kuei-chü*) mirrors find their place midway in the series, as type 6; these are sub-divided into three sub-types, as described above (see p. 210).

The report considers these types in relation to the periodization suggested for the graves. The TLV mirrors were found in graves dated in periods IIIb, IV and V of the following schema:[18]

I   Mid western Han and somewhat later
II Mid western Han and somewhat later

213

Ways to Paradise

IIIa Late western Han
IIIb Wang Mang and somewhat later

IV   Early eastern Han
V   Middle eastern Han
VI   Late eastern Han

The report classifies nine of these mirrors as type 6 (i), two as type 6 (ii), and four as type 6 (iii).[19] In the absence of fuller details and better facsimiles, very little comment can be added to this distinction, which is far less fine than that of the criteria adopted in the foregoing pages on the basis of a much larger number of TLV mirrors. In general, however, there seems to be no great inconsistency.[20] The evidence of Shao-kou can be modified, supplemented and in some ways supported by the discoveries made subsequently at other sites, whose reports have appeared later. The examples of mirrors that are given under (B) below have been selected from the very large number of mirrors whose discovery has been subsequently reported in the pages of the Chinese archaeological journals.

Notes to Appendix four

1. Karlgren (1941).
2. Karlgren (1941), p. 114.
3. See Watson (1972), p. 97. Recent archaeological finds include one Ts'ao-yeh mirror (without TLV marks) from the tombs of Man-ch'eng, which were sealed shortly before 100 BC (see KK 1972.1, p. 17, fig. 14). Perhaps the earliest datable example of a Ts'ao-yeh mirror which bears the TLV marks comes from the graves of Shih-chai-shan of c. 100 BC (see A 0002).
4. Bulling (1960), p. 21.
5. Bulling (1960), pp. 36 f., 41, fig. C and plate 29.
6. See the notes to X 1004 and X 1005 in Appendix One. It should be noted that X 1004 has been accepted as authentic by K. Tomioka (*Kōkogaku zasshi* VII, 5 (1917), pp. 243 f., and VIII, 5 (1918), pp. 243 f.) who refers to the inclusion of the mirror in the collection of Mo Yu-chih. Tomioka is followed by Nakayama and K. Takahashi in *Kōkogaku zasshi* IX, 12 (1919), pp. 692 f.
7. Bulling (1960), p. 59, with reference to her plate 42a.

Appendix four - Types of mirrors and their distribution

8. See Shao-kou, pp. 160 f., and 235 f., for general considerations and conclusions regarding the sequences for different types of artefact.
9. For a description of these features, see Appendix One above.
10. In Moriya, p. 2.
11. Komai, p. 96; Hayashi (1973, 1), p. 15.
12. Other groups include one of 500 graves in Yü-hsien, Ho-nan, where a total of 99 mirrors were found in the 263 graves examined (KKHP 1959.1, p. 61); and a further group in the western suburbs of Lo-yang where, out of a total number of over 400 graves, 217 are identified as Han; of the 175 mirrors found at the sites, 47 were of TLV pattern (KKHP 1963.2, pp. 1 f., 22 and 49, table 3).
13. Two examples suffice to illustrate this point. (i) D 2022; this was found at a site which has been identified as the capital of the kings of Ch'u, and whose contents vary from *Chan-kuo* times to Han. (ii) See WW 1956.12, p. 39 and frontispiece for a *Ts'ao-yeh* mirror that was found in a grave of the Sung period, along with mirrors and porcelains made long after the Han dynasty.
14. Shao-kou, pp. 160 f. The report gives the number of iron mirrors as 9 (see p. 160) but 8 only are shown in the list on p. 198 (Table 45).
15. I.e. 16 were at the left side of the head, 12 at the right; 3 were by the breast or the shoulder; 3 were at the feet.
16. For a literary reference in this connection, on the occasion of the burial of an empress dowager, see HHS 10A.7a. See also KKHP 1958.4, p. 85 for the discovery of five mirrors at Ying-ch'eng-tzu, all with traces of textile wrappings. See also Komai, p. 15.
17. For a further example, see KK 1959.3, p. 149.
18. Shao-kou, pp. 235, 239. Table 66 (*ibid.* p. 237) which sets out the numbers of the different types of mirror found at sites according to the scheme of periodization is reproduced on p. 217.
19. Shao-kou, p. 168, table 30.
20. Details of the 15 TLV mirrors appear as follows in Shao-kou tables 30 and 66. Examples of type 6 (i) were found in graves 111 and 1005 (period III); 38, 41 and 59B (period IIIb); 104 (period III–IV); and 21, 1023 (period IV). The two mirrors of type 6 (ii) were found in graves 60 (period IIIb) and 1028A (period III); and the four mirrors of type 6 (iii) were from graves 25 (period IV), 1007 (period IV–V), 117 (period V) and 20 (period VI). The dating suggested for grave 25, i.e. period IV, early eastern Han, is somewhat at variance with the conclusions reached above, as the mirror in question (25: 15; see Shao-kou, fig. 74A, no. 5 and Plate 44, no. 3) would be classified here in sub-type X 20. For a further possible inconsistency, which arises in the case of a mirror which bears the date of AD 6, see Appendix Five below.

(A) The graves of Shao-kou and their evidence for dating

(i) Classification

The following list summarizes the types of mirror distinguished in the report on the graves from Shao-kou and draws attention to some corresponding terms that are used elsewhere. The list does not attempt to include all the terms that are used in other scholars' classifications.

Shao-kou, pp. 160 f.	Number of sub-types	Figure	Karlgren (1941): category	Shodō: term used	Bulling (1960): term used
1 *P'an-chih*	—	69.1	E, F	*P'an-chih*	*Shou-chou* 'winding dragon'

Ways to Paradise

Shao-kou, pp. 160 f.	Number of sub-types	Figure	Karlgren (1941): category	Shodō: term used	Bulling (1960): term used
2 *Ts'ao-yeh*	—	69.2	K	*Ssu-ju ts'ao-yeh*	*Ts'ao-yeh*
3 *Hsing-yün* or *Po-ju*	—	69.3 69.4	—	—	Hundred nipples
4 *Jih-kuang, Chao-ming, lien hu wen*	3	i 69.5 ii 69.6; 71.1,2 iii 70.1	—	*Ching-pai*	Inscription mirrors
5 *Pien-hsing ssu ch'ih wen*	—	71.3,4,5	J	—	Mirrors with four snakes
6 *Kuei-chü*	3	i 71.6; 72; 73; 74A.1,2 ii 74B.3 iii 74A.4,5	L	*Fang-ko ssu-shen*	TLV
7 *Ssu-ju*	5	i 74A.6 ii 74B.1 iii 74B.2; 75.1,2 iv 75.3	J	—	—
8 *Yün lei wen lien hu wen, Ch'ang i tzu sun lien hu wen*	2	i 75.4,5 ii 76.1; 77.1	—	*Ching-pai*	*Ching-pai Ming-kuang*
9 *K'uei-feng, Shuang-k'uei*	2	i 77.2 ii 76.2	—	*K'uei-feng*	—
10 *Pien-hsing ssu yeh wen*	—	77.3	—	—	*Shou-shou*
11 *Pien-hsing ssu yeh ssu feng*	—	77.4	—	*Shou-shou*	*Shou-shou*
12 *Jen wu hua hsiang*	—	77.5	—	*Hua-hsiang*	*Hua-hsiang*
13 *San shou*	—	77.6	—	—	—
14 *Niu*	—	Plate 46.2	—	—	—

(ii) Distribution

The following table, which is reproduced from Shao-kou, p. 237, Table 66, shows the distribution of mirrors of various types in those graves, which can be dated in one of the periods I to VI (for these periods, see p. 213–14). As all the graves where mirrors were found cannot necessarily be dated, the table does not include a record of all the mirrors which were found on the Shao-kou site. For details of

Appendix four – Types of mirrors and their distribution

some types of mirror, see Tables 27–32 (Shao-kou, pp. 160 f.); for a summary of the style and contents of each grave, see Table 67.

Type	I	II	IIIA	IIIB	IV	V	VI
2	1						
3	4	3					
4 i		3	8	5			
4 ii		3	10	6			
5			9	2			
7			3	1	2		
4 iii				1			
6				4	3	2	
8 i						4	
9						1	
8 ii						1	5
11							1
12							1
10							2
13							1
Iron							7

(B) Supplementary evidence

The following examples have been chosen to supplement the evidence of the report from Shao-kou, and that of Appendix One above, regarding the sequences and chronology of various types of mirror. The description of the types of mirror follows the scheme that is adopted in Shao-kou (for TLV mirrors, the classification adopted in the foregoing pages has been inserted in parentheses). In general the facsimiles and information that are available are far from clear or complete, very often because only the preliminary reports of an excavation have been published. As the list has been compiled to aid in establishing chronological sequences, two TLV mirrors which are included above in Appendix One and which derive from comparatively well dated sites, have been included below (A 0002 and C 1101). The lists are arranged as follows:

  (i) Mirrors of types earlier than TLV
  (ii) TLV mirrors
  (iii) TLV mirrors of irregular types
  (iv) Mirrors of types that were probably concurrent with TLV
  (v) Mirrors of types which emerged after TLV
  (vi) Mirrors with an inscription of the type *Wei chih san kung* (see p. 176 note 49 to Appendix One)
  (vii) TLV mirrors found in Japan

Ways to Paradise

The dating that is entered in the lists is usually as suggested in the reports of WW, KK etc., and is subject to revision in the light of evidence that has come to light since those publications appeared.

(i) Mirrors of types earlier than TLV

Site	Type of mirror (Shao-kou)	Suggested date of site	Notes	References
Ch'ang-sha (Ma-wang-tui)	1	c. 168 BC		MWT (Report), p. 128, fig. 111, and Plate 178
Ho-pei (Man-ch'eng)	2	113–104 BC		KK 1972.1, p. 17, fig. 14
Shan-tung (Lin-i)	2	shortly after 134 BC	from grave M2; in the adjoining M 1 (dated 140–118) one type 4 mirror was found	WW 1974.2, pp. 18, 26, figs. 38, 39
Kiang-su (Lien-shui)	(one mirror with decor of pre-Han type; *cf.* Karlgren (1941) type C; mirror carries three rings at the edge, but no central boss)	c. 112 BC. See KK no. 2, 1973, p. 87 for association of the grave with Liu Ying, noble of Chan, deprived of his nobility in 112 BC (HS 15A.50b)	For a similar mirror, i.e. with external rings but no boss, from a *Chan-kuo* grave; see WW 1972.5, Plate 1	KK 1973.2, p. 82, Plate 12.1
Ch'ang-sha	1	early west Han	Items 333.1; 342.3; 407.10	Ch'ang-sha, pp. 83 f., Plates 43, 44
	5	early west Han	Item 122.5	Ch'ang-sha, Plate 44
	2	late west Han	Item 339.18	Ch'ang-sha, p. 116, Pl. 67.1
Lo-yang	2	38–6 BC		KK 1964.8, p. 405, fig. 3.2

(ii) TLV mirrors

Site	Type	Suggested date	Notes	References
Yün-nan (Shih-chai-shan)	(A)	c. 100 BC		see Appendix One, A 0002
Si-an Hung-ch'ing	(A)	from mid to late[a] west Han	Item 121.7	KK 1959.12, p. 666, Fig. 2.2
Ch'ang-sha	(C 11)	late west Han		see Appendix One, C 1101

[a] Dating suggested in KK, *loc. cit.*, p. 667, largely on the basis of mirror types of the 55 Han tombs discussed; see also p. 220 below.

Appendix four – Types of mirrors and their distribution

Site	Type of mirror (Shao-kou)	Suggested date of site	Notes	References
Hu-pei (Han-yang)	(C 31)	not later than western Chin	Item 13; cloud-scroll replaced by patterned scroll	KK 1966.4, p. 196, and fig. 4
Ch'ang-sha	(C 22)	between Ling ti (167–189) and early *Liu-ch'ao* period	see note (b) below	KK 1957.5, p. 72
Lo-yang (west. suburbs)	(C 41)	middle east Han	Item 10025.1	KKHP 1963.2, p. 24, fig. 21.3
Kiang-si (Nan-ch'ang)	(C)(c) (D 20)	late east Han	items 1.14 and (d) 1.15	KK 1966.3, p. 150, fig. 5
Ch'ang-sha	(D 20) (D)	Hsüan ti to Yüan ti	four other mirrors found, of Shao-kou types 3 i, 5 and 7	KK 1966.4, p. 186, p. 185, fig. 5, and Plate 3
Ssu-ch'uan	(D 20)	*Liu-ch'ao*	KK compares with X 9001	KK 1958.7, p. 28, Plate 9

(b) The mirror has no inner inscription, and there is a decorative scroll in place of a cloud-scroll. The same tomb yielded a mirror in high relief, with inscription referring to the Queen Mother of the West.

(c) Inscription not legible in the facsimile.

(d) Item 1.3 from the same grave, is of Shao-kou type 8 ii.

(iii) TLV mirrors of irregular types

Site	Type of mirror	Suggested date of site	Notes	References
Lo-yang	one with Vs; one with Ts, Ls; one with Ts (cross bars only)	Wang Mang or later; middle east Han; middle east Han; (see KKHP, *loc. cit.*, table 6)	total of 175 mirrors (47 TLV) found at this site. See items 3006.3; 7011.2; 9014.1	KKHP 1963.2, p. 23, fig. 20.3; Plates 7.3, 9.5
Kuang-tung (Fo-shan-shih)	one with Ts	middle east Han?	Item 4.8	KK 1964.9, pp. 456–7, fig. 6
Ho-nan (Ying-yang)	two with Ts	late east Han	two TLV mirrors (types C 41, D 20) at the same site	WW 1960.5, p. 65, figs. 8–11
Nanking	TLV, with Ls facing left	east Han	22 mirrors at the site (a)	KK 1959.1 p. 22, Plate 6, 3–6
Si-an	one with Vs	Sui dynasty		WW 1957.8, p. 65

(a) These included examples of Shao-kou types 4 i, 7 and 12, and one with a depiction of the Queen Mother of the West.

Ways to Paradise

(iv) *Mirrors of types that were probably concurrent with TLV*

Site	Type of mirror (Shao-kou)	Suggested date of site	Notes	References
Hu-nan (Hsiang-hsiang)	3 4 i 4 ii 4 iii	west Han	11 mirrors altogether	KK 1966.5, pp. 247, 270
Nan-king	3	mid west Han	4 mirrors altogether	WW 1973.4, p. 24, figs. 19, 20
Si-an (Hung-ch'ing)	3 4 i 4 ii 4 iii 5 8	from mid to late west Han	18 mirrors altogether, including one TLV; see under (ii) above	KK 1959.12, p. 666, items 119.6; 011.1; 017.2; 142.13; 06.14; 110.13; Plate 4.8; figs. 3.2; 2.1; 2.4
Ho-nan (Cheng-chou)	4 i	mid to late west Han		WW 1972.10, p. 45, fig. 4.1
Kuang-si (Ho-p'u)	4 ii	late west Han [a]		KK 1972.5, p. 27
Ho-nan (Chi-yüan)	4 ii	late west Han to Wang Mang		WW 1973.2, p. 46, fig. 3
Korea (Lo-lang)	4 iii		C 4123 found at the same site	Lo-lang (Wang Kuang) p. 41, Plate 79
Lo-yang [b]	4 iii	late west Han		KKHP 1964.2, p. 123, fig. 11
Lo-yang (no. 81)	4	33–6 BC	inscription illegible on the facsimile	KK 1964.8, p. 405, fig. 3.1

[a] For the bronze vessels found at this site see J. Rawson in *Oriental Art*, vol. XIX, No. 4, winter 1973.

[b] From the tomb with decorated pediments showing the *ssu shen*, etc.

(v) *Mirrors of types which emerged after TLV* [a]

Site	Type of mirror (Shao-kou)	Suggested date of site	Notes	References
Shan-tung (T'eng-hsien)	7 iii 8 13	east Han	eleven [b] mirrors altogether	KK 1963.8, pp. 426–8
Kuei-chou (An-shun)	high relief	late east Han		KK 1972.2, p. 37, fig. 4
Kiang-si (Nan-ch'ang)	11 high-relief, with characters in blocks	early Liu-ch'ao		KK 1965.9, p. 460, fig. 2

[a] See KK 1955.6, Plate 16 and 1955.6, pp. 101 f. for consideration of mirrors from Shao-hsing, with particular reference to high relief mirrors, such as Shao-kou type 12. Examples are also seen as follows: for eastern Han, Hu-nan no. 85, and suppl. nos. 12, 13; *Che-kiang* nos. 28–30; for Nan-pei ch'ao, *Ssu-ch'uan* nos. 40, 41; *Hu-nan* suppl. nos. 14–16; *Che-kiang* nos. 31–37.

[b] These include two examples of Shao-kou 8, four of Shao-kou 7 iii and three of Shao-kou 13; classification of the others is difficult owing to the quality of the facsimiles.

Appendix four – Types of mirrors and their distribution

(vi)   Mirrors with an inscription of the type Wei chih san kung [a]

Site	Suggested date	Notes	References
Ho-nan (Cheng-chou)	late east Han	Item M 13.1	KK 1966.5, p. 249 fig. 3.1
Ho-pei (Shih-chia-chuang)	late east Han		WW 1959.4, p. 72, fig. 3
Si-an (north suburbs)	east Han		WW 1960.5, p. 69, fig. 5
An-hui (Ho-fei)	from the end of east Han to middle Liu-ch'ao		KK 1957.1, p. 34
Hu-pei (Sui hsien)	see note [b] below	Item 3.21	KK 1966.2, p. 90, fig. 6.2
Kiang-si (Jui-ch'ang)	west Chin		KK 1974.1, p. 32

[a] These are instances in which this formula is seen without further text. For an example where it appears as part of a long inscription, see WW 1966.12, p. 54 (and plate on p. 52). This mirror is engraved in high relief, with an inscription of 48 characters, set in 12 square blocks. The formula is included towards the end of the inscription, which dates the mirror at AD 167.

[b] See KK *loc. cit*, p. 91, where this type of mirror is taken as a criterion for late dating (in this case in the *San-kuo* period).

(vii)   TLV mirrors found in Japan[a]

1. Yamakawa no. 15. In this irregular mirror the Ls face left instead of right; the inscription is replaced by a series of decorative marks of a type that is seen in late Han mirrors fashioned in high relief (e.g., Bulling (1960), Plates 75, 78, 79); and the outer band is formed of a geometrical, diamond pattern in place of a cloud-scroll. The *ssu shen* and animals have been replaced by curvilinear patterns. There are four bosses in the inner square; each T is bounded by two large bosses, set unusually close to the centre; and there are four smaller bosses set intermediately at the heads of the Vs.

2. Yamakawa no. 20. This mirror is of a regular TLV pattern, as far as may be determined from the facsimile; there is an inner inscription (the Twelve Branches); 12 inner and 8 outer bosses; the *ssu shen* (details uncertain); degree markings; chevron pattern and cloud-scroll. The outer inscription is illegible.

3. Suzuki, H., p. 7, fig. 7. In this imitation the Ls face left instead of right; the central square includes 12 bosses and considerable decoration, but no characters. There are four pairs of animals (not the *ssu shen*),

[a] For this aspect of the subject, see Umehara (1955), pp. 254 f.; and Suzuki, pp. 5–6, and the short entry for *Hō-sei-kyō* in the *Dictionary of Japanese Archaeology*, p. 493 (*Nihon kōkogaku jiten*, Tokyo, 1962).

and in place of the outer inscription, chevrons and cloud-scroll, there is a patterned geometric scroll.

4. See Umehara (1955), pp. 255–6, for a mirror found at Inari, Kyoto; there are irregular features, as in nos. 1 and 3 above; and it is 'decorated on the back with a pipe-like design projecting from the outer band' (Umehara, *loc. cit.*).

Appendix five

Mirrors dated to a specified year

It has been suggested above that there are reasons for believing that the two TLV mirrors whose inscriptions bear the dates of AD 10 and AD 15 are spurious, in the sense that they were made long after the dates specified, at a time when antiquaries were evincing a striking interest in artefacts of an earlier age. These suspicions are somewhat supported by an examination of other mirrors whose inscriptions mention comparatively early dates, and by the existence of similar grounds for suspicion for most of the mirrors dated in this way before AD 145. The following mirrors are concerned.

(a) Umehara (1943), no. 1 (pp. 6–7 and Plate I); and Umehara (1955), p. 239, fig. 1.

According to the classification of the Shao-kou report this mirror would be placed in type 8, and dated in period V, i.e. in the middle of the eastern Han. However, the inscription bears the date of AD 6. The mirror was found in Korea, as a result of a privately conducted excavation; and if it is accepted as a genuine product of that date, it constitutes reason to modify the conclusions reached in Shao-kou. However, there are some odd and somewhat inconsistent features on the mirror. The inscription is in 'squared characters', which are not seen in mirrors which may be accepted as dating from that time (i.e. Wang Mang's dynasty of Hsin). In addition the mirror bears two bands of chevron decoration, which are not seen in other mirrors of type 8. These features may either be regarded as signs of individual designing which were tried before the style of type 8 mirrors became rigidly fixed; alternatively they may be regarded as signs of subsequent fabrication, in which the details chosen by the artist from earlier practices were not completely true to type.

(b) Liu 16.65a

Unfortunately the details of this remarkable example are by no means clear, and certain basic information, such as the depth of the relief, is not available. The design of the mirror is entirely different from any that are known for the Han or the Hsin periods, and the text of the inscription, which mentions a date corresponding with AD 8, is of a form that varies radically from others of that time. The text bears a propagandist message of support for the Hsin dynasty that is couched in terms that are reminiscent of Wang Mang's proclamation of accession (HS 99A.35b; HFHD, vol. 3, p. 255).

The inscription dates the mirror in the following terms: *Hsin Ch'u-shih yüan nien sui tsai mou-ch'en*. Ch'u-shih was adopted as the regnal title on the day *mou-wu* of the eleventh month of the third year of Chü-she, i.e. 31 December AD 8 (HS 99A.35a; HFHD, vol. 3, p. 251 f.). However, the dynastic title of Hsin, which is also inscribed on the mirror, was not adopted until ten days later, i.e. on the day *mou-ch'en*, or 10 January AD 9 (HS 99A.36a; HFHD, vol. 3, p. 257); and an edict of that very day ordered a further change of regnal title, to Shih chien kuo, to take effect five days later (HS 99A.36a; HFHD, vol. 3, p. 258). Thus, the initial part of the formula used for dating the mirror was valid for the very short period of six days, i.e. 10 to 15 January AD 9; and strictly speaking the mirror should have been designed and completed within that very short space of time.

Three further factors have a bearing on the authenticity of the mirror.

(1) The style of dating a year by reference to the terms of the sexagenary cycle, as is done here, is not seen on Han mirrors, and it is questionable whether it was used on official documents at the time.
(2) There is some doubt regarding the expression actually adopted for the regnal title from 31 December AD 8 (see HFHD, vol. 3, p. 252, note 35.3, for the question whether the title was Ch'u-shih or Shih-ch'u).
(3) the calligraphic style of the inscription is archaised, being very different from that of mirrors whose inscriptions refer to the Hsin dynasty. (For the use of archaised styles of calligraphy see Appendix six.)

(c) X 1004, i.e. Umehara (1943), no. 2 (pp. 7–9 and Plate II); see pp. 170, 210 above and Appendix one

(d) X 1005, i.e. Umehara (1943), no. 3 (pp. 9–11 and Plate I); see pp. 170, 210 above and Appendix one

(e) Umehara (1943), no. 4 (pp. 11–12 and Plate III)

The style of this mirror approximates to those of types 8.1 and 8.2 of Shao-kou, which are dated in the middle or later part of eastern Han. The inscription, which is placed in a somewhat different situation as compared with other examples of these types, dates the piece in AD 64, and it is not beyond the bounds of possibility that it was added

PLATE XXVII
Decorated ends of the third coffin, tomb no. 1 Ma-wang-tui; 92 by 89 cm; original colouring, gold, white, scarlet and black.

PLATE XXVIII
The suppliant's path to paradise; from a fresco at Ying-ch'eng-tzu, Liaoning; approximately 3 by 2½ metres. The suppliant is shown in a series of postures in the lower register, and re-appears in the upper register, accompanied by an acolyte, to be greeted by the creatures who inhabit the world to come.

Appendix five – Mirrors dated to a specified year

subsequently to the manufacture of the mirror, at the cost of defacing part of the original decoration. As Umehara points out there is a further oddity in the terms of the four character inscription of the centre, which reads *I san po ching*. Despite these peculiarities, however, Umehara accepts the mirror and its inscription as genuine.

(f) Umehara (1943), no. 5 (pp. 12–14 and Plate IV)

The inscription is of TLV sub-type C 31 as described above, with the peculiar feature, not seen in mirrors of that sub-type, that the date of manufacture is specified, i.e. as the ninth month of the seventh year of Yung-p'ing (AD 64). In the main text of the inscription, the usual character *hsien* has been replaced by *i*.

The mirror does not carry the characteristic features of TLV mirrors, although there is an attempt to reproduce some of the *ssu shen*. The double line of chevron markings and the degree markings seen here also appear both on TLV and on other types. While it is not unusual to find that an inscription which appears typically on TLV mirrors is used on types evolved at a later stage, the attachment of this inscription to a design which does not bear the appropriate symbols would seem to be extremely odd for AD 64, i.e. at a time when TLV mirrors were in fashion. Umehara considers and rejects the supposition that the inscription was added at a later date, subsequently to the original manufacture.

(g) Umehara (1943), no. 6 (pp. 14–16 and Plate V)

The inscription of this mirror invokes the power of the King Father of the East and the Queen Mother of the West in order to procure the blessing of longevity, and specifies a date corresponding to AD 105. If this can be accepted as genuine it is of considerable importance in marking the existence of the cult at this time. However, there are reasons for doubting the validity of the inscription.

The inscription refers to an amnesty dated on the day *ping-wu* in the fifth month of the first year of Yüan-hsing, but according to the reconstructions of the calendar there was no day named with that term in the fifth month. HHS 4.15a dates the amnesty, together with the decision to adopt the *nien-hao* Yüan-hsing, on the day *keng-wu* of the fourth month; this date is likewise incorrect, as such a day did not occur during the month. Possibly the correct version is carried in the *Hou Han chi* 14.15a, which dates the amnesty on *ping-wu* in the fourth month, i.e. 24 May. Umehara observes the presence of several anomalies in the inscription and notes the difficulty of the dating.

(h) Umehara (1943), no. 7 (pp. 16–17).

This mirror was discovered in west China in 1937. It is reported to have carried two inscriptions, of which one specifies the day *Jen-wu* in the fifth month of the first year of Yüan-hsing (i.e. 9 July AD 105). In the absence of a facsimile (none was available to Umehara) comment would be inappropriate.

The next example included in Umehara (1943) (i.e. no. 8, pp. 17–19, Plate VI) is dated in AD 145. (For an irregular TLV mirror whose inscription refers to the first year of Yung-ho, see X 9001 in Appendix one.)

Appendix six[*]

Decorative features and calligraphic styles in mirrors

The foregoing study of the different types of TLV mirror and their inscriptions suggests that the pattern was first seen, decoratively, on Ts'ao-yeh and Shou-chou mirrors, where it was accompanied by short and simple inscriptions expressing a hope or prayer for earthly happiness. Later the pattern appears symbolically, in order to ensure felicity in a wider context and in a higher form of existence; and at this stage the design may have been affected by the shape of the diviner's board. In the first stages of the regular TLV mirrors the prayers for cosmic bliss were implicit (sub-type D 10); but they shortly became explicit (sub-types C 11, C 12, C 19). They were concerned next with philosophical aspects (sub-types of C 2) and later, by way of a transitional stage (sub-types of C 3), with the paradisal aspirations (sub-types of C 4 and C 50).

Such were the mirrors produced when the fashion for TLV was at its height and in its purest form. Later when the symbolism and its significance had been forgotten, features of the design were used irregularly, improperly, or purely for decorative purposes (sub-types C 13, D 20 and X); and the design occasionally incorporates allusions to a further stage of imagery, that of the Queen Mother of the West.

In historical terms, a growing popularity was attending the spread of the ideas of *Wu hsing* and Yin Yang from perhaps 60 BC onwards, and their propagation is associated with names such as Liu Hsiang (79–8 BC), Liu Hsin (died AD 23) and Wang Mang. It may therefore be asked whether a corresponding development may be traced in the decorative features of the mirrors, accompanying the changes noted in the types and contents of the inscriptions. The main contributors to this aspect of the subject are Karlgren, Umehara, Miss Bulling, Suzuki and Hayashi.[1]

In general, precise criteria cannot be formulated so as to trace the chronological development of different decorative details. The period in which the TLV mirrors developed is in any event relatively short,

[*] For notes, see p. 229.

and it is unlikely that an orderly line of ancestry can be traced, whereby one form yielded place to another. There are however some points which can be recognized as parts of an overall tendency, and which may apply to the development of mirrors and their designs both before and after the period when TLV mirrors were at the height of their popularity.

As time proceeded, so the mirrors became thicker and carried heavier rims. The central boss developed from a somewhat slender loop to become a heavy knob; and low relief patterns gave place to modelling in high relief. Miss Bulling[2] has also observed that 'In general, there is a growing tendency in the course of the later part of the first century BC and AD to simplify the designs of the central fields.' Attention will be directed here to two further aspects only: the number of animals depicted on the mirrors; and the calligraphic style of the inscriptions.

There is a general tendency for the number of the animals, birds and mythological creatures to diminish. Some of the regular types (e.g., C 2103, C 3101) are embellished by a large number of animals, in which the four beasts of the cosmos take pride of place (see Plates XII–XIV). This large number may perhaps be compared with the number seen on the diviner's boards, but in the absence of more examples of those boards such comparison cannot be taken too far.

However, it seems that in time the multiplicity and charming variety of animals gave place to a mere four pairs of animals only; and whereas the size of the animals and birds had varied considerably when they were depicted in large numbers, when they were reduced to eight only these are moulded in the same uniform size (e.g., C 4112, C 4126; see Plate XV). Sometimes the pairs are shown confronting one another; sometimes they consist of two mirror images of the same creature. These pairs are then reduced even further, until some mirrors were adorned with the four animals alone and sometimes these were shown bestriding the Ts rather than being enclosed within them.[3] As a final development, when the TLV style has given place to its successors, there are a number of examples of mirrors fashioned in high relief in which four, or then three, animals are depicted.[4]

In his study of the development of Han and Huai styles, Karlgren discusses the different types of script that are seen in the inscriptions.[5] He traces the evolution of the *li-shu* style, its particular forms in those inscriptions and the stages whereby this style became modified, to reach a point of close affinity with its successor, i.e. *k'ai-shu*. While noting that the sample of inscriptions open to inspection is small, Karlgren concludes on statistical grounds that during the period 109 to 3 BC there was a decreasing use of Lesser Seal and an increasing

Appendix six – Decorative features and calligraphic styles in mirrors

use of 'modernised script', i.e. *li-shu*, modified in the way described.

Five major calligraphic styles may be distinguished in the outer inscriptions of TLV mirrors:

1. Squared characters; stylization has been effected by reducing curved lines to straight lines wherever possible. The style is seen on Ts'ao-yeh mirrors (e.g., Bulling (1960), Plate 15) and on a mirror of that type which bears the TLV marks (A 0001). It is also seen on other mirrors that are not of TLV type (e.g., Lo-yang no. 66; Ch'ang-sha, Plate 67, no. 3). The style is seen on a few regular TLV mirrors such as C 1901, C 1902, C 2404 (see Plates VIII, XI).
2. Lesser Seal; for the short currency of this script, see Karlgren and Bulling.⁶ The style is exemplified in Bulling *ib.*, Plate 8, and TLV mirrors such as B 0001, B 0002, B 0003.
3. *Li-shu*; the normal style used in most of the regular types of TLV mirrors, e.g., C 1201, C 1206 (see Plate VII).
4. Ornate *li-shu*, developed in a somewhat precious way that varies from the *pa-fen* style of the eastern Han period stone stele (*pa-fen* would hardly be suitable for inscription on the narrow bands of the mirrors);⁷ e.g., C 1302, C 1903, X 1006, X 9003 (see Plates IX, XX).
5. An archaised script, which attempts to simulate some versions of Greater Seal, in a complex and somewhat unrealistic manner; e.g., X 1002, X 1004.

Notes to Appendix six

1. See Karlgren (1941), pp. 39 f. on rims; p. 70 on background patterns; pp. 81 f. on dragons; p. 96 on Shou-chou mirrors; Umehara (1943), pp. 135 f; Bulling (1960), pp. 59 f. for centre-fields, border patterns, animal figures and immortals; H. Suzuki, in Moriya, pp. 3 f.; and Hayashi (1973, 1), pp. 14 f.
2. Bulling (1960), p. 61.
3. See C 2404, D 2009, D 2018 (Plates XI, XVIII).
4. See Bulling (1960), Plate 65 (dated AD 189 and not 139, as printed); for three-animal type mirrors, see Shao-kou type 13 (as noted in Appendix Four above), Shao-kou, fig. 77.6; Lo-yang (mirrors), p. 99.
5. Karlgren (1947), pp. 19 f. For a summary of the different types of script, see WW 1962.6, pp. 30 f. and the introductory chapters by Umehara and Kanda Kiichirō in Shodō (pp. 1–10 and 13–21). For other references, see note 30 to chapter Three above.
6. Karlgren (1941), pp. 15 f.; Bulling (1960), p. 16.
7. For examples of *pa-fen* styles, see Shodō Plates 100, 101, 118, 119.

List of books cited and abbreviations used

The following list is not intended to be a full bibliography of works which relate to the subjects under study in this book. In general it does not include publications which have appeared since 1974. An asterisk* marks titles which are mentioned by other scholars but which have not been available for consultation directly.

Unless stated otherwise, references to Chinese texts are to the *Ssu-pu ts'ung-k'an* print. A number of modern Chinese writings are not signed individually and appear simply under the name of the committee responsible for the work. In the list which follows the use of the term 'Anon' has been reduced to a minimum, in order to avoid inconvenience; where possible, catch-words from the title of a book have been adopted as abbreviations (e.g., Ch'ang-sha or Wu-wei).

Figures in brackets [ ] refer to the list of characters for Chinese and Japanese titles which follow below.

An Chih-min 'Ch'ang-sha hsin fa-hsien ti hsi Han po-hua shih t'an'; KK 1973.1, pp. 43–53 [1]

Anon (1) 'Kuan-yü Ch'ang-sha Ma-wang-tui i hao Han mu ti tso-t'an chi-yao'; by the editorial board of *Kaogu*; KK 1972.5, pp. 37–42. [2]

Anon (2) 'Tso-t'an Ch'ang-sha Ma-wang-tui i hao Han mu'; WW 1972.9, pp. 52–73 [3]

Anon (3) 'Ch'ang-sha Ma-wang-tui i hao Han mu kuan-kuo mu-ts'ai chien-ting'; by the Timber Research Department, Kiangsi; KK 1973.2, p. 128 [4]

Anon (4) 'Ch'ang-sha Ma-wang-tui Han mu nü shih chin-hsing liao chieh-p'ou wei k'o-hsüeh yen-chiu t'i-kung liao feng-fu tz'u-liao'; WW 1973.7, p. 73 [5]

Anon (5) 'Ma-wang-tui i hao Han mu nü shih yen-chiu ti chi ko wen-t'i'; WW 1973.7, pp. 74–80 [6]

Anon (6) 'Ch'ang-sha Ma-wang-tui i hao Han mu ch'u-t'u ti jung-chuan chin'; KKHP 1974.1, pp. 175–186 [7]

Anon (7) 'Ch'ang-sha Tzu-tan-k'u chan-kuo mu-kuo mu'; WW 1974.2, pp. 36–40 [8]

Anon (8) 'Ch'ang-sha Ma-wang-tui erh, san hao Han mu fa-chüeh chien pao'; WW 1974.7, pp. 39–48 [9]

Bauer W. Bauer, *China und die Hoffnung auf Glück*; München, 1971 (English edition: *China and the search for happiness*; New York, 1976)

List of books cited and abbreviations used

Bielenstein	Hans Bielenstein, 'The Restoration of the Han Dynasty'; BMFEA 26, 1954, pp. 1–209
Biot	E. Biot, *Le Tcheou-li*; Paris, 1851
Blacker	Carmen Blacker, *The Catalpa Bow*; London, 1975
BMFEA	Bulletin of the Museum of Far Eastern Antiquities
Bodde (1961)	Derk Bodde, 'Myths of Ancient China'; originally published in S. N. Kramer, *Mythologies of the Ancient World*, New York, 1961; reprinted in Chun-shu Chang, *The Making of China*, New Jersey, 1975
Bodde (1975)	Derk Bodde, *Festivals in Classical China*, Princeton, 1975
Boyle	J. A. Boyle, 'The Hare in Myth and Reality: a Review Article'; *Folklore* 84, 1973, pp. 313–26
Bulling (1955)	A. Bulling, 'The Decoration of some mirrors of the Chou and Han Periods'; Artibus Asiae, 18.1, 1955, pp. 20–43
Bulling (1960)	A. Bulling, *The Decoration of Mirrors of the Han Period*; Ascona, 1960
Bulling (1974)	A. Bulling, 'The Guide of the Souls picture in the western Han tomb in Ma-wang-tui near Ch'ang-sha'; *Oriental Art* XX.2, 1974, pp. 158–73
Bushell	S. W. Bushell, *Chinese Art*, vols. I–II; London, 1904
Butterworth	E. A. S. Butterworth, *The Tree at the Navel of the Earth*; Berlin, 1970
Cammann (1948)	Schuyler Cammann, 'The "TLV" pattern on cosmic mirrors of the Han Dynasty'; JAOS 68, 1948, pp. 159–67
Cammann (1950)	Schuyler Cammann, 'Suggested origin of the Tibetan Mandala paintings'; *The Art Quarterly*, Spring 1950, pp. 107–17
Cammann (1953)	Schuyler Cammann, 'Types of Symbols in Chinese Art', in Arthur F. Wright, *Studies in Chinese Thought*, University of Chicago Press, 1953, pp. 195–231
Chan	Wing-tsit Chan, *A Source Book in Chinese Philosophy*; London, 1963
Chang	Chang An-chih, 'Hsi Han po-hua ti i-shu ch'eng-chiu'; WW 1973.9, pp. 66–70 [10]
Chang Hsin-cheng	Chang Hsin-cheng, *Wei shu t'ung-k'ao*; Shanghai, 1957 [11]
Chang Hung-yüan	Chang Hung-yüan, 'Ch'ang-sha Han mu chih-hsiu p'in ti t'i-hua ho yin-hua'; WW 1972.9, pp. 50–1 [12]
Chang Kwang-chih	Chang Kwang-chih, *Early Chinese Civilisation: Anthropological Perspectives*; Cambridge, Massachusetts, and London, 1976
Ch'ang-sha	*Ch'ang-sha fa-chüeh pao-kao*; Peking, 1957 [13]
Chavannes (1893)	Edouard Chavannes, *La sculpture sur pierre en Chine au temps des deux dynasties Han*: Paris, 1893
Chavannes (1913)	Edouard Chavannes, *Mission Archéologique dans la Chine Septentrionale*; Paris, 1913
Chavannes	See also MH
Chekiang	*Che-chiang ch'u-t'u t'ung ching hsüan-chi*, ed. Wang Shih-lun; Peking, 1958 [14]
Ch'en (1936)	Ch'en Meng-chia, 'Ku wen-tzu chung chih Shang Chou chi-ssu'; *Yen-ching hsüeh-pao* 19, 1936, pp. 91–155 [15]
Ch'en (1965)	Ch'en Meng-chia, 'Han chien nien-li piao-hsü'; KKHP 1965.2, pp. 103–49 [16]

Ch'en Chih	Ch'en Chih, 'Ch'ang-sha Ma-wang-tui i hao Han mu ti jo-kan wen-t'i k'ao-shu'; WW 1972.9, pp. 30–5 [17]
Cheng (1933)	Cheng Te-k'un, 'The Travels of Emperor Mu'; *Journal of the North China Branch of the Royal Asiatic Society*, 64, 1933, pp. 124–142
Cheng (1957)	Cheng Te-k'un, '*Yin-yang Wu-hsing* and Han Art'; HJAS 20, 1957, pp. 162–86
Cheng (1963)	Cheng Te-k'un, *Archaeology in China*; vol. 3, *Chou China*; Cambridge, 1963
Ch'iu Hsi-kuei	Ch'iu Hsi-kuei, 'Ts'ung Ma-wang-tui i hao Han mu "ch'ien-ts'e" t'an kuan-yü ku li ti i-hsieh wen-t'i'; KK 1974.1, pp. 46–55 [18]
Chow	Fong Chow, 'Ma-wang-tui: a Treasure-trove from the Western Han Dynasty'; *Artibus Asiae* XXXV, 1/2, 1973, pp. 5–24
Chu Hung-fu	Chu Hung-fu and Wang Lin-yao, 'Ch'ang-sha Ma-wang-tui i hao Han mu chung ch'u-t'u ti k'un-ch'ung shih-t'i'; KK 1973.1, pp. 62–4 [19]
Chu-shu chi-nien	See Fan
Ch'u tz'u	References are to the SPPY edition
Ch'ü	T'ung-tsu Ch'ü, *Han Social Structure*; Seattle and London, 1972
Couvreur	S. Couvreur, *Li Ki ou Mémoires sur les Bienséances et les Cérémonies*; Ho Kien Fou, 1913
Creel (1970)	Herrlee G. Creel, *The Origins of Statecraft in China*, volume One; Chicago, 1970
Creel (1974)	Herrlee G. Creel, *Shen Pu-hai A Chinese Political Philosopher of the Fourth Century B.C.*; Chicago, 1974
Cull	See Yetts
CYYY	Bulletin of the Institute of History and Philology, Academia Sinica, Shanghai and Taipei
de Bary	W. de Bary *et al.*, *Sources of Chinese Tradition*; New York, 1960
Diény	J-P. Diény, *Les Dix-neuf Poèmes Anciens*; Paris, 1963
Doi	Doi Yoshiko, 'Hakuga no etoki'; *Shūkan Asahi*, supplement 9–10, 1972, pp. 86–9 [20]
Dubs (1942)	Homer H. Dubs, 'An ancient Chinese mystery cult'; *Harvard Theological Review*, XXXV, 1942, pp. 221–40
Dubs (1958)	Homer H. Dubs, 'The beginning of Chinese astronomy'; JAOS 78.4, 1958, pp. 295–300
Dubs (1959)	Homer H. Dubs, 'Han "Hill Censers"'; *Studia Serica Bernhard Karlgren dedicata*, Copenhagen, 1959, pp. 259–64
Dubs	See also HFHD
Eberhard (1942)	W. Eberhard, *Lokalkulturen im alten China*, vols. 1–2; Leiden, 1942
Eberhard (1970)	W. Eberhard, *Sternkunde und Weltbild im alten China*; *gesammelte Aufsätze*; Chinese Materials and Research Aids Center, Taipei, 1970
Eichhorn	Werner Eichhorn, *Die Religionen Chinas*; Stuttgart, 1973
Eliade (1954)	Mircea Eliade, *The Myth of the Eternal Return*; New York, 1954
Eliade (1957)	Mercia Eliade, *Myths, Dreams and Mysteries*; London, 1957
Eliade (1958)	Mircea Eliade, *Patterns in Comparative Religion*; London and Sydney, 1958
Eliade (1961)	Mircea Eliade, *Images and Symbols*; London, 1961

List of books cited and abbreviations used

Eliade (1964)	Mircea Eliade, *Shamanism: Archaic Techniques of Ecstasy*; London, 1964
Erkes	Eduard Erkes, 'Chinesisch-Amerikanische Mythen Parallelen'; *T'oung Pao* 24, 1926, pp. 32–53
Evans and Thomson	George Ewart Evans and David Thomson, *The Leaping Hare*; London, 1972
Fairbank	Wilma Fairbank, *Adventures in Retrieval: Han Murals and Shang bronze molds*; Cambridge, Massachusetts, 1972
Fan	Fan Hsiang-yung, *Ku-pen chu-shu chi-nien chi-chiao ting-pu*; Shanghai, 1956 [21]
Fan Ning	Fan Ning, 'Niu-lang chih-nü ku-shih ti yen-pien'; *Wen-hsüeh i-ch'an tseng-k'an* 1, pp. 421–33, Peking, 1955 [22]
Feng	Feng Yün-p'eng and Feng Yün-yüan, *Chin so*; 1821 (partly reproduced in Uchino); ch. 6 (foliation as in Uchino) [23]
Finsterbusch	Käte Finsterbusch, *Verzeichnis und Motivindex der Han-Darstellungen*; Wiesbaden, vol. 1, 1966, vol. 2, 1971
Forke	Alfred Forke, *Lun-heng*, vols. 1–2; original edition 1907; reprinted New York, 1962
Frazer	James George Frazer, *The Worship of Nature*; London, 1926
Freedman	See Granet (Freedman)
Fu-chai	*Fu-chai ts'ang ching*, ed. Ch'en Chieh-ch'i; Shanghai, 1925 [24]
Gotō	Gotō Shūichi, *Kan shiki kyō* (*Nihon kōkogaku taikei*, 1), 1926 [25]
Graham	A. C. Graham, *The Book of Lieh-tzu*; London, 1960
Granet (1926)	Marcel Granet, *Danses et Légendes de la Chine ancienne*; Paris, 1926
Granet (Freedman)	Marcel Granet, *The Religion of the Chinese People* (translated and edited by M. Freedman); Oxford, 1975
Hansford	S. Howard Hansford, *Chinese Carved Jades*; London, 1968
Harada	See Lo-lang (Harada)
Hawkes	David Hawkes, *Ch'u Tz'u, The Songs of the South*; Oxford, 1959
Hayashi (1969)	M. Hayashi, 'Chūgoku kodai no saigyoku, zuigyoku'; THG 40, 1969, pp. 161–323 [26]
Hayashi (1971)	M. Hayashi, 'Chōsha shutsudo So hakusho no jū ni shin no yurai'; THG 42, 1971, pp. 1–63 [27]
Hayashi (1973,1)	M. Hayashi, 'Kan kyō no zuhyō ni, san ni tsuite'; THG 44, 1973, pp. 1–65 [28]
Hayashi (1973,2)	M. Hayashi, 'Chōsha Baōtai ichi gō bo shutsudo no hakuga'; Museum 267, Tokyo, 1973, pp. 4–14 [29]
Hayashi (1973,3)	M. Hayashi, 'Haigyoku to shu'; THG 45, 1973, pp. 1–57 [30]
Hayashi (1974)	M. Hayashi, 'Kandai kishin no sekai'; THG 46, 1974, pp. 223–306 [31]
Hervouet (1964)	Yves Hervouet, *Un poète de cour sous les Han: Sseu-ma Siang-jou*; Paris, 1964
Hervouet (1972)	Yves Hervouet, *Le chapitre 117 du Che-ki*; Paris, 1972
HFHD	Homer H. Dubs, *The History of the Former Han Dynasty*, vols. 1–3, Baltimore and London, 1938–55
HHS	*Hou-Han-shu* and *Hsü-Han-shu*; references are to Wang Hsien-ch'ien, *Hou-Han-shu chi-chieh*, Ch'ang-sha, 1915 [32]
Hightower	James Robert Hightower, *The Poetry of T'ao Ch'ien*, Oxford, 1970

233

Higuchi	T. Higuchi, *Kodai Chūgoku wo hakkutsusuru*; Tokyo, 1975 [33]
HJAS	Harvard Journal of Asiatic Studies
HNT	*Huai-nan-tzu*; references are to Liu Wen-tien, *Huai-nan hung-lieh chi-chieh*; Commercial Press, 1926 (reprinted, Taipei, 1969) [34]
HS	*Han-shu*; references are to Wang Hsien-ch'ien, *Han-shu pu-chu*, Ch'ang-sha, 1900 [35]
Hsi Han po-hua	*Hsi Han po-hua* (album of photographs of the painting from Ma-wang-tui); Peking, 1972 [36]
Huai-nan-tzu	See HNT
Huang	Huang Sheng-chang and Niu Chung-hsün, 'Yu kuan Ch'ang-sha Ma-wang-tui Han mu ti li-shih wen-t'i'; WW 1972.9, pp. 22–9 [37]
Hulsewé (1955)	A. F. P. Hulsewé, *Remnants of Han Law*; Leiden, 1955
Hulsewé (1965)	A. F. P. Hulsewé, 'Texts in Tombs'; Asiatische Studien xviii/xix, 1965, pp. 78–79
Hulsewé (1975)	A. F. P. Hulsewé, 'The problem of the authenticity of *Shih-chi*, ch. 123, the memoir on Ta Yüan'; *T'oung Pao*, vol LXI, 1–3, 1975, pp. 83–147
Hu-nan	*Hu-nan ch'u-t'u t'ung ching t'u-lu*; Peking, 1960 [38]
I-nan	Tseng Chao-yü, *I-nan ku hua-hsiang shih-mu fa-chüeh pao-kao*; Shanghai, 1956 [39]
Izushi	Y. Izushi, *Shina shinwa densetsu no kenkyū*; Tokyo, 1943 [40]
JAOS	Journal of the American Oriental Society
Kaltenmark	Max Kaltenmark, *Le Lie-sien tchouan*; Peking, 1953
Kao	Kao Yao-t'ing, 'Ma-wang-tui i hao Han mu sui-tsang-p'in chung kung-shih yung ti shou lei'; WW 1973.9, pp. 76–8 [41]
Kao Ming	Kao Ming, 'Ch'ang-sha Ma-wang-tui i hao Han mu "Kuan jen" yung'; KK 1973.4, pp. 255–57 [42]
Kaplan	Sidney M. Kaplan, 'On the Origin of the TLV Mirror'; *Revue des Arts Asiatiques*, XI, 1937, pp. 21–4
Karlgren (1931)	Bernhard Karlgren, 'The early History of the Chou Li and Tso Chuan texts'; BMFEA 3, 1931, pp. 1–59
Karlgren (1934)	Bernhard Karlgren, 'Early Chinese Mirror Inscriptions'; BMFEA 6, 1934, pp. 9–79
Karlgren (1941)	Bernhard Karlgren, 'Huai and Han'; BMFEA 13, 1941, pp. 1–125
Karlgren (1944)	Bernhard Karlgren, 'Glosses on the Siao Ya Odes'; BMFEA 16, 1944, pp. 25–169
Karlgren (1946)	Bernhard Karlgren, 'Legends and Cults in Ancient China'; BMFEA 18, 1946, pp. 199–365
Karlgren (1950)	Bernhard Karlgren, *The Book of Odes*; Stockholm, 1950
Karlgren (GSR)	Bernhard Karlgren, 'Grammata Serica Recensa'; BMFEA 29, 1957, pp. 1–332
Kinenkyō	See Umehara (1943)
KK	*Kaogu* (sometimes written *Kao ku*, *K'ao-ku*) and its predecessor *K'ao-ku t'ung-hsün* [43]
KKHP	*K'ao-ku hsüeh-pao* (also written *Kaogu Xuebao*) [44]
Komai	K. Komai, *Chūgoku kokyō no kenkyū*; Tokyo, 1953 [45]
Kominami	I. Kominami, 'Seiōbo to shichi seki denshō'; THG 46, 1974, pp. 33–81 [46]

List of books cited and abbreviations used

Ku	Ku T'ieh-fu, 'Shih lun Ch'ang-sha Han mu ti pao-ts'un t'iao-chien'; KK 1972.6, pp. 53–8 [47]
Kuo Mo-jo	Kuo Mo-jo, 'T'ao-tu, Nü-kua, Chia-ling'; WW 1973.1, pp. 2–6 [48]
Kuo Mo-jo	See also Lo-yang (2)
Lao	Lao Kan, *Chü-yen Han-chien t'u-pan chih pu*; Taipei, 1957 [49]
Laufer (1909)	Berthold Laufer, *Chinese pottery of the Han Dynasty*; Leiden, 1909
Laufer (1911)	Berthold Laufer, *Chinese Grave Sculptures of the Han Period*; New York, London and Paris, 1911
Layard	J. W. Layard, *The Lady of the Hare*; London, 1944
Liebenthal	W. Liebenthal, 'The immortality of the soul in Chinese thought'; *Monumenta Nipponica* VIII, 1952, pp. 327 f.
Liu	Liu T'i-chih, *Hsiao-chiao-ching-ko chin-wen t'a-pen*; 1935 (partly reproduced in Uchino) [50]
Liu Ping-sen	Liu Ping-sen, 'Lin mo Ma-wang-tui hsi Han po-hua ti tien-ti t'i-hui'; WW 1973.9, pp. 71–5 [51]
Lo	Lo Chen-yü, *Ku ching t'u-lu*; 1916 [52]
Lo K'un	Lo K'un, 'Kuan-yü Ma-wang-tui Han mu po-hua ti shang-t'ao'; WW 1972.9, pp. 48–9 [53]
Lo-lang (Harada)	Y. Harada and K. Tazawa, *Rakurō, A Report on the Excavation of Wang Hsü's tomb in the Lo-lang province, an ancient Chinese colony in Korea*; Tokyo, 1930 [54]
Lo-lang (Painted Basket)	*Rakurō saikyō tsuka, the Tomb of painted basket of Lo-lang*; Kyoto, 1934 [55]
Lo-lang (Wang Kuang)	*Rakurō Ō Kō bo, the Tomb of Wang Kuang of Lo-lang*; Kyoto, 1935 [56]
Lo-yang (1)	'Lo-yang hsi Han pi-hua mu fa chüeh pao-kao'; KKHP 1964.2, pp. 107–24 [57]
Lo-yang (2)	'Lo-yang hsi Han mu pi-hua'; with a short explanation signed by Kuo Mo-jo; *Wen-wu ching-hua* 3, 1964, pp. 1–5 [58]
Lo-yang (Mirrors)	*Lo-yang ch'u-t'u ku ching liang Han pu fen*; Peking, 1959 [59]
Lo Yung-lin*	Lo Yung-lin, 'Shih lun niu-lang chih-nü'; *Min-chien wen-hsüeh chi-k'an ti erh pen*, Shanghai, 1957 [60]
Loewe (1966)	Michael Loewe, *Imperial China: The historical background to the modern age*; London, 1966
Loewe (1967)	Michael Loewe, *Records of Han Administration*, vols. 1–2; Cambridge, 1967
Loewe (1968)	Michael Loewe, *Everyday Life in Early Imperial China during the Han Period 202 BC–AD 220*; London, 1968
Loewe (1974,1)	Michael Loewe, *Crisis and Conflict in Han China*; London, 1974
Loewe (1974,2)	Michael Loewe, 'The campaigns of Han Wu-ti'; *Chinese Ways in Warfare*, edited by Frank A. Kierman and John K. Fairbank, Cambridge, Massachusetts, 1974
Loewe (1977)	Michael Loewe, 'Manuscripts found recently in China: a preliminary survey'; *T'oung Pao*, vol. LXIII, 2–3, 1977, pp. 99–136
Loewe (1978)	Michael Loewe, 'Man and Beast; the Hybrid in early Chinese art and literature'; *Numen*, xxv, 2, pp. 97–117
Lun-heng	References are to Huang Hui, *Lun-heng chiao-shih*; a reprint of Hu Shih's personally annotated copy, Taipei, 1969 (A. Forke, *Lun-heng: Philosophical Essays of Wang Ch'ung*, Shanghai and Leipzig, 1907–11; reprinted New York, 1962) [61]

Ma (1972)	Ma Yung, 'Tai hou ho Ch'ang-sha kuo ch'eng-hsiang'; WW 1972.9, pp. 14–21 [62]
Ma (1973)	Ma Yung, 'Lun Ch'ang-sha Ma-wang-tui i hao Han mu ch'u-t'u po-hua ti ming-ch'eng ho tso-yung'; KK 1973.2, pp. 118–25 [63]
Major	John S. Major, *Topography and Cosmology in Early Han Thought: Chapter Four of the* Huai-nan-tzu; doctoral thesis presented to Harvard University, 1973. I am indebted to the author for permission to quote from this work
Maspero (1924)	Henri Maspero, 'Légendes mythologiques dans le *Chou king*'; *Journale Asiatique*, CCIV, January to March 1924, pp. 1–100
Maspero (1950)	Henri Maspero, *Mélanges posthumes sur les religions et l'histoire de la Chine*; Paris, 1950
Maspero (1965)	Henri Maspero, *La Chine Antique*; revised edition, Paris, 1965
Mayers	W. F. Mayers, *The Chinese Reader's Manual*; Shanghai, 1924
MH	Edouard Chavannes, *Les Mémoires Historiques de Se-ma Ts'ien*; Paris, 1895–1905; republished, with an additional volume, Paris, 1967
Miyazaki	I. Miyazaki, 'Tai kō fujin setsu ni gigi ari'; *Shūkan Asahi*, supplement 9–10, 1972, pp. 133–4 [64]
Mizuno*	S. Mizuno, 'Hakucho hakki hakushin hakkyoku'; *Tōyōshi kenkyū*, NS, 1, 5–6, 1947, pp. 39–45 [65]
Moriya	*Moriya Kōzō shūshū hōkaku kiku shishin kyō zuroku*; Kyoto, 1969 [66]
MWT (report)	*Ch'ang-sha Ma-wang-tui i hao mu*, vols. 1–2; Peking, 1973 (Japanese edition, Heibonsha, Tokyo, 1976) [67]
MWT (summary)	*Ch'ang-sha Ma-wang-tui i hao Han mu fa-chüeh chien-pao*; Peking, 1972 (partly translated into English in Chow, pp. 15 f.) [68]
Nakayama	H. Nakayama, 'Koshiki Shina kyōkan enkaku'; *Kōkogaku zasshi* IX (1918–19), 2, pp. 85–101; 3, pp. 145–58; 4, pp. 189–212; 5, pp. 280–300; 6, pp. 323–40; 7, pp. 381–96; and 8, pp. 465–81 [69]
Needham	Joseph Needham, *Science and Civilisation in China*, vols. 1– ; Cambridge, 1954–
Ngo	Ngo Van Xuyet, *Divination Magie et Politique dans La Chine ancienne*; Paris, 1976
Nishimura	H. Nishimura (ed.), *Kan dai no bijutsu*; Osaka Municipal Museum of Arts, 1974 [70]
Niu	See Huang
Nott	S. C. Nott, Chinese Jade throughout the Ages; London, 1936
Olcott	W. T. Olcott, *Sun Lore of All Ages*, New York and London, 1914
Painted Basket	See Lo-lang (Painted Basket)
Pokora	Timotheus Pokora, *Hsin-lun (New Treatise) and other writings by Huan T'an (43 BC–28 AD)*; Ann Arbor, 1975
Rawson and Ayers	Jessica Rawson and John Ayers, *Chinese Jade throughout the Ages*; catalogue of an exhibition organized by the Arts Council of Great Britain and the Oriental Ceramic Society; London, 1975
Rudolph and Wen	Richard C. Rudolph and Yu Wen, *Han Tomb Art of West China*; Berkeley and Los Angeles, 1951

List of books cited and abbreviations used

Salmony	Alfred Salmony, *Antler and Tongue: an Essay on Ancient Chinese symbolism*; Ascona, 1954.
SC	*Shih-chi*; references are to Takigawa Kametarō, *Shiki kaichū kōshō*; Tokyo, 1932–34 [71]
Schipper	Kristofer Schipper, *L'Empereur Wou des Han dans la Légende Taoiste*; Paris, 1965
Schlegel	Gustav Schlegel, *Uranographie Chinoise*; The Hague, 1875
Schwabe	J. Schwabe, *Archetyp und Tierkreis, Grundlinien einer komischen Symbolik und Mythologie*; Basel, 1951
Seidel	Anna K. Seidel, 'The Image of the Perfect Ruler in Early Taoist Messianism: Lao-tzu and Li Hung'; *History of Religions*, 9, 2–3, 1969–70, pp. 216–47
Shan-hai-ching	See SHC
Shan-tung	*Shan-tung wen-wu hsüan-chi*, Peking, 1959 [72]
Shang	Shang Chih-t'an, 'Ma-wang-tui i hao Han mu "fei i" shih shih'; WW 1972.9, pp. 43–7 [73]
Shao-kou	*Lo-yang Shao-kou Han mu*; Peking, 1959 [74]
SHC	*Shan-hai-ching*; references are to the SPPY edition [75]
Shensi	*Shen-hsi sheng ch'u-t'u t'ung ching*; Peking, 1959]76]
Shih-chai-shan	*Yün-nan Chin-ning Shih-chai-shan ku mu-ch'ün fa-chüeh pao-kao*; Peking, 1959 [77]
Shih Wei	Shih Wei, 'Ch'ang-sha Ma-wang-tui i hao Han mu ti kuan-kuo chih-tu'; KK 1972.6, pp. 48–52 [78]
Shodō	*Shodō zenshū*; Heibonsha, Tokyo, vol 2, 1958 [79]
Sieffert	René Sieffert, 'La Lune au Japon'; in *La Lune Mythes et Rites* (see s.v. Soymié), pp. 323–37
Sivin	N. Sivin, 'Cosmos and Computation in Early Chinese Mathematical Astronomy'; *T'oung Pao*, LV 1–3, 1969, pp. 1–73
Soper	Alexander C. Soper, 'The purpose and date of the Hsiao-t'ang shan offering shrines: a modest proposal'; *Artibus Asiae*, XXXVI.4, 1974, pp. 249–66
Soymié	Michel Soymié, 'La Lune dans les religions Chinoises'; in *La Lune Mythes et Rites* (series *Sources Orientales*, Paris, 1962), pp. 289–319
SPPY	*Ssu-pu pei-yao* [80]
SPTK	*Ssu-pu ts'ung-k'an* [81]
Ssu-ch'uan	*Ssu-ch'uan Han tai hua-hsiang chuan t'a-p'ien*; Shanghai, 1961 [82]
Ssu-ch'uan (mirrors)	*Ssu-ch'uan sheng ch'u-t'u t'ung ching*; Peking, 1960 [83]
Stith Thompson	See Thompson
Sun (1)	Sun Tso-yün, 'Ch'ang-sha Ma-wang-tui i hao Han mu ch'u-t'u hua-fan k'ao-shih'; KK 1973.1, pp. 54–61 [84]
Sun (2)	Sun Tso-yün, 'Ma-wang-tui i hao Han mu ch'i kuan hua k'ao-shih'; KK 1973.4, pp. 247–54 [85]
Sun (3)	Sun Tso-yün, 'Lo-yang hsi Han Pu Ch'ien-ch'iu mu pi-hua k'ao-shih; WW 1977.6, pp. 17–22 [86]
Suzuki	H. Suzuki, 'Tai kō fujin no itai ha kataru'; *Shūkan Asahi*, supplement 9–10, 1972, p. 90 [87]
Suzuki, H.	Suzuki Hiroshi, explanatory description of the plates included in *Moriya*; Moriya, pp. 1–39

T'ang	*T'ang Sung t'ung ching*, edited by Shen Ts'ung-wen; Peking, 1958 [88]
THG	*Tōhō gakuhō*, Kyoto [89]
Thompson	Stith Thompson, *Motif-Index of Folk-Literature*; Copenhagen, 1955
Thomson	See Evans
Tjan	Tjan Tjoe Som, *Po Hu T'ung: the comprehensive discussions in the White Tiger Hall*; Leiden, 1949
TPYL	*T'ai-p'ing yü-lan* [90]
Uchino	K. Uchino, *Kan Gi hibun kimbun kyōmei sakuin*; Tokyo, 1966 [91]
Umehara (1920)	S. Umehara, *Kankyō no kenkyū*; Kyoto, 1920 [92]
Umehara (1933)	S. Umehara, *Shōkō kokyō shūei*; Kyoto, 1933 [93]
Umehara (1943)	S. Umehara, *Kan Sangoku Rikuchō kinen kyō zusetsu*; Kyoto, 1943 [94]
Umehara (1955)	S. Umehara, 'The late Mr. Moriya's collection of Ancient Chinese Mirrors' (translated by J. Harada); *Artibus Asiae*, XVIII, 1955, pp. 238–56
Umehara and Fujita	Umehara Sueji and Fujita Ryōsaku, *Chōsen ko bunka sōkan*, vol. 3, Tenri, 1959 [95]
von Zach	E. von Zach, *Die Chinesische Anthologie*; Cambridge, Massachusetts, 1958
Waley (1933)	Arthur Waley, 'The Book of Changes'; BMFEA 5, 1933, pp. 121–42
Waley (1937)	Arthur Waley, *The Book of Songs*; London, 1937
Waley (1946)	Arthur Waley, *Chinese Poems*; London, 1946
Waley (1955)	Arthur Waley, *The Nine Songs*; London, 1955
Waley (1955a)	Arthur Waley, 'The Heavenly Horses of Ferghana'; *History Today*, V.2, 1955, pp. 95–103
Wang Hsü	See Lo-lang (Harada)
Wang Kuang	See Lo-lang (Wang Kuang)
Wang Lin-yao	See Chu Hung-fu
Wang-tu (1955)	*Wang-tu Han mu pi-hua*; Peking, 1955 [96]
Wang-tu (1959)	*Wang-tu erh hao Han mu*; Peking, 1959 [97]
Watson (1963)	William Watson, *Handbook to the collections of early Chinese Antiquities*; London, 1963
Watson (1972)	William Watson, *Ancient Chinese Bronzes*; London, 1972
Watson (1973)	William Watson, *The Genius of China*; London, 1973
Watson, B.	Burton Watson, *Records of the Grand Historian of China*, vols. 1–2, New York and London, 1961
Wen-hua	*Wen-hua ta-ko ming ch'i-chien ch'u-t'u wen-wu*, vol. 1; Peking, 1972 [98]
Wen Yu	See Rudolph and Wen
Wu Shih-ch'ang	Wu Shih-ch'ang, 'Ts'ung Ma-wang-tui Han mu ch'u-t'u ti "Yü-mao t'ieh hua chüan" tao *Hung-lou-meng* chung ti "ch'üeh chin ch'iu"'; WW 1973.9, pp. 61–5 [99]
Wu-Tso-jen	Wu Tso-jen, 'Tu Ma-wang-tui hsi Han po-hua hou'; WW 1972.9, pp. 41–2 [100]
Wu-wei	*Wu-wei Han chien*; Peking, 1964 [101]
WW	*Wen wu*, and its predecessor *Wen-wu ts'an-k'ao tzu-liao* [102]

List of books cited and abbreviations used

Yamakawa	S. Yamakawa, *Baisenkyo zō Nihon shutsudo Kanshiki kyō zushū*; Osaka, 1923 [103]
Yang (1947)	L. S. Yang, 'A Note on the So-called TLV Mirrors and the game *Liu-po*'; HJAS 9, 1917, pp. 202–6
Yang (1952)	L. S. Yang, 'An Additional Note on the Ancient Game *Liu-po*'; HJAS 15, 1952, pp. 124–39
Yang Po-chün	Yang Po-chün, 'Lüeh t'an wo kuo shih-chi shang kuan-yü shih-t'i fang-fu ti chi-tsai ho Ma-wang-tui i hao Han mu mu chu wen-t'i'; WW 1972.9, pp. 36–40 [104]
Yen-t'ieh lun	See YTL
Yetts	W. P. Yetts, *The Cull Chinese Bronzes*; London, 1939
Ying-ch'eng-tzu	*Ying-ch'eng-tzu*; Archaeologia Orientalis, vol. IV; Tokyo and Kyoto, 1934 [105]
YTL	*Yen-t'ieh lun*; references are to Wang Li-ch'i, *Yen-t'ieh lun chiao-chu*, Shanghai, 1958; the page number is preceded by the number of the section (*p'ien*) in parentheses [106]
Yü Sheng-wu	Yü Sheng-wu, 'Kuan-yü Ch'ang-sha Ma-wang-tui i hao Han mu nei kuan kuan-shih ti chieh-shuo'; KK 1973.2, pp. 126–7 [107]
Yü Ying-shih	Yü Ying-shih, 'Life and Immortality in the Mind of Han China'; HJAS 25, 1964–5, pp. 80–122
Yüan	Yüan K'o, *Chung-kuo ku-tai shen-hua*; Shanghai, 1951 [108]

1) 安志敏　長沙新發現的西漢帛畫試探

2) 關于長沙馬王堆一號漢墓的座談記要

3) 座談長沙馬王堆一號漢墓

4) 長沙馬王堆一號漢墓棺槨木材的鑒定

5) 長沙馬王堆漢墓女尸進行了解剖為科學研究提供了豐富資料

6) 馬王堆一號漢墓女尸研究的幾個問題

7) 長沙馬王堆一號漢墓出土的絨圈錦

8) 長沙子彈庫戰國木槨墓

9) 長沙馬王堆二,三號漢墓發掘簡報

10) 張安志　西漢帛畫的藝術成就

11) 張心澂　偽書通考

12) 張宏源　長沙漢墓織綉品的提花和印花

13) 長沙發掘報告

14) 浙江出土銅鏡選集　王士倫

15) 陳夢家　古文字中之商周祭祀 燕京學報

16) 漢簡年曆表叙

17) 陳直　長沙馬王堆一號漢墓的若干問題考述

18) 裘錫圭從馬王堆一號漢墓"遣冊"談關于古隸的一些問題

19) 朱弘復　王林瑤　長沙馬王堆一號漢墓中出土的昆蟲尸体

List of books cited and abbreviations used

20) 土居淑子　帛畫のえとき　週刊朝日
21) 范祥雍　古本竹書紀年輯校訂補
22) 范寧　牛郎織女故事的演變　文學遺產增刊
23) 馮雲鵬　馮雲鵷　金索
24) 簠齋藏鏡　陳介祺
25) 後藤守一　漢式鏡　日本考古學大系
26) 林巳奈夫　中國古代の祭玉, 瑞玉
27) 長沙出土楚帛書の十二神の由來
28) 漢鏡の圖柄二、三について
29) 長沙馬王堆一號墓出土の帛畫
30) 佩玉と綬
31) 漢代鬼神の世界
32) 王先謙　後漢書集解
33) 樋口隆康　古代中國を發掘する
34) 劉文典　淮南鴻烈集解
35) 王先謙　漢書補注
36) 西漢帛畫

37) 黃盛璋　鈕仲勛　有關長沙馬王堆漢墓的歷史地理問題
38) 湖南出土銅鏡圖錄
39) 曾昭燏　沂南古畫象石墓發掘報告
40) 出石誠彥　支那神話傳說の研究
41) 高耀亭　馬王堆一號漢墓隨葬品中供食用的獸類
42) 高明　長沙馬王堆一號漢墓"冠人"俑
43) 考古　考古通訊
44) 考古學報
45) 駒井和愛　中國古鏡の研究
46) 小南一郎　西王母と七夕傳承
47) 顧鐵符　試論長沙漢墓的保存條件
48) 郭沫若　桃都，女媧，加陵
49) 勞榦　居延漢簡圖版之部
50) 劉體智　小校經閣金文拓本
51) 劉炳森　臨摹馬王堆西漢帛畫的點滴体會

List of books cited and abbreviations used

52) 羅振玉　古鏡圖錄
53) 羅琨　關于馬王堆漢墓帛畫的商討
54) 原田淑人　田澤金吾　樂浪
55) 樂浪彩篋冢
56) 樂浪王光墓
57) 洛陽西漢壁畫墓發掘報告
58) 洛陽西漢墓壁畫　郭沫若　文物精華
59) 洛陽出土古鏡　兩漢部分
60) 羅永麟　試論牛郎織女　民間文學集刊　第二本
61) 黃暉　論衡校釋
62) 馬雍　軑侯和長沙國丞相
63) 論長沙馬王堆一號漢墓出土帛畫的名稱和作用
64) 宮崎市定　軑侯夫人説に疑義あり　週刊朝日
65) 水野清一　博箸博冢博鎮博局　東洋史研究

66) 守屋孝藏蒐集　方格規矩四神鏡圖錄

67) 長沙馬王堆一號漢墓

68) 長沙馬王堆一號漢墓發掘簡報

69) 中山平次郎　古式支那鏡鑑沿革　考古學雜誌

70) 西村兵部　漢代の美術

71) 瀧川龜太郎　史記會注考證

72) 山東文物選集

73) 商志䫞　馬王堆一號漢墓"非衣"試釋

74) 洛陽燒溝漢墓

75) 山海經

76) 陝西省出土銅鏡

77) 雲南晉寧石寨山古墓群發掘報告

78) 史為　長沙馬王堆一號漢墓的棺椁制度

79) 書道全集　平凡社

80) 四部備要

List of books cited and abbreviations used

81) 四部叢刊
82) 四川漢代畫像磚拓片
83) 四川省出土銅鏡
84) 孫作云　長沙馬王堆一號漢墓出土畫幡考釋
85) 馬王堆一號漢墓漆棺畫考釋
86) 洛陽西漢卜千秋墓壁畫考釋
87) 鈴木尚　軑侯夫人の遺体は語る
88) 唐宋銅鏡　沈從文
89) 東方學報
90) 太平御覽
91) 内野熊一郎　漢魏碑文金文鏡銘索引
92) 梅原末治　鑑鏡の研究
93) 紹興古鏡聚英
94) 漢三國六朝紀年鏡圖説
95) 梅原末治,藤田亮策　朝鮮古文化綜鑑
96) 望都漢墓壁畫
97) 望都二號漢墓

98) 文化大革命期間出土文物
99) 吳世昌 從馬王堆漢墓出土的"羽毛貼花絹"到《紅樓夢》中的"雀金裘"
100) 吳作人 讀馬王堆西漢帛畫后
101) 武威漢簡
102) 文物，文物參考資料
103) 山川七左衛門 梅仙居藏日本出土漢式鏡圖集
104) 揚伯峻 略談我國史籍上關于尸體防腐的記載和馬王堆一號漢墓墓主問題
105) 營城子
106) 王利器 鹽鐵論校注
107) 于省吾 關于長沙馬王堆一號漢墓內棺棺飾的解說
108) 袁珂 中國古代神話

Glossary of Chinese and Japanese proper names and terms

An Ch'i 安期
An-hsi 安息
An-shun 安順
Chan 鱣
Chan-kuo 戰國
Ch'an 蟬
Chang 張
Chang 杖
Chang Ch'ien 張騫
Chang Heng 張衡
Chang Hua 張華
Chang I 張揖
Chang-wei 章尾
Ch'ang-ho 閶闔
Ch'ang i tzu sun lien-hu wen 長宜子孫連弧文
Ch'ang-sha 長沙
Ch'ang-sha Ch'u mu po-hua 長沙楚墓帛畫
Chao 昭
Chao-hun 招魂
Chao-ming 昭明
Ch'ao Ts'o 鼌錯
Chen-chiang 鎮江
Cheng-chou 鄭州
Cheng Chung 鄭眾
Cheng Hsüan 鄭玄
Cheng-i 正義
Ch'eng-hsiang 丞相
Ch'eng-huang 乘黃

Ways to Paradise

Chi (in the ten stems) 己	Chiao 鵁
Chi (services) 祭	Chieh ch'ung 介蟲
Chi 基	Chien (commentary) 箋
Chi-an 輯安	Chien (mirror) 鑑
Chi-yüan 濟源	Chien-chang 建章
Ch'i (seven) 七, 柒	Chien-mu 建木
Ch'i (board) 綦	Chien-p'ing 建平
Ch'i (type of horse) 騏	Ch'ien-niu 牽牛
Ch'i-chiao wen 乞巧文	Chih-nü 織女
Ch'i chung ch'ing ch'i 七種青氣	Ch'ih Sung 赤誦 (松)
	Ch'ih-tao-i 赤道儀
Ch'i hsiang 七襄	Chin-ch'eng 金城
Ch'i sheng 七勝	Chin Cho 晉灼
Chia chih 甲之	Chin-ch'üeh-shan 金雀山
Chia Ch'ung 賈充	Chin-shu 晉書
Chia-hsiang 嘉祥	Chin-wen ku-lin 金文詁林
Chia I 賈誼	Ching (essence) 精
Chiang-hsia 江夏	Ching (mirror) 鏡
Chiang-ling 江陵	Ching ch'u sui-shih-chi 荊楚歲時記
Ch'iang 羌	

Glossary of names and terms

Ching-pai 精白
Ching Wen 靜聞
Ching-yüan 景元
Ch'ing (green) 青
Ch'ing (musical instrument) 磬
Ch'ing-ch'iu 青丘
Chiu-chang suan-shu 九章算術
Chiu-ch'üan 酒泉
Chiu-ssu 九思
Chiu-t'an 九歎
Chiu yang 九陽
Chiu yeh 九野
Ch'iung-ch'iung chü-hsü 蛩蛩距虛
Chou ch'u 周處
Chou-Fa-kao 周法高
Chou-i 周易
Chou-li 周禮
Chu chüeh 朱爵

Chu Hsi 朱熹
Chu Lung 燭龍
Chu Po 朱博
Chu-shu chi-nien 竹書紀年
Chu Yu-tseng 朱右曾
Ch'u 楚
Ch'u Shao-sun 褚少孫
Ch'u-shih 初始
Ch'u tz'u 楚辭
Chuan Hsü 顓頊
Chuang-tzu 莊子
Ch'un-ch'iu fan-lu 春秋繁露
Ch'un-ch'iu yüan-ming-pao 春秋元命苞
Chung 蚤
Chung-hua shu-chü 中華書局
Chung-shan 中山

249

Ways to Paradise

Chü-hsü 巨虛
Chü-mang 句芒
Chü-she 居攝
Chü-yen 居延
Chü-yen Han-chien 居延漢簡
k'ao-cheng 考證
Chüan 卷
Ch'ü-ju 瞿如
Ch'ü Yüan 屈原
Ch'üan Tsu-wang 全祖望
Chün (commandery) 郡
Chün 踆
Chün-wu 踆烏
Daedong kang 大洞紅
Densetsu sesshōseki 傳說殺生石
Fan Hsiang-yung 范祥雍
Fang (constellation) 方
Fang-chang 方丈

Fang-hu 方壺
Fang-ko ssu-shen 方格四神
Fang-shih 方士
Fei-huang 飛黃
Fei-lien 飛廉
Fen-yin 汾陰
Feng 封
Feng-ch'ang 奉常
Feng-huang-shan 鳳凰山
Feng-su t'ung-i 風俗通義
Feng-t'u-chi 風土記
Fo-shan-shih 佛山市
Fu 傅
Fu An 傅安
Fu Hsi 伏羲
Fu-sang 扶桑
Fu Sheng 伏生
Hai 海

Glossary of names and terms

Hai-nei-ching 海內經

[Hai-nei] shih chou chi 海內十洲記

Hai-wai-ching 海外經

Han emperors:
    Ai ti 7–1 BC 哀帝
    Chang ti AD 75–89 章帝
    Chao ti 87–74 BC 昭帝
    Ching ti 157–141 BC 景帝
    Kao tsu 202–195 BC 高祖
    Ling ti AD 167–89 靈帝
    Wen ti 180–157 BC 文帝
    Wu ti 141–87 BC 武帝

Han-shu 漢書

Han Wei ts'ung-shu 漢魏叢書

Han Wu ku-shih 漢武故事

Han Wu-ti nei-chuan 漢武帝內傳

Han-yang 漢陽

Hao 好

Hao-I-hsing 郝懿行

Heng 姮

Heng O 姮娥

Hitomi T. 人見輝人

Ho-fei 合肥

Ho ku 河鼓

Ho-lin-ko-erh 和林格爾

Ho-p'u 合浦

Hō-sei-kyō 仿製鏡

Hou 侯

Hou Han-shu 後漢書

Hou Han-chi 後漢記

Hou t'u 后土

Hsi, Ho 羲和

Hsi Hsia sung 西狹頌

Hsi lao (mu) 西姥

Hsi mu 西母

Hsi wang mu 西王母

251

Ways to Paradise

Hsi wang mu chuan 西王母傳

Hsiang (chancellor) 相

Hsiang (loosen clothing) 襄

Hsiang-hsiang 湘鄉

Hsiao Chi 蕭吉

Hsiao t'ang shan 孝堂山

Hsiao-wei 校尉

Hsiao ya 小雅

Hsien 仙

Hsien Men 羨門

Hsien Men shih fa 羨門式法

Hsien-ti chuan 獻帝傳

Hsin 新

Hsin Ch'u-shih yüan nien 新初始元年

sui tsai mou-ch'en 歲在·戊辰

Hsin Chui 辛追

Hsin-fan 新繁

Hsin T'ang-shu 新唐書

Hsin-yang 信陽

Hsing 形

Hsing ching 星經

Hsing-yün 星雲

Hsiu 宿

Hsü Ch'i hsieh-chi 續齊諧記

Hsü Han-shu 續漢書

Hsü Shen 許慎

Hsü ti 須抵

Hsüan-chung-chi 玄中記

Hsüan-tsung hsiang-chuan 玄中象傳

Hsün-tzu 荀子

Hu 狐

Hu-liang 壺梁

Hua-hsiang 畫像

Hua Yang 華陽

Glossary of names and terms

Hua-yin 華陰	I-wen lei-chü 藝文類聚
Huai 槐	Inaba 稻羽
Huai-nan-tzu 淮南子	Jan 然
Huan Lin 桓驎	Jen 人
Huan T'an 桓譚	Jen huang 人皇
Huang 璜	Jen-wu 壬午
Huang-ch'u 黃初	Jen-wu hua-hsiang 人物畫像
Huang ch'üan 黃泉	
Huang-tao-i 黃道儀	Jih-kuang 日光
Huang-ti 黃帝	Jih shih chia mou 日時加某
Hun 魂	
Hung-ch'ing 洪慶	Jih-wei-shu 日緯書
Hung-ming-chi 弘明集	Jo 弱
Hung Ying-ming 洪應明	Jo-mu 若木
Huo Kuang 霍光	Ju 如
I 佚	Jui-ch'ang 瑞昌
I (archer) 羿	K'ai-ming 開明
I-ching 易經	K'ai-shu 楷書
I-nan 沂南	Kan-ch'üan 甘泉
I san po ching 宜三百竟	Kan lu 甘露

Ways to Paradise

Kan Pao 干寶
Kan Te 甘德
Kanda Kiichirō 神田喜一郎
Kao-tsu 高祖
K'ao-kung-chi 考工記
Keng Ping 耿秉
Keng-wu 庚武
Kojiki 古事記
Kōkogaku zasshi 考古學雜誌
Kominami 小南
Kou 鉤
Kou-mang 句芒
Ku hsiao-shuo kou-ch'en 古小說鉤沈
Ku K'ai-chih 顧愷之
Kuang wu 廣武
Kuang-ya 廣雅
Kuei (return) 歸

Kuei (spirit) 鬼
Kuei-chü 規矩
Kuei-yang 桂陽
K'uei-feng 夔鳳
Kun 鯀
K'un-lun 崑崙
Kung Kung 共工
Kuo (headdress) 幗
Kuo (family) 郭
Kuo Hsien 郭憲
Kuo P'u 郭璞
Kuo Sung 郭頌
Lao 老
Lao Kan 勞榦
Li 厲
Li-chi 禮記
Li Ch'ih 黎秩
Li Fu 黎扶
Li Fu-jen tien-chieh 李夫人典戒

Glossary of names and terms

Li Hsi 李豨
Li Hsien 李賢
Li-huo-lun 理惑論
Li-kuang 栗廣
Li Kuang-li 李廣利
Li P'eng-tsu 黎彭祖
Li-sao 離騷
Li Shao-chün 李少君
Li-shu 隸書
Li Tao-yüan 酈道元
Li Ts'ang 黎蒼
Liang 兩
Lieh 列
Lieh-hsien-chuan 列仙傳
Lieh-tzu 列子
Lien-hu wen 連弧文
Lien-shui 漣水
Lin-ch'iang 臨羌
Lin-i 臨沂
Ling-hsien 靈憲

Ling-ling 零陵
Liu 劉
Liu (Minister of Kung Kung) 柳
Liu Chao 劉昭
Liu Fu 劉復
Liu fu 六府
Liu Hsiang 劉向
Liu Hsin 劉歆
Liu jen 六壬
Liu Pang 劉邦
Liu-po 六博
Liu Tsung-yüan 柳宗元
Liu Ying 劉應
Lu-an chuan-shuo 陸安傳說
Lu wu 陸吾
Lü 呂
Lü shih ch'un-ch'iu 呂氏春秋
Luan-huang 鸞皇

255

Ways to Paradise

Lüan Ta 欒大	Mou-wu 戊午
Lung 龍	Mu (mother) 母
Ma-ch'eng 馬成	Mu (acre) 畝
Ma Chi 馬岌	Mu (Duke of Ch'in) 穆
Ma-wang-tui 馬王堆	Mu (King of Chou) 穆, 繆
Man-ch'eng 滿城	Mu-lien-li 才連理
Mao 卯	Mu T'ien-tzu chuan 穆天子傳
Meng 蒙	
Meng K'ang 孟康	Na-lü 挐閭
Ming-ch'i 明器	Nan-ch'ang 南昌
Ming-kuang 明光	Nan-yang 南陽
Ming shih 明視	Nan-yüeh 南越
Ming-t'ang 明堂	Nihon kōkogaku jiten 日本考古學辭典
Mizuno 水野	
Mo-tsui-tzu 磨咀子	Niu 鈕
Mo-tzu 墨子	Nü Kua (Wa) 女媧
Mo Yu-chih 莫友之	Pa-fen 八分
Mou 謀	Pan Ku 班固
Mou-ch'en 戊辰	Pan-liang 半兩
Mou tzu 牟子	P'an-ch'ih 蟠螭

Glossary of names and terms

Pao	保
Pao-p'u-tzu	抱朴子
Pao-yen-t'ang pi-chi (Kuang chi) 寶顏堂秘笈（廣集）	
Pei-ching ta-hsüeh yen-chiu-so kuo-hsüeh-men chou-k'an 北京大學研究所國學門週刊	
P'ei	沛
P'ei Sung-chih	裴松之
P'eng-hu	蓬壺
P'eng-lai	蓬萊
Pi	璧
Pi-yung	辟雍
Piao	瘭
Pieh-kuo tung ming chi 別國洞冥記	
Pien-hsing ssu ch'ih wen Pien-hsing ssu-yeh ssu-feng Pien-hsing ssu yeh wen 變形四蠍文	
	四葉四鳳
	四葉紋
Ping-wu	丙午
Po-hu-t'ung	白虎通
Po-ju	百乳
Po-na-pen	百衲本
Po-t'u	白兔
Po-wu-chih	博物志
P'o	魄
Pu	不
Pu Ch'ien-ch'iu	卜千秋
San-kuo-chih	三國志
San-shou	三獸
San tsu wu	三足烏
San wei	三危
Sha-tzu-t'ang	沙子塘
Shan (mountain)	山
Shan (ceremony)	禪
Shan-hai-ching	山海經
Shang-fang	尚方

Ways to Paradise

Shang-shu ta-chuan	尚書大傳	Shih Sheng-han	石聲漢
Shang ti	上帝	Shih-yü	世語
Shao-fu	少府	Shoseki meihin sōkan	
Shao-hsing	紹興		書跡名品叢刊
Shao-kuang	少廣	Shou-chou	壽州
Shao-ssu-ming	少司命	Shou-shou	獸首
Shen Ch'in-han	沈欽韓	Shu	銖
Shen-i-ching	神異經	Shu-ching	書經
Shen Pu-hai	申不害	Shuang-k'uei	雙夔
Shen Yüeh	沈約	Shui-ching-chu	水經注
Sheng (crown)	勝	Shuo-fu	說郛
Sheng (rope)	繩	Shuo-wen	說文
Shih	式, 栻, 拭	Shuo-yüan	說苑
Shih-chai-shan	石寨山	So-yin	索隱
Shih-chi	史記	Ssu chi	四極
Shih-chia-chuang	石家莊	Ssu-ch'uan Han tai tiao-su i-shu	
Shih-ching	式經		四川漢代彫塑藝術
Shi-ch'u	始初		
Shih-li-p'u	十里鋪	Ssu chung	四仲
Shih Shen	石申	Ssu-hsüan fu	思玄賦

Glossary of names and terms

Ssu ju (ts'ao yeh) 四乳（草葉）

Ssu-ma Ch'ien 司馬遷

Ssu-ma Hsiang-ju 司馬相如

Ssu-min yüeh-ling (chiao-chu) 四民月令校注

Ssu-ming 司命

Ssu shen 四神

Ssu-shen-ching 四神鏡

Ssu wei 四維

Sui-hsien 隨縣

Sui-ning 睢寧

Sui-te 綏德

Ta-chao 大招

Ta Ch'in 大秦

Ta-fen-t'ou 大墳頭

Ta-hsing-po 大行伯

Ta-jen fu 大人賦

Ta-mang-ching 大荒經

Ta-ssu-ming 大司命

Ta Tai li-chi 大戴禮記

Ta T'ang liu tien 大唐六典

Ta-tung 大東

Ta Yüan 大宛

Tai (commandery) 代

Tai (countess) 軑

T'ai 泰

T'ai-ch'ang 太常

T'ai-chen ch'en ying chih kuan 太真晨嬰之冠

T'ai-chi 太極

T'ai-i 太一

T'ai shan 泰山

T'ai shih 太氏

T'ai-yang 太陽

T'ai yin 太尹

Tan-erh 儋耳

T'ang-ho 唐河

T'ang ku 湯谷

T'ang liu tien 唐六典

259

Ways to Paradise

T'ang wen 湯問	Ts'ao-yeh 草葉
Tao 道	Tso chuan 左傳
T'ao Ch'ien 陶潛	Tsou 騶
T'ao-tu (shan) 桃都山	Tsou Yen 騶衍
T'eng-hsien 滕縣	Ts'ui Shih 崔定
Ti 帝	Tsung Lin 宗懍
T'iao 蜩	Ts'ung-shu chi-ch'eng 叢書集成
T'iao-chih 條支	
T'ien (Heaven) 天	Tu 杜
T'ien (surname) 田	Tu Kung-chan 杜公瞻
T'ien kang 天剛	Tu-shuo 度朔
T'ien ma 天馬	Tu Yeh 杜鄴
T'ien wen 天問	T'u-p'o 兔魄
Ting-wei 丁未	Tun-huang 敦煌
Tomioka 冨岡	Tung Chung-shu 董仲舒
Tou 竇	Tung-fang Shuo 東方朔
Ts'ai Yung 蔡邕	Tung-hai 東海
Tsao-fu 造父	Tung-kuan Han-chi 東觀漢記
Ts'ao Chih 曹植	

Glossary of names and terms

Tung wang fu (kung) 東王父（公）

T'ung-shan 銅山

T'ung-t'ien-t'ai 通天臺

Tzu, ch'ou 子丑

Tzu-tan-k'u 子彈庫

Tz'u-yün 慈雲

Wang Chang 王章

Wang Ch'iao 王僑

Wang Ch'ung 王充

Wang Hsien-ch'ien 王先謙

Wang I 王逸

Wang Kuang 王光

Wang Kuo-wei 王國維

Wang Mang 王莽

Wang-shan 望山

Wang Shao-ying 汪紹楹

Wang-tu 望都

Wei 魏

Wei Chih san kung 位至三公

Wen-hai ch'u-pan-she 文海出版社

Wen I-to 聞一多

Wen-wu ching-hua 文物精華

Wo-wei 渥洼

Wu (surname) 吳

Wu (in the Twelve Branches) 午

Wu (Warrior) 武

Wu, chi (in the Ten Stems) 戊己

Wu-cheng Jao (Chao) 務成昭

Wu ching t'ung-i 五經通義

Wu Chün 吳均

Wu hsing 五行

Wu hsing ta-i 五行大義

Wu Jui 吳芮

261

Ways to Paradise

Wu Liang 武梁
Wu shu 五銖
Wu ts'an 五殘
Wu-tsang-ching 五藏經
Wu-wei 武威
Wu Yüeh ch'un-ch'iu 吳越春秋
Yang Hsiung 楊雄
Yang-kuan-ssu 楊官寺
Yang Pao 楊寶
Yang-t'ien-hu 仰天湖
Yao 堯
Yen 弇
Yen Shih-ku 顏師古
Yen Tzu 弇茲
Yin 銀
Yin-shou 尹壽
Ying-ch'eng 郢稱
Ying-ch'eng-tzu 營城子
Ying-chou 瀛洲
Ying-hu 瀛壺
Ying Lung 應龍
Ying Shao 應劭
Ying-shih 營室
Ying-yang 滎陽
Yu 有
Yu (in the Twelve Branches) 酉
Yung 雍
Yung Chih 勇之
Yung-ho 永和
Yung-p'ing 永平
Yü (The Great) 禹
Yü (weather bird) 䳗
Yü Ch'iang 禺疆
Yü-han-shan-fang chi-i-shu 玉函山房輯佚書
Yü Hao-liang 于豪亮
Yü-hsien 禹縣

Glossary of names and terms

Yü-ti-t'u 輿地圖
Yü-t'u 玉兔
Yüan (surname) 袁
Yüan (locusts) 蝝
Yüan-hsing 元興

Yüan-yu 遠遊
Yüeh 越
Yün-lei-wen 雲雷文
Yün-meng 雲夢

Index

acupuncture 139
alchemy 138
Algonquin, Great Hare of 133
amnesty 225
An Ch'i 37
An-hsi 95
animals 78, 79, 147; the four, see ssu shen; grateful 151; horned 43; man's relations to 131
antlers, king of 198
archaised script 229
Aristotle 132
armed guardian 106
ascent, to life of immortals 167
astronomy 2, 71; in art 54, 129; at court 78; instruments 134
attendants, for the dead 13
axis, of universe 83

banner, function of funerary 30
banquet, scene of 45
bat, in painting 46
bell, in painting 55 f.; in rites 135
birds, as bridge 121; human-headed 40, 139; in inscriptions 177; in painting 55 f.; 'Seldom Seen' 125; in the sun 127 f.; as symbols 140; the three 90 f., 116 f.; three-headed 140, 157; three-legged 54, 94, 106, 108, 128 f., 157; two-legged 50 f.; two-tailed 39
body, preservation intact 29
bosses, on mirrors 72, 79, 83, 228; see TLV mirrors
Browne, Sir Thomas 132
Brundage collection 152
Buddhism 16, 21, 87, 122 f., 132–3, 139, 148, 155
burial practices 9, 11, 13

calendar 1, 2, 134
calligraphic styles 27, 228 f.
canopies, on mirrors 73–4
cardinal points (*ssu chi*) 74
cassia tree 140
catalpa wood 23
causeway, in painting 46
cave paintings 131
cave, of Queen Mother of West 91
centre of world 72
Ch'ang-an, building at 15, fig. 1
Chang Ch'ien 98
Chang Heng 2, 54, 128; vision of 16
Ch'ang-ho 49, 97, 142

Chang Hua 155
Ch'ang-sha, kingdom 20
change, operation of 3
Changes, Book of 5, 15, 84, 134–5, 192
Cheng Chung 77
Ch'eng-hsiang 136
ch'eng-huang 56
chevron ornament 69, 161, 180, 183
ch'i hsiang 113, 119
Chia-hsiang, reliefs from 108
chieh ch'ung 146
chien (mirror) 65
Chien-chang palace 38
Ch'ien-niu, see Oxherd
Ch'ih Sung 122
chih-nü, see weaving maid
Ch'in, empire 8, 20 f.; first emperor 162; Mu Duke of 42
Chin-ch'eng 96
Chin-ch'üeh-shan 142
ching (mirror) 65
ch'ing (musical instrument) 44
Ch'ing-ch'iu 108
Ching Ch'u sui-shih-chi 115, 154
Chiu chang suan shu 134
Chiu-ch'üan 101
chiu yang 51, 52, 141
Ch'iung-ch'iung chü-hsü 198
Chou, kings of 8; Mu king of 92
Chou-li 44, 49, 56, 140
Ch'u, culture of 18, 57
Chu Hsi 33
Chu lung 57 f.
Chu Po 174
Ch'u Shao-sun 77, 128
Chu-shu-chi-nien 92, 95; text of 149
Ch'u tz'u 17, 18, 33, 53, 58; *Chao-hun* 11, 18, 33, 45, 49, 51–2, 136; *Li-sao* 47 f., 199; *Nine Songs* 48 f., 199; *Shao-ssu-ming* 33, 136; *Ta-shao* 33, 58, 136; *Ta-ssu-ming* 33, 49, 136; *T'ien-wen* 43 f., 54 f., 108, 133 f., 199; *Yüan-yu* 42 f., 51, 136, 149, 153
Chuang-tzu 3, 51, 89, 110
Ch'un-ch'iu yüan-ming-pao 54, 128 f.
chün wu 128
Chü (Kou)-mang 42
Chü-hsü 198
Chü-yen 26–7
Chüan Hsü 139
circle, degrees of 85; the Han 160, 173, 207
circlets, see medallions
cloud-scroll 69, 70, 161, 167 f., 180 f.

Index

coffins, of Ma-wang-tui 23; multiple 136; in painting 46; Pl. XXVI–VII; figs. 4, 5
coins 147, 170 f.; at Ma-wang-tui 26–7; replica 137
communication, between Heaven, Earth and Man 8 f., 97, 134
compass, points of 160
compasses, draftsman's 73, 77
Confucian attitude 4, 6 f., 58, 88
Confucius 4
constellations 73; meeting of 112 f.
copper, supplies of 166, 196
corners, of the heavens 74
cosmology 4, 31, 60, 72, 96 f., 122
cosmos, favoured position in 61; four nodal points of (*ssu wei*) 73, 77 f., 83, 176; order of 3, 6, 81 f., 94 f., 112, 119 f., 146, 161 f.; ropes of (*sheng*) 4, 74, 77, 79
crow, in the sun 127 f.
crown, *see sheng* (s.v. Queen Mother of the West)
cup holders 90, 107 f.

death, consequences of 9; life after 2, 9
deathlessness 58, 93 f., 100, 116 f., 121
decoration, of mirrors 62 f., 70
degree markings 75, 160
demon riders 56
diameters, of TLV mirrors 64, 144, 176 f.
Dipper, the 52, 75, 77, 78
divination 9, 61, 76, 80, 84, 135, 146 f.
diviners' boards 60 f., 71, 75 f., 82, 85, 147, 159, 168, 204 f., figs. 11, 12; animals of 75, 79, 207; bosses of 205; degree marks, diagonal paths 75, 205; inscriptions 205 f.; pivot 75, 204 f.
dragons 40, 50, 52–3
dragon and tiger 105 f.

Earth Queen 97 f., 118
eclipses 55
Egypt, mythology of 127, 133
elixir, plant, drug of 16, 54 f., 59, 70, 94, 106 f., 112, 122 f., 168
embroidery 73
emperor, capacity of 8
errors, in inscriptions 160; *see* omissions
evil, problem of 2 f., 7, 84
exorcism 140

fang-shih 15, 97, 125, 163
Fei-huang 56
Fei-lien 46
Feng and *shan* rites 37
Feng-su t'ung-i 49, 149, 153
Feng-t'u-chi 153
five, as principle of the cosmos 60

Five Phases (use of term 134); 7 f., 31, 34, 60, 69, 70, 79, 83 f., 115, 129, 161 f., 174, 192, 211, 227
Five Powers (*ti*) 97 f., 118
figurines 13, 25
foreign tribes' submission 165, 194
four animals, beasts, *see ssu shen*
fox, 56; nine-tailed 108 f., 152
frescoes 13, 25
Fu An 2
Fu Hsi 57 f., 89, 111, fig. 9
funerary furnishings 13, 25, 33
Fu-sang tree 16, 50 f., 111, 128, 141

gaming boards 99; incident with 147
geomancers' compass 85, 206
giant 43, 140
gilding, on mirrors 160
globes, in painting 56
gnomon boards 63, 71
Golden Lower Mantle 192
golden sparrow 100
government, authority of 2
Grand Unity 38, 97 f., 118, 142
grapes 118

Hall, of Flowery Delights 116 f., 120
Han Fei 94
Han-shu 95 f., 150, 154
Han Wu ku-shih 116 f., 119
Han Wu-ti nei-chuan 118
hare 52 f., 106 f., 110, 112; characteristics of 132, 157; in Japan 133; on painting 133; in the moon 127 f.; in mythology 131 f.
harmony, of universe 7
Heaven, with earth, man 7, 15, 21, 31, 78, 83, 97; pillar of 125; power of 7, 52; worship of 8, 15, 21, 97 f.
Hegn O 54 f., 94
Herb of Life 106, 198, 200
hexagrams, the sixty-four 5
hierogamies, cosmic 155
hill censer 148
Hippocrates 132
Ho-lin-ko-erh 129
holy mountains 38
honey dew, *see kan lu*
horses, of heaven 56, 97, 142; on painting 55
Hou t'u 97 f., 118
hound, of heaven 99
Hsi and Ho 52
Hsi Hsia sung, stele 153
Hsi lao, Hsi mu, Hsi wang mu 88, 95; *see* Queen Mother of West
Hsi wang mu chuan 149
Hsiao-t'ang shan 151
Hsien Men 139

265

Hsin, dynasty 163 f., 170 f., 202
hsing 9 f.
Hsüan-chung-chi 54
Hsüan-tsung hsiang-chuan 155
Hsün-tzu 95
Hua Yang 108
Huai-nan-tzu 1, 4, 18, 45, 47, 50, 53 f., 60, 74, 76, 84 f., 89, 93 f., 108, 112, 121, 124, 128, 146, 155
Huan T'an 135
Huang ch'üan 10 f., 111
Huang ti 15, 37, 89, 97, 118
hun 9 f., 33
Huo Kuang 135
hybrid creatures 89, 91, 139, 140, 152, 156

I, partner of Heng O 54, 55, 94
I-ching 5, 15, 84, 134–5, 192
I-nan 13, 103, 110, 122
immortality 15, 30 f., 70; see deathlessness
immortals, life of 60, 69, 72, 83 f., 110 f., 122, 161, 167, 198
Inaba, white hare of 133
incense 154
inscriptions, see diviners' board, mirrors, and TLV mirrors
intermediaries 15, 97, 125, 163
inventory, of funerary goods 26, 30
invocation of soul, see summons
iron mirrors 213

jade, for the dead 12, 135; Gate 118; *huang* 44, 140; mountains 90; *pi* 30, 40, 44, 72; screen 103 f., 119 f., Pl. XXIII; springs of 198 f.; suits 12
Japan, hare in 133; imperial palace 129; mirrors in 65, 221
Jen Huang 110
Jih shih chia mou 147
Jih-wei-shu 154
Jo-mu 111
Jo River 90, 95 f.
jujubes 118, 138, 167, 175, 198

K'ai-ming 110, 152
k'ai-shu 228
kan lu 38, 56, 91, 139, 143
Kan Pao 38
Kan Te 128, 154
Keng Ping 135
King, Father of the East 88, 105, 110, 121 f., 163, 174, 225; on mirrors 122; Pl. XXIII, fig. 21
kingdoms, of Han empire 21
Kojiki 133
Korea, diviners' boards from 205; mirror from 223

Ku K'ai-chih, scroll 65
Kuang-ya 53
kuei 10
K'un-lun 15 f., 34, 73, 89 f., 97 f., 108 f., 124 f., 155
Kung Kung 110
Kuo, family shrine 129
Kuo (headdress) 105
Kuo Hsien 128
Kuo P'u 42, 58, 90, 93, 128, 130, 148

lacquer wares 18, 25
lamps, of nine lights 116; in Taoist ritual 108
leaders of the months 206
leopards 46
Lesser seal script 228 f.
leviathans 43
li (constellation) 90
Li-chi 135
Li-huo lun 135
Li Kuang-li 143
Li Shao-chün 37
li-shu 160, 169, 178, 228 f.
Lieh-tzu 38, 40, 45, 93, 149
Liu Hsiang 52, 54, 70, 124, 128, 135, 148, 153, 155, 227
Liu Hsin 2, 148, 227
Liu, imperial family 21
Liu-jen board 78
Liu Pang 57
Liu-po board 63, 71, 72, 82, 84, 110, 145, 147; fig. 14
Liu Tsung-yüan 153
Lo-lang 71, 111
Lo-yang 15, 54, 125
Lord of the Lives 33, 48, 49
Lu wu 152
Luan huang 47
Lun-heng 9, 13
Lü, family of 21
Lü shih ch'un-ch'iu 74, 143, 146
Lüan Ta 38

Ma-wang-tui, sequence of tombs 29; tomb no. 1, dating of 27; excavation of 17, figs. 3–5; identification of 27; inventory 27; painting from 17 f., 127, 129, fig. 7 (see painting); tomb no. 3, painting from 31
magnetic compass, needle 85, 147
magpies 93, 114
man, elements of 9 f.; force of 4
Man-ch'eng 62, 214
manikins 25, 119, 141
mansions, the 28, 85, 147, 204 f.
mathematics 2

Index

medallions, of bird and toad 84, 127 f., 160, 166 f., 173, 179
medicine 2
meeting, of partners 116, 124; *see* Queen, and Weaver and Oxherd
milfoil 76
military expansion, of Han 174
Milky Way 112, 114, 121; as home of dead 115
ming-shih 133
Ming-t'ang 155, 202
mirrors, cords for 213; dating of 62, 70, 151, 223 f.; in daily life 147; decorative features 227; distribution of 209 f., 216; early types 218, Pl. II, IV; high relief 66, 151, 163, 174, Pl. XXII, XXIV; inscriptions on 66, 71, 155; iron 213; in Japan 221; manufacture 64; post Han makes 69, 220, Pl. XXV; reasons for burial 64; from Shao-kou 215 f.; simplification of design 228; spurious examples 70; of T'ang dynasty 67, 103; with three rings 173; types of 66, 209 f.; *see also* TLV mirrors
modernist attitude 76, 134
moon 53, 127 f.; as symbol 55, 132
moulds, in making mirrors 64
moutnains, of cosmos 74, 110; *see* pillar
Mu, king of Chou 101, 118 f., 122
Mu-lien-li 111
Mu t'ien tzu chuan 92 f., 143
mummification 18
musical instruments 26, 44, 55
myth, of seasonal meetings 86 f., 92, 100 f.
mythological creatures 23, 160, fig. 5
mythology, of China 18, 31, 53, 124; of Japan 108; Jewish 127

Na Chi 101
Na-lü people 95
naturalist attitude 3 f.
nature, festivals 88; order of 5 f.
nine, as a number 108; of heavens 108; of lamps 108, 111, 116 f.; of a monster 110; of walls 108
nineteen, hymns 97, 142; Old Poems 113
nodal points, of cosmos, *see* cosmos
Nü Kua 57 f., fig. 9

offerings, to ancestral shrine 10
old age, obliviousness of 167; prevention of 128
omens, for good 108, 124
omissions, in inscriptions 169, 173, 175, 179, 196, 198
oracle bones, shells 76, 84, 88
owls 42, 100

Oxherd 112 f., 153

paintings at Ma-wang-tui; from tomb no. 1 17 f., fig. 7; alternation in 39; central figure 46, 57 f., 108; composition 34; function 30; size 30; 'space fillers' in 44, 47, 57; upper part 47 f., vertical part 35 f.; from tomb no. 3, 31
Pao-p'u-tzu nei p'ien 144
paradise, journey to 33, 46, 51, 59
partnership, of persons, stars 88
patterned scroll 169
peaches, peach tree 30, 111, 116 f., 138
P'eng-lai 16 f., 34, 37 f., 56, 59, 97
phenomena, strange 5, 7, 98, 134
Pi-yung 202
Pieh-kuo tung ming chi 154
pillars 122; of copper 125; of cosmos 110; of paradise 48 f.; of Queen Mother of West 91
pillow, from Wang-tu 122
pivot, of cosmos 93; of diviners' boards 204
Pliny 132
Po-hu-t'ung 108, 152
p'o 9 f.
po-t'u 133
Po-wu-chih 116, 119, 154, 157
Pool of heaven 50
prayer for skills 114
prophylactic function, of mirrors 64
Pu Ch'ien-ch'iu 59, 134, 140, fig. 16
purification, of palace 154

Queen Mother of the West 16, 33, 34, 52, 54 f., 59, 86 f., 227, Pl. I, XXI, XXII, XXIII, figs. 15, 18, 19, 21, 22; advent of 98 f., 116; attributes of 103 f. (armed guardian 106; birds 117, 124; cosmic tree, pillar 110; dragon and tiger 105 f.; hare 106, 122 f., 140; nine-tailed fox 108 f., 124; *sheng* 103 f., 111, 115, 117, 119, 122, 140, fig. 17; suppliants 106, 124; three-legged birds 106; toad 106, 140); breaks *sheng* 95; in cave 91, 94; cult of 12, 70, 163; and deathlessness 89, 92; as hybrid creature 89, 90; iconography of 101 f.; and K'un-lun 73, 89 f., 93 f., 124; meeting, with Mu king of Chou 92, 118 f., with Han Wu ti 112, 115 f., 120; messenger of 100; myth of 97; powers over cosmos 95, 112; references on mirrors and inscriptions 60, 69, 83, 101, 122, 151, 155, 162 f., 168, 174 f., 200, 225; and seasonal festivals 100, 119; shrine for 101; and stars 90, 115; with symbols of sun, moon 127, 130 f.; and weaving 105, 115

Ways to Paradise

Queen of Sheba 89
quincunx 160

Ra, Egyptian sun god 127
radio-carbon dating 18
rank, reduction of 137
rebirth 87
reformist attitude 76, 83, 134
regnal titles 224
religious building 15
replica coins 27
ring, in artistic devices 56, 139, Pl. XXVI, fig. 8
River's drum 112
'ropes', of universe; *see* cosmos

sash 44
sculptures 13
seasonal festivals 100; meetings 86, 119 f.
sericulture 120
serpent 43
serpentine legs, tails 57, 59, 107, 140
set square 73, 77
seventh day, meetings on 114, 116 f., 119 f., 125
Sha-tzu-t'ang 13, 23, 27, 44, 139, Pl. XXVI
Shaman 91; use of mirrors 65
Shan-hai-ching 17, 18, 42, 43, 50, 53, 56, 57, 89, 91 f., 106, 108, 110, 115, 128, 130, 155, 198; compilation of 148
Shantung, relief from 57
Shang-fang 166, 175, 179 f., 194, 196, 198, 200
Shang ti, *see* Ti
Shang Yang 94
Shao-fu 166, 175
Shao-hsing 220
Shao-kou, graves 62, 210, 212, 215
Shao-kuang 89, 110, 148
Shen-i-ching 111, 155
Shen Pu-hai 94, 146, 147
sheng 90 f., 95, 119 f., fig. 17; *see* Queen Mother of the West
shih, *see* diviners' boards
Shih-chai-shan 62, 158
Shih-chi 18, 77, 83, 93, 95, 128, 150, 154
Shih-ching 64, 112, 205
Shih chou chi 153
Shih-li-p'u 139
Shih Shen 154
Shou-chou mirrors 67, 69, 81, 158, 209 f., 213, 227, Pl. IV, V
Shu-ching 134
Shui-ching-chu 155
Shun 95
Shuo-wen 2
Silk Roads 118

sophora tree 93
soteriological cult, of Queen Mother of West 98 f.
square, on TLV mirrors 69
squared characters 229
ssu chi 74
Ssu-ma Ch'ien 1
Ssu-ma Hsiang-ju 1, 49, 93 f., 124, 130, 150
Ssu-min yüeh-ling 114
ssu shen (four animals) 15, 69 f., 79, 82, 84, 140, 160 f., 174, 178, 186, 196, 210, 225
ssu wei, *see* cosmos
straight-eyed men 150
Sui-ning, relief from 108
summons, to soul 11 f., 33, 140; *see* Chao-hun, Ta-chao (s.v., *Ch'u tz'u*)
sun, symbol of 127 f.; valley of 16; eight, nine and ten suns 50 f.
sun-dials 71
sunspots 128, 156
suppliants 106 f., Pl. XXVIII
supplication 108
Sung, king of 77
sweet dew, *see* Kan lu
symbols 15, 108, 123; of birth, death, rebirth 133; in Chien-chang palace 38; as escort for dead 8, 12; of sun, moon 127 f.; of TLV mirrors 70 f., 83, 162, 168

Ta-hsing-po 106
Ta-jen-fu 49, 149
Ta Tai Li-chi 146
Tai, countess of 29; nobility of 28 f., 137
T'ai, Mount 97, 118, 200
T'ai chi 73
T'ai i (Grand Unity) 38, 97 f., 118, 142
T'ai-yang 128
talismans 25, 30, 88, 99, 101
Tan-yang 196
T'ang-ku 51
T'ang liu tien 78, 147
Tao 5, 89; Taoist attitude 3 f., 76, 122; ritual 88, 108, 118
T'ao Ch'ien 93, 156
T'ao-tu, mountain 111
tassels, of Ma-wang-tui painting 30
Ten stems 85, 204 f.
T'eng-hsien, relief from 107
Three Dangers, mountain 95
Ti, Shang ti 8, 10 f., 40-9, 52-9, 97, 141
T'iao-chih 95, 150
T'ien ma, *see* horses of heaven
TLV marks 60, 66, 81
TLV mirrors 60 f., Pl. VI-XX, figs. 10, 13, 23-6; bosses on 69, 159, 169, 173, 210, 228; choice examples 166-7; circlets in 117, 166; classification of 158 f., 209 f.;

Index

evolution of 66 f.; extra ring in 82, 159; function of TLV marks 81, 159, 160; gilding on 160, 173; inscriptions of 12, 60 f., 159 f., 169 (classification of inscriptions 63, 161; dates of 62, 68, 174, 177; in lines of poetry 194, 202; starting point 160; style of script 228; texts of 192 f.); irregular types 68, 169, 219; from known sites 218; late fabrication 170; list of those surveyed 177 f.; makers of 166 f., 174 f., 192 f.; manufacture of 165, 166, 170; purpose of 80 f.; square centre of 159; symbolism of 83 f., 162; system of reference 61. References to particular examples follow:

  A 0002; 158
  C 1101; 68, 79, 159, 167, 210
  C 1201; 160
  C 1202; 160
  C 1205; 144
  C 1303; 165
  C 1304; 165
  C 2102; 166
  C 2103; 228
  C 2104; 71, 166
  C 2105; 166
  C 2106; 166
  C 3101; 228
  C 3103; 167
  C 4102; 167
  C 4103; 167
  C 4108; 167
  C 4112; 228
  C 4126; 228
  C 4208; 145, 172
  C 5001; 101
  C 5002; 101, 145, 159
  D 2001; 168
  D 2004; 163, 169
  D 2015; 73
  D 2022; 167, 215
  X 1001; 79
  X 1004; 101, 105, 145, 170, 210, 224
  X 1005; 145, 170, 176, 210, 224
  X 1007; 170, 172
  X 1009; 176
  X 2001; 176
  X 2008; 170
  X 9001; 170, 226
  X 9005; 72, 170

toad 52 f., 106, 127, 131 f., 140; three-legged 54
tokens, exchange of 98 f., 119
tombs, structure of 13, 18, 21 f.
Topsell, Edward 157
towers, of paradise 48
transformation, of body 140

tree, of cosmos, heaven 93, 110 f.
Trigrams, the eight 5, 77
Tsao-fu 93
Ts'ao-yeh mirrors 67, 69, 81, 158, 209 f., 214, 227, Pl. II, III
Tso chuan 9
Tsou Yen 96
Tu Kung-chan 119
t'u-p'o 133
Tu-shuo, Mount 137
Tu Yeh 99
Tun-huang, strips from 26–7
Tung Chung-shu 1, 6, 21, 83, 87, 96, 98, 101, 115, 118, 124, 162–3
Tung-fang Shuo 117, 118, 120, 128, 153 f.
Tung-kuan Han-chi 129, 152
T'ung-shan 129
T'ung T'ien t'ai 97
Tung wang fu (kung), see King Father of the East
turtles 40, 43, 146, 147; mountains of 90
twelve, as principle of the cosmos 60
Twelve Branches 77, 79, 82 f., 159, 165, 204 f.
Twelve *shen* 204 f.
Tz'u-yün, reliefs from 108

unicorn sheep 160
universe, *see* cosmos

vase, of P'eng-lai 38 f., 43
victory, celebration of 30
violence, occurrence of 4 f.

Wang Ch'iao 122
Wang Ch'ung 2, 9, 87, 129; attitude to death 16
Wang I 58
Wang Mang 42, 70, 77, 78, 83, 85, 162 f., 172, 174, 210, 211, 223, 227; in inscriptions 69, 170
Wang-tu 13, 103, 122, Pl. XXI
wardens, of paradise 48
water-clock 1
Weaver and Oxherd, myth of 87, 93, 112 f., fig. 20
weaving, and the *sheng* 105, 113 f.; maid, (constellation) 112 f., 125, 155
Wei, king of 147
wei chih san kung 176, 209, 221
western regions 95
wheelwright's shop, on relief 131, fig. 19
white, on P'eng-lai 45; deer, hare, tiger 108
wine goblet 111; warmer (of 26 BC) 108, 111
winged men 83, 84, 122, fig. 5
woman, in painting; at apex 57; on dragon 53

269

wu hsing, see Five Phases
Wu, king of 147
wu, chi, in inscriptions 204 f., 208
Wu Jui, king of Ch'ang-sha 20, 29
Wu Liang shrines 103, 106
Wu ti, Han emperor 37, 92, 97, 108, 111, 128, 162, 174; meeting with Queen Mother 115 f., 121 f.
wu ts'an, constellation 90
Wu-tsang-ching 89, 148
Wu-wei, texts from 2, 26
Wu Yüeh ch'un-ch'iu 152

Yang Hsiung 93
Yang-kuan-ssu 129
Yang Pao 100
yellow, power of, see *Huang ti*
Yellow Springs 10, 11, 13, 111

Yen, Mount 93
Yen Tzu 43
Yin, Yang 6, 8, 15, 31, 40, 58, 60, 69, 87, 105, 126, 129, 164–6, 196, 227
Ying-ch'eng-tzu, frescoes of 15, 33, 46, 59, 106, Pl. XXVIII
Ying lung 53
Ying-shih 115
Ying Shao 47
Yü-hsien, graves of 215
Yü, the Great 53, 95, 108, 148
Yü, weather bird 72
Yü Ch'iang 40, 42, 43, 89
yü-t'u 133
Yung Chih 38

zigzag pattern, see chevron

For Product Safety Concerns and Information please contact our EU representative GPSR@taylorandfrancis.com
Taylor & Francis Verlag GmbH, Kaufingerstraße 24, 80331 München, Germany